THE MARCH OF FREEDOM

THE
MARCH
OF
FREEDOM

Modern Classics in Conservative Thought

(New and Expanded Edition)

Edited with Commentaries by
Edwin J. Feulner Jr.

Published by Heritage Books
an activity of The Heritage Foundation
214 Massachusetts Ave., NE, Washington, DC 20002

Printed in the United States of America
First edition published in 1998 by Spence Publishing Company

The Library of Congress has cataloged the original edition as follows:
The march of freedom : modern classics in conservative thought /
    edited by Edwin J. Feulner Jr.
        p. cm.
    Includes bibliographic references.
    isbn 0-9653208-8-x (hardcover).
    1. Conservatism—United States. i. Feulner, Edwin J.
jc573.2.u6m347 1998   98-
10678
320. 52'0973=dc21

ISBN 0-743665-0-1 (Paperback)

Book and cover design by Elizabeth Brewer © The Heritage Foundation

Cover photograph copyright © Punchstock, 2003.

Distributed to the trade by
National Book Network
Lanham, MD

For Linda

Contents

Foreword to the New Edition

The five years since the first edition of *The March of Freedom* appeared in 1998 have been among the most tumultuous in our nation's history, encompassing the razor-thin presidential election of 2000, the horrifying events of September 11, 2001, the ouster of the extremist Taliban government of Afghanistan, a short-lived but stubborn recession, and the swift liberation of Iraq from the totalitarian grip of Saddam Hussein in the spring of 2003.

Not since Abraham Lincoln, perhaps, has a new American president confronted so divided a nation as did George W. Bush in January 2001. His swearing-in was overshadowed by the disputed nature of his victory—narrowly losing the popular vote to Democratic Vice President Al Gore and winning the electoral college by just one vote more than the needed 270. A cautious Bush began his presidency by focusing on tax cuts and educational reform as reflections of his "compassionate" conservatism. By mid-July, the president was receiving modestly favorable public approval ratings of 57 percent; his major accomplishment was a monumental tax cut of $1.6 trillion, although most of the reductions were scheduled for later in the decade.

And then came September 11 and the worst terrorist attacks ever on U.S. soil. Hijacked airplanes smashed into the silver towers of the World Trade Center in New York City, the mammoth Pentagon in Washington, D.C., and the Pennsylvania countryside, killing three thousand innocent people and sweeping away the political and social detritus of the previous year. The nation was no longer divided into Bush red and Gore blue (as depicted in a much-reproduced electoral map of the 2000 presidential results) but united in red, white, and blue.

President Bush moved quickly to rally America and the world. Congress overwhelmingly authorized an initial $40 billion for the war on terrorism. NATO invoked Article 5 of its charter for the first time ever, declaring that an attack on one member was an attack on all. A tidal wave of patriotism inundated the nation: military enlistments surged; thousands lined up to give blood; tens of millions of dollars in donations for the victims and their families poured into the Red Cross, the Salvation Army, and other charitable organizations; attendance doubled and tripled at churches and synagogues; and there was a runaway sale of American flags.

Aided by the public's tendency to rally around the president in a time of crisis, Bush's public approval topped 90 percent, the highest level of any president since the advent of polling. The president who had once seemed to spend almost as much time at his Texas ranch as the White House became a constant and reassuring public presence, rarely out of sight. The Jeffersonian Republican who favored limited, decentralized government called for the federal authority to fight a protracted conflict, help industries hit hard by terrorism, and rejuvenate a stalled economy. Far from having a nervous breakdown over the first major terrorist attack on their homeland, Americans remained calm and collected. "The can-do pioneers who tamed a wild continent," wrote *The Economist,* "and then helped to win three world confrontations have not disappeared after all."

As I write this new introduction on the second anniversary of 9/11, some things have inevitably changed. President Bush's popularity has leveled off to a more normal rating in the mid-fifties. Bipartisanship in Congress has faded as the fundamental differences between Republicans and Democrats have surfaced on core issues like taxes and spending. Patriotism has become a little passé in some quarters, especially in the academy. But I firmly believe that America will not return to its pre-September 11 way of life. The terrorist attacks were a defining moment in modern American history, like the assassination of John F. Kennedy, the Tet offensive, and the fall of the Berlin Wall.

The president and the nation face formidable challenges at home and abroad: securing the peace and preparing the way for representative government in Iraq; locating Osama bin Laden and putting al-Qaeda out of business permanently; stimulating the U.S. economy without running up giant deficits and increasing the power of government. Such a balancing act of economics and politics will require extraordinary skill. In this time of crisis—and I believe it is accurate to say we are still in a crisis—the Bush administration and the nation can call upon the myriad resources of a mature conservative movement.

Two of the more prominent conservative organizations engaged in the battle of ideas celebrate anniversaries this year—The Heritage Foundation marks its thirtieth year, the Intercollegiate Studies Institute (ISI), its fiftieth. We are but two of the many institutions on the Right committed to limited government, individual freedom and responsibility, the free market, a strong national defense, and traditional American values. I am confident that Heritage, ISI, and all the other truly conservative organizations will continue to articulate the right policies and plans, to publish the right books and journals, to sponsor the right speakers and seminars, because we rest securely on the priceless principle of ordered liberty about which Russell Kirk, F. A. Hayek, Richard Weaver, Whittaker Chambers, and the other contributors herein write so eloquently and persuasively.

This new edition of *The March of Freedom* is enhanced by the presence of the free market economist Ludwig von Mises, the foreign policy analyst and practitioner Jeane Kirkpatrick, and the sociologist

Robert Nisbet, all of whose perceptive insights into the workings of the market and of the world offer further evidence as to why the conservative movement continues to be a major player in the political and economic realms of the nation.

— Edwin J. Feulner Jr.
October 2003

Introduction

Nowadays conservatism is not only the dominant but also the sole intellectual tradition in America. This is a claim borrowed from Lionel Trilling, who applied it in the 1950s to liberalism, not conservatism. "It is the plain fact," he wrote, "there are no conservative ideas in general circulation," but only "irritable mental gestures which seem to resemble ideas."

The past four decades have seen a dramatic reversal of fortunes—among the most dramatic in American political history. The conservative case for freedom and markets, virtue and families, has been proven like Copernicus's case for the movement of the earth: because it corresponds to the unavoidable reality.

Arguments for capitalism and traditional morality and against socialism and paternalism—once hotly contested—have been transformed into broadly shared assumptions. I am not referring to the ebb and flow of political and party fortunes, influenced by personalities, circumstances, and electoral strategy (or the lack thereof). I am referring to a tide of ideas running through our times, lapping on the shores of many nations—the intellectual triumph of the philosophy of freedom over the various utopias of central planning.

Thus, those who do not understand the conservative movement—its history and heroes and ideals—do not understand the modern history of America. This book is intended as an overview of this vigorous, varied movement and an introduction to the conservative canon.

Any introduction to conservatism would seem to require a definition of conservatism. And yet, those of us who have worked in this cause, argued for it, and organized for it still have a hard time defining it. Conservative history is, in part, a continuing, combative quest for self-definition—a goal that remains elusive.

This leads to recurring stories and articles predicting that conservatism is on the verge of disintegration—about to collapse under the weight of its own internal contradictions. What platform could possibly unite midwestern businessmen and New York neoconservative intellectuals? Libertarians and the religious right? But this assertion betrays a fundamental misunderstanding.

Conservatism is not a political party, with a shared platform, hashed out by lobbying and majority vote. According to Russell Kirk, it is "neither a religion nor an ideology," and it possesses "no Holy Writ and no _Das Kapital_ to provide dogmata." It is, instead, a broad social movement of diverse but reinforcing beliefs, gathering travelers on the same journey—pilgrims who argue over the topography of their promised land but move in the same direction.

As a witness to the conservative renaissance, I can attest to one fact: It has always been this way. This movement has never spoken with one voice and is unlikely to start. Even in the small circle of its beginnings, debate was nothing if not spirited. In 1962, Frank Meyer attacked Russell Kirk as a "New Hegelian" Statist of the American Right. Max Eastman resigned from the _National Review_ editorial board after attacking Meyer for "pre-liberal ecclesiastical authoritarianism." Kirk once announced he felt closer to socialist Norman Thomas than libertarian Murray Rothbard. William F. Buckley chastised Milton Friedman for making _laissez-faire_ a "dogmatic theology." Whittaker Chambers directed his ire against objectivist Ayn Rand, concluding, "From almost any page of *Atlas Shrugged*, a voice can be heard, from painful necessity, commanding: 'To a gas chamber—go!'" As conservatism reached new heights of influence in the 1980s, the same fissures were obvious. "On one side," recalls sociologist Peter Berger, "there were people who thought that being born again was some sort of Hindu superstition, while people on the other side thought that Groton was a throat disease."

For four decades, conservatism has encompassed ex-Communists, traditionalists, religious conservatives, libertarians, Southern Agrarians, fusionists, traditional (European) liberals, supply-siders, and neoconservatives, all fighting for attention, converts, and elbow room. And in all their exasperating diversity, they have performed feats of persuasion and influence on an epic scale, turning a "remnant" into an intellectual movement into a political revolution.

It is easy to forget how unlikely this once seemed. American history offers individual conservative heroes—from John Adams to Calvin Coolidge—but no example of a coherent, conservative movement. In the 1950s, argues historian George Nash, "No articulate, coordinated, self-consciously conservative intellectual force existed in the United States." The intellectual and political classes were self-consciously left-liberal, and they were flush with confidence after their victory against Japan and Germany. Conservatives, such as they were, were identified exclusively with their opposition to World War II and the New Deal—hardly winning issues in the context of the times. Peter Viereck observed in 1949: "To be praised as conservative has become an insuperable political handicap." Raymond English referred to conservatism as "the forbidden faith," while Clinton Rossiter dubbed it "the thankless persuasion." In one American city at the time, a man was arrested for disturbing the peace, accused, according to the police report, of "using abusive language, calling people conservatives and all that."

The stirrings of a conservative response began with a trio of books and the creation of a journal. First, in 1944, came Friedrich

von Hayek's *The Road to Serfdom,* providing an ethical defense of
free markets and a classical liberal critique of planned economies.
Years later, a liberal Harvard historian called publication of that
book "a major event in the intellectual history of the United States."
In 1952, Whittaker Chambers revealed his story and his soul in
Witness, recasting the contest of communism and democracy as an
enduring, spiritual contest of good and evil. In 1953 came Russell
Kirk's *The Conservative Mind,* providing American conservatism
with an intellectual pedigree reaching back to Edmund Burke. The
journal, founded by William F. Buckley, was *National Review,* giving conservatism an infusion of self-confidence and wit, and separating it decisively from isolationism, conspiracy theories, and
anti-Semitism, defining the principled mainstream of the movement.
This trio and journal provided the building blocks for a foundation
of a new conservatism: libertarian (eventually including Milton
Friedman), anti-Communist (including James Burnham), and traditionalist (joined by Robert Nisbet)—all balanced by the diplomacy of Bill Buckley.

In this respected and respectable form, conservatism influenced
a generation of political leaders, finding resonance in both political parties. In 1964, Senator Barry Goldwater concentrated that
influence in the Republican Party by winning its nomination and
began to change the landscape of American politics. When Goldwater took the podium at the San Francisco Cow Palace on July
16, his nomination marked a milestone of conservative confidence.
After hearing his unapologetically conservative call to arms
("extremism in the defense of liberty is no vice") one reporter
expressed shock, "My God, he's going to run as Barry Goldwater."

The Goldwater movement made enemies (Norman Mailer in
Esquire compared the San Francisco convention to a Nazi rally)
and inspired lifelong activists. On college campuses, it excited
unprecedented enthusiasm, along with a sense of rebellion. One
student conservative explained, "You walk around with your Goldwater button, and you feel the thrill of treason." Because of the

role of his campaign in the advance of conservative ideas, Goldwater's eventual loss has been called "the most fruitful defeat of modern times." Immediately after the election, cars across America sprouted bumper stickers reading: "Twenty-seven million Americans can't be wrong." That figure, it turned out, was a baseline, not a high-water mark.

Following the election, two Southern Democrats in the House of Representatives were stripped of their seniority in retaliation for their support of Goldwater—an attempt to prevent any Southern flirtation with the Republican Party. It didn't work. In every election since 1964, Republican candidates for House seats have gotten more votes than in the one before, creating the stronghold of the Republican majority that arrived thirty years later. And the 1964 election also brought a conservative actor named Ronald Reagan to the national stage, with a televised speech on behalf of Goldwater's campaign. That speech powerfully tied conservatism to populism and optimism, expanding its appeal to secretaries and steelworkers—people eventually known as Reagan Democrats.

In the next decade and a half, the conservative movement gained the momentum of three groups of potent reinforcements. In the fall of 1965, a group of New York intellectuals—mostly former leftists—founded a journal called *The Public Interest* and a trend called neoconservatism. Irving Kristol, Norman Podhoretz, Daniel Bell, Seymour Lipset, Midge Decter, James Q. Wilson, and others pointed out the limits of liberal social policy, revealed its unintended, counterproductive consequences, and argued for the importance of virtue in society. They helped conservatives accept the civil rights movement, established social science as an ally, and proved, contra John Stuart Mill, that conservatism was anything but the "stupid party."

In the mid-1970s, religious conservatives, assaulted by the organized irreligion of government, awoke to assume a public role, providing conservatism with grassroots activism and moral passion. At the same time, a handful of supply-siders, led by Jack Kemp and championed by the editorial page of the *Wall Street Journal*, defined a hopeful economic philosophy of low tax rates, increased productivity and investment, and expanded growth. "Supply side economics," observes William Kristol, "became the governing doctrine of the Republican Party in 1980 and the governing doctrine of the nation in '81." In this period of conservative vitality, Democratic Senator Daniel Patrick Moynihan announced that "something momentous has happened in American life; the Republican Party has become the party of ideas." And they were conservative ideas.

Barry Goldwater had managed to carry only five states in his run for President. Beginning in 1980, Ronald Reagan carried ninety-three states in forty-eight months, based on an effective, productive alliance of economic and social concerns. By 1983—twenty years after conservatism had been called the "forbidden faith"—twice as many Americans identified themselves in polls as "conservatives" than as "liberals." The Reagan administration brought a generation of bright, educated young conservatives to Washington, occupying congressional staffs, agency appointments, conservative publications, and think tanks—with many passing through the doors of The Heritage Foundation. It established a resentment of overgrown government, a resistance to high tax rates, and a concern about judicial activism at the center of American politics. And, above all, it refused to accept the permanent division of the globe into slave and free, establishing conservatism as an aggressive defender of liberty in a world weary of poverty and oppression. A far cry from conservative opposition to World War II.

The congressional elections of 1994—with their historic shift to a Republican majority—confirmed that conservatism is not an aberration, based on the winning personality and moving rhetoric of Ronald Reagan. It is the most serious, sustained political movement since progressivism. It is reinforced by philosophic sophistication, historical learning, literary achievement, and populist outrage. And it has sent liberalism into a crisis of faith—a series of constantly revised visions—having watched its traditional ideals and goals transformed from inevitable into incredible.

"The trouble," writes Norman Podhoretz, "is that thirty years of shuffling have blurred the creed, so that liberalism now resembles a person who has undergone 27 face-lifts; the natural contours have disappeared ... Mainstream liberalism ... has become vaporous. There are no deep channels of energy." Liberals hear the beating waves of the conservative tide on the shores of their own St. Helena, confined to universities and newsrooms.

As I've argued, this does not always guarantee day-to-day political success for conservative candidates, particularly when conservative themes are insincerely but effectively copied. Still, we have seen the strength of conservatism become deeper than the results of the last election. Today's conservative movement has its own think tanks, publishing houses, radio talk shows, magazines, foundations, and journals. It has developed, in the words of the former *Washington Post* writer and present Clinton staffer Sidney Blumenthal, a "counter-establishment"—not by joining the current establishment, but creating a new one to supplant the old.

This has been a conscious goal of The Heritage Foundation—to be a permanent Washington presence. We have set out to make conservative ideas not just respectable but mainstream. To set the terms of national policy debate. To offer, not a lament for a lost America, but positive, practical, free market alternatives to the failed liberal policies of the old order.

In 1980, we issued the first *Mandate For Leadership*—a detailed series of policy proposals, running 1,093 pages, which spent three weeks on the *Washington Post* bestsellers list. Designed as "a blueprint for conservative government," it was the result of an effort that had never been previously undertaken. We took the lead in popularizing the Reagan Doctrine of supporting anti-Communist freedom fighters in Nicaragua and Afghanistan. We gave aggressive support to tax cuts in the 1980s, which created the longest economic boom in American history. And we have served as the neutral common ground for the conservative movement—a place to act on our agreements and to disagree with civility.

This intellectual, political, and institutional success presents a temptation: to forget that these gains were not ordained by history but won by courage. The popularity of conservative ideas creates the possibility of shallow assent—a failure to appreciate that conservatism is richer than talk radio, and once was costly to confess. It is the story of men and women who often risked reputations, careers, and lives to break from communism, colleagues, or convention. It is the story of giants of thought and action, who lived some of the most interesting lives of the twentieth century. It is the story of four decades of careful, costly intellectual struggle. It is the story of white-heat conviction that illuminates our age. And it is the story that occupies these essays.

Conservatism may not be an ideology, to be declared in a manifesto, but it is also far from a passing fashion. This book, I hope and expect, will reveal to the careful reader some principles that have emerged out of conservative practice. I won't attempt an exhaustive list, but there is a set of ideals to look out for.

At the outset, it is worth noting that conservatism is not a blind defense of the status quo—a confusion that has occasionally led to the journalistic baptism of Joseph Stalin or Fidel Castro as a "conservative." This is the most common caricature of conservatism. (In the early part of the last century, a French observer claimed that if British conservative Lord Liverpool has been present at the Creation, he would have said, "*Mon Dieu, conserve le chaos!*") Sometimes conservatives themselves have reinforced this perception. Evelyn Waugh once bitterly complained that the Conservative Party had "never put the clocks back by a single minute."

No, conservatism is not simply resistance to change. It is more than a fearful habit of mind. American conservatism, as it has developed, has a content, which sharply distinguishes it from the aristocratic conservatism of Europe, or the authoritarian conservatism of South America. It is not just a variant, it is a different breed.

- AMERICAN CONSERVATISM IS HIGHLY suspicious of promised utopia and earthly salvation. The purpose of politics is not redemptive, it is to carve out a system of justice, moral order and freedom, recognizing that human beings are neither perfect nor perfectible. When governments seek after utopia they end in oppression and disaster, because man and society are infinitely complex, and cannot be reshaped by an aristocracy of experts. Humility is the only proper attitude for governing authorities.

- Conservatives—all conservatives from libertarian to traditional-ist—believe that social power is a zero-sum game. When it is taken by government it is lost by individuals. This calls for prudent restraints on the role and reach of government. "There must be a stopping point," argues Charles Murray, "some rule by which governments limit what they do for people—not just because of budget constraints, not just because of infringements on freedom (though either of these might be a sufficient reason in itself), but because happiness is impossible unless people are left alone to take trouble over important things."

- Conservatives tend to believe there is a close and necessary connection between property and freedom—that economic freedom is an essential part of human freedom. Economic markets, when left to themselves, often have unexpected and positive social benefits. And this should not surprise us, because they are based on cooperation rather than coercion. It has been noted by conservatives that to prosper as a Socialist you need to threaten people, while to prosper as a capitalist you need to please them.

- Conservatives often teach that the order of society depends directly on the moral order found in the souls of citizens—that freedom must be tempered by internal restraint, so our laws can be permissive while our society is not. Put another way, liberty unconstrained by character can destroy freedom, and freedom itself must be defined as something better and higher than grinning decadence. This points to the centrality of character-building institutions in society, particularly families, churches, and synagogues, because they uphold the moral order that makes freedom functional, initiating men and women in the elevating traditions of the human race—loyalty and love, diligence and duty.

- Conservatives usually believe that individual liberty is protected in the preservation of national sovereignty, making national defense a high moral duty.

- Conservatives tend to judge social policies by their outcomes not their intentions, arguing that humanitarianism should do something positive for actual humans. Citizens, in short, should seek to do good, not just to feel good. So conservatives are critical of the embarrassing legacy of Great Society goodness without wisdom—the reduction of citizens to serfs, and the creation of whole communities where the funerals of young people are common, and their weddings are rare.

- Though conservatives are not wedded to the status quo, they are wary of radical change based on abstract theories. They tend to prefer settled institutions, values, and traditions, embodying what G.K. Chesterton called "the democracy of the dead"—an approach which "refuses to submit to the small and arrogant oligarchy of those who happen merely to be walking about." This leads, as Michael Oakeshott terms it, to "the politics of repair" rather than "the politics of destruction and creation."

- And, though this is not universal, many conservatives share a sense of reverence, a belief in two worlds—one physical and one moral and spiritual—that stand in judgment of our own. When Ralph de Toledano was sent proof sheets of a novel he had written, he noticed that his publishers had removed the capital letters from Heaven and Hell. Toledano corrected each instance and sent back the proofs. His publisher called and said, "Ralph, we have a set of style rules over here we must observe. Why do you insist on capitalizing Heaven and Hell?" "Because," replied Toledano, "they're places. You know, like Scarsdale." And this has an influence on the way many conservatives approach life and politics.

- George Santayana observed, "The consciousness that the human spirit is derived and responsible, that all its functions are heritages and trusts, involves a sentiment of gratitude and duty which we may call piety." And that piety is common in the conservative movement, among men and women of every religious tradition and, sometimes, none at all.

These are some of the themes of the conservative restoration. I find all of them compelling and none of them contradictory. The danger of division, as I have seen it, comes when one conservative value—either freedom or moral order—is elevated to an absolute, to which everything else is sacrificed. So perhaps the highest conservative virtue is prudence—the balance of valid and competing truths.

In my own case, three men have had the greatest impact on my thinking—Russell Kirk, Friedrich von Hayek, and Milton Friedman. In the same room, they would have had (and did have) fascinating, heated arguments. But I don't believe my respect for them is schizophrenic. All shared a revulsion against "gnosticism" and "social engineering." All would admit that a vigorous economy depends on strong families and communities, and that economic policy has an important influence on the social fabric. And all of them refreshed and revived the conservative faith.

I hope that this book will introduce or reintroduce many to this faith—and then encourage many to cross the bridge from thought to action, matching principle with participation. There is unfinished business for American conservatism until the family is honored, the nanny state is finally fired, and freedom no longer needs champions. There is room for new, epic accomplishments in this living tradition—this great and honorable adventure.

Near the end of his life, Whittaker Chambers wrote: "Escapism is laudable, perhaps the only truly honorable course for humane men—but only for them. Those who remain in the world, if they will not surrender on its terms, must maneuver within its terms. That is what conservatives must decide: how much to give in order to survive at all; how much to give in order not to give up basic principles. And of course that results in a dance along a precipice. Many will drop over, and always, the cliff dancers will hear the screaming curses of those who fall, or be numbed by the sullen silence of those ... who will not join the dance."

Consider this book a formal invitation to join the dance.

Acknowledgments

These essays have appeared annually since Christmas 1986 as "President's Essays" from The Heritage Foundation. Several friends originally encouraged me to bring them together in a single collection. Hence, this volume.

Over the years, I have relied on the assistance of a number of individuals in the preparation of this series. Specifically, my colleagues on the Board of Trustees of The Heritage Foundation, especially our chairman, David Brown, Larry Arnn, and Frank Shakespeare and the late Bill Simon kept the inspiration alive. Our honorary trustee, Jack Eckerd, was enthusiastic about them early in this effort. Many of my Heritage staff colleagues have been very helpful, and I owe particular thanks to Herb Berkowitz, Adam Meyerson, Edwin Meese, Bridgett Wagner, Lee Edwards, Matthew Spalding, and Phil Truluck for their ideas and insights, and to Mark Esper, Kathy Rowan, Missy Stephens, Ann Klucsarits, and Michelle Smith for their production assistance. "Eagle Eye" Richard Odermatt has been Heritage's walking style manual and proofreader for more than twenty years, and his unique skills have again saved me from several glaring errors.

The wise counsel of the late Don Lipsett, founder of The Philadelphia Society, inspired this series almost two decades ago. His gentle prodding, especially in the early years, kept me focused when it seemed that the "urgent might overwhelm the important" and a year might be missed. His able successor, Bill Campbell; the Society's Secretary, Vic Milione, President Emeritus of the Intercollegiate Studies Institute, and his successor, Ken Cribb; and the late Henry Regnery, publisher of so many extraordinary works of seminal influence on the conservative movement, have all guided and advised me over the years.

My wife, Linda, to whom this volume is dedicated, has waged these battles with me for more than thirty years. Her unfailing good humor, encouragement, and support have given me the stamina to continue when the prospects for conservatism seemed particularly dark and depressing.

Of course, my debt, and that of all who believe in the conservative vision, is primarily to these thinkers and writers whose work undergirds the "spirit of liberty" around the world. Therefore, I gratefully acknowledge permission to reprint the following essays in this volume:

"The Conservative Framework and Modern Realities" by William F. Buckley Jr., from *Up from Liberalism*. Copyright © 1959, 1964, 1968, and 1997 by William F. Buckley Jr. Used by permission of the Wallace Literary Agency, Inc.

"Enlivening the Conservative Mind" by Russell Kirk, from *Prospects for Conservatives*. Copyright © 1989 by Russell Kirk. Reprinted by arrangement with Regnery Publishing, Inc., Washington, D.C.

"Responsibility and Freedom" by F.A. Hayek from *The Constitution of Liberty*, pp. 71–84. Copyright © 1960 by the University of Chicago. Reprinted by permission.

Introduction and Chapters 1 & 2, from *Capitalism and Freedom* by Milton Friedman, pp. 1–36. Copyright © 1960 by the University of Chicago. Reprinted by permission.

"Freedom, Tradition, Conservatism" by Frank S. Meyer, from *What Is Conservatism?* by ISI Books. Copyright © 1964 by Intercollegiate Studies Institute. Reprinted by permission.

"A Letter to the Young" by Midge Decter, from *Liberal Parents, Radical Children*. Copyright © 1975 by Midge Decter. Reprinted by permission of Midge Decter.

"Isaiah's Job" by Albert Jay Nock, from *Free Speech and Plain Language*. Copyright © 1937 by Albert Jay Nock. Copyright renewed 1963 by Frances J. Nock and Samuel Nock. Reprinted by permission of William Morrow & Company, Inc.

"A Letter to My Children" by Whittaker Chambers, from *Witness*. Copyright © 1952 by Whittaker Chambers. Reprinted by permission of Random House, Inc.

"Errand into the Wilderness" by Michael Novak, from *Political Passages: Journey Through Two Decades*. Copyright © 1988 by Michael Novak. Reprinted by permission of Michael Novak.

"The Economic Necessity of Freedom" by Wilhelm Roepke, from *Modern Age*, Summer, 1959. Copyright © 1959 by Intercollegiate Studies Institute. Reprinted by permission.

"Up from Liberalism" by Richard M. Weaver, from *Life Without Prejudice and Other Essays*. Copyright © 1966 by Richard M. Weaver. Reprinted by arrangement with Regnery Publishing, Inc., Washington, D.C.

"Liberty and Property" by Ludwig von Mises, from a lecture by Ludwig von Mises presented at the ninth meeting of the Mont Pelerin Society, Princeton University, October 1958. Copyright ©

PART ONE

Conservative Minds

The Heritage Foundation Collection, 1988

Chapter 1

William F. Buckley Jr.

Commentary by Edwin J. Feulner Jr. (1994)

Founder of *National Review*, host of *Firing Line*, writer of spy novels, sailor in all weather, player of the harpsichord, lover of the Latin Mass, and definitive authority on God and man at Yale, William F. Buckley Jr. is quite simply the most famous conservative of his generation. When he broke upon the intellectual scene in 1955, with the publication of *God and Man at Yale*, Ronald Reagan was still a card-carrying Democrat, and conservatism as we know it today was barely a glimmer in Russell Kirk's eye. In the four decades that have followed, Bill Buckley has been the leader of America's conservative insurrection—a revolution hatched in the cramped offices of *National Review* and fed on Pat Buckley's chicken salad sandwiches. The long march up from liberalism has led through the wilderness of Goldwater's defeat, to the promised land of Reagan's victory, and over the corpse of communism. At every stage of the journey, Bill Buckley has confidently called the cadence. And all the while, he has conducted a running seminar on the art of writing and the art of living.

If, as George Orwell insisted, "political chaos is connected with the decay of language," then the reordering of American politics is inseparable from Bill Buckley's resurrection of rhetoric. He is an orator in an age of mutterers. A rhetorical pyro-technician for whom every day is the Fourth of July. A polemicist with the power to convince or enrage but never to disappoint. An elegant eulogist who expands our empathy into places we never expected. An essayist with no patience for the shapeless, the careless, the colorless. A verbal craftsman with an unfailing ear for the rhythm of words. A philosopher who adds the fuel of ideas to the fire of political debate.

It is difficult now to remember how isolated the conservative remnant seemed in the 1940s and early 1950s, meeting by torchlight in its catacombs. In August of 1945, Churchill was defeated and a newly elected Labor majority in England walked into Parliament singing the "Red Flag," a leftist battle hymn unsung since the Spanish Civil War. At home, the Republican Party adopted a program that was little more, in Buckley's words, than "measured socialism." Historian Morton Smith stated that conservatism "is all but dead in our present world."

It was not true, but it felt like it was true. Ronald Reagan joked that he had received his first issue of *National Review* "in a plain, brown wrapper." "The few spasmodic victories conservatives are winning," Buckley wrote in 1954, "are aimless, uncoordinated and inconclusive. This is so ... because many years have gone by since the philosophy of freedom has been expounded systematically, brilliantly and resourcefully."

But midway through the 1950s, the philosophy of freedom found its voice—systematic, brilliant, resourceful—and it belonged to a freshly minted graduate of Yale. In a swirl of passionate public controversy (with Vidal, Mailer, Kempton, Galbraith, Baldwin), the young Buckley introduced liberals to humility and inspired conservatives to confidence. His arguments were illuminated by the lightning of wit and suffused with scholarship. They made right reason seem plausible, then inevitable. It soon became clear that Buckley was not just developing a following, but a movement.

William F. Buckley Jr., with his drawled "Waal ..." and suits that seem to come pre-rumpled from the cleaners, is one of the most recognizable men in America. But to those who know him, he is most easily recognized for acts of personal kindness and unexpected generosity. It is unprecedented that a life of such intense argument should yield so many friends. Friends in trouble who have discovered bills mysteriously paid. Friends who have found the private Buckley unfailingly tolerant of the failings of others. When Bill was running for Mayor of New York City against John Lindsay and Abraham Beame, *New York Times* columnist Murray Kempton observed, "The only one in the group I would dare call collect long distance for a loan is William F. Buckley."

The public style is playfully self-confident ("I don't stoop to conquer. I merely conquer.") But his polemic always has a purpose; his erudition always serves an ideal. He is impatient, for example, with the tart skepticism of H.L. Mencken ("He debunked for the sake of debunking," Buckley has observed). His own approach he describes as knowing "about the quality of reverence and feeling it strongly and feeling that the holy things should be treated venerably." In this category he counts his Church, his nation, and his alma mater. When he has been critical of these things, it is always evidence of loyalty and love, never disdain.

He has demonstrated that wit is possible without cynicism; that a pundit can also be a pilgrim. "I am not tortured by the problems that torture a great many other people," he writes, "because I do very sincerely and very simply believe in God and in the whole of the Christian experience. And there are enough resources in it to show me where to go." It is the key to understanding both his character and his politics. "I myself believe that the duel between Christianity and atheism is the most important in the world."

Liberalism's chief flaw, Buckley argues, is spiritual: its skepticism and relativism; its elevation of method over substance; its defense of freedom as an end in itself. It "has no eschatology; no vision, no fulfillment, no point of arrival." Freedom, while the highest goal of democracy, cannot be the highest goal of civilization. It is a road on which we travel, not a house for us to live in. Our true destination is defined by the creed we hold about the cosmos in which we live. Liberalism's epistemological relativism reduces everything, including politics, to unsignifying sound and fury. "It cannot care deeply, and so cannot be cared about deeply," he writes. "There is nothing there of ultimate meaning to care for, though there is much there to despise." It is a political faith crippled by moral apathy, unable to distinguish between noble and base, just and unjust, or to "call for the kind of passionate commitment that stirs the political blood."

William Buckley was born November 24, 1925, sixth of ten children—nine of whom would go on to write or work for *National Review*. His father was an oilman of imposing presence ("He worshipped three earthly things: learning, beauty, and his family"). His mother, a woman of gregarious, Southern grace ("She was wonderfully content making others happy by her vivacity, her delicate beauty, her habit of seeing the best in everyone"). Before his teens, Bill's cosmopolitan upbringing had made stops in Venezuela, France, and England. A precocious youth, he was fluent in French and Spanish before entering prep school, and already possessed of strong, early convictions. As a boy of six, he sent a letter to the King of England demanding that His Majesty repay his war debts to the United States. At age fifteen, he received a note from his father admonishing him "to be more moderate in the expression of your views and [to] try to express them in a way that would give as little offense as possible." "That must have been," wrote one biographer, "the most wasted piece of advice since the Prime Minister counseled Edward VIII against hanging out with divorcees."

At Yale, Bill proved a natural debater and rose to the chairmanship of the *Yale Daily News*. Invited to give the university's annual Alumni Address, his speech urged Yale to declare "active Christianity the first basis of enlightened thought and action" and "communism, socialism, collectivism ... inimical to the dignity of the individual." The Administration promptly censored it. *God and Man at Yale,* written a year after graduation, extended and developed this critique of anti-Christian and collectivist bias in higher education. It was praised in the *Saturday Review* as having "a clarity, a sobriety, and an intellectual honesty that would be noteworthy if it came from a college president." The book's criticisms clearly struck a nerve (McGeorge Bundy pronounced its author "a twisted and ignorant young man"). They also struck a chord. Buckley's bombshell became a best-seller, launching his career.

At this point, the narrative of Bill Buckley's life becomes a biography of the conservative movement. A few days short of his thirtieth birthday, he founded *National Review*. Forrest Davis, editor of *The American Mercury*, recalls his first meeting with Buckley, who was traveling to Washington to recruit writers for his new journal: "This positive kid came into the restaurant, with his tie half off, sat down, kicked off his shoes, and became the focus of the whole table's attention. By the time he left the restaurant, he had its staff almost fighting for the chance to serve him. I thought, 'Here's a man who's going somewhere.'" From the first issue, the new magazine invited strong reactions. Author Dwight Macdonald charged it with "brutality," "banality" and "vulgarity"—the work of "half-educated provincials." Even the faithful had some initial doubts. Russell Kirk wrote T.S. Eliot that the magazine evinced "too much Yale undergraduate spirit." But that spirit proved a weapon of enduring value, managing the difficult task of being literate about the illiterate, witty about the witless. It not only jousted with the Black Knight of liberalism and collectivism, but revealed it, on closer inspection, as a tattered, toothless scarecrow. After the Chernobyl meltdown: "The Soviet Union has finally contrived to give power to the people." On the CIA: "The attempted assassination of Sukarno last week had all the earmarks of a CIA operation. Everyone in the room was killed except Sukarno." On a suggested advertising campaign for the *New York Times* classified section: A smiling picture of Castro above the slogan, "I Got My Job Through the *New York Times*."

The magazine found an immediate influence because it managed to bring together (and hold together) a group of brilliant, contentious, sometimes difficult men—James Burnham, Russell Kirk, Frank Meyer, Willi Schlamm. The glue that maintained this united conservative front was Bill Buckley's personality. "Morale at NR," writes Garry Wills, "was kept up, in the early years, almost as an army's is. And the source of the unifying spirit was evident. Things lit or dimmed at NR with the coming or going of ... Bill's laugh."

Beyond this task, the magazine acted as the Buckley Writing Academy—cultivating talent like George Will, Garry Wills, Chilton Williamson, and Richard Brookhiser. It became, through the quality of its writing and the force of its personalities, the single place to talk directly to the entire conservative movement. The place Ronald Reagan chose to write, after the Goldwater defeat, that conservatism was not routed, just its "false image." The place Patrick Moynihan chose to announce the failure of his pet project, guaranteed income programs ("And so you turn out to be right," he congratulated Buckley).

In a life hectic with accomplishment, *National Review* is Bill Buckley's proudest achievement. Once, when asked by supporters to run for governor of New York, he replied, "I could not make the time to run for governor, given my obligations to *National Review*. My friends couldn't understand my priorities. But I was very content with them." The attention he lavished was rewarded: Many conservatives learned in its pages, for the first time, that they were not alone. Listen to two witnesses:

Peggy Noonan: "I started reading NR, and it sang to me. They saw it the way I was seeing it: America was essentially good, the war is being fought for serious and valid reasons, the answer to every social ill is not necessarily a social program, when you let a government get too big you threaten your own liberties—and God is real as a rock. I was moved, and more. It assuaged a kind of loneliness. Later I found that half the people in the Reagan administration had as their first conservative friend that little magazine."

Pat Buchanan: "It is difficult to exaggerate the debt conservatives of my generation owe *National Review* and Bill Buckley.

Before I read NR, there was virtually nothing I read that supported or reinforced what I was coming to believe. We young conservatives were truly wandering around in a political wilderness,
wondering if there was anyone of intelligence and wit, any men of
words, who thought and felt and believed as we did…. For us, what
National Review did was take the word *conservatism,* then a
synonym for stuffy orthodoxy, Republican stand-pat-ism and economic self-interest, and convert it into the snapping pennant of a
fighting faith."

In 1965, Bill Buckley raised that pennant in a run for Mayor of
New York City, his only excursion into electoral politics. Though
he refused to display what he called "the usual neurotic confidence
of all political candidates," the race was not a lark. "My motives
were didactic, not political." A showing of 13.4 percent for a conservative in Gotham was more than respectable, but Bill's head was
never turned by politics. "As one gets older, one has to decide
whether to be a critic or a statesman…. When Ronald Reagan
offered me the ambassadorship to Afghanistan, I said, 'Yes, but only
if you give me fifteen divisions of bodyguards.' I was offered the
United Nations and I said no. It is an illusion that you need to be
a formal member of government to have real power." He believes,
with good reason, that his voice is better amplified by writing than
running. In 1970 he was asked, "What would you feel about running for a seat in the House?" "God, no," he replied. "Not unless
I can have all the seats simultaneously"

Recounting Bill Buckley's accomplishments becomes difficult,
because his cruising speed is several gears higher than most. His life
reveals not a minute that the locust has eaten. In 1960, he helped
organize Young Americans for Freedom. In 1961, he was instru-
mental in founding the New York Conservative Party; *Firing Line*
was started in 1966, quickly earning an Emmy. Given the breadth
of his interests, it is not surprising that he has published books on
everything from Joe McCarthy to celestial navigation, from national service to children's literature. His passion for sailing has carried

him in the wake of Columbus across the Atlantic and then across the Pacific for good measure. At age fifty, he began a series of ten best-selling spy novels. The week he went into semi-retirement from *National Review*, he performed a harpsichord concerto with the North Carolina Symphony. "I get bored," he says, "winding my watch." But we who are privileged to watch him are never bored.

Two great contributions define Bill Buckley's place in the history of conservative thought. The first is his built-in, shockproof, ideological balance detector. Conservatism is notoriously difficult to define and any of its elements—freedom, order, tradition—can be taken to extremes that undermine the whole. There is a line beyond which an emphasis becomes a mania; and beyond which a political movement is disqualified from the task of governing. It has been Bill's role to grab the wheel and give it a sharp turn when conservative thought veered toward "crackpot alley."

Never was this role more important than when the movement was still a kicking fetus. Conservatism in the 1950s was colorful, eccentric—and largely irrelevant. Some taught that theism was weakness and altruism a crime. Others accused Dwight Eisenhower of being a communist agent. In both cases, Bill Buckley shored up the ideological levies that defined the course of the conservative mainstream. The result was a movement prepared for Goldwater and respectability, and then for Reagan and power.

Buckley's second contribution has been to lend conservatism an intellectual style that challenges its designation by J.S. Mill as "the stupid party." ("As the intelligent are liberals," Maurice Baring once commented, "I am on the side of the idiots.") For the liberal establishment, Buckley's besetting sin was not his conservatism, but his intelligence and wit—the fact that he is both conservative and interesting. This was a threat like none it had ever seen—the prospect of defeat on its own turf and terms. During his run for Mayor of New York, Buckley was informed that "a senior editor of the *New York Times* confessed ... that he had taken to dispatching different reporters to Buckley's press conferences because 'everyone who came back after a couple of them said he was going to vote for [him].'" Even the liberal palace guard could no longer be trusted.

The select company of those represented in these essays is familiar company for Bill Buckley. Albert J. Nock was a friend of Bill's family during his youth, often lunching at their home in Connecticut. Frank Meyer, Russell Kirk, and James Burnham were fellow-laborers in the vineyards of *National Review*. Michael Novak was a religion editor at the magazine. Whittaker Chambers and Bill developed a close, spiritual friendship which lasted until Chambers' death in 1961 (recorded in the moving volume *Odyssey of a Friend*). Bill Buckley, it seems, has always been the epicenter of rumbles on the right.

"The Conservative Framework and Modern Realities" is taken from *Up From Liberalism*, published in 1959. It is a meditation on the meaning of conservatism—a creed so easy to live for and so difficult to define. Buckley, elsewhere, admits the challenge: "I have never failed to dissatisfy an audience that asks the meaning of conservatism." Usually his mischievous response is to quote Richard Weaver: "A paradigm of essences toward which the phenomenology of the world is in continuing approximation." Here his answer is more clearly developed. Conservatism, he argues, is not an ideology, but it does have discernable principles at its core. Such principles must respect political reality, yet there are limits to maneuver—issues, times, and places where conservatism can bend but must not break. The result is a balancing act, "a dance along a precipice." But the currency in which our success is counted is always human freedom, not as an end but a means—the power to "live my life an obedient man, but obedient to God, subservient to the wisdom of my ancestors; never to the authority of political truths arrived at yesterday at the voting booth."

Buckley commends a conservatism that is principled, but not dogmatic; that balances long-term goals with the politics of the present. The objective is not the consistency of simple minds—the clean, well-lit, padded room of a single idea. It is to skillfully adjust to current circumstances until all our fundamental commitments—freedom, order, community, justice—are aligned in the same conservative vision. This allows for vigorous disagreement on the right over policy without recourse to anathema and schism because our unity is found in broad themes, not specific measures. "It is not a single conservative's responsibility or right to draft a concrete program—merely to suggest the principles that should frame it." But those principles remain the best hope of every future we can imagine.

I first met William Buckley in the fall of 1964 at the organizing committee meeting for the Philadelphia Society, also attended by Don Lipsett, Frank Meyer, and Milton Friedman. According to the early records of the group, Bill Buckley loaned the Society its first one hundred for organizing expenses at that meeting. (Since I was an impecunious graduate student at the Wharton School, it was highly unlikely that I would be in the position to have start-up funds for such a risky venture.) Thirty years later, the Philadelphia Society continues to fill a vital role as a meeting place for American conservatives. Bill has a talent for encouraging the small beginnings of great things. He is a gardener who has seen redwoods grow to maturity.

His association with The Heritage Foundation is a long one. He was a featured speaker in 1980 at the dedication of the Noble and Coors Buildings, our first Heritage headquarters. He also spoke when we dedicated the Fertig Board Room in our current building. But off the public platform, the private Buckley has been a friend of mine and of Heritage. Bill's talent for hospitality and his unfailing good humor have steadied and unified the conservative movement. At his semi-annual dinners and discussions, all the disparate factions of conservatism are invited and reminded of the battle against a common enemy that is more important than the squabbles among natural allies.

Over the years, Bill Buckley has baffled opponents with his insistent, infectious cheerfulness—the attitude of a man continually surprised by joy. This has strengthened the conservative cause, but its source is deeper than the ideology it enriches. Even Bill Buckley's spirited conservatism reveals an underlying and unsettling realism. "It is undoubtedly necessary," Buckley writes, "every now and then, to bare one's teeth; and we do so, preferably, in the course of smiling. But the smiles have a way of freezing, as sadness rolls in. The joys of warmaking [for conservative causes] presuppose the eventual stillness of victory: and that, so far as I can see, is beyond our reach. Perhaps it was meant to be so." But there is more to say—infinitely more. When asked by one interviewer whether "most dogmas, theological as well as ideological, do not crumble sooner or later," he replied, "Most, but not all." How, the interviewer persisted, could he be so sure? Because, Buckley affirmed, "I know that my Redeemer liveth."

With G.K. Chesterton, William F. Buckley asserts that "the men signed of the Cross of Christ go gaily in the dark." And the darkness itself is lifted as men and women follow his example.

William F. Buckley Jr.

The Conservative Framework and Modern Realities

> ... an essay such as this is far more important for what it destroys—or to speak more accurately for the destruction which it crystallizes, since the ultimate enemy of myth is circumstance—than for what it creates. This is sharply at odds with the conventional wisdom. The latter sets great store by what it calls constructive criticism. And it reserves its scorn for what it is likely to term a purely destructive or negative position. In this, as so often, it manifests a sound instinct for self-preservation.
>
> — J. K. Galbraith, *The Affluent Society*

Up where from liberalism? There is no conservative political manifesto which, as we make our faltering way, we can consult, confident that it will point a sure finger in the direction of the good society. Indeed, sometimes the conservative needle appears to be jumping about as on a disoriented compass. My professional life is lived in an office battered by every pressure of contemporary conservatism. Some of the importunities upon a decent American conservatism are outrageous, or appear so to me,

From William F. Buckley Jr., *Up from Liberalism* (1959).

at any rate. (*"We should have high tariffs because the farmers have high subsidies, and they shouldn't, by the way."*) Some are pathological *("Alaska is being prepared as a mammoth concentration camp for pro-McCarthyites.")* Some are deeply mystical (*"The state can do no good."* My answer: It can arrest Communists, can't it?); some ambitiously spiritual (*"Conservatism has no extrinsic significance except in relation to religion."*) Some urge the schematization of conservatism (*"What passes for conservatism these days is nothing more than sentimentality and nostalgia. Let us give it structure ..."*); or the opposite (*"Beware the ideologization of conservatism."*)

Still, for all the confusion and contradiction, I venture to say it is possible to talk about "the conservative position" and mean something by it. At the political level, conservatives are bound together for the most part by negative response to liberalism; but altogether too much is made of that fact. Negative action is not necessarily of negative value. Political freedom's principal value is negative in character. The people are politically stirred principally by the necessity for negative affirmations. Cincinnatus was a farmer before he took up his sword, and went back to farming after wielding some highly negative strokes upon the pates of those who sought to make positive changes in his way of life.

The weakness of American conservatives does not reduce neatly to the fact that some want tariffs, others not. Dr. Robert Oppenheimer was much taken during the 1950s by what goes by the name of "complementarity," a notion having to do with revised relationships in the far reaches of philosophical thought, where "opposites" come under a single compass, and fuse into workable philosophical and physical unities. No doubt Physicist Oppenheimer was sticking an irreverent finger in the higher chemistry of metaphysics: but his theory, like the Hegelian synthesis, served to remind us that there is almost always conceivable the vantage point from which the seemingly incongruous, the apparently contradictory, can be viewed in harmony. A navigator for whom two lighthouses can mark extreme points of danger relative to his present position, knows that by going back and making a wholly different approach, the two lighthouses will fuse together to form a single object to the vision, confirming the safety of his position. They are then said to be "in range."

There is a point from which opposition to the social security laws and a devout belief in social stability are in range; as also a determined resistance to the spread of world Communism—and a belief in political noninterventionism; a disgust with the results of modern education—and sympathy for the individual educational requirements of the individual child; a sympathetic understanding of the spiritual essence of human existence—and a desire to delimit religious influence in political affairs; a patriotic concern for the nation and its culture—and a genuine respect for the integrity and differences of other peoples' culture; a militant concern for the Negro—and a belief in decentralized political power even though, on account of it, the Negro is sometimes victimized; a respect for the omnicompetence of the free marketplace—and the knowledge of the necessity for occupational interposition. There is a position from which these views are "in range"; and that is the position, generally speaking, where conservatives now find themselves on the political chart. Our most serious challenge is to restore principles— the right principles; the principles liberalism has abused, forsaken, and replaced with "principles" that have merely a methodological content—our challenge is to restore principles to public affairs.

I mentioned in the opening pages of this book that what was once a healthy American pragmatism has deteriorated into a wayward relativism. It is one thing to make the allowances to reality that reality imposes, to take advantage of the current when the current moves in your direction, while riding at anchor at ebb tide. But it is something else to run before political or historical impulses merely because fractious winds begin to blow, and to dismiss resistance as foolish, or perverse idealism. And it is supremely wrong, intellectually and morally, to abandon the norms by which it becomes possible, viewing a trend, to pass judgment upon it; without which judgment we cannot know whether to yield, or to fight.

Are we to fight the machine? Can conservatism assimilate it? Whittaker Chambers once wrote me that "the rockcore of the Conservative Position can be held realistically only if Conservatism will accommodate itself to the needs and hopes of the masses—needs and hopes which like the masses themselves, are the product of machines."

It is true that the masses have asserted themselves, all over the world; have revolted, Ortega said, perceiving the revolutionary quality of the cultural convulsion. The question: how can conservatism accommodate revolution? Can the revolutionary essence be extravasated and be made to diffuse harmlessly in the network of capillaries that rushes forward to accommodate its explosive force? Will the revolt of the masses moderate when the lower class is risen, when science has extirpated misery, and the machine has abolished poverty? Not if the machines themselves are irreconcilable, as Mr. Chambers seemed to suggest when he wrote that "… of course, our fight is with machines," adding: "A conservatism that cannot face the facts of the machine and mass production, and its consequences in government and politics, is foredoomed to futility and petulance. A conservatism that allows for them has an eleventh-hour chance of rallying what is sound in the West."

What forms must this accommodation take? *The welfare state!* is the non-Communist answer one mostly hears. It is necessary, we are told, to comprehend the interdependence of life in an industrial society, and the social consequences of any action by a single part of it, on other parts. Let the steel workers go on strike, and sparkplug salesmen will in due course be out of work. There must be laws to mitigate the helplessness of the individual link in the industrial chain that the machine has built.

What can conservatism do? Must it come to terms with these realities? "To live is to maneuver [Mr. Chambers continued]. The choices of maneuver are now visibly narrow. In the matter of social security, for example, the masses of Americans, like the Russian peasants in 1918, are signing the peace with their feet. I worked the hay load last night against the coming rain—by headlights, long after dark. I know the farmer's case for the machine and for the factory. And I know, like the cut of haybale cords in my hands, that a conservatism that cannot find room in its folds for these actualities is a conservatism that is not a political force, or even a twitch: it has become a literary whimsy."

Indeed. The machine must be accepted, and conservatives must not live by programs that were written as though the machine did not exist or could be made to go away; that is the proper kind of realism. The big question is whether the essential planks of conservatism were anachronized by the machine; the big answer is that they were not. "Those who remain in the world, if they will not surrender on its terms, must maneuver within its terms [said Mr. Chambers]. That is what conservatives must decide: how much to give in order to survive at all; how much to give in order not to give up the basic principles. And, of course, that results in a dance along a precipice. Many will drop over, and, always, the cliff-dancers will hear the screaming curses of those who fall, or be numbed by the sullen silence of those, nobler souls perhaps, who will not join in the dance." We cliff-dancers, resolved not to withdraw into a petulant solitude, or let ourselves fall over the cliff into liberalism, must do what maneuvering we can, and come up with a conservative program that speaks to our time.

It is the chronic failure of liberalism that it obliges circumstance—because it has an inadequate discriminatory apparatus which might cause it to take any other course. There are unemployed in Harlan County? *Rush them aid.* New Yorkers do not want to pay the cost of subways? Get someone else to pay it. Farmers do not want to leave the land? *Let them till it,* buy and destroy the produce. Labor unions demand the closed shop? *It is theirs.* Inflation goes forward in all industrial societies? *We will have continued inflation.* Communism is in control behind the Iron Curtain?

Coexist with it. The tidal wave of industrialism will sweep in the welfare state? *Pull down the sea walls.*

Conservatism must insist that while the will of man is limited in what it can do, it can do enough to make over the face of the world, and that the question that must always be before us is, what shape should the world take, given modern realities? How can technology hope to invalidate conservatism? Freedom, individuality, the sense of community, the sanctity of the family, the supremacy of the conscience, the spiritual view of life—can these verities be transmuted by the advent of tractors and adding machines? These have had a smashing social effect upon us, to be sure. They have created a vortex into which we are being drawn as though irresistibly; but that, surely, is because the principles by which we might have made anchor have not been used, not because of their insufficiency or proven inadaptability. "Technology has succeeded in extracting just about the last bit of taste from a loaf of bread," columnist Murray Kempton once told me spiritedly. "And when we get peacetime use of atomic energy, we'll succeed in getting all the taste out!"

How can one put the problem more plainly? I assume by now Mrs. Kempton has gone to the archives, dusted off an ancient volume, and learned how to bake homemade bread. And lo! the bread turns out to be as easy to make as before, tastes as good as before, and the machine age did not need to be roasted at an *auto-da-fé* to make it all possible. A conservative solution to that problem. But when the atom does to politics what it threatens to bread, what then is the solution? Can one make homemade freedom, under the eyes of an omnipotent state that has no notion of or tolerance for, the flavor of freedom?

Freedom and order and community and justice in an age of technology: that is the contemporary challenge of political conservatism. How to do it, how to live with mechanical harvesters and without socialized agriculture. The direction we must travel requires a broadmindedness that, in the modulated age, strikes us as antiquarian and callous. As I write there is mass suffering in Harlan County,

Kentucky, where coal mining has become unprofitable, and a whole community is desolate. The liberal solution is: immediate and sustained federal subsidies. The conservative, breasting the emotional surf, will begin by saying that it was many years ago foreseeable that coal mining in Harlan County was becoming unprofitable, that the humane course would have been to face up to that realism by permitting the marketplace, through the exertion of economic pressures of mounting intensity, to require resettlement that was not done for the coal miners (they were shielded from reality by a combination of state and union aid)—any more than it is now being done for marginal farmers; so that we are face-to-face with an acute emergency for which there is admittedly no thinkable alternative to immediate relief—if necessary (though it is not) by the federal government; otherwise, by the surrounding communities, or the state of Kentucky. But having made arrangements for relief, what then? Will the grandsons of the Harlan coal miners be mining coal, to be sold to the government at a pegged price, all this to spare today's coal miners the ordeal of looking for other occupations?

The Hoover Commission on government reorganization unearthed several years ago a little rope factory in Boston, Massachusetts, which had been established by the federal government during the Civil War to manufacture the textile specialties the Southern blockade had caused to be temporarily scarce. There it was, ninety years after Appomattox, grinding out the same specialties, which are bought by the government, and then sold at considerable loss. "Liquidate the plant," the Hoover Commission was getting ready to recommend. Whereupon a most influential Massachusetts Senator, Mr. John F. Kennedy, interceded. "You cannot," he informed a member of the Commission, "do so heinous a thing. The plant employs 136 persons, whose only skill is in making this specialty." "Very well then," said the spokesman for the Commission, anxious to cooperate. "Suppose we recommend to the Government that the factory retain in employment every single present employee until he quits, retires, or dies—but on the understanding that none of them is to be replaced. That way we can at least look forward to the eventual liquidation of the plant. Otherwise, there will be 136 people making useless specialties generations hence; an unreasonable legacy of the Civil War."

The Senator was unappeased. What a commotion the proposal would cause in the textile-specialty enclave in Boston! The solution, he warned the Commission, was intolerable, and he would resist it with all his prodigious political might.

The relationship of forces being what it is, the factory continues to operate at full force.

To be sure, a great nation can indulge its little extravagances, as I have repeatedly stressed; but a long enough series of little extravagances, as I have also said, can add up to a stagnating if not a crippling economic overhead. What is disturbing about the Civil War factory incident is first the sheer stupidity of the thing, second the easy victory of liberal sentimentalism over reason. Subsidies are the form that modern circuses tend to take, and, as ever, the people are unaware that it is they who pay for the circuses.

But closing down the useless factories—a general war on featherbedding—is the correct thing to do, if it is correct to cherish the flavor of freedom and economic sanity. There is a sophisticated argument that has to do with the conceivable economic beneficences of pyramid building, and of hiring men to throw rocks out into the sea. But even these proposals, when advanced rhetorically by Lord Keynes, were meliorative and temporary in concept: the idea was to put the men to work until the regenerative juices of the economy had done their work. Now we wake to the fact that along the line we abandoned our agreement to abide, as a general rule, by the determinations of the marketplace. We once believed that useless textile workers and useless coal miners—and useless farmers and useless carriage-makers and pony expressmen—should search out other means of employment.

It is the dawning realization that under the economics of illusion, pyramid building is becoming a major economic enterprise in

America, that has set advanced liberals to finding more persuasive ways to dispose of the time of the textile specialty workers. And their solution—*vide* Galbraith—is great social enterprises, roads, schools, slum clearance, national parks. The thesis of the Affluent Society is that simple. We have (1) an earned surplus, (2) unemployment, (3) "social imbalance" (i.e., too many cars, not enough roads; too much carbon monoxide, not enough air purification; too many children, not enough classrooms.) So let the government (1) take over the extra money, (2) use it to hire the unemployed, and (3) set them to restoring the social balance, i.e., to building parks, schools, roads.

The program prescribed by Mr. Galbraith is unacceptable, conservatives would agree. Deal highhandedly as he would have us do with the mechanisms of the marketplace, and the mechanisms will bind. Preempt the surplus of the people, and surpluses will dwindle. Direct politically the economic activity of a nation, and the economy will lose its capacity for that infinite responsiveness to individual tastes that gives concrete expression to the individual will in material matters. Centralize the political function, and you will lose touch with reality, for the reality is an intimate and individual relationship between individuals and those among whom they live; and the abstractions of widescreen social draftsmen will not substitute for it. Stifle the economic sovereignty of the individual by spending his dollars for him, and you stifle his freedom. Socialize the individual's surplus and you socialize his spirit and creativeness; you cannot paint the *Mona Lisa* by assigning one dab each to a thousand painters.

Conservatives do not deny that technology poses enormous problems; they insist only that the answers of liberalism create worse problems than those they set out to solve. Conservatives cannot be blind, or give the appearance of being blind, to the dismaying spectacle of unemployment, or any other kind of suffering. But conservatives can insist that the statist solution to the problem is inadmissible. It is not the single conservative's responsibility or right to draft a concrete program—merely to suggest the principles that should frame it.

What then is the indicated course of action? It is to maintain and wherever possible enhance the freedom of the individual to acquire property and dispose of that property in ways that he decides on. To deal with unemployment by eliminating monopoly unionism, featherbedding, and inflexibilities in the labor market, and be prepared, where residual unemployment persists, to cope with it locally, placing the political and humanitarian responsibility on the lowest feasible political unit. Boston can surely find a way to employ gainfully its 136 textile specialists—and its way would be very different, predictably, from Kentucky's with the coal miners; and let them be different. Let the two localities experiment with different solutions, and let the natural desire of the individual for more goods, and better education, and more leisure, find satisfaction in individual encounters with the marketplace, in the growth of private schools, in the myriad economic and charitable activities which, because they took root in the individual imagination and impulse, take organic form, And then let us see whether we are better off than we would be living by decisions made between nine and five in Washington office rooms, where the oligarchs of the Affluent Society sit, allocating complaints and solutions to communities represented by pins on the map.

Is that a program? Call it a No-Program, if you will, but adopt it for your very own. I will not cede more power to the state. I will not willingly cede more power to anyone, not to the state, not to General Motors, not to the CIO. I will hoard my power like a miser, resisting every effort to drain it away from me. I will then use my power, as I see fit. I mean to live my life an obedient man, but obedient to God, subservient to the wisdom of my ancestors; never to the authority of political truths arrived at yesterday at the voting booth. That is a program of sorts, is it not?

It is certainly program enough to keep conservatives busy, and liberals at bay. And the nation free.

The Heritage Foundation Collection, 1987

CHAPTER 2

Russell Kirk

Commentary by Edwin J. Feulner Jr. (1992)

Not by force of arms are civilizations held together, but by subtle threads of moral and intellectual principle.

— Russell Kirk

An omnivorous reader, prolific writer, deep thinker, and teller of tall tales, Russell Kirk was a Hamlet who did not hesitate to protect his patrimony. Gladly battling the slings and arrows of outrageous liberals, this contemplative man of action took verbal arms against a sea of troubles and, by opposing, tried to end them. As scholar, lecturer, essayist, and critic, he wielded "the sword of imagination" in defense of "the permanent things" and the "unbought grace of life," repelling Philistine and barbarian alike. From the ramparts of custom, tradition, and convention, he lobbed metaphorical bombs at the mad metaphysicians of libertarianism and the "squalid oligarchs" of *laissez-faire* capitalism.

A critic for all seasons, he denounced the automobile as "a mechanical Jacobin," and reviled television as an electronic demon.

No friend of modernism, he condemned materialism and all its works, including secularism, utilitarianism, positivism, statism, progressivism, and atheism, to say nothing of "power-tipsy professors," "Behemoth" Universities, and "quarter-educated" collegians. An advocate of audacious conservatism, Kirk was unafraid to extol unfashionable virtues and unpopular principles. He unblushingly called for the reinstatement of manners and morals and praised prudence and humility as the basis of sound public policy. Describing wisdom and virtue as the proper end of education, he campaigned for a return to classical learning, the liberal arts, and Christian principles. In literature, he advocated reviving high moral standards, and in life argued for the return of chivalry and manliness.

Although Russell was every inch a man of letters, my long-time friend was also very much a man of the world. Christening himself a "bohemian Tory," he explained that he had lived in "garrets," "cellars," and "forest cabins," as well as mansions and villas, happily feasting on "ducks' eggs and goats' milk in the Hebrides," or dining in style at "the great country houses of Scotland." With typical self-deprecation, he called himself a "connoisseur of slums and strange corners," numbering among them the "Skid Rows of Detroit and Los Angeles," "the literacy circles of London and Madrid," and the "backwoods from Beaver Island to Morocco." Although he was a great walker, known to cover forty miles in a day, it would be more accurate to describe him as an explorer and a pilgrim, a student of the human heart, who took the haunts of men as his text. Such a description would have pleased Kirk, who once told an audience at The Heritage Foundation that a conservative is "a pilgrim in a realm of mystery and wonder, where duty, discipline, and sacrifice are required."

Another realm of mystery where he distinguished himself is the crepuscular land of ghost and goblin. Endowed with what he calls a "Gothic mind" that would "exchange any number of neo-classical pediments for one poor battered gargoyle," he wrote spiritual thrillers like his novel, *Lord of the Hollow Dark*, as well as "fearsome" stories, such as those collected in *Watchers at the Strait Gate*. By his own admission, these "grimly amusing tales," which he considered "experiments in moral imagination," feature "retributive ghosts, malign magicians, blind angels, beneficent phantoms, conjuring witches, demonic possession, creatures of the twilight" and "divided selves." Sometimes composed in what Kirk called "my ancestral spooky house at Mecosta," where his mother's kin, the Johnsons—teetotalers and Spiritualists—held seances, these stories, he insisted, were actually a conservative undertaking. Since "all important literature has some ethical end," tales of the preternatural, he asserted, "can be an instrument for the recovery of moral order." Indeed, he saw the uncanny tale as a means of "expressing truths enchantingly."

Although Russell Kirk's best-known book, *The Conservative Mind*, published in 1953, is not a work of enchantment, it certainly broke the spell under which American conservatism had languished for more than a hundred years. Today it is hard to imagine the disarray in which right-thinking men and women found themselves forty years ago. As Richard Brookhiser quips, in those days, "The American right wing was an intellectual rag-tag, about as coherent as the Iranian parliament," boasting "robber barons and free-enterprisers; Communists turned Americans; America Firsters turned McCarthyites; Midwestern Republicans and Confederates." Derided by the intelligentsia, ignored by the media, and unsung even by its adherents, conservatism was so ill-regarded that the very notion of a conservative mind was considered oxymoronic.

The publication of Kirk's landmark study, hailed by Whittaker Chambers as one of the most important books of the twentieth century, changed all that. Kirk showed conclusively that conservatism had an illustrious lineage; proved that many of the finest British and American thinkers—including Burke, Coleridge, John Adams, and John Calhoun—to say nothing of luminaries such as de Tocqueville, Newman, Disraeli, Santayana, and Irving Babbitt—espoused this philosophy; and demonstrated that much of America's success derived from her conservative principles. Attacking popular slurs against traditionalists head-on, Kirk asserted that conservatism is "something more than mere defense of shares and dividends and something nobler than mere dread of what is new."

His book was not only, as Lee Edwards asserts, "a brilliant distillation of conservative thinking over the past 150 years," but also "a scathing indictment of every liberal nostrum, from the perfectibility of man to economic egalitarianism." Kirk unmasked the shallow rationalism of the cynical French *philosophes*, unveiled the egotistical underpinnings of Rousseau's romantic sentimentalism; exposed the heartlessness of utilitarianism and the absurdity of its founder; revealed the philosophical superficiality of Comte's positivism; and disclosed the spiritual bankruptcy of materialism in all its malefic forms.

In addition, his book set forth six "canons" or principles that provided a credo for American conservatives: (1) "belief in a transcendent order," including natural law; (2) respect for the "variety and mystery of human existence"; (3) recognition that civilization requires classes and orders; (4) acknowledgment of the crucial link between freedom and private property; (5) adherence to custom, convention, and prescription; (6) awareness that change is not necessarily reform, and agreement that Providence plays the final role in the affairs of men. Ironically, *The Conservative Mind*, originally titled *The Conservatives' Rout* in manuscript form, was the beginning of their triumph.

Although reviewers remarked that Kirk's study seemed to have emerged out of nowhere (intellectual shades of "Who was that masked man?" his heritage, upbringing, temperament, and education had conspired for thirty years to help him write it. Even so, few would have predicted that the little boy born in 1918 in Plymouth, Michigan, to a young railway engineman and his book-loving wife, would one day be hailed as the "American Cicero." In one of Sears and Roebuck's new, pre-fabricated bungalows near the railyards, Russell passed a "cheerful infancy." He learned patience from his father, who was descended from a long line of Scottish farmers, and inherited a vivid imagination from his "tiny, tender, romantic" mother, who read him Lewis Carroll, Stevenson, and Grimm, as well as tales of King Arthur and the Round Table. Although bookish, the child never liked school, preferring long walks with his grandfather, a small-town banker, who helped young Russell look for Indian arrowheads and talked with him about everything from the character of Richard III to the cruelty of the Assyrians. From him Russell learned to love history, initially reading the work of Ridpath and H.G. Wells, and later devouring Herodotus, Thucydides, Xenophon, Polybius, Livy, and Tacitus.

Before Kirk had reached the age of ten, his mother had launched him on the novels of Hawthorne, Fenimore Cooper, Hugo, Dickens and Twain. A little later, Russell encountered Sir Walter Scott and Shakespeare—a discovery that intensified his life-long love for literature. His imagination was also stimulated by summer visits to the "enchanted world of Mecosta," the town founded by his great-grandfather, Amos Johnson. In this little, one-street village of two hundred souls, which would have made "a perfect set for a Western shootout," he grew to value continuity, community, and a sense of connectedness to the past. The family home (where he returned to live permanently in 1953) was set on a "bleak ridge," called "Piety Hill" by the hard-drinking lumberjacks of the previous century who didn't know what to make of the "temperance people"— Russell's ancestors—who lived there. The house itself was magic: "over everything brooded an air of faded splendours, vanished lands, and baffled expectations."

Although the Depression hit the Kirks hard, it did not interrupt Russell's two favorite pastimes—reading and walking—nor did it prevent him from going to college. Winning a scholarship to Michigan State College (now University), he earned his BA in 1940, and then received a fellowship to attend Duke, where he completed his MA in history a year later. His thesis, on John Randolph of Roanoke, the brilliant, eccentric, conservative Congressman from

Virginia, later provided the material for Kirk's first book, *Randolph of Roanoke*. At the same time, Russell discovered Edmund Burke, whose *Reflections on the Revolution in France* struck him with all the force of revelation: converting "prejudice into an apprehension of the wisdom of our ancestors."

After graduating, Russell headed north to Michigan, where he worked at the gargantuan Ford Motor plant, which for him epitomized the "soulless corporation." Rescued by the draft, he was inducted into the Army's Chemical Warfare Service and stationed in a remote area of Utah. Marooned in "the heart of the Great Salt Lake Desert," the young staff sergeant read by the hour—Conrad and Shakespeare, Ibsen and Sophocles, Marcus Aurelius and Epictetus—and as he read, sitting on the great sand dunes, he began to believe that man is more than a handful of dust and to suspect that a beneficent Being may have put him here. Although Russell felt God's presence in the desert, it was not until twenty years later that he was baptized, when he converted to Roman Catholicism in 1964.

Returning to his alma mater after the war, Kirk taught the history of civilization—an enterprise he compares to "Cyclops leading the blind." Pressured by administrators in "the petrified forest of academe" to earn a doctorate, he embarked for the British Isles, where he enrolled at Saint Andrews, the oldest Scottish university. There, in his late twenties, he began writing his dissertation on the major conservative writers of Britain and America—which several years later became *The Conservative Mind*. After its publication, Kirk resigned from Michigan State, determined to live the life of a man of letters—subsisting, if necessary, on the peanut butter and crackers that had successfully taken him through nine years of college and graduate school.

With the publication of his seminal work, Russell Kirk assumed the role he played for almost forty years—the conscience of the conservative movement. Perhaps more than anyone in our century, he revitalized conservative thought, galvanized its adherents into forming a movement, and restored its intellectual respectability. As scholar, journalist, editor, lecturer, and teacher, he fought to preserve what T. S. Eliot calls "the permanent things." In books such as *A Program for Conservatives* (1954), *The American Cause* (1957), *The Intelligent Woman's Guide to Conservatism* (1957), *Edmund Burke: A Genius Reconsidered* (1967), *The Roots of American Order* (1974), *Reclaiming a Patrimony* (1982), and *The Wise Men Know What Wicked Things Are Written on the Sky* (1987), Kirk battled "outrages against our common cultural heritage."

As an acute critic of modern education, he tirelessly upheld virtue and wisdom as the twin goals of learning, denouncing the kind of "tapioca pudding" curriculum that transforms students into mindless automatons. In *Academic Freedom* (1955), *The Intemperate Professor* (1965), and *Decadence and Renewal in the Higher Learning* (1978), he unerringly pointed to the liberal follies that are the scourge of academe. As a social critic, notably in *Beyond the Dreams of Avarice* (1956), *Enemies of the Permanent Things* (1969), and *Eliot and His Age* (1971), Kirk championed the return to a civilized society in which virtue and knowledge would flourish. In fact, the influence of Russell's work was so far-reaching that even the world of ghosts and goblins acknowledged his accomplishments—in the form of the Count Dracula Society's award for outstanding Gothic fiction.

Russell also rode in the lists as a defender of conservatism, using his journalistic gifts. For a quarter-century, he skewered scholastic tomfoolery in "From the Academy," his column in *National Review*, and for half as long, regaled readers of his nationally syndicated newspaper column, "To the Point," with right-thinking on everything from Ayn Rand to euthanasia. He also made his mark as an editor—both literally and figuratively. With the founding of *Modern Age* (1957), America's first conservative quarterly for scholars, Russell ended the liberal monopoly on intellectual journals, and by founding and editing the *University Bookman* (1960), which features literate reviews of serious books—often ignored elsewhere—he struck yet another blow against the liberal conspiracy to muzzle conservatives.

Despite his renown as a scholar, author, and editor, Kirk was probably best known as a lecturer and teacher. For over forty years, he lectured at universities around the globe, speaking at hundreds of colleges in this country alone. In addition, he was a stalwart supporter of the Intercollegiate Studies Institute (ISI), frequently conducting seminars under its auspices.

In fact, it was at such a gathering, in 1962, in Detroit, that I first met Dr. Kirk. At that time, he was already a star in the conservative firmament, and although he has described himself in those days as "roly-poly and benign," most of us students were still somewhat in awe of him. Had we known that he was an eater of beaver and a smoker of "dark, thick" Burmese cigars, "looking and tasting ... like torpedoes," we probably would have addressed him with even greater trepidation. As we shook hands on that frosty night in Detroit, little did I know that twenty years later, Russell Kirk would be a Heritage Distinguished Fellow or that two of his books, *Reclaiming a Patrimony* (1982) and *The Wise Men Know What Wicked Things Are Written on the Sky* (1987), would be composed of lectures that he delivered at The Heritage Foundation. Little did I know that I would have the honor of presenting Kirk with the inaugural Henry Salvatori Prize awarded by the Intercollegiate Studies Institute in 1991.

In addition to the myriad students who met Kirk at collegiate lectures, ISI forums, and symposia at The Heritage Foundation, countless others profited from his personal instruction at what has been called "Mecosta U." Indeed, for almost forty years, Mecosta has been a kind of Midwestern Mecca for Young Conservative scholars. Today, even after Russell's passing, it remains a haven under the direction of his widow, Annette. They still come in droves—descending on this sleepy Michigan town, flooding the Kirks' Italianate brick house, fanning out over Piety Hill, and congregating on the path to Russell's library in an old Dutch barn that used to be a toy factory. Some participate in ISI seminars or take classes, but many come as solitary seekers. Attracted by the Kirks' kindness, some are neither students nor conservatives, but simply souls in search of the kind of haven that Piety Hill provides.

Over the years, Russell, his indefatigable wife, Annette, and their four lovely daughters have welcomed a virtual army of visitors to their home. With great generosity they have taught, tutored, nursed, and nurtured an unbelievable array of guests, including "unwed mothers, half-reformed burglars, ... Vietnamese ... families, waves of Ethiopians, Poles fled from martial law, freedom-seeking Croats, students disgusted with their colleges, and a diversity "of waifs and strays from Progress." Many who come to Piety Hill marvel at the intrepidity of a family that offers hospitality on such a scale and some wonder what motivates such generosity. The answer lies in the Kirks' shared commitment to Christian principles and their common belief in the Burkean idea that all members of society—the living and the dead, as well as the yet-to-be-born—are tied together in a community of souls.

Russell Kirk also belonged to a smaller and more select company: the circle of those who have shaped conservatism for our time. Like the others of this circle, he advanced the conservative cause not only by what he has done but also by what he has been. Many of these other writers have been Kirk's colleagues; most have been his friends; and all have been fellow defenders of "the unbought grace of life." Kirk knew and admired Richard Weaver and Wilhelm Roepke, and corresponded with Albert Jay Nock. Kirk and Frank Meyer, both long-time contributors to *National Review*, were intellectual sparring partners who defined conservatism as we know it today; and Whittaker Chambers helped launch *The Conservative Mind* by encouraging *Time* to devote the entire book review section of the July 6, 1953, issue to what Russell modestly called "my fat book."

In one important respect, however, Kirk differed from these other men: he was never a liberal. Unlike them, he did not convert to conservatism after freeing himself from the snares of socialism or the shackles of communism. "From the hour I began to reason, and possibly from the hour I began to feel," he wrote, "I have been a conservative." Indeed, his life's work was to conserve "the three great bodies of principle ... that tie together modern civilization"— the Christian faith, humane letters, and the social and political institutions that define the culture we cherish. When that life's work was completed in 1994, he died one of conservatism's greatest minds and largest hearts.

In "Enlivening the Conservative Mind," Kirk urges all of us to defend this culture as a patrimony too precious to squander. Making an impassioned plea for the preservation of "the permanent things," he reminds us that ours is a country well worth loving and that we are the stewards as well as the beneficiaries of the gifts she has given us. Despite the incivility, "uglification," materialism, crassness, irreverence, and immorality that he sees all around him, Kirk is not discouraged. In fact, he predicts that if conservatives "take up the weapons of reason and imagination," they have every reason to anticipate victory.

Although some consider cheerful conservatism a contradiction in terms, it was Kirk's very conservatism that gave him hope, for, as Edmund Burke reminds us, the goodness of one person, the courage of one man, the strength of one individual can turn the course of history and renew an entire civilization. As supporters of free enterprise, believers in democracy, and guardians of the Judeo-Christian principles on which America was founded, we are committed to the idea that one person—even fighting against seemingly impossible odds—can change the world. We would do well to remember T. S. Eliot's words that Kirk often quoted with approval: "there is no such thing as a Lost Cause because there is no such thing as a Gained Cause. We fight because we know that our defeat and dismay may be the preface to our successors' victory." The Sage of Mecosta knew that "in every period, some will endeavor to pull down the permanent things, and others will defend them manfully." Russell Kirk cast his lot with those manning the barricades, and he invites us to be his comrades in arms.

Russell Kirk

Enlivening the Conservative Mind

One of America's wittier public men, Eugene McCarthy, remarked in 1985 that nowadays he employs the word "liberal" as an adjective merely. This is a measure of the ascendancy of the conservative mentality in recent years—which incidentally has involved the ascendancy of the conservative side of Mr. McCarthy's own mind and character.

Perhaps it would be as well, most of the time, to use the word "conservative" as an adjective chiefly. For there exists no Model Conservative, and conservatism is no ideology: it is a state of mind, a type of character, a way of looking at the order of the common-wealth. The conservative movement or body of opinion can accommodate a considerable diversity of views on a good many subjects, there existing no Test Act or Thirty-Nine Articles of the conservative creed. In essence, the conservative person is simply one who finds the permanent things more pleasing than Chaos and old Night. This is by way of preface to some desultory observations on what the conservative mind seems to require nowadays.

In America, the great wave of public opinion sweeps in a conservative direction today, carrying all before it: as Tocqueville instructs us, such is the way with opinion in democratic nations generally. Both foreign affairs and domestic questions impel the

From Russell Kirk, *Prospects for Conservatives* (1989).

nation toward long-range conservative policies. Yet could the tremendous conservative successes in public opinion, during recent years, conceivably cease? Might the wave of democratic opinion begin to sweep back again, an ebb-tide, carrying out to the great deep much American flotsam?

Yes.

From what cause?

Stupidity.

It was not altogether without reason, a century ago, that John Stuart Mill called conservatives "the stupid party." Four decades ago, when in Britain the Attlee government abolished the university seats in the House of Commons, Winston Churchill declared that the Socialists were "against brains." But a good many conservatively-inclined folk, near the end of this century, finding themselves only second best in the pursuit of stupidity, try harder.

Some years ago I remarked in the course of a speech that conservative imagination is required in our time. From the audience, a conservative man of business retorted, "We don't need any imagination: we're practical." That is what I mean.

Less than forty years ago there commenced a renewal—regarded by liberals and radicals as a recrudescence—of conservative thought and imagination. Like Fabianism in Britain two generations earlier, but proceeding in an opposite direction, this "New Conservatism" became an intellectual foundation for grand-scale victories at the polls thirty years later. In the United States, as earlier in Britain, persuasive ideas combined or coincided with favorable circumstances; and thus the course of a great nation's policies was altered mightily.

In Britain, however, the intellectual successes of the Fabians and the electoral victories of the Labour party were followed by the development of periodicals, book-publishing firms, and university associations favorable to socialism. In the United States, *au contraire,* relatively few intellectual gains for the conservative interest have occurred since 1953—the year marked by the publication of serious books by Robert Nisbet, Daniel Boorstin, Clinton Rossiter, this present writer, and other scholars and men of letters of a conservative inclination; a year in which liberals began to listen.

True, several magazines of a conservative cast are published today, although none of tremendous circulation. But also new liberal or radical publications have sprung-up. Major book-review media are markedly more hostile toward any book suspected of political conservatism or religious orthodoxy than they were in the Fifties. As for book publishing, in the year 1953 there existed but one consistent reputable conservative publisher of serious books. And today, among the editors of New York firms there prevails a powerful prejudice against the very word "conservative."

In universities and colleges, staffs are far more dominated by radicals than they were at the beginning of the Fifties; the extremists of the Sixties now have become professors entrenched behind tenure. The larger foundations, most of them, are dominated by a Ford Foundation humanitarian mentality, which assesses the Fiend according to the degree of his conservatism.

Thus the conservative movement is enfeebled, intellectually and in backing, at the very hour of its popular ascendancy. This may become a fatal impoverishment.

For the most pressing need of the conservatives in the United States is to quicken their own right reason and moral imagination. The rising generation, already won to a kind of unthinking conservatism of self-interest on nearly every college campus, must be made aware that conservative views and policies can be at once intellectually reputable and interestingly lively.

Ballot-box victories are undone in short order, if unsupported by the enduring art of persuasion. A political movement that fancies it can subsist by slogans, and by an alleged "pragmatism," presently is tumbled over by the next political carnival, shouting fresher slogans.

I am not implying that conservative folk should set to forming a conservative ideology; for conservatism is the negation of

ideology. The conservative public man turns to constitution, custom, convention, ancient consensus, prescription, precedent, as
guides—not to the narrow and fanatic abstractions of ideology. I
am saying, rather, that unless conservatives show the rising generation what requires to be conserved, and how to go about the work
of preservation with intelligence and imagination—why, the present wave of conservative opinion will break upon a stern and rock-
bound coast, perhaps with a savage behind every giant tree.

The existence of various factions within the conservative movement is not in itself alarming. All large-scale political movements
of reform, in the beginning, are alliances of various groups and
interests that share chiefly a dislike of what has been the dominant
political power. Journalists, for their own delectation, invent or cry
up such labels as "Old Right," "Traditionalists," "Neoconservatives," "Libertarians," "New Right," "Fundamentalist Right,"
"Paleoconservatives," and the like. But these categories overlap and
intermingle. The more eccentric members of this loose coalition
may be expected to fall away into fresher eccentricities—and no
great loss will result. Various emphases upon this or that aspect of
public policy will linger among the several conservative groupings;
but enough common ground can be cultivated to maintain substantial agreement on some large questions—supposing that narrow
ideology is abjured. If, to the contrary, conservative leaders complacently fancy that guessing and muddling through may suffice—
why, then future historians may describe the attempt to wake
conservative minds and hearts during the latter half of the twentieth century as an intellectual Mississippi Bubble.

For despite the apparent success of candidates nominally conservative in the elections of the Eighties—in Britain, Germany, and
France, too, besides the United States—the public measures of the
Western democracies have been little altered for the better as yet. As
Disraeli put it, prevailing opinions generally are the opinions of the
generation that is passing. Party leaders, legislators, and principal
civil servants—also judges, or perhaps especially judges—received a

liberal indoctrination in the course of formal education, most of them; they may sense the public's desire for a repudiation of doctrinaire liberalism, and even honestly desire to respond to that public mood; yet they lack knowledge of principles or policies of an alternative sort.

It would require many pages to analyze the survival, and even enlargement, of what Sidney Hook called "ritualistic liberalism." How conservative can a country be considered, for instance, when various state legislatures and municipal councils confer special class privileges upon self-proclaimed pathics, so damaging the fundamental social institution, the family—an institution already much weakened by technological and moral changes? And confer those privileges and immunities at the very time when homosexuality spreads a ghastly disease, with increasing speed? There could be no more telling illustration of what Malcolm Muggeridge calls "the Great Liberal Death-Wish."

Or if one turns to the foreign policies of the United States, one encounters very little amendment of the liberal illusions under which both Democratic and Republican administrations have labored most of the twentieth century. Dense ignorance of the complexities of order in Africa does not deter senators from the folly of meddling; they appear bent upon bringing down the government, and perhaps the whole social order, of a friendly power. If the meddling policy fails—why, senators will instruct us, all the same, "The democratic ideal has been vindicated!"

Often, in short, the politician who calls himself a conservative may have failed to put on the mind of the principal conservative thinkers of yesteryear. The fundamental division among conservative groups today, it seems to me, is the gulf fixed between (on the one side) all those conservative men and women who, taking long views, argue that intellectual activity and rousing of the imagination are required urgently; and (on the other side of the canyon) all those professedly "pragmatic" persons who think of a conservative government as one that holds office through placating or serving certain powerful interests—and so warding off radical interests.

The ideologue does not govern well; but neither does the time-server, the placeman (as he was called in the eighteenth century). Conservative people in politics need to steer clear of the Scylla of abstraction and the Charybdis of opportunism. So it is that folk of conservative inclination ought to decline the embraces of such categories of American political zealots or charlatans as I list below:

Those who demand that the National Parks be sold to private developers.

Those who declare that "the test of the market" is the whole of political economy and of morals.

Those who fancy that foreign policy can be conducted with religious zeal on a basis of absolute rights and absolute wrongs.

Those who, in the belief that there exists a malign "elite," cry, with Carl Sandburg, "The people, yes!"

Those who assure the public that great corporations can do no wrong.

Those who confound public liberties with private license.

And various other folk who abjure liberalism but seem incapable of conserving anything worth keeping.

After this commination, is anyone left within the conservative ramparts? Yes.

There survives, even unto our day, a conservative cast of mind and character capable of reflection, sound sentiments, and sacrifice. That sort of conservative mentality was discerned in America by Tocqueville a century and a half ago, by Henry Maine and James Bryce a century gone, by Julián Marías a quarter of a century ago. If waked in mind and conscience, such men and women—really quite numerous in these United States—are capable of an enduring conservative reform and reinvigoration. But if the trumpet give an uncertain sound, who shall go forth to the battle?

Indulge me now in an exhortation of a kind too rarely addressed to American conservatives—an appeal for the preservation of a country worth loving.

"To make us love our country," Edmund Burke says, "our country ought to be lovely." The effective conservatives of the rising generation may be the poet and the philosopher, the artist and the builder. I believe, with Burke, that before we can learn to love humanity, or even the nation, we must "learn to love the little platoon we belong to in society." Men who would sever society from its traditional roots, out of a lust for abstract efficiency or equality, destroy the sources of loyalty to a country.

"There ought to be a system of manners in every nation which a well-formed mind would be disposed to relish": this sentence Burke prefaces to his observations on the love of country. Well, the traditional system of manners is much decayed nowadays throughout Western society, and particularly in America; and as for loveliness, Western civilization, since Burke's age, seems to have been intent upon one of the principal studies in the curriculum of Alice's Mock Turtle, Uglification. "I have always been of the mind that in a democracy manners are the only effective weapon against the bowie-knife," James Russell Lowell observes in one of his letters, "the only thing that will save us from barbarism." Manners, and the visible loveliness of a society in which taste and feeling have their due, are a cement of loyalty.

Now it would be laborious and painful to recite here a catalog of the incivility of our age; nor would it be useful, for we see all about us, every day, that disheartening contempt for station, and age, and sex, and character, which is a degradation of the democratic dogma. We see it in the Capitol at Washington, and we see it on every city bus. "One man is as good as another, or maybe a little better": this presumption, induced by the gutter press, the decay of liberal education, and the diminished influence of the religious concepts of hierarchy and veneration, ultimately may overthrow both republican government and the complex technological achievement of modern civilization. Instead of endeavoring to make most men into gentlemen, we have been intent upon reducing any surviving gentlemen to the condition and manners of proletarians.

Dr. Johnson did not recognize the word "civilization" as legitimate English: "civility," he told Boswell, was the proper term to describe a high civil social order. In its traditional usage, "civility" imports both the idea of citizenship and the state of being civilized, as well as good breeding and courtesy. Once the kind of civility represented by manners is cast aside, the responsibilities of citizenship and the very foundation of civilized existence are in peril. Similarly, the words "generosity" and "generation" come from the same root; and when a society has treated with contempt the chivalric idea of high breeding, then the very life of that society, the process of its generation, is threatened.

> *I know the Table Round, my friends of old;*
> *All brave, and many generous, and some chaste.*

Mannerless nations, in civil societies, end in servility to some strong brute who does not require the trappings of a moral imagination; and peoples without respect for generous hearts presently lose even the love for giving life to the next generation, and make some Alfred Kinsey the dreary keeper of their conscience.

The beauty of manners which a well-informed mind is disposed to cherish—this is a form of beauty which is withering even as we describe it; and as it withers, the higher loyalty to our country is correspondingly weakened. And I believe that the other chief visible sign of a country's loveliness—its physical being, its scenery, architecture, art, and pattern of town and country—is desperately sick among us. The triumph of the mass-mind in the realm of art is in part the consequence of certain powerful causes which also crushed or distorted the traditional framework of society; and the revolt of the masses is in part itself the cause of the degradation of a country's beauty. The industrial revolution, for instance, created the modern industrial masses; it also overwhelmed those established artistic skills and handicrafts which were joined to traditional art, and substituted new patterns of life and new methods of design for the prescriptive framework of the arts. These causes and consequences are too intricate for any adequate description here. To put the matter briefly, I think that since Burke wrote we have seen a progressive degeneration of the arts and the very physical aspect of most modern states.

One may see the process being completed by the wreckers' bulldozers almost anywhere in Britain, nowadays; and as for America, the spectacle of the devastation of our country's loveliness is so gigantic as almost to defy description. I find it curious to reflect that Harriet Martineau once remarked that Milton must have been thinking of southern Michigan when he wrote the garden parts of *Paradise Lost*. In southern Michigan (where I was born) the process of alteration now rushes on at vertiginous speed. We sweep away our trees, our hills, our very churches, out of our passion for unchecked motion. An infatuation with haste is one of the marks of a profound social boredom; and this is stamped upon our character. No consideration prevails against the lust for speed. The endeavors of our National Trust to preserve our old buildings are insignificant in comparison with the furious energy of the traffic engineer and the tasteless entrepreneur. No people in all history have been so insensitive to ugliness as are we Americans today, making our roads hideous with billboards and our magazines hideous with vulgarity. There has been some improvement of domestic architecture among us, if we compare our present standards with those of 1910 or 1920; but this amelioration has been offset by the spreading blight of jerry-built little houses thrusting into the countryside from every town, as if we were determined to realize one of Karl Marx's fondest dreams, that town and country should merge in one amorphous blur. One of the dreariest experiences a man of some taste can have is to drive along a road in Michigan, say, or Tennessee, dotted with grotesque shacks and trailers and motels, blotting out the natural charm of what once was handsome country; and nothing is better calculated to stimulate reflections on how the decay of taste and the decay of the traditional framework of society are joined.

Nor is vulgarity confined to the classes vulgar in the old sense, in our society. A glance at the architecture of most American universities ought to suggest to any reasonable observer that taste is nearly dead at the top of our society, as well as at the bottom. Most recent building at our institutions of higher learning is monstrous; it is not "modern," and not "traditional"; certainly it almost never is "functional." The university may have a well-endowed school of architecture, with a complex hierarchy of professors; but the proof of the pudding is in the buildings the university erects; and, with a very few exceptions, that proof informs us that our professors of architecture are quacks: they have neither taste nor technical skill. "Administration" buildings look like factories, but are less efficient than the most decrepit little office tucked away in some Oxford quadrangle; classroom buildings have corridors too narrow to let the students into their rooms without interminable queuing, and the rooms themselves are cursed with bad proportions and over-heating; chapels look as if they were designed by the League of Militant Atheists, to make a mockery of religion. I touch upon these matters because they suggest how thoroughly the decay of taste and skill has worked its way upward among us, as well as downward. The only considerable accomplishment of the modern age in building is in steel-and-concrete construction; but that is the work of the engineer, really, not of the architect; and ordinarily it is quite indifferent to beauty.

Probably it is not possible—to employ a phrase of Chesterton's—to "rouse a great wild forest passion in a little Cockney heart." Though the average countryman and the average townsman in our time suffer from a pronounced degradation of taste, still the average man never has had much of an eye for beauty. In former times, however, the average man felt some degree of respect for fine buildings and scenes because he endeavored to copy the taste of his superiors; he deferred to their aesthetic judgment. Now he has lost the quality of deference, or perhaps has lost any true superiors. Sir Osbert Sitwell tells us that there is no such thing as folk-art, and no such thing as folk-costume: these are simply imitations, commonly delayed in time, of the art and dress of the upper classes. Lord Raglan insists that there really is no such thing as folklore: the traditional tales of a people are simply the popularized versions of stories which had their origin among the aristocracy. So it is with the sense of beauty. We are foolish if we expect to summon forth a native and untutored love of beautiful things from the vulgar heart; appreciation of natural and artistic beauty is the fruit of long study and discipline; and if the classes which encouraged that study and that discipline are depressed, or if they neglect their old function of forming the taste of a nation, then surely the mass of the people will be indifferent, or perhaps hostile, to the charm of nature and the charm of art.

Tocqueville, in the second part of *Democracy in America,* predicts that in a classless society, dedicated to economic egalitarianism, and indifferent to traditional freedom, the arts must perish, as much else perishes under democratic despotism:

> Not only would a democratic people of this kind show neither aptitude nor taste for science, literature, or art, but it would probably never arrive at the possession of them. The law of descent would of itself provide for the destruction of large fortunes at each succeeding generation, and no new fortunes would be acquired. The poor man, without either knowledge or freedom, would not so much as conceive the idea of raising himself to wealth; and the rich man would allow himself to be degraded to poverty, without a notion of self-defense. Between these two members of the community complete and invincible equality would soon be established. No one would then have time or taste to devote himself to the pursuits or pleasures of the intellect, but all men would remain paralyzed in a state of common ignorance and equal servitude.
>
> When I conceive a democratic society of this kind, I fancy myself in one of those low, close, and gloomy abodes where the light which breaks in from without soon faints and fades away. A

sudden heaviness overpowers me, and I grope through the surrounding darkness to find an opening that will restore me to the
air and the light of day.

Tocqueville proceeds to point out that the only security against
the coming of such a regime, the death of all art, is the preservation of the rights of property, the rights of bequest and inheritance,
and the traditional liberties of persons, in democratic society—in
short, the exertion of constitutional and moral checks upon the levelling appetite. He also observes that a number of very large fortunes is more beneficial to the arts and the welfare of a community
generally than is a greater number of modest fortunes; for the mil-
lionaire can afford to patronize the arts on a large scale, or to undertake enterprises of an enduring and noble character, while the man
with only modest wealth does not have sufficient surplus to achieve
any work of much beauty or permanence.

Now I think that in the English-speaking nations we have
come very close to the classless and tasteless society which Tocqueville dreaded, and that chiefly within the present century. We
still have men of wealth; but as their consideration and influence
have been injured by the leveling temper of the time, they have
lost proportionately their own sense of duty toward the arts and
a high culture. In his chapter entitled "The Poor Rich," in *The
Mechanical Bride*, Marshall McLuhan maintains that our leading classes are failing to perform their old roles as patrons of
learning and skill:

> The very conditions of success render the rich suspicious of those
> failures whom they might be expected to assist. They have no train-
> ing or taste which would enable them to select struggling artists or
> writers who might be worthy of aid. In these matters, therefore,
> they work through the dealers in old pictures or distribute many
> tiny gratuities through bureaucratic foundations which are run on
> the most finicky, academic lines. This, of course, overlooks those

endowments for hospitals and libraries which are intended as family monuments. And it is not true to say that the rich are niggardly. The point here is simply that they are timid and unresourceful in a way which stands in stark contrast to the zip and push that has put them where they are.

Privilege, in any society, is the reward of duties performed; and the guardianship of culture being one of the chief duties of any leading class, it is not surprising that when rich men cease to be patrons of arts and letters, presently they cease to be rich. Yet in our time, perhaps, the leading classes have been as much deprived of their responsibilities as they have been derelict in their fulfillment. A society intent upon employing the power of positive law to force existence down to an egalitarian Dead Sea will destroy beauty as it destroys inequality. Some friends of the planned economy talk hopefully of a future in which state subsidies, or the surviving funds of great impersonal foundations, will undertake the patronage of arts and letters. I am unable to share their optimism: the record of the state and the foundation as patrons, thus far, is not heartening; the millionaires themselves did better. When states have been discerning patrons in modern times, ordinarily those states have been monarchies. Soviet patronage of arts and letters worked the death of arts and letters. Though great American foundations accomplish good, it not good of this sort. The typical foundation bureaucrat is a world away from the aristocratic virtuoso or dilettante.

I suggest, therefore, that if we love beauty, we will be wise not to destroy those classes, and that pattern of society, which support the unbought grace of life. The rich man often has failed to do what he ought for the life of art and the life of the mind; yet the failure of the commissar would be infinitely more lamentable. To recur to my example of architecture and town-planning, the outward aspect of life under a collectivistic state, devoid of all the complexity and variety of traditional existence, would be a hideous monotony. In the monolithic hive-building of Le Corbusier at Marseilles, in the lofty wastes of Stuyvesant Town, in the dreary streets of the British New Towns, in the cartoon by Osbert Lancaster called "The Drayneflete of the Future," we behold the hulk of this architecture, and the spirit which would brood over the unfortunate beings condemned to inhabit these barracks. If Gothic architecture was the highest achievement of man in the arts, surely this architecture of the future (despite all the perfection of technology which it represents) is the lowest, lower than the log-cabin or the igloo or the hogan; and the men and women who submitted to this new order would have forgotten altogether the unbought grace of life.

Loyalty to a nation comes in part from the appreciation of intangible values: equal justice under law, security of life and property, a common religious faith, a common literature of elevation, the knowledge of a great history. These things, I believe, are even more important than manners and beauty. But these intangibles commonly are taken for granted by most people; only a small minority really are aware that justice and freedom and order are not the gifts of nature, like sun and rain, but are the product of tradition and of the strenuous effort of our ancestors. Wrong though they may be, most people tend to judge their society not by its intangible qualities, but by its immediate influence upon their own temper. I have chosen, therefore, to emphasize the qualities of loveliness which encourage loyalty to a nation, because almost no one else is saying anything about these, and because they more directly influence popular opinion, even though the people who are so influenced may be unaware of the source of their prejudices.

"To make us love our country, our country ought to be lovely." Is it possible to love the gritty squalor of the Black Belt of Chicago, or Main Street in Los Angeles? Conceivably; but it is wiser not to put that strain upon loyalty. The better natures among us, surely will be hard put to it to love America if it becomes a nation wholly mannerless, an uncivil society, in which "tough-mindedness" is praised as a cardinal virtue, in which generosity and charity are scorned as weakness, in which all great literature, and the whole stock of a moral imagination, is rejected out of a lust for the gratification of carnal appetites and a taste for second-hand narrations of violence and concupiscence. The conservative of reflection will not be afraid to defend the manners and the tastes of a gentle and generous nature, in this industrial age.

With similar resolution, the thinking conservative will struggle to preserve the face of his country from disfigurement, and the character of his cities from proletarian hideousness. Whenever a project for material change is put forward, he will ask first of all *not* the question, "Is there money in it for us?" but "Will it make men love their country?" He knows that money is made for men, not men for money; he knows that men work and fight for a country which appeals to their hearts, rather than their pocketbooks. In reconciling necessary change with the elements that hold men's loyalties, he will put the considerations that pertain to traditional living first, and the considerations that pertain to material aggrandizement second. Such choices will arise with great frequency in the next few years, and it is time conservatives began to face them frankly. The current American passion for turnpikes, freeways, and gigantic roadways under other labels is an instance of my meaning. Scarcely a voice is raised in protest when such a project destroys hundreds of farms, demolishes interesting old neighborhoods, parts an urban district forever into halves, or dehumanizes a landscape. No balance between the claims of efficiency and the claims of stability is attempted. Here is the pure Utilitarian mind at work, contemptuous of beauty and of social roots. The conservative thinks otherwise. When the conservative turns planner, his impulse is not to drive men out of their accustomed ways of life, but to reconcile economic change with all the amenities and decencies of traditional existence; and when he is told that some great new development is underway, he does not exult, "How rich shall we get!" but inquires, "Can money pay for this break with beauty and tradition?"

For that reason, the conservative distrusts the typical social planner, trained in Benthamite methods, blind to individuality and true order, intent only upon Efficiency and Simplicity. Our cities and the whole face of our country urgently require restoration and improvement, and the conservative is going to have to undertake that duty, unless he is ready to let it go to the Utilitarian by default. But when he turns his hand to prudent reform, the conservative remembers that the reform ought to be the voluntary work of the people concerned in it; that it ought to be a local undertaking, so far as possible, not a centralized Grand Design; that its object is to keep men human, not to make them into units for efficient industrial production; that individuality, not collectivism, ought to govern the architectural and social features of such a reform. The face of any civilized country comes to resemble the minds of the people who inhabit it; the country dominated by avarice and compulsion will tend to be ugly, but the country inspired by charity and wise choice will tend to be beautiful.

In a bungalow across an alley from the Pere Marquette station, at a town twenty miles out of Detroit, seventy-four years ago, I entered this world. By chance riding past my birthplace, in recent years, I found it had become a doghouse: a kennel for pedigreed poodles. Similar changes had occurred meanwhile in the world at large.

We boys of the North End used to play the old game of prisoners' base, after nightfall, in the railroad yards that lay five minutes' trot from my house, freight engines puffing about us, and occasionally a nocturnal passenger-train sweeping by us. I would stare invisible at the passengers' white faces, behind the windows of parlor car or coach, wondering what they did and whither they journeyed. Well, all those travellers are gone into the dark now, presumably. The very roundhouse and rip-track have been demolished since my day in that town; no passenger trains run over those tracks nowadays; and my grandparents and parents, who lived in that big bungalow by the station, were buried long ago. My grandmother's elaborate garden, with its brick walks, is now an asphalt parking-lot.

Even now, on many summer nights, one can hear the boys of the North End shouting in the railway yards, joyfully playing prisoners' base. Most of the town's fine old houses have been swept away, but a cultural continuity persists, and a spirit of community. The changes in Plymouth, Michigan, over seven decades, are less drastic than those which have occurred in most of the world during that time, Michigan having been exempted from war and revolution; but they may be sufficiently representative of what large alterations new technology and the swelling of population have worked in America.

Despite those changes, the town where I was born remains a town of churches, conservative in its politics, neighborly and cheerful enough, conscious of its identity. Yet it is beleaguered: I am told that gangs out of Detroit ravage the belt of public parks that swing round the town, so that almost nobody out of Plymouth ventures so far as the picnic tables. The parks' comfort stations are permanently closed.

These circumstances too sufficiently symbolize developments, or rather decadence, in the world at large. Picnics have become perilous round the globe, and nearly everywhere somebody malignly smashes the plumbing. About the shores of the surviving islands of civility, among them my town of Plymouth, pirates cruise by night and by day. If anything is to be conserved, the conservators must take up now the weapons of reason and imagination.

Near the end of the twentieth century, the human condition fast becomes a global game of prisoners' base, kidnappers and hostages, ideology justifying every atrocity. Ignorant armies, supplied with the weapons of annihilation, clash by night on our darkling plain. By Anno Domini 2000, what will remain?

This, as I write, is the prospect which conservatives confront. Their obligation is the recovery of moral order and political order, a task to stagger Hercules. Their adversaries are the Four Horsemen of the Apocalypse—in particular that Fourth Horseman, who is called Revolution. Yet my young comrades and I, pursued and pursuing through the ponds and scrub of the Pere Marquette railway yards in the dark, rescued prisoners from the enemies' base:

we found it possible to win against odds. If we defy the Four Horse-men, it may come to pass that the Permanent Things will not fall trophy to Chaos and old Night.

The Heritage Foundation Collection, 1990

CHAPTER 3

F. A. Hayek

Commentary by Edwin J. Feulner Jr. (1993)

Economic and political freedom are inseparable.

— F. A. Hayek

riedrich von Hayek was much more than a Nobel-prize-winning economist. He was also a philosopher and a prophet. A world renowned scholar, this courtly Austrian aristocrat was one of the twentieth century's most influential intellectuals. Having earned three doctorates—in law, the social sciences, and economics—he ranged fearlessly over many fields—exhibiting an enviable mastery in numerous disciplines. Publishing ground-breaking work not only in economics, but also in political theory, legal philosophy, psychology, and the history of ideas, Hayek was the antithesis of the pedantic professor who specializes in the parochial and the picayune.

He was intrigued by the mind of man, the markets he has made, and the way that those markets have made man and society what they are. Hayek's fascination with markets and monetary theory, however, did not lead him into the mechanistic madness that some-times befalls unwary economists. Instead, he employed economics to investigate the mind of man, using the knowledge he gained to unveil the totalitarian nature of socialism and to explain how it inevitably leads to "serfdom." A metaphysical Paul Revere, for sixty years he sounded the alarm that the foes of freedom were on the march. Armed with meticulous scholarship and inexorable logic, he cut the advocates of planned economies off at their intellectual knees, leaving them without a theoretical leg to stand on.

Like all great men, he was something of a paradox, a man who transcended the very categories that he exemplified. A contempla-tive who made things happen, he mobilized the mind of nations, helping to turn back the seemingly inevitable socialist juggernaut. The founding father of economic policies later invoked by Ronald Reagan and Margaret Thatcher, Hayek deliberately shunned poli-tics. Although an inveterate debater, he resolutely avoided "move-ments" and "schools." A stickler for technical competence and a student of the scientific method, he was the first to acknowledge the insufficiency of technique and the limits of rationalism. At ease on the dizzy heights of abstruse monetary policy, he was the pri-mary popularizer of free-market ideas to the Western World.

Indeed, he may well be the only Nobel-prize-winning economist ever to have had a major work—*The Road to Serfdom*—abridged in the *Reader's Digest*, where it became an international best seller. Although immersed in the critical questions of his time, Hayek was also prescient, foreseeing the collapse of communism more than a half century before it happened. His greatest discov-ery, however, came from his paradoxical recognition that in the largest of all economies of scale—the real world—the bottom line is the mind and soul of man. Armed with this seemingly uneconom-ical truth, this most self-effacing of men intellectually swashbuck-led his way into the history of ideas.

Although Hayek did brilliant research on money, credit, capi-tal, interest, and monetary cycles; on socialism, planning, and free enterprise; on liberty and the law; on the errors of scientism; and on the best ways to ensure a free society guided by the rule of law, his greatest contribution lay in his discovery of a simple yet profound truth: man does not and cannot know everything and when he acts as if he does, disaster follows.

Hayek's stunningly simple insight was that the biblical warning, "pride goeth before a fall," applies to societies as well as individuals, and that hubris is a tragic flaw not only for ancient Greek heroes, but also for modern nation states. He recognized that socialism, the collectivist state, and planned economies represent the ultimate form of hubris, for those who plan them attempt—with insufficient knowledge—to redesign the nature of man. In so doing, they arrogantly disregard traditions that embody the wisdom of generations; impetuously disregard customs whose purpose they do not understand; and blithely confuse the law written on the hearts of men—that they cannot change—with administrative rules that they can alter at whim. For Hayek, such presumption was not only "fatal conceit," but also "the road to serfdom"—the title of his famous denunciation of socialism, published in 1944.

In this book, as in much of Hayek's other writing on law, liberty, economics, society, and morals, he serves not only as a scholar, but also as a prophet. Unwilling to limit himself to arid Benthamitic calculations or even the higher reaches of economic theory, where none but intellectual alpinists venture, he set his sights on the twin peaks of philosophy and morals. From their summits he brought back what he had learned, assuming the unwelcome role of a prophet. Virtually alone in the halls of academe, he read the words written on the walls of the civilization of the West. What he deciphered was not, like Daniel's message to Nebuchadnezzar, "You have been weighed in the balance and found wanting: this night you shall die," but its purport was similar. What Hayek read—written by Adam Smith's "invisible hand"—was that socialism leads to slavery and that those who try to control an economy are guilty not only of fatal conceit but also of factual error—which inevitably dooms planned economies.

For this insight, Hayek received a prophet's reward. He was accused of *lèse majesté*: how dare he relate the world of debits and credits to the drama of the human heart; what audacity to link supply and demand to the rise and fall of nations; what cheek to identify socialism, then widely hailed as the salvation of the West as the inevitable prelude to totalitarianism. He was labeled an *enfant terrible*—spewing out unfashionable ideas—without proper respect for the findings of his colleagues. Daring to tell the truth, he courted academic ostracism, castigation, and invective from those who had committed their lives, their liberty, and their sacred tenure to the proposition that socialism was the road to freedom and prosperity. Along with a small band of associates (most notably, Ludwig von Mises), Hayek exposed this vision as a mirage, and converted a large portion of the public to his point of view. How did he do it?

The story begins with the forces and people who made him what he was. Born on May 8, 1899, Friedrich August von Hayek ("Fritz" to his friends; simply "Professor" to several generations of us) first saw the light of day in turn-of-the-century Vienna. One grandfather was a well-known zoologist and the other a professor of constitutional law, who later became the President of the Statistical Commission of Austria. Hayek's father, August, was a doctor, as well as a professor of botany at the University of Vienna; and his two brothers became, respectively, professors of anatomy and chemistry—footsteps in which Hayek's two children—a biologist and a bacteriologist—followed.

Unsure whether to become an economist or psychologist himself, Friedrich was rescued from indecision by a brief stint in the Austrian army during the First World War. Far from leaving an indelible imprint on him, his time as an officer primarily provided him with anecdotal reminiscences: He once reported that his most memorable adventure had been spilling and trying to recapture a bucket of eels destined for his fellow soldiers' breakfast. After the war, he enrolled at the University of Vienna, where he received a doctorate of laws in 1921, and a second doctorate in the social sciences two years later.

Initially a moderate socialist, Hayek changed his allegiance under the influence of his mentor, Ludwig von Mises. From 1927 until 1931, Friedrich acted as the older man's assistant and then served as Director of the Austrian Institute for Economic Research, which he and von Mises had founded. Simultaneously, Friedrich lectured in economics at his alma mater, but even if he had not been an economist, he could hardly have escaped the issue of inflation—as his salary increased *two hundred times* in eight months—barely keeping pace with prices that doubled daily.

After publishing *Monetary Theory and the Trade Cycle* (1929), Hayek was invited, in 1931, to give a series of lectures at the London School of Economics, later published as *Prices and Production*. Shortly thereafter, he was appointed Tooke Professor of Economic Science and Statistics at the University of London, where he stayed until 1950. While there, he not only became a British citizen, but also published two of his most famous works, *The Pure Theory of Capital* (1941) and *The Road to Serfdom* (1944).

The publication of *The Road to Serfdom*, which made him something of a household name—especially in America—earned him the enmity of most of his left-leaning colleagues. Perhaps in part because of this work's great success in the United States, Hayek agreed to take a position as Professor of Social and Moral Sciences at the University of Chicago, where he published *The Counter-Revolution of Science* (1952) and *The Constitution of Liberty* (1960). Returning to continental Europe in 1962, Hayek accepted a professorship at the University of Freiburg, where he completed his *Studies in Philosophy, Politics and Economics* (1967). After teaching there five years, he "retired" to his native Austria, where he taught for ten more years at the University of Salzburg, while working on his three-volume masterpiece, *Law, Legislation and Liberty* (1973, 1975, 1979). To those astounded at the pace that he kept up even as an octogenarian, he explained, "Some years ago I tried old age, but discovered I didn't like it."

Doubtless, receiving the Nobel Prize for economics in 1974, and the Companion of Honour of the British Empire in 1984, reinvigorated him, as did the growing recognition among his fellow economists that he had been right about socialism. Another source of joy was the continuing vitality of the Mont Pelerin Society, which he had founded. In convoking this group of scholars, named for the Swiss mountain where the thirty-nine original members first met in 1947, Hayek hoped not only to increase "the chances of preserving a free civilization," but also "to make the building of a free society once more an intellectual adventure, a deed of courage." As President of the Mont Pelerin Society from its founding until 1960, and thereafter as its honorary head, Hayek influenced not only his colleagues in economics, but also innumerable younger scholars in a variety of disciplines. As one of the young men who benefited tremendously from participating in the Mont Pelerin Society, I can testify to the enormous influence that he and the Society have had on several generations of scholars and policymakers.

As I look back over my own intellectual evolution, F. A. Hayek looms large at every turn along the way. When I first read *The Road to Serfdom* as an undergraduate at Regis in the sixties, I was electrified by its relevance, accuracy, and eloquence. Not only was it a "recent" book—published after I had been born—but also a sophisticated philosophical critique of the absurdities then being promoted by leftists in Washington and in the media. A few years later, when a Richard Weaver Fellow at the London School of Economics, I had the good fortune—in February of 1965—to meet Professor Hayek when he came to give a guest lecture. On that occasion, a group of us (graduate students from the UK, Portugal, Brazil, India, and France) enjoyed a half-hour coffee with him, queried him about his recently published book, *The Constitution of Liberty*, and even dared to suggest that we start a group to study his works. He graciously suggested a name—the Old Whig Society—which we immediately adopted. Under that title, it flourished for several years, irritating our intellectual adversaries to the point that they vandalized our publications and stole our cash box. Whether this was dictated by ideological opposition or crass greed, we never discovered, but I argued that it had to be ideological because I thought that the sum in question, three shillings sixpence, ruled out enlightened self interest as a motive. Thirty years ahead of time, we experienced the throes of "political correctness," the scourge of campus life today.

In 1968, Professor Hayek kindly invited me to the Mont Pelerin Society's meeting in Aviemore, Scotland, as one of his designated guests. Since then, I have been intimately involved in its affairs, especially since being elected Treasurer in 1978. With great graciousness, the Professor also welcomed me to his home in Germany on a number of occasions and even allowed our son and me to pay a call on him in 1990, when he was already suffering from the illness from which he would die two years later.

Since Professor Hayek's death in March of 1992, I recall with great pleasure the times that my wife Linda and I were able to repay his hospitality by hosting dinner parties in his honor at our home. Several of these occurred after he had agreed to become a Distinguished Fellow at The Heritage Foundation, where we were fortunate to have him as scholar-in-residence on three separate occasions.

As Milton Friedman, his fellow Nobelist, has observed, "Hayek's influence has been tremendous. His work is incorporated in the body of technical economic theory; has had a major influence on economic history, political philosophy and political science; [and] has affected students of the law, of scientific methodology, and even of psychology." But, as Friedman rightly recognizes, all of these achievements "are secondary to Hayek's influence in strengthening the moral and intellectual support for a free society." It was this achievement for which President Bush conferred the Presidential Medal of Freedom on Professor Hayek, *in absentia*, saying that he had "done more than any thinker of our age to explore the promise and contours of liberty."

The breadth of this exploration is indicated by the number of volumes in Hayek's collected works (projected to number twenty-two), currently being published by the University of Chicago under the joint editorship of the late Professor William Bartley and Professor Stephen Kresge. In recognition of Hayek's contribution to the cause of freedom everywhere, The Heritage Foundation is proud to be one of the institutions working to bring this monumental undertaking to fruition. In so doing, we walk in the footsteps of the Professor himself, who believed, as we do, that ideas are what count—a belief that history has vindicated many times over.

In "Responsibility and Freedom," chapter five of *The Constitution of Liberty* (1960), Friedrich von Hayek makes a compelling case for two of the most important ideas of all. He emphasizes that liberty cannot exist without responsibility—a virtue that contemporary man has rejected. Hayek attributes this rejection to modern man's disinclination to carve out a life for himself; reluctance to accept blame if he fails; misunderstanding of the nature of free will; and belief that the laws of science govern his behavior—thus absolving him of responsibility for his own conduct.

Hayek is quick to point out, however, that although freedom imposes the "burden" of making man responsible for his "own fate," it also confers the "privilege" of allowing him to use his abilities, and to employ them to help others. The author considers this vital, for, he insists, "one of the main conditions of ... [men's] happiness [is] that they make the welfare of other people their chief aim." Hayek does not, however, endorse "general altruism," which he castigates as "a meaningless conception," emphasizing that man can care only for *specific* individuals in *concrete* circumstances. Stressing that "responsibility must be both definite and limited," Hayek decries the modern tendency to burden man with vague, diffuse duties. Today, when victimization is so much in vogue, reading "Freedom and Responsibility" has the bracing effect of a long walk in cold, clear air. Moreover, now, when we as a nation are debating what each of us owes his fellow Americans, Hayek's words concerning the folly of general altruism have never seemed more relevant.

Although "Freedom and Responsibility" is clearly an essay for our time, some might wonder why I include in this volume the work of a man whose famous epilogue to *The Constitution of Liberty* is entitled "Why I Am Not a Conservative." I can only reply that even though Professor Hayek considered himself a nineteenth-century liberal, he made common cause with conservatives; and fought for freedom, decency, civility, and truth, espousing a unique blend of liberal conservatism that he christened "Old Whiggism."

Like the others whose work appears in this volume, he spent his life defending the principles on which our civilization is based. Like Whittaker Chambers and Frank Meyer, he recognized communism as a deadly false religion; like Richard Weaver, he believed passionately in the power of ideas; like his colleague Wilhelm Roepke, he made a foolproof case for the foolishness of socialism; and like Michael Novak and Albert Jay Nock, he defended the free market against all comers. Finally, like Russell Kirk, Professor Hayek was convinced that tradition is often wiser than the wisdom of men and that to cast it aside wantonly is "the fatal conceit" the title of his last book, published in 1988, when he was nearly ninety years old.

This last work provides a fitting coda to Hayek's life, for he was keenly aware of the importance of humility, of being willing to participate in something bigger than himself and beyond his imagining. In participating in the market, democracy, and life itself, he believed that we are all involved in such an enterprise, "a game" of high seriousness. In fact, he once wrote that he had "fallen ... in love" with the Greek word *katallattein* after he discovered that it meant not only "to exchange," but also "to admit into the community," and "to change from enemy to friend." He believed that exchange in the market—"by which we ... induce the stranger to welcome and serve us"—should be called "the game of *catallaxy*." This idea greatly attracted him, for he was convinced that the market is "a game which serves to elicit from each player the highest and [most] worth-while contribution to the common pool...."

Conservatives ought always to recall that the true purpose of the "game of exchange" is *catallaxy*, to make friends of our enemies.

F. A. Hayek

Responsibility and Freedom

> *It is doubtful that democracy could survive in a society*
> *organized on the principle of therapy rather than judg-*
> *ment, error rather than sin. If men are free and equal, they*
> *must be judged rather than hospitalized.*

> — E. D. Wormuth

    1.   Liberty not only means that the individual has both the opportunity and the burden of choice; it also means that he must bear the consequences of his actions and will receive praise or blame for them. Liberty and responsibility are inseparable. A free society will not function or maintain itself unless its members regard it as right that each individual occupy the position that results from his action and accept it as due to his own action. Though it can offer to the individual only chances and though the outcome of his efforts will depend on innumerable accidents, it forcefully directs his attention to those circumstances that he can control as if they were the only ones that mattered. Since the individual is to be given the opportunity to make use of circumstances that may be known only to him and since, as a rule, nobody else can know whether he has made the best use of them or not, the presumption is that the out-

From F. A. Hayek, *The Constitution of Liberty* (1960). The E. D. Wormuth quote is taken from *The Origins of Modern Constitutionalism* (New York, 1949), p. 212.

come of his actions is determined by them, unless the contrary is quite obvious.

This belief in individual responsibility, which has always been strong when people firmly believed in individual freedom, has markedly declined, together with the esteem for freedom. Responsibility has become an unpopular concept, a word that experienced speakers or writers avoid because of the obvious boredom or animosity with which it is received by a generation that dislikes all moralizing. It often evokes the outright hostility of men who have been taught that it is nothing but circumstances over which they have no control that has determined their position in life or even their actions. This denial of responsibility is, however, commonly due to a fear of responsibility, a fear that necessarily becomes also a fear of freedom.[1] It is doubtless because the opportunity to build one's own life also means an unceasing task, a discipline that man must impose upon himself if he is to achieve his aims, that many people are afraid of liberty.

2.   The concurrent decline in esteem for individual liberty and individual responsibility is in a great measure the result of an erroneous interpretation of the lessons of science. The older views were closely connected with a belief in the "freedom of the will," a conception that never did have a precise meaning but later seemed to have been deprived of foundation by modern science. The increasing belief that all natural phenomena are uniquely determined by antecedent events or subject to recognizable laws and that man himself should be seen as part of nature led to the conclusion that man's

---

1. This old truth has been succinctly expressed by G. B. Shaw: "Liberty means responsibility. That is why most men dread it." *(Man and Superman: Maxims for Revolutionaries* [London], 1903, p. 229.) The theme has, of course, been treated fully in some of the novels of F. Dostoevski (especially in the Grand Inquisitor episode of *The Brothers Karamazov*), and there is not much that modern psychoanalysts and existentialist philosophers have been able to add to his psychological insight. But see E. Fromm, *Escape from Freedom* (New York, 1941 English ed. entitled *The Fear of Freedom*); M. Grene, *Dreadful Freedom* (Chicago: University of Chicago Press, 1948); and O. Veit, *Die Flucht vor der Freiheit* (Frankfort on the Main, 1947). The converse of the belief in individual responsibility and connected respect for the law which prevail in free societies is the sympathy with the lawbreaker which seems to develop regularly in unfree societies and which is so characteristic of nineteenth-century Russian literature.

actions and the working of his mind must also be regarded as necessarily determined by external circumstances. The conception of universal determinism that dominated nineteenth-century science[2] was thus applied to the conduct of human beings, and this seemed to eliminate the spontaneity of human action. It had, of course, to be admitted that there was no more than a general presumption that human actions were also subject to natural law and that we actually did not know how they were determined by particular circumstances except, perhaps, in the rarest of instances. But the admission that the working of man's mind must be believed, at least in principle, to obey uniform laws appeared to eliminate the role of an individual personality which is essential to the conception of freedom and responsibility.

The intellectual history of the last few generations gives us any number of instances of how this determinist picture of the world has shaken the foundation of the moral and political belief in freedom. And many scientifically educated people today would probably agree with the scientist who, when writing for the general public, admitted that freedom "is a very troublesome concept for the scientist to discuss, partly because he is not convinced that, in the last analysis, there is such a thing."[3] More recently, it is true, physicists have, it would seem with some relief, abandoned the thesis of universal determinism. It is doubtful, however, whether the newer conception of a merely statistical regularity of the world in any way affects the puzzle about the freedom of the will. For it would seem that the difficulties that people have had concerning the meaning of voluntary action and responsibility do not at all spring from any necessary consequence of the belief that human action is causally determined but are the result of an intellectual muddle, of drawing conclusions which do not follow from the premises.

---

2. For a careful examination of the philosophical problems of general determinism see K. R. Popper *The Logic of Scientific Discovery—Postscript: After Twenty Years* (London, 1959); cf. also my essay "Degrees of Explanation," *British Journal for the Philosophy of Science*, Vol. VI (1955).

3. C. H. Waddington, *The Scientific Attitude* ("Pelican Books" [London, 1941]), p. 110.

It appears that the assertion that the will is free has as little meaning as its denial and that the whole issue is a phantom problem,[4] a dispute about words in which the contestants have not made clear what an affirmative or a negative answer would imply. Surely, those who deny the freedom of the will deprive the word "free" of all its ordinary meaning, which describes action according to one's own will instead of another's; in order not to make a meaningless statement, they should offer some other definition, which, indeed, they never do.[5] Furthermore, the whole suggestion that "free" in any relevant or meaningful sense precludes the idea that action is necessarily determined by some factors proves on examination to be entirely unfounded.

The confusion becomes obvious when we examine the conclusion generally drawn by the two parties from their respective positions. The determinists usually argue that, because men's actions are completely determined by natural causes, there could be no justification for holding them responsible or praising or blaming their actions. The voluntarists, on the other hand, contend that, because there exists in man some agent standing outside the chain of cause and effect, this agent is the bearer of responsibility and the legitimate object of praise and blame. Now there can be little doubt that, so far as these practical conclusions are concerned, the voluntarists are more nearly right, while the determinists are merely confused.

---

4 This was already clearly seen by John Locke (*An Essay Concerning Human Understanding*, Book II, chap. xxi, sec. 14, where he speaks of the "unreasonable because unintelligible Question, viz. *Whether Man's Will be free, or not?* For if I mistake not, it follows from what I have said, that the question itself is altogether improper"), and even by T. Hobbes, *Leviathan*, ed. M. Oakeshott (Oxford, 1946), p. 137. For more recent discussions see H. Gomperz, *Das Problem der Willensfreiheit* (Jena, 1907); M. Schlick, *Problems of Ethics* (New York, 1939); C. D. Broad, *Determinism, Indeterminism, and Libertarianism* (Cambridge, England, 1934); R. M. Hare, *The Language of Morals* (Oxford, 1952); H. L. A. Hart, "The Ascription of Responsibility and Rights," *Proc. Arist. Soc.,* 1940–41, reprinted in *Logic and Language*, ed. A. Flew (1st ser.; Oxford, 1951); P. H. Nowell-Smith, "Free Will and Moral Responsibility," *Mind*, Vol. LVII (1948), and the same author's *Ethics* ("Pelican Books" [London, 1954]); J. D. Mabbott, "Freewill and Punishment," in *Contemporary British Philosophy*, ed. H. D. Lewis (London, 1956); C. A. Campbell, "Is Free Will a Pseudo-Problem?" *Mind*, Vol. LX (1951); D. M. MacKay, "On Comparing the Brain with Machines" (British Association Symposium on Cybernetics), *Advancement of Science*, X (1954), esp. 406; *Determinism and Freedom in the Age of Modern Science*, ed. S. Hook (New York: New York Press, 1958); and H. Kelsen, "Causality and Imputation," *Ethics*, Vol. LXI (1950–51).

5 Cf. David Hume, *An Enquiry Concerning Human Understanding*, in *Essays*, ii, 79: "By liberty, then, we can only mean *a power of acting or not acting, according to the determination of the will.*" See also the discussion in my book, *The Sensory Order* (London and Chicago: University of Chicago Press, 1952), secs. 8.93–8.94.

The peculiar fact about the dispute is, however, that in neither case do the conclusions follow from the alleged premises. As has often been shown, the conception of responsibility rests, in fact, on a determinist view,[6] while only the construction of a metaphysical "self" that stands outside the whole chain of cause and effect and therefore could be treated as uninfluenced by praise or blame could justify man's exemption from responsibility.

3.   It would be possible, of course, to construct, as illustration of an alleged determinist position, a bogey of an automaton that invariably responded to the events in its environment in the same predictable manner. This would correspond, however, to no position that has ever been seriously maintained even by the most extreme opponents of the "freedom of the will." Their contention is that the conduct of a person at any moment, his response to any set of external circumstances, will be determined by the joint effects of his inherited constitution and all his accumulated experience, with each new experience being interpreted in the light of earlier individual experience a cumulative process which in each instance produces a unique and distinct personality. This personality operates as a sort of filter through which external events produce conduct which can be predicted with certainty only in exceptional circumstances. What the determinist position asserts is that those accumulated effects of heredity and past experience constitute the whole of the individual personality, that there is no other "self" or "I" whose disposition cannot be affected by external or material influences. This means that all those factors whose influence is sometimes inconsistently denied by those who deny the "freedom of the will," such as reasoning or argument, persuasion or censure,

---

6 Though this contention still has the appearance of a paradox, it goes back as far as David Hume and apparently even Aristotle. Hume stated explicitly (*Treatise*, II, 192): " 'Tis only upon the principles of necessity, that a person acquires any merit or demerit from his actions, however the common opinion may incline to the contrary." On Aristotle see Y. Simon, *Traité du libre arbitre* (Liége, 1951), and K. E Heman, *Des Aristoteles Lehre von der Freiheit des menschlichen Willens* (Leipzig, 1887), quoted by Simon. For recent discussions see R. E. Hobart, "Free Will as Involving Determination and Inconceivable without It," *Mind*, Vol. XLIII (1934); and P. Foot, "Free Will as Involving Determinism," *Philosophical Review*, Vol. LXVI (1957).

or the expectation of praise or blame, are really among the most
important factors determining the personality and through it the
particular action of the individual. It is just because there is no separate "self" that stands outside the chain of causation that there is
also no "self" that we could not reasonably try to influence by
reward or punishment.[7]

That we can, in fact, often influence people's conduct by education and example, rational persuasion, approval or disapproval,
has probably never been seriously denied. The only question that
can be legitimately asked is, therefore, to what extent particular
persons in given circumstances are likely to be influenced in the
desired direction by the knowledge that an action will raise or lower
them in the esteem of their fellows or that they can expect reward
or punishment for it.

Strictly speaking, it is nonsense to say, as is so often said, that "it
is not a man's fault that he is as he is," for the aim of assigning responsibility is to make him different from what he is or might be. If we
say that a person is responsible for the consequences of an action,
this is not a statement of fact or an assertion about causation. The
statement would, of course, not be justifiable if nothing he "might"
have done or omitted could have altered the result. But when we use
words like "might" or "could" in this connection, we do not mean
that at the moment of his decision something in him acted otherwise
than was the necessary effect of causal laws in the given circumstances. Rather, the statement that a person is responsible for what
he does aims at making his actions different from what they would
be if he did not believe it to be true. We assign responsibility to a man,
not in order to say that as he was he might have acted differently, but
in order to make him different. If I have caused harm to somebody

---

7 The most extreme deterministic position tends to deny that the term "will" has any meaning (the word has
indeed been banned from some kinds of super-scientific psychology) or that there is such a thing as voluntary
action. Yet even those who hold that position cannot avoid distinguishing between the kinds of actions that
can be influenced by rational considerations and those that cannot. This is all that matters. Indeed, they will
have to admit, what is in effect a *reductio ad absurdum* of their position, that whether a person does or does
not believe in his capacity to form and carry out plans, which is what is popularly meant by his will being free
or not, may make a great deal of difference to what he will do.

by negligence or forgetfulness, "which I could not help" in the circumstances, this does not exempt me from responsibility but should impress upon me more strongly than before the necessity of keeping the possibility of such consequences in mind.[8]

The only questions that can be legitimately raised, therefore, are whether the person upon whom we place responsibility for a particular action or its consequences is the kind of person who is accessible to normal motives (that is, whether he is what we call a responsible person) and whether in the given circumstances such a person can be expected to be influenced by the considerations and beliefs we want to impress upon him. As in most such problems, our ignorance of the particular circumstances will regularly be such that we will merely know that the expectation that they will be held responsible is likely, on the whole, to influence men in certain positions in a desirable direction. Our problem is generally not whether certain mental factors were operative on the occasion of a particular action but how certain considerations might be made as effective as possible in guiding action. This requires that the individual be praised or blamed, whether or not the expectation of this would in fact have made any difference to the action. Of the effect in the particular instance we may never be sure, but we believe that, in general, the knowledge that he will be held responsible will influence a person's conduct in a desirable direction. In this sense the assigning of responsibility does not involve the assertion of a fact. It is rather of the nature of a convention intended to make people observe certain rules. Whether a particular convention of this kind is effective may always be a debatable question. We shall rarely know more than that experience suggests that it is or is not, on the whole, effective.

Responsibility has become primarily a legal concept, because the law requires clear tests to decide when a person's actions create an

---

8 We still call a man's decision "free," though by the conditions we have created he is led to do what we want him to do, because these conditions do not uniquely determine his actions but merely make it more likely that anyone in his position will do what we approve. We try to "influence" but do not determine what he will do. What we often mean in this connection, as in many others, when we call his action "free," is simply that we do not know what has determined it, and not that it has not been determined by something.

obligation or make him liable to punishment. But it is, of course,
no less a moral concept, a conception which underlies our view of
a person's moral duties. In fact, its scope extends considerably
beyond what we commonly consider as moral. Our whole attitude
toward the working of our social order, our approval or disapproval
of the manner in which it determines the relative position of different individuals, is closely tied up with our views about responsibility. The significance of the concept thus extends far beyond the
sphere of coercion, and its greatest importance perhaps lies in its
role in guiding man's free decisions. A free society probably
demands more than any other that people be guided in their action
by a sense of responsibility which extends beyond the duties exacted by the law and that general opinion approve of the individuals'
being held responsible for both the success and the failure of their
endeavors. When men are allowed to act as they see fit, they must
also be held responsible for the results of their efforts.

4.   The justification for assigning responsibility is thus the presumed effect of this practice on future action; it aims at teaching
people what they ought to consider in comparable future situations.
Though we leave people to decide for themselves because they are,
as a rule, in the best position to know the circumstances surrounding their action, we are also concerned that conditions should permit them to use their knowledge to the best effect. If we allow men
freedom because we presume them to be reasonable beings, we also
must make it worth their while to act as reasonable beings by let-
ting them bear the consequences of their decisions. This does not
mean that a man will always be assumed to be the best judge of his
interests; it means merely that we can never be sure who knows
them better than he and that we wish to make full use of the capacities of all those who may have something to contribute to the common effort of making our environment serve human purposes.

The assigning of responsibility thus presupposes the capacity on
men's part for rational action, and it aims at making them act more

rationally than they would otherwise. It presupposes a certain minimum capacity in them for learning and foresight, for being guided by a knowledge of the consequences of their action. It is no objection to argue that reason in fact plays only a small part in determining human action, since the aim is to make that little go as far as possible. Rationality, in this connection, can mean no more than some degree of coherence and consistency in a person's action, some lasting influence of knowledge or insight which, once acquired, will affect his action at a later date and in different circumstances.

The complementarity of liberty and responsibility means that the argument for liberty can apply only to those who can be held responsible. It cannot apply to infants, idiots, or the insane. It presupposes that a person is capable of learning from experience and of guiding his actions by knowledge thus acquired; it is invalid for those who have not yet learned enough or are incapable of learning. A person whose actions are fully determined by the same unchangeable impulses uncontrolled by knowledge of the consequences or a genuine split personality, a schizophrenic, could in this sense not be held responsible, because his knowledge that he will be held responsible could not alter his actions. The same would apply to persons suffering from really uncontrollable urges, kleptomaniacs or dipsomaniacs, whom experience has proved not to be responsive to normal motives. But so long as we have reason to believe that a man's awareness that he will be held responsible is likely to influence his actions, it is necessary to treat him as responsible, whether or not in the particular instance this will have the desired effect. The assigning of responsibility is based, not on what we know to be true in the particular case, but on what we believe will be the probable effects of encouraging people to behave rationally and considerately. It is a device that society has developed to cope with our inability to look into other people's minds and, without resorting to coercion, to introduce order into our lives.

This is not the place to enter into a discussion of the special problem raised by all those who cannot be held responsible and to whom the argument for liberty therefore does not or cannot wholly apply. The important point is that being a free and responsible member of the community is a particular status that carries with it a burden as well as a privilege; and if freedom is to fulfill its aim, this status must not be granted at anybody's discretion but must automatically belong to all who satisfy certain objectively ascertainable tests (such as age), so long as the presumption that they possess the required minimum capacities is not clearly disproved. In personal relations the transition from tutelage to full responsibility may be gradual and indistinct, and those lighter forms of coercion which exist between individuals and with which the state should not interfere can be adjusted to degrees of responsibility. Politically and legally, however, the distinction must be sharp and definite and be determined by general and impersonal rules if freedom is to be effective. In our decisions as to whether a person is to be his own master or be subject to the will of another, we must regard him as being either responsible or not responsible, as either having or not having the right to act in a manner that may be unintelligible, unpredictable, or unwelcome to others. The fact that not all human beings can be given full liberty must not mean that the liberty of all should be subject to restrictions and regulations adjusted to individual conditions. The individualizing treatment of the juvenile court or the mental ward is the mark of unfreedom, of tutelage. Though in the intimate relations of private life we may adjust our conduct to the personality of our partners, in public life freedom requires that we be regarded as types, not as unique individuals, and treated on the presumption that normal motives and deterrents will be effective, whether this be true in the particular instance or not.

5.   There is much confusion of the ideal that a person ought to be allowed to pursue his own aims with the belief that, if left free, he will or ought to pursue solely his selfish aims.[9] The freedom to

---

9. Cf. T. N. Carver, *Essays in Social Justice* (Cambridge: Harvard University Press, 1922), and the first essay in my *Individualism and Economic Order* (London and Chicago, 1948).

pursue one's own aims is, however, as important for the most altruistic person, in whose scale of values the needs of other people occupy a very high place, as for any egotist. It is part of the ordinary nature of men (and perhaps still more of women) and one of the main conditions of their happiness that they make the welfare of other people their chief aim. To do so is part of the normal choice open to us and often the decision generally expected of us. By common opinion our chief concern in this respect should, of course, be the welfare of our family. But we also show our appreciation and approval of others by making them our friends and their aims ours. To choose our associates and generally those whose needs we make our concern is an essential part of freedom and of the moral conceptions of a free society.

General altruism, however is a meaningless conception. Nobody can effectively care for other people as such; the responsibilities we can assume must always be particular, can concern only those about whom we know concrete facts and to whom either choice or special conditions have attached us. It is one of the fundamental rights and duties of a free man to decide what and whose needs appear to him most important.

The recognition that each person has his own scale of values which we ought to respect, even if we do not approve of it, is part of the conception of the value of the individual personality. How we value another person will necessarily depend on what his values are. But believing in freedom means that we do not regard ourselves as the ultimate judges of another person's values, that we do not feel entitled to prevent him from pursuing ends which we disapprove so long as he does not infringe the equally protected sphere of others.

A society that does not recognize that each individual has values of his own which he is entitled to follow can have no respect for the dignity of the individual and cannot really know freedom. But it is also true that in a free society an individual will be esteemed according to the manner in which he uses his freedom. Moral esteem would be meaningless without freedom: "If every action which is good or evil in a man of ripe years were under pittance and prescription and compulsion, what were virtue but a name, what praise would be due to well-doing, what gramercy to be sober, just, or continent?"[10] Liberty is an opportunity for doing good, but this is so only when it is also an opportunity for doing wrong. The fact that a free society will function successfully only if the individuals are in some measure guided by common values is perhaps the reason why philosophers have sometimes defined freedom as action in conformity with moral rules. But this definition of freedom is a denial of that freedom with which we are concerned. The freedom of action that is the condition of moral merit includes the freedom to act wrongly: we praise or blame only when a person has the opportunity to choose, only when his observance of a rule is not enforced but merely enjoined.

That the sphere of individual freedom is also the sphere of individual responsibility does not mean that we are accountable for our actions to any particular persons. True, we may lay ourselves open to censure by others because we do what displeases them. But the chief reason why we should be held wholly responsible for our decisions is that this will direct our attention to those causes of events that depend on our actions. The main function of the belief in individual responsibility is to make us use our own knowledge and capacities to the full in achieving our ends.

6.　　The burden of choice that freedom imposes, the responsibility for one's own fate that a free society places on the individual, has under the conditions of the modern world become a main source of dissatisfaction. To a much greater degree than ever before, the success of a man will depend not on what special abilities he

---

10. John Milton, *Areopagitica* ("Everyman" ed. [London, 1927]), p. 18. The conception of moral merit depending on freedom was already emphasized by some of the Scholastic philosophers and again especially in the German "classical" literature (cf., e.g., F. Schiller, *On the Aesthetic Education of Man* [New Haven: Yale University Press, 1954], p. 74: "Man must have his freedom to be ready for morality").

possesses in the abstract but on these abilities being put to the right use. In times of less specialization and less complex organization, when almost everybody could know most of the opportunities that existed, the problem of finding an opportunity for putting one's special skills and talents to good use was less difficult. As society and its complexity extend, the rewards a man can hope to earn come to depend more and more, not on the skill and capacity he may possess, but on their being put to the right use; and both the difficulty of discovering the best employment for one's capacities and the discrepancy between the rewards of men possessing the same technical skill or special ability will increase.

There is perhaps no more poignant grief than that arising from a sense of how useful one might have been to one's fellow men and of one's gifts having been wasted. That in a free society nobody has a duty to see that a man's talents are properly used, that nobody has a claim to an opportunity to use his special gifts, and that, unless he himself finds such opportunity, they are likely to be wasted, is perhaps the gravest reproach directed against a free system and the source of the bitterest resentment. The consciousness of possessing certain potential capacities naturally leads to the claim that it is somebody else's duty to use them.

The necessity of finding a sphere of usefulness, an appropriate job, ourselves is the hardest discipline that a free society imposes on us. It is, however, inseparable from freedom, since nobody can assure each man that his gifts will be properly used unless he has the power to coerce others to use them. Only by depriving somebody else of the choice as to who should serve him, whose capacities or which products he is to use, could we guarantee to any man that his gifts will be used in the manner he feels he deserves. It is of the essence of a free society that a man's value and remuneration depend not on capacity in the abstract but on success in turning it into concrete service which is useful to others who can reciprocate. And the chief aim of freedom is to provide both the opportunity and the inducement to insure the maximum use of the knowledge that an individual can acquire. What makes the individual unique in this respect is not his generic but his concrete knowledge, his knowledge of particular circumstances and conditions.

7.   It must be recognized that the results of a free society in this respect are often in conflict with ethical views that are relics of an earlier type of society. There can be little question that, from the point of view of society, the art of turning one's capacity to good account, the skill of discovering the most effective use of one's gift, is perhaps the most useful of all; but too much resourcefulness of this kind is not uncommonly frowned upon, and an advantage gained over those of equal general capacity by a more successful exploitation of concrete circumstances is regarded as unfair. In many societies an "aristocratic" tradition that stems from the conditions of action in an organizational hierarchy with assigned tasks and duties, a tradition that has often been developed by people whose privileges have freed them from the necessity of giving others what they want, represents it as nobler to wait until one's gifts are discovered by others, while only religious or ethnic minorities in a hard struggle to rise have deliberately cultivated this kind of resourcefulness (best described by the German term *Findigkeit*)— and are generally disliked for that reason. Yet there can be no doubt that the discovery of a better use of things or of one's own capacities is one of the greatest contributions that an individual can make in our society to the welfare of his fellows and that it is by providing the maximum opportunity for this that a free society can become so much more prosperous than others. The successful use of this entrepreneurial capacity (and, in discovering the best use of our abilities, we are all entrepreneurs) is the most highly rewarded activity in a free society, while whoever leaves to others the task of finding some useful means of employing his capacities must be content with a smaller reward.

It is important to realize that we are not educating people for a free society if we train technicians who expect to be "used," who are incapable of finding their proper niche themselves, and who regard it as somebody else's responsibility to ensure the appropriate use of their ability or skill. However able a man may be in a particular field, the value of his services is necessarily low in a free society unless he also possesses the capacity of making his ability known to those who can derive the greatest benefit from it. Though it may offend our sense of justice to find that of two men who by equal effort have acquired the same specialized skill and knowledge, one may be a success and the other a failure, we must recognize that in a free society it is the use of particular opportunities that determines usefulness and must adjust our education and ethos accordingly. In a free society we are remunerated not for our skill but for using it rightly; and this must be so as long as we are free to choose our particular occupation and are not to be directed to it. True, it is almost never possible to determine what part of a successful career has been due to superior knowledge, ability, or effort and what part to fortunate accidents; but this in no way detracts from the importance of making it worthwhile for everybody to make the right choice.

How little this basic fact is understood is shown by such assertions, made not only by socialists, as that "every child has a natural right, as citizen, not merely to life, liberty, and the pursuit of happiness, but to that position in the social scale to which his talents entitle him."[11] In a free society a man's talents do not "entitle" him to any particular position. To claim that they do would mean that some agency has the right and power to place men in particular positions according to its judgment. All that a free society has to offer is an opportunity of searching for a suitable position, with all the attendant risk and uncertainty which such a search for a market for one's gifts must involve. There is no denying that in this respect a free society puts most individuals under a pressure which is often resented. But it is an illusion to think that one would be rid of such pressure in some other type

---

11. C. A. R Crosland, *The Future of Socialism* (London, 1956), p. 208.

of society; for the alternative to the pressure that responsibility for one's own fate brings is the far more invidious pressure of personal orders that one must obey.

It is often contended that the belief that a person is solely responsible for his own fate is held only by the successful. This in itself is not so unacceptable as its underlying suggestion, which is that people hold this belief because they have been successful. I, for one, am inclined to think that the connection is the other way round and that people often are successful because they hold this belief. Though a man's conviction that all he achieves is due solely to his exertions, skill, and intelligence may be largely false, it is apt to have the most beneficial effects on his energy and circumspection. And if the smug pride of the successful is often intolerable and offensive, the belief that success depends wholly on him is probably the pragmatically most effective incentive to successful action; whereas the more a man indulges in the propensity to blame others or circumstances for his failures, the more disgruntled and ineffective he tends to become.

8.   The sense of responsibility has been weakened in modern times as much by overextending the range of an individual's responsibilities as by exculpating him from the actual consequences of his actions. Since we assign responsibility to the individual in order to influence his action, it should refer only to such effects of his conduct as it is humanly possible for him to foresee and to such as we can reasonably wish him to take into account in ordinary circumstances. To be effective, responsibility must be both definite and limited, adapted both emotionally and intellectually to human capacities. It is quite as destructive of any sense of responsibility to be taught that one is responsible for everything as to be taught that one cannot be held responsible for anything. Freedom demands that the responsibility of the individual extend only to what he can be presumed to judge, that his actions take into account effects which are within his range of foresight, and particularly that he be responsible only for

his own actions (or those of persons under his care)—not for those of others who are equally free.

Responsibility, to be effective, must be individual responsibility. In a free society there cannot be any collective responsibility of members of a group as such, unless they have, by concerted action, all made themselves individually and severally responsible. A joint or divided responsibility may create for the individual the necessity of agreeing with others and thereby limit the powers of each. If the same concerns are made the responsibility of many without at the same time imposing a duty of joint and agreed action, the result is usually that nobody really accepts responsibility. As everybody's property in effect is nobody's property, so everybody's responsibility is nobody's responsibility.[12]

It is not to be denied that modern developments, especially the development of the large city, have destroyed much of the feeling of responsibility for local concerns which in the past led to much beneficial and spontaneous common action. The essential condition of responsibility is that it refer to circumstances that the individual can judge, to problems that, without too much strain of the imagination, man can make his own and whose solution he can, with good reason, consider his own concern rather than another's. Such a condition can hardly apply to life in the anonymous crowd of an industrial city. No longer is the individual generally the member of some small community with which he is intimately concerned and closely acquainted. While this has brought him some increase in independence, it has also deprived him of the security which the personal ties and the friendly interest of the neighbors provided. The increased demand for protection and security from the impersonal power of the state is no doubt largely the result of the disappearance of those smaller communities of interest and of

---

12. Cf. also the observation by J. Huizinga, *Incertitudes* (Paris, 1939), p. 216: "Dans chaque groupe collectif une partie du jugement de l'individu est absorbée avec une partie de sa responsabilité par le mot d'ordre collectif. Le sentiment d'être tous ensemble responsables de tout, accroit dans le monde actuel le danger de l'irresponsabilité absolue de l'action des masses."

the feeling of isolation of the individual who can no longer count on the personal interest and assistance of the other members of the local group.[13]

Much as we may regret the disappearance of those close communities of interest and their replacement by a wide-flung net of limited, impersonal, and temporary ties, we cannot expect the sense of responsibility for the known and familiar to be replaced by a similar feeling about the remote and the theoretically known. While we can feel genuine concern for the fate of our familiar neighbors and usually will know how to help when help is needed, we cannot feel in the same way about the thousands or millions of unfortunates whom we know to exist in the world but whose individual circumstances we do not know. However moved we may be by accounts of their misery, we cannot make the abstract knowledge of the numbers of suffering people guide our everyday action. If what we do is to be useful and effective, our objectives must be limited, adapted to the capacities of our mind and our compassions. To be constantly reminded of our "social" responsibilities to all the needy or unfortunate in our community, in our country, or in the world, must have the effect of attenuating our feelings until the distinctions between those responsibilities which call for our action and those which do not disappear. In order to be effective, then, responsibility must be so confined as to enable the individual to rely on his own concrete knowledge in deciding on the importance of the different tasks, to apply his moral principles to circumstances he knows, and to help to mitigate evils voluntarily.

---

13. See D. Riesman, *The Lonely Crowd* (New Haven: Yale University Press, 1950).

The Heritage Foundation Collection,

Chapter 4

Milton Friedman

Commentary by Edwin J. Feulner Jr. (1997)

P romoter of free markets and free minds; father of floating currency, stable money and the volunteer army; guiding light of the "Chicago School"; critic of the chaos that flows from central planning; sworn enemy of the free lunch: Milton Friedman is the spokesman and symbol of the remarkable revival of neoclassical economics in our time. As a groundbreaking scholar, influential teacher, intimidating debater, television personality, widely read columnist and advisor to presidents and prime ministers, he has defended the efficiency and nobility of markets and revealed the justice found in freedom. Evidence of his dazzling brilliance ranges from discoveries in statistics made fifty years ago (still known as the "Friedman Test") to his early advocacy of school choice, deregulation and the flat tax, which have reshaped policy debate in America and around the world.

In a career of constructive controversy, he has deflated the pretensions of Keynesian technocrats and proven, with moral passion and economic sophistication, that the tradition of Adam Smith is the wave of the world's future. In the process, Milton Friedman has become, in the words of the *Economist* and the estimation of countless others, "the greatest economist of the 20th century."

His continuing influence is felt in the American government, where House Majority Leader Richard Armey comments, "One of the great privileges of this job is that I dare call Milton Friedman friend. This is like a miracle in my life." On the flip side, Robert Rubin, secretary of the treasury in the Clinton administration, has proclaimed, "We're not a set of Milton Friedmans"—which is both accurate and unfortunate.

Yet the broadest measure of Friedman's influence is found in the capitalist renaissance beyond America's borders.

- A *New York Times* reporter interviews the vice mayor of Dong-guan, forty miles from Hong Kong, a former member of the Red Guard, whose fervor earned him a private reception with Mao Zedong. "Times have changed," the article observes. "These days, Lau says his favorite economist is Milton Friedman, the American conservative who stresses the importance of monetary policy and decries big government. It is a bit like George Bush saying his favorite economist is Karl Marx."
- A correspondent for the *Chicago Tribune* interviews Naidansuren-gin Zolzhargal, the twenty-six-year-old director of the Mongolian Stock Exchange and director of the State Bank of Mongolia. "Zolzhargal," the reporter notes, "says his idol is Nobel laureate economist Milton Friedman."
- A *New York Times* reporter files a story from Khartoum, Sudan. "With a copy of the Koran in one hand and the economic theories of Milton Friedman in the other, the Sudanese government is trying to wed unbridled capitalism to militant Islam."

"The tide of ideas isn't local," Milton Friedman has argued. "It's international; it's worldwide." And throughout the world, Friedman has become the breathing, bespectacled example of how human freedom can be advanced with academic integrity and articulate zeal. His direct influence can be traced in places as diverse as Thatcher's Britain, the Czech Republic, South Korea, Portugal, Spain, and Chile—where the "Chicago Boys," including some of

Friedman's students, created a free-market showcase by cutting public spending, attacking inflation, reducing tariffs, and inviting foreign investment. At one point, University of Chicago graduates included the Chilean ministers of finance, planning, and the treasury; the budget director; and president and vice president of the central bank.

Martin Anderson, former chief domestic policy advisor to President Reagan, concludes, "If you step back and look at all the sweeping political and economic changes in the United States and even in other countries, a lot of people have had an important effect. But if you had to say one person who had the most impact, it's Milton Friedman."

John Maynard Keynes famously said that we are unconsciously ruled by dead economists. Our world is increasingly, consciously, and gratefully governed by the ideas of a distinguished living economist. In many ways, this can be called the age of Friedman.

Milton Friedman has conducted his crusade for liberty with a distinctive style that can both intimidate and disarm. He is a natural debater, for whom passionate, principled argument is a way of life. His son, David, recalls that until the age of fifteen in the Friedman household, "It had not occurred to me that there were forms of conversation that didn't involve argument and analysis." And when he debates, Friedman can be devastating. During one forum on the military draft, a general insisted on using the term "mercenaries" in his argument against a volunteer army. "You could see Milton getting more and more agitated," recalls Martin Anderson. "Finally he went up to the mike and said to the general, 'If you will stop calling young men who volunteer to serve their country mercenaries, then I will not start calling people who are drafted slaves." Some of Friedman's opponents have wisely sent up a white flag when it comes to verbal combat. John Kenneth Galbraith concedes, "Milton Friedman is a superb debater ... I've always avoided debating him."

Yet this debating skill is leavened with wit, proving that the "dismal science" is anything but dismal in his hands. In reference to his height—five feet, two inches—he claims that he lost an inch from carrying the "weight of the world" on his shoulders. When Richard Nixon opined that "We are all Keynesians now," Friedman immediately wrote Galbraith a note: "You must be as chagrined as I am to have Nixon for your disciple."

Milton Friedman's defining attitude is an infectious confidence, which has given conservative (and classical liberal) economics its forward momentum. A student skit from the University of Chicago in the 1950s included the line: "Mr. Friedman, is it correct that you have discovered *Truth*, and that you are now simply verifying it empirically?" Once, when hiring an administrative assistant who lacked an economics background, Friedman reassured her: "You don't have to worry about not knowing anything about economics. There are many people who studied economics for years and don't know anything about economics. Stick with me and you'll learn the correct way."

Chairman of the Federal Reserve Alan Greenspan, who has called Friedman one of the most productive intellects of the century, comments: "As far as Milton Friedman is concerned, if something is true, it's true. He talks the same way to an eighteen-year-old college student as he does to the President of the United States." And he has regularly and persuasively talked with both.

Born in 1912, Milton Friedman is the product of America's hard, rich immigrant experience. His parents emigrated from a province of the Austro-Hungarian Empire in the late nineteenth century. From the age of fourteen, his mother worked as a seamstress in a New York sweat shop, an institution Friedman vigorously defends as a source of low-skill, low-paying jobs. "Sweatshops serve a very useful function. If present-day labor laws had been in effect in the 19th century, you never would have been able to have all the immigration you did."

As a child, Friedman showed a talent for mathematics, graduating from high school before his sixteenth birthday and dreaming of becoming an actuary for an insurance company. But at Rutgers

College, where he was a student of Arthur Burns (later chairman of the Council of Economic Advisers and chairman of the Federal Reserve), Friedman fell in love with economics. Graduating in 1932, at the darkest moment of the Great Depression, he was offered a scholarship to the University of Chicago.

That university, he remembers, "exposed me to a cosmopolitan and vibrant intellectual atmosphere of a kind that I had never dreamed existed. I have never recovered." The University of Chicago's economics department was populated by free-market giants, including Frank Knight, Jacob Viner, and Henry Simons. Here Friedman also encountered another formative influence—a fellow graduate student in economics named Rose Director, who became his wife and frequent collaborator. Her husband, she recalls, was supremely studious, with little interest in things non-academic. Once, before they were married, she dragged him to the symphony in New York in a vain attempt to civilize him. "When I saw that he sat beside me reading a book while the music was on, I gave up."

After wartime work in Washington (where his efforts led to income tax withholding from paychecks to fund the war effort), Friedman returned to the University of Chicago, this time as a professor. Lindley Clark, editor and columnist at the *Wall Street Journal*, was one of Friedman's students in the late 1940s. He remembers him as "exciting, even exhilarating" teacher who, unlike some colleagues, "wasn't always canceling classes because his advice was wanted in Washington."

The University of Chicago, after World War II, was in the midst of a conservative golden age. Richard Weaver taught English and rhetoric. Friedrich von Hayek lectured on social philosophy. Leo Strauss attacked relativism and revisited Athens and Jerusalem in political philosophy. And Milton Friedman began a thirty-year run of scholarly achievements that changed the landscape of American economics. In 1950, he wrote a landmark piece on flexible exchange rates which has been called a "modern classic." In the early 1960s, he authored, with Anna Schwartz, the 860-page *A Monetary*

History of the United States, reconstructing money supply data back
to the Civil War from old bank records. Other works dealt with
consumption theory, statistics and economic methodology. "People at MIT and Harvard didn't know what they were going to work
on until Milton made a speech," says fellow University of Chicago
Nobel Laureate, the late George Stigler. His influence transformed
an academic department into a movement, the "Chicago School,"
of which Friedman was the spiritual leader. One professor at the
time was led to conclude, "At most universities, people are either
conservatives or liberals, but at Chicago, you are either a libertarian or an authoritarian."

Along the way, Friedman participated in the founding of the
Mont Pelerin Society on April 1, 1947—an organization which has
been called a "kind of Comintern for the free-market." Convened
by Hayek in Switzerland, the meeting attracted thirty-nine prominent European and American scholars and connected Friedman to
an international network of like-minded intellectuals. The tone of
that first conference was somber. Its concluding declaration warned
that "the position of the individual and the voluntary group are
progressively undermined by extensions of arbitrary power." Yet
the effect was encouraging. "The importance of that meeting,"
Friedman observes, "was that it showed us we were not alone." It
was a "rallying point," he says, for outnumbered troops.

Friedman's rising star was quickly noticed in Washington. He
turned down an invitation from President Eisenhower to serve on
his Council of Economic Advisers. "I really thought I could be much
more helpful and useful in the world at large as a maverick than I
could be in Washington as a civil servant." But Washington kept
insisting. In 1964, Friedman served as economic adviser to
candidate Barry Goldwater.

But through it all, Friedman remained a maverick, unafraid to
criticize slipshod economic thinking, whatever its source. When
President Nixon imposed wage and price controls in 1971, Friedman wrote in the *New York Times*: "The controls are deeply and

inherently immoral. By substituting the rule of men for the rule of law and for voluntary cooperation in the marketplace, the controls threaten the very foundations of a free society. By encouraging men to spy and report on one another, by making it in the private interest of large numbers of citizens to evade controls, and by making actions illegal that are in the public interest, the controls undermine individual morality."

In this period, one of Friedman's great achievements was the all-volunteer military. Beginning at a University of Chicago conference in December of 1966, Friedman debated vigorously against the draft. Eventually, he served on the presidential commission that voted to terminate it. And our experience since the summer of 1973, culminating in the Gulf War, has confirmed Friedman's faith in the ability and commitment of soldiers who give their service without compulsion.

In 1966—the same year that William Buckley started "Firing Line"—Friedman began his regular column in *Newsweek*, dueling with liberal economist Paul Samuelson, and spreading his ideas to a broader popular audience. In 1967, he was elected president of the American Economic Association. In 1969 he was featured on the cover of *Time*, in which he was called a "maverick messiah." Historian George Nash observes: "Here was a man of increasing prestige within his profession, a man whom even opponents respected as one of the very best American economists, who was articulating conservative viewpoints with a felicitous combination of learning and wit."

The Nobel Prize came in 1976, the two hundredth anniversary of Adam Smith's *Wealth of Nations* and Thomas Jefferson's Declaration of Independence, statements of economic and social freedom that Friedman has given new vigor and voice. In that same year, he left the University of Chicago. "I reached the age of 65 and had graded enough exam papers." But a broader exercise in teaching was just beginning. On January 11, 1980—a landmark date in American conservatism—the first episode of Friedman's "Free to

Choose" aired on PBS, making a compelling case to millions of viewers on the essential connection between capitalism and human freedom. The ten-part series took Friedman from Hong Kong harbor, to the Glasgow classroom where Adam Smith lectured, to a Japanese electronics factory, to the ornate boardroom of the New York Federal Reserve. The book based on the series, and written with his wife Rose, was simultaneously on the bestseller list of every English-speaking nation in the world. One reviewer commented, "The Friedmans come out swinging on page one of the Preface and do not let up until the last page of Appendix B." Ronald Reagan called it "must reading for everyone."

In 1988, Milton Friedman was awarded the Presidential Medal of Freedom. He now lives in San Francisco and is a senior research fellow with the Hoover Institution. His overriding interest, he says, remains the same: "To try to understand as much as I can of the world around me—and to enjoy myself in the process. And no doubt, one has to confess, not only to understand, not only to enjoy—but to reform."

I first met Professor Milton Friedman in 1964 when he was a visiting professor of economics at Columbia University. The late Don Lipsett arranged a meeting with Frank Meyer, William F. Buckley, Milton, himself, and me at the Sheraton-Atlantic Hotel in New York City. This was the organizing meeting of what would become the Philadelphia Society. Incidentally, this was also the first time that Friedman and Buckley had met each other. I was very much the junior man at the meeting, but plans were laid for a major American institution patterned after the international Mont Pelerin Society as an interdisciplinary organization of academics, businessmen, journalists, and others involved in studying and promoting the Free Society.

After our initial 1964 meeting, I came to know Milton and Rose as active participants in the public policy process, as well as participants in both Philadelphia Society and Mont Pelerin Society meetings. Milton's acuity was never sharper or more pithy than the time in 1968 at the Chicago meeting of the Philadelphia Society when he challenged me for my support of revenue sharing. Suffice it to say that in this case, like so many others before and since that meeting, Friedman was right and I was wrong, despite the seeming political attractiveness of the idea at the time.

The active involvement of both Milton and Rose in the Fiftieth Anniversary Special Gathering of the Mont Pelerin Society in Mont Pelerin, Switzerland, was a special occasion for all 120 of us who participated in it. To many of us, this was the capstone of his career as the leading intellectual light of the worldwide movement for liberty, especially since he was the only member of the Society who attended both the founding meeting and this golden anniversary celebration.

Milton Friedman carefully defines himself as a free market liberal, not as a conservative—a liberal in the classical sense, concerned primarily with the freedom of individuals. But it is impossible to deny that Friedman's greatest influence has been on, and come through, the American conservative movement, which has this same concern at its core.

In *Free to Choose*, he talks of "the importance of the intellectual climate of opinion, which determines the unthinking preconceptions of most people and their leaders, their conditioned reflexes to one course of action or another." Friedman's contribution to conservatism has been to influence that climate like the thaw after an ice age.

First, he has been able to thoroughly discredit the idea, common since the Great Depression, that capitalism is inherently flawed and requires the "fine-tuning" of government to avoid excess and disaster. This has been the central conceit of the Keynesian state, administered by educated elites, adjusting tax and spending policies to tame the business cycle. As late as December 1965, *Time* could run a cover story on John Maynard Keynes, concluding, "Today, some twenty years after his death, his theories are the prime influence on the world's free economies, especially on America's.

Keynes and his ideas still make some people nervous, but they have been so widely accepted that they constitute both the new orthodoxy in the universities and the assumption of economic management in Washington."

Friedman attacked these beliefs at their root. He ambitiously argued that the Great Depression was not caused by the "defects" of capitalism but by government incompetence. Going back to the 1930s, he demonstrated that the one-third fall in GNP was due to a one-third cut in the money supply from 1929 to 1933. "The Great Depression in the United States, far from being a sign of the inherent instability of the private enterprise system, is a testament to how much harm can be done by mistakes on the part of a few men when they wield vast power over the monetary system of the country."

This astonishing revision of the conventional wisdom changed the entire context of economic policy. Keynesians argued that an unstable private sector must be stabilized by the public sector. Friedman showed that an essentially stable private sector has been the victim of irrational shocks by government. In the process, he made it academically and intellectually respectable to believe there was life left in Adam Smith, even after the soup lines of the 1930s.

Second, Milton Friedman has shown, in case after case, that government interventions in free markets are not only ineffective, but result in the exact opposite of their intended purpose. He has called this the "invisible foot"—the unseen force that makes things go terribly and perversely wrong with social programs. The minimum wage, instead of helping poor people, eliminates low-paying, entry-level jobs. Price controls on energy actually resulted in the energy shortage and crisis of the 1970s. Public housing has led to inhuman living conditions. "The government solution to a problem," Friedman concludes, "is usually as bad as the problem."

Yet, on the other side of this ledger, when free markets are allowed and encouraged to work, they often prove an unsuspected, constructive power to solve social problems—in education and the protection of workers, consumers, and the environment.

Freedom leads, not just to economic efficiency, but to social justice. And this has led Friedman beyond the realm of economic theory to draw the hopeful policy implications of his ideas. Above any conservative economist of his time, he understands the inadequacy of a vision without a task. He has not only criticized current social and economic arrangements, he has proposed specific, free-market alternatives like school vouchers, the flat tax and deregulation. His brainstorms have provided conservatives with a positive agenda. Friedman is a realist with a passion for the possible, who sees his role not only in the demolition of bad ideas, but the construction of better ones. And this has helped turn free market economics into a force of hopeful reform.

Third, and most important, Friedman has made a case with passion and power that economic, social, and political freedom are inseparable—part of the same yearning of the human spirit. He has defended "the fundamental proposition that freedom is one whole, that anything that reduces freedom on one part of our lives is likely to affect freedom in the other parts." "It is widely believed that politics and economics are separate and largely unconnected; that individual freedom is a political problem and material welfare is an economic problem ... Such a view is a delusion," wrote Friedman in 1962. "On one hand, freedom in economic arrangements is itself a component of freedom broadly understood, so economic freedom is an end in itself. In the second place, economic freedom is also an indispensable means toward achievement of political freedom."

This is perhaps the most revolutionary idea of the twentieth century, with more dramatic promise than anything claimed by Marx, and it is a profoundly conservative concept. What Jefferson called the "disease of liberty" cannot be quarantined; it is bound to spread rapidly, as a number of the world's tyrants have discovered to their discomfort. Economic freedom is connected not only to the liberation of men and women from poverty, but their liberation from tyranny and torture, and from the oppression of conscience and information. Friedman argues that the finest achievement of capitalism is not the accumulation of wealth and property but "the opportunities it offers to men and women to extend and develop and improve their capacities." And Friedman's unquestioned success in making this case is the primary reason William Buckley refers to him simply as "my hero."

This essay is one of the classic statements of the philosophy of freedom. *Capitalism and Freedom*—dubbed by some followers as "Capitalism and Friedman"—is described by George Nash as "one of the most significant works of conservative scholarship of the 1960s." It has been in print for thirty-five years, sold over half a million copies and been translated into Spanish, French, Swedish, Italian, German, Japanese, Hebrew, Icelandic, Arabic, Russian, and Portuguese.

With typical iconoclasm, Milton Friedman launches his defense of liberty with an attack on John Kennedy's call to ask what "we can do for our country." In place of this concept, Friedman elevates another objective: "We take freedom of the individual, or perhaps of the family, as our ultimate goal in judging social arrangements." His reasons are practical, noble, and compelling: because social progress—in art, ideas, and the relief of misery—results from a social climate of variety and diversity; because free markets are a necessary condition for political freedom (though not a sufficient one); because "democratic socialism" can never be democratic; and, most important, because freedom and justice head in the same direction, rewarding merit and allowing for coordination without coercion. Opposing free markets is a serious matter, because "underlying most arguments against the free market is a lack of belief in freedom itself."

This essay is a bold assault on the core convictions of modern liberalism by a classical liberal in the tradition of Adam Smith. And it reveals a conviction at the heart of modern conservatism: that justice, opportunity, and even social morality depend on personal liberty and limited government—on structures of freedom that honor accomplishment and cherish human dignity.

There is no more articulate voice in defense of freedom than Milton Friedman. But he is careful to note that, while freedom is the highest goal of society, it cannot be the highest goal of individuals. "In a society, freedom has nothing to say about what an individual does with his freedom; it is not an all-embracing ethic. Indeed, a major aim of the liberal is to leave the ethical problem for the individual to wrestle with. The really important ethical problems are those that face an individual in a free society—what he should do with his freedom."

In mid-1998, Milton and Rose Friedman's joint autobiography will be published by the University of Chicago Press. At that time, the same publisher will release a new edition of *Capitalism and Freedom*. We hope that this excerpt from that seminal work will pique the interest of the new generation to reflect on the timeless principles of liberty as expounded by Milton Friedman a generation ago.

Economic and social freedom, Friedman reminds us, is not a state of nature, but it is also not a state of grace. It creates the space where souls can make their own choices, informed by bishops and, rabbis, poets, and philosophers. "The central and supreme object of liberty," said Lord Acton, "is the reign of conscience." And in the end they are inseparable.

Milton Friedman

Capitalism and Freedom

Introduction

In a much quoted passage in his inaugural address, President Kennedy said, "Ask not what your country can do for you— ask what you can do for your country." It is a striking sign of the temper of our times that the controversy about this passage centered on its origin and not on its content. Neither half of the statement expresses a relation between the citizen and his government that is worthy of the ideals of free men in a free society. The paternalistic "what your country can do for you" implies that government is the patron, the citizen the ward, a view that is at odds with the free man's belief in his own responsibility for his own destiny. The organismic, "what you can do for your country" implies that government is the master or the deity, the citizen, the servant or the votary. To the free man, the country is the collection of individuals who compose it, not something over and above them. He is proud of a common heritage and loyal to common traditions. But he regards government as a means, an instrumentality, neither a grantor of favors and gifts, nor a master or god to be blindly worshipped and served. He recognizes no national goal except as it is the consensus of the goals that the citizens severally serve. He

From Milton Friedman, *Capitalism and Freedom* (1962).

recognizes no national purpose except as it is the consensus of the purposes for which the citizens severally strive.

The free man will ask neither what his country can do for him nor what he can do for his country. He will ask rather "What can I and my compatriots do through government" to help us discharge our individual responsibilities, to achieve our several goals and purposes, and above all, to protect our freedom? And he will accompany this question with another: How can we keep the government we create from becoming a Frankenstein that will destroy the very freedom we establish it to protect? Freedom is a rare and delicate plant. Our minds tell us, and history confirms, that the great threat to freedom is the concentration of power. Government is necessary to preserve our freedom, it is an instrument through which we can exercise our freedom; yet by concentrating power in political hands, it is also a threat to freedom. Even though the men who wield this power initially be of good will and even though they be not corrupted by the power they exercise, the power will both attract and form men of a different stamp.

How can we benefit from the promise of government while avoiding the threat to freedom? Two broad principles embodied in our Constitution give an answer that has preserved our freedom so far, though they have been violated repeatedly in practice while proclaimed as precept.

First, the scope of government must be limited. Its major function must be to protect our freedom both from the enemies outside our gates and from our fellow-citizens: to preserve law and order, to enforce private contracts, to foster competitive markets. Beyond this major function, government may enable us at times to accomplish jointly what we would find it more difficult or expensive to accomplish severally. However, any such use of government is fraught with danger. We should not and cannot avoid using government in this way. But there should be a clear and large balance of advantages before we do. By relying primarily on voluntary cooperation and private enterprise, in both economic and other activities, we can ensure that the private sector is a check on the powers of the governmental sector and an effective protection of freedom of speech, of religion, and of thought.

The second broad principle is that government power must be dispersed. If government is to exercise power, better in the county than in the state, better in the state than in Washington. If I do not like what my local community does, be it in sewage disposal, or zoning, or schools, I can move to another local community, and though few may take this step, the mere possibility acts as a check. If I do not like what Washington imposes, I have few alternatives in this world of jealous nations.

The very difficulty of avoiding the enactments of the federal government is of course the great attraction of centralization to many of its proponents. It will enable them more effectively, they believe, to legislate programs that—as they see it—are in the interest of the public, whether it be the transfer of income from the rich to the poor or from private to governmental purposes. They are in a sense right. But this coin has two sides. The power to do good is also the power to do harm; those who control the power today may not tomorrow; and, more important, what one man regards as good, another may regard as harm. The great tragedy of the drive to centralization, as of the drive to extend the scope of government in general, is that it is mostly led by men of good will who will be the first to rue its consequences.

The preservation of freedom is the protective reason for limiting and decentralizing governmental power. But there is also a constructive reason. The great advances of civilization, whether in architecture or painting, in science or literature, in industry or agriculture, have never come from centralized government. Columbus did not set out to seek a new route to China in response to a majority directive of a parliament, though he was partly financed by an absolute monarch. Newton and Leibnitz; Einstein and Bohr; Shakespeare, Milton, Pasternak; Whitney, McCormick, Edison, and Ford; Jane Addams, Florence Nightingale, and Albert Schweitzer; no one of these opened new frontiers in human knowledge and understanding, in literature, in technical possibilities, or in the relief of human misery in response to governmental directives. Their achievements were the product of individual genius, of strongly held minority views, of a social climate permitting variety and diversity.

Government can never duplicate the variety and diversity of individual action. At any moment in time, by imposing uniform standards in housing, or nutrition, or clothing, government could undoubtedly improve the level of living of many individuals; by imposing uniform standards in schooling, road construction, or sanitation, central government could undoubtedly improve the level of performance in many local areas and perhaps even on the average of all communities. But in the process, government would replace progress by stagnation, it would substitute uniform mediocrity for the variety essential for that experimentation which can bring tomorrow's laggards above today's mean.

This book discusses some of these great issues. Its major theme is the role of competitive capitalism—the organization of the bulk of economic activity through private enterprise operating in a free market—as a system of economic freedom and a necessary condition for political freedom. Its minor theme is the role that government should play in a society dedicated to freedom and relying primarily on the market to organize economic activity.

The first two chapters deal with these issues on an abstract level, in terms of principles rather than concrete application. The later chapters apply these principles to a variety of particular problems.

An abstract statement can conceivably be complete and exhaustive, though this ideal is certainly far from realized in the two chapters that follow. The application of the principles cannot even conceivably be exhaustive. Each day brings new problems and new circumstances. That is why the role of the state can never be spelled out once and for all in terms of specific functions. It is also why we need from time to time to re-examine the bearing of what we hope are unchanged principles on the problems of the day. A by-product is inevitably a retesting of the principles and a sharpening of our understanding of them.

It is extremely convenient to have a label for the political and economic viewpoint elaborated in this book. The rightful and proper label is liberalism. Unfortunately, "As a supreme, if unintended compliment, the enemies of the system of private enterprise have thought it wise to appropriate its label,"[1] so that liberalism has, in the United States, come to have a very different meaning than it did in the nineteenth century or does today over much of the Continent of Europe.

As it developed in the late eighteenth and early nineteenth centuries, the intellectual movement that went under the name of liberalism emphasized freedom as the ultimate goal and the individual as the ultimate entity in the society. It supported laissez faire at home as a means of reducing the role of the state in economic affairs and thereby enlarging the role of the individual; it supported free trade abroad as a means of linking the nations of the world together peacefully and democratically. In political matters, it supported the development of representative government and of parliamentary institutions, reduction in the arbitrary power of the state, and protection of the civil freedoms of individuals.

Beginning in the late nineteenth century, and especially after 1930 in the United States, the term liberalism came to be associated with a very different emphasis, particularly in economic policy. It came to be associated with a readiness to rely primarily on the state rather than on private voluntary arrangements to achieve objectives regarded as desirable. The catchwords became welfare and equality rather than freedom. The nineteenth-century liberal regarded an extension of freedom as the most effective way to promote welfare and equality; the twentieth-century liberal regards welfare and equality as either prerequisites of or alternatives to freedom. In the name of welfare and equality, the twentieth-century liberal has come to favor

---

1. Joseph Schumpeter, *History of Economic Analysis* (New York: Oxford University Press, 1954) p. 394.

a revival of the very policies of state intervention and paternalism against which classical liberalism fought. In the very act of turning the clock back to seventeenth-century mercantilism, he is fond of castigating true liberals as reactionary!

The change in the meaning attached to the term liberalism is more striking in economic matters than in political. The twentieth-century liberal, like the nineteenth-century liberal, favors parliamentary institutions, representative government, civil rights, and so on. Yet even in political matters, there is a notable difference. Jealous of liberty, and hence fearful of centralized power, whether in governmental or private hands, the nineteenth-century liberal favored political decentralization. Committed to action and confident of the beneficence of power so long as it is in the hands of a government ostensibly controlled by the electorate, the twentieth-century liberal favors centralized government. He will resolve any doubt about where power should be located in favor of the state instead of the city, of the federal government instead of the state, and of a world organization instead of a national government.

Because of the corruption of the term liberalism, the views that formerly went under that name are now often labeled conservatism. But this is not a satisfactory alternative. The nineteenth-century liberal was a radical, both in the etymological sense of going to the root of the matter, and in the political sense of favoring major changes in social institutions. So too must be his modern heir. We do not wish to conserve the state interventions that have interfered so greatly with our freedom, though, of course, we do wish to conserve those that have promoted it. Moreover, in practice, the term conservatism has come to cover so wide a range of views, and views so incompatible with one another, that we shall no doubt see the growth of hyphenated designations, such as libertarian-conservative and aristocratic-conservative.

Partly because of my reluctance to surrender the term to proponents of measures that would destroy liberty, partly because I cannot find a better alternative, I shall resolve these difficulties by using the word liberalism in its original sense—as the doctrines pertaining to a free man.

I

The Relation Between Economic Freedom and Political Freedom

It is widely believed that politics and economics are separate and largely unconnected; that individual freedom is a political problem and material welfare an economic problem; and that any kind of political arrangements can be combined with any kind of economic arrangements. The chief contemporary manifestation of this idea is the advocacy of "democratic socialism" by many who condemn out of hand the restrictions on individual freedom imposed by "totalitarian socialism" in Russia, and who are persuaded that it is possible for a country to adopt the essential features of Russian economic arrangements and yet to ensure individual freedom through political arrangements. The thesis of this chapter is that such a view is a delusion, that there is an intimate connection between economics and politics, that only certain combinations of political and economic arrangements are possible, and that in particular, a society which is socialist cannot also be democratic, in the sense of guaranteeing individual freedom.

Economic arrangements play a dual role in the promotion of a free society. On the one hand, freedom in economic arrangements is itself a component of freedom broadly understood, so economic freedom is an end in itself. In the second place, economic freedom is also an indispensable means toward the achievement of political freedom.

The first of these roles of economic freedom needs special emphasis because intellectuals in particular have a strong bias against regarding this aspect of freedom as important. They tend to express contempt for what they regard as material aspects of life, and to regard their own pursuit of allegedly higher values as on a different plane of significance and as deserving of special attention.

For most citizens of the country, however, if not for the intellectual, the direct importance of economic freedom is at least comparable in significance to the indirect importance of economic freedom as a means to political freedom.

The citizen of Great Britain, who after World War II was not permitted to spend his vacation in the United States because of exchange control, was being deprived of an essential freedom no less than the citizen of the United States, who was denied the opportunity to spend his vacation in Russia because of his political views. The one was ostensibly an economic limitation on freedom and the other a political limitation, yet there is no essential difference between the two.

The citizen of the United States who is compelled by law to devote something like 10 percent of his income to the purchase of a particular kind of retirement contract, administered by the government, is being deprived of a corresponding part of his personal freedom. How strongly this deprivation may be felt and its closeness to the deprivation of religious freedom, which all would regard as "civil" or "political" rather than "economic," were dramatized by an episode involving a group of farmers of the Amish sect. On grounds of principle, this group regarded compulsory federal old-age programs as an infringement of their personal individual freedom and refused to pay taxes or accept benefits. As a result, some of their livestock were sold by auction in order to satisfy claims for social security levies. True, the number of citizens who regard compulsory old age insurance as a deprivation of freedom may be few, but the believer in freedom has never counted noses.

A citizen of the United States who under the laws of various states is not free to follow the occupation of his own choosing unless he can get a license for it, is likewise being deprived of an essential part of his freedom. So is the man who would like to exchange some of his goods with, say, a Swiss for a watch but is prevented from doing so by a quota. So also is the Californian who was thrown into jail for selling Alka Seltzer at a price below that set by the manufacturer under so-called "fair trade" laws. So also is the farmer who cannot grow the amount of wheat he wants. And so on. Clearly, economic freedom, in and of itself, is an extremely important part of total freedom.

Viewed as a means to the end of political freedom, economic arrangements are important because of their effect on the concentration or dispersion of power. The kind of economic organization that provides economic freedom directly, namely, competitive capitalism, also promotes political freedom because it separates economic power from political power and in this way enables the one to offset the other.

Historical evidence speaks with a single voice on the relation between political freedom and a free market. I know of no example in time or place of a society that has been marked by a large measure of political freedom, and that has not also used something comparable to a free market to organize the bulk of economic activity.

Because we live in a largely free society, we tend to forget how limited is the span of time and the part of the globe for which there has ever been anything like political freedom: the typical state of mankind is tyranny, servitude, and misery. The nineteenth century and early twentieth century in the Western world stand out as striking exceptions to the general trend of historical development. Political freedom in this instance clearly came along with the free market and the development of capitalist institutions. So also did political freedom in the golden age of Greece and in the early days of the Roman era.

History suggests only that capitalism is a necessary condition for political freedom. Clearly it is not a sufficient condition. Fascist Italy and Fascist Spain, Germany at various times in the last seventy years, Japan before World Wars I and II, tzarist Russia in the decades before World War I—are all societies that cannot conceivably be described as politically free. Yet, in each, private enterprise was the dominant form of economic organization. It is therefore clearly possible to have arrangements that are fundamentally capitalist and political arrangements that are not free.

Even in those societies, the citizenry had a good deal more freedom than citizens of a modern totalitarian state like Russia or Nazi Germany, in which economic totalitarianism is combined with political totalitarianism. Even in Russia under the Tzars, it was possible for some citizens, under some circumstances, to change their jobs without getting permission from political authority because capitalism and the existence of private property provided some check to the centralized power of the state.

The relation between political and economic freedom is complex and by no means unilateral. In the early nineteenth century, Bentham and the Philosophical Radicals were inclined to regard political freedom as a means to economic freedom. They believed that the masses were being hampered by the restrictions that were being imposed upon them, and that if political reform gave the bulk of the people the vote, they would do what was good for them, which was to vote for laissez faire. In retrospect, one cannot say that they were wrong. There was a large measure of political reform that was accompanied by economic reform in the direction of a great deal of laissez faire. An enormous increase in the well-being of the masses followed this change in economic arrangements.

The triumph of Benthamite liberalism in nineteenth-century England was followed by a reaction toward increasing intervention by government in economic affairs. This tendency to collectivism was greatly accelerated, both in England and elsewhere, by the two world wars. Welfare rather than freedom became the dominant note in democratic countries. Recognizing the implicit threat to individualism, the intellectual descendants of the Philosophical Radicals— Dicey, Mises, Hayek, and Simons, to mention only a few—feared that a continued movement toward centralized control of economic activity would prove *The Road to Serfdom*, as Hayek entitled his penetrating analysis of the process. Their emphasis was on economic freedom as a means toward political freedom.

Events since the end of World War II display still a different relation between economic and political freedom. Collectivist economic planning has indeed interfered with individual freedom. At least in some countries, however, the result has not been the suppression of freedom, but the reversal of economic policy. England again provides the most striking example. The turning point was perhaps the "control of engagements" order which, despite great misgivings, the Labour party found it necessary to impose in order to carry out its economic policy. Fully enforced and carried through, the law would have involved centralized allocation of individuals to occupations. This conflicted so sharply with personal liberty that it was enforced in a negligible number of cases, and then repealed after the law had been in effect for only a short period. Its repeal ushered in a decided shift in economic policy, marked by reduced reliance on centralized "plans" and "programs," by the dismantling of many controls, and by increased emphasis on the private market. A similar shift in policy occurred in most other democratic countries.

The proximate explanation of these shifts in policy is the limited success of central planning or its outright failure to achieve stated objectives. However, this failure is itself to be attributed, at least in some measure, to the political implications of central planning and to an unwillingness to follow out its logic when doing so requires trampling rough-shod on treasured private rights. It may well be that the shift is only a temporary interruption in the collectivist trend of this century. Even so, it illustrates the close relation between political freedom and economic arrangements.

Historical evidence by itself can never be convincing. Perhaps it was sheer coincidence that the expansion of freedom occurred at the same time as the development of capitalist and market institutions. Why should there be a connection? What are the logical links between economic and political freedom? In discussing these questions we shall consider first the market as a direct component of freedom, and then the indirect relation between market arrangements and political freedom. A by-product will be an outline of the ideal economic arrangements for a free society.

As liberals, we take freedom of the individual, or perhaps the family, as our ultimate goal in judging social arrangements. Freedom as a value in this sense has to do with the interrelations among people; it has no meaning whatsoever to a Robinson Crusoe on an isolated island (without his Man Friday). Robinson Crusoe on his island is subject to "constraint," he has limited "power," and he has only a limited number of alternatives, but there is no problem of freedom in the sense that is relevant to our discussion. Similarly, in a society freedom has nothing to say about what an individual does with his freedom; it is not an all-embracing ethic. Indeed, a major aim of the liberal is to leave the ethical problem for the individual to wrestle with. The "really" important ethical problems are those that face an individual in a free society—what he should do with his freedom. There are thus two sets of values that a liberal will emphasize—the values that are relevant to relations among people, which is the context in which he assigns first priority to freedom; and the values that are relevant to the individual in the exercise of his freedom, which is the realm of individual ethics and philosophy.

The liberal conceives of men as imperfect beings. He regards the problem of social organization to be as much a negative problem of preventing "bad" people from doing harm as of enabling "good" people to do good; and, of course, "bad" and "good" people may be the same people, depending on who is judging them.

The basic problem of social organization is how to coordinate the economic activities of large numbers of people. Even in relatively backward societies, extensive division of labor and specialization of function is required to make effective use of available resources. In advanced societies, the scale on which coordination is needed, to take full advantage of the opportunities offered by modern science and technology, is enormously greater. Literally millions of people are involved in providing one another with their daily bread, let alone with their yearly automobiles. The challenge to the believer in liberty is to reconcile this widespread interdependence with individual freedom.

Fundamentally, there are only two ways of coordinating the economic activities of millions. One is central direction involving the use of coercion—the technique of the army and of the modern totalitarian state. The other is the voluntary cooperation of individuals—the technique of the market place.

The possibility of coordination through voluntary cooperation rests on the elementary—yet frequently denied—proposition that both parties to an economic transaction benefit from it, *provided the transaction is bilaterally voluntary and informed.*

Exchange can therefore bring about coordination without coercion. A working model of a society organized through voluntary exchange is a *free private enterprise exchange economy*—what we have been calling competitive capitalism.

In its simplest form, such a society consists of a number of independent households—a collection of Robinson Crusoes, as it were. Each household uses the resources it controls to produce goods and services that it exchanges for goods and services produced by other households, on terms mutually acceptable to the two parties to the bargain. It is thereby enabled to satisfy its wants indirectly by producing goods and services for others, rather than directly by producing goods for its own immediate use. The incentive for adopting this indirect route is, of course, the increased product made possible by the division of labor and specialization of function. Since the household always has the alternative of producing directly for itself, it need not enter into any exchange unless it benefits from it. Hence, no exchange will take place unless both parties do benefit from it. Cooperation is thereby achieved without coercion.

Specialization of function and division of labor would not go far if the ultimate productive unit were the household. In a modern society, we have gone much farther. We have introduced enterprises which are intermediaries between individuals in their capacities as suppliers of service and as purchasers of goods. And similarly, specialization of function and division of labor could not go very far if we had to continue to rely on the barter of product for product. In consequence, money has been introduced as a means of facilitating exchange, and of enabling the acts of purchase and of sale to be separated into two parts.

Despite the important role of enterprises and of money in our actual economy, and despite the numerous and complex problems they raise, the central characteristic of the market technique of achieving co-ordination is fully displayed in the simple exchange economy that contains neither enterprises or money. As in that simple model, so in the complex enterprise and money exchange economy, co-operation is strictly individual and voluntary *provided*: (a) that enterprises are private, so that the ultimate contracting parties are individuals and (b) that individuals are effectively free to enter or not to enter into any particular exchange, so that every transaction is strictly voluntary.

It is far easier to state these provisos in general terms than to spell them out in detail, or to specify precisely the institutional arrangements most conducive to their maintenance. Indeed, much of technical economic literature is concerned with precisely these questions. The basic requisite is the maintenance of law and order to prevent physical coercion of one individual by another and to enforce contracts voluntarily entered into, thus giving substance to "private." Aside from this, perhaps the most difficult problems arise from monopoly—which inhibits effective freedom by denying individuals alternatives to the particular exchange—and from "neighborhood effects"—effects on third parties for which it is not feasible to charge or recompense them. These problems will be discussed in more detail in the following chapter.

So long as effective freedom of exchange is maintained, the central feature of the market organization of economic activity is that it prevents one person from interfering with another in respect of most of his activities. The consumer is protected from coercion by the seller because of the presence of other sellers with whom he can deal. The seller is protected from coercion by the consumer because of other consumers to whom he can sell. The employee is protected from coercion by the employer because of other employers for whom he can work, and so on. And the market does this impersonally and without centralized authority.

Indeed, a major source of objection to a free economy is precisely that it does this task so well. It gives people what they want instead of what a particular group thinks they ought to want. Underlying most arguments against the free market is a lack of belief in freedom itself.

The existence of a free market does not of course eliminate the need for government. On the contrary, government is essential both as a forum for determining the "rules of the game" and as an umpire to interpret and enforce the rules decided on. What the market does is to reduce greatly the range of issues that must be decided through political means, and thereby to minimize the extent to which government need participate directly in the game. The characteristic feature of action through political channels is that it tends to require or enforce substantial conformity. The great advantage of the market, on the other hand, is that it permits wide diversity. It is, in political terms, a system of proportional representation. Each man can vote, as it were, for the color of tie he wants and get it; he does not have to see the color the majority wants and then, if he is in the minority, submit.

It is this feature of the market that we refer to when we say that the market provides economic freedom. But this characteristic also has implications that go far beyond the narrowly economic. Political freedom means the absence of coercion of a man by his fellow men. The fundamental threat to freedom is power to coerce, be it in the hands of a monarch, a dictator, an oligarchy, of a momentary majority. The preservation of freedom requires the elimination of such concentration of power to the fullest possible extent and the dispersal and distribution of whatever power cannot be eliminated— a system of checks and balances. By removing the organization of economic activity from the control of political authority, the market eliminates this source of coercive power. It enables economic strength to be a check to political power rather than a reinforcement.

Economic power can be widely dispersed. There is no law of conservation which forces the growth of new centers of economic strength to be at the expense of existing centers. Political power, on the other hand, is more difficult to decentralize. There can be numerous small independent governments. But it is far more difficult to maintain numerous equipotent small centers of political power in a single large government than it is to have numerous centers of economic strength in a single large economy. There can be many millionaires in one large economy. But can there be more than one really outstanding leader, one person on whom the energies and enthusiasms of his countrymen are centered? If the central government gains power, it is likely to be at the expense of local governments. There seems to be something like a fixed total of political power to be distributed. Consequently, if economic power is joined to political power, concentration seems almost inevitable. On the other hand, if economic power is kept in separate hands from political power, it can serve as a check and a counter to political power.

The force of this abstract argument can perhaps best be demonstrated by example. Let us consider first, a hypothetical example that may help to bring out the principle involved, and then some actual examples from recent experience that illustrate the way in which the market works to preserve political freedom.

One feature of a free society is surely the freedom of individuals to advocate and propagandize openly for a radical change in the structure of society—so long as the advocacy is restricted to persuasion and does not include force or other forms of coercion. It is a mark of the political freedom of a capitalist society that men can openly advocate and work for socialism. Equally, political freedom in a socialist society would require that men be free to advocate the introduction of capitalism. How could the freedom to advocate capitalism be preserved and protected in a socialist society?

In order for men to advocate anything, they must in the first place be able to earn a living. This already raises a problem in the socialist society, since all jobs are under the direct control of political authorities. It would take an act of self-denial whose difficulty is underlined by experience in the United States after World War II with the problem of "security" among federal employees, for a socialist government to permit its employees to advocate policies directly contrary to official doctrine.

But let us suppose this act of self-denial to be achieved. For advocacy of capitalism to mean anything, the proponents must be able to finance their cause—to hold public meetings, publish pamphlets, buy radio time, issue newspapers and magazines, and so on. How could they raise the funds? There might and probably would be men in the socialist society with large incomes, perhaps even large capital sums in the form of government bonds and the like, but these would of necessity be high public officials. It is possible to conceive of a minor socialist official retaining his job although openly advocating capitalism. It strains credulity to imagine the socialist top brass financing such "subversive" activities.

The only recourse for funds would be to raise small amounts from a large number of minor officials. But this is no real answer. To tap these sources, many people would already have to be persuaded, and our whole problem is how to initiate and finance a campaign to do so. Radical movements in capitalist societies have never been financed this way. They have typically been supported by a few wealthy individuals who have become persuaded—by a Frederich Vanderbilt Field, or an Anita McCormick Blaine, or a Corliss Lamont, to mention a few names recently prominent, or by a Friederick Engels, to go farther back. This is a role of inequality of wealth in preserving political freedom that is seldom noted—the role of the patron.

In a capitalist society, it is only necessary to convince a few wealthy people to get funds to launch any idea, however strange, and there are many such persons, many independent foci of support. And, indeed, it is not even necessary to persuade people or financial institutions with available funds of the soundness of the ideas to be propagated. It is only necessary to persuade them that the propagation can be financially successful; the newspaper or magazine or book or other venture will be profitable. The competitive publisher, for example, cannot afford to publish only writing with which he personally agrees; his touchstone must be the likelihood that the market will be large enough to yield a satisfactory return on his investment.

In this way, the market breaks the vicious circle and makes it possible ultimately to finance such ventures by small amounts from many people without first persuading them. There are no such possibilities in the socialist society; there is only the all-powerful state.

Let us stretch our imagination and suppose that a socialist government is aware of this problem and is composed of people anxious to preserve freedom. Could it provide the funds? Perhaps, but it is difficult to see how. It could establish a bureau for subsidizing subversive propaganda. But how could it choose whom to support? If it gave to all who asked, it would shortly find itself all out of funds, for socialism cannot repeal the elementary economic law that a sufficiently high price will call forth a large supply. Make the advocacy of radical causes sufficiently remunerative, and the supply of advocates will be unlimited.

Moreover, freedom to advocate unpopular causes does not require that such advocacy be without cost. On the contrary, no society could be stable if advocacy of radical change were costless, much less subsidized. It is entirely appropriate that men make sacrifices to advocate causes in which they deeply believe. Indeed, it is important to preserve freedom only for people who are willing to practice self-denial, for otherwise freedom degenerates into license and irresponsibility. What is essential is that the cost of advocating unpopular causes be tolerable and not prohibitive.

But we are not yet through. In a free market society, it is enough to have the funds. The suppliers of paper are as willing to sell it to the *Daily Worker* as to the *Wall Street Journal*. In a socialist society, it would not be enough to have the funds. The hypothetical supporter of capitalism would have to persuade a government factory making paper to sell to him, the government printing press to print his pamphlets, a government post office to distribute them among the people, a government agency to rent him a hall in which to talk, and so on.

Perhaps there is some way in which one could overcome these difficulties and preserve freedom in a socialist society. One cannot say it is utterly impossible. What is clear, however, is that there are very real difficulties in establishing institutions that will effectively preserve the possibility of dissent. So far as I know, none of the people who have been in favor of socialism and also in favor of freedom have really faced up to this issue, or made even a respectable start at developing the institutional arrangements that would permit freedom under socialism. By contrast, it is clear how a free market capitalist society fosters freedom.

A striking practical example of these abstract principles is the experience of Winston Churchill. From 1933 to the outbreak of World War II, Churchill was not permitted to talk over the British radio, which was, of course, a government monopoly administered by the British Broadcasting Corporation. Here was a leading citizen of his country, a member of Parliament, a former cabinet minister, a man who was desperately trying by every device possible to persuade his countrymen to take steps to ward off the menace of Hitler's Germany. He was not permitted to talk over the radio to the British people because the BBC was a government monopoly and his position was too "controversial." Another striking example, reported in the January 26, 1959 issue of *Time*, has to do with the "Blacklist Fadeout." Says the *Time* story,

> The Oscar-awarding ritual is Hollywood's biggest pitch for dignity, but two years ago dignity suffered. When one Robert Rich was announced as top writer for *The Brave One*, he never stepped forward. Robert Rich was a pseudonym, masking one of about 150 writers ... blacklisted by the industry since 1947 as suspected Communists or fellow travelers. The case was particularly embarrassing because the Motion Picture Academy had barred any

Communist or Fifth Amendment pleader from Oscar competition. Last week both the Communist rule and the mystery of Rich's identity were suddenly rescripted.

Rich turned out to be Dalton (*Johnny Got His Gun*) Trumbo, one of the original "Hollywood Ten" writers who refused to testify at the 1947 hearings on Communism in the movie industry. Said producer Frank King, who had stoutly insisted that Robert Rich was "a young guy in Spain with a beard": "We have an obligation to our stockholders to buy the best script we can. Trumbo brought us *The Brave One* and we bought it"...

In effect it was the formal end of the Hollywood black list. For barred writers, the informal end came long ago. At least 15% of current Hollywood films are reportedly written by blacklist members. Said producer King, "There are more ghosts in Hollywood than in Forest Lawn. Every company in town has used the work of the blacklisted people. We're just the first to confirm what everybody knows."

One may believe, as I do, that communism would destroy all of our freedoms, one may be opposed to it as firmly and as strongly as possible, and yet, at the same time, also believe that in a free society it is intolerable for a man to be prevented from making voluntary arrangements with others that are mutually attractive because he believes in or is trying to promote communism. His freedom includes his freedom to promote communism. Freedom also, of course, includes the freedom of others not to deal with him under those circumstances. The Hollywood blacklist was an unfree act that destroys freedom because it was a collusive arrangement that used coercive means to prevent voluntary exchanges. It didn't work precisely because the market made it costly for people to preserve the blacklist. The commercial emphasis, the fact that people who are running enterprises have an incentive to make as much money as they can, protected the freedom of the individuals who were blacklisted by providing them with an alternative form of employment, and by giving people an incentive to employ them.

If Hollywood and the movie industry had been government enterprises or if in England it had been a question of employment by the British Broadcasting Corporation it is difficult to believe that the "Hollywood Ten" or their equivalent would have found employment. Equally, it is difficult to believe that under those circumstances, strong proponents of individualism and private enterprise—or indeed strong proponents of any view other than the status quo—would be able to get employment.

Another example of the role of the market in preserving political freedom was revealed in our experience with McCarthyism. Entirely aside from the substantive issues involved, and the merits of the charges made, what protection did individuals, and in particular government employees, have against irresponsible accusations and probing into matters that it went against their conscience to reveal? Their appeal to the Fifth Amendment would have been a hollow mockery without an alternative to government employment.

Their fundamental protection was the existence of a private-market economy in which they could earn a living. Here again, the protection was not absolute. Many potential private employers were, rightly or wrongly, averse to hiring those pilloried. It may well be that there was far less justification for the costs imposed on many of the people involved than for the costs generally imposed on people who advocate unpopular causes. But the important point is that the costs were limited and not prohibitive, as they would have been if government employment had been the only possibility.

It is of interest to note that a disproportionately large fraction of the people involved apparently went into the most competitive sectors of the economy—small business, trade, farming—where the market approaches most closely the ideal free market. No one who buys bread knows whether the wheat from which it is made was grown by a Communist or a Republican, by a constitutionalist or a Fascist, or, for that matter, by a Negro or a white. This illustrates how an impersonal market separates economic activities from political views and protects men from being discriminated against in their economic activities for reasons that are irrelevant to their productivity—whether these reasons are associated with their views or their color.

As this example suggests, the groups in our society that have the most at stake in the preservation and strengthening of competitive capitalism are those minority groups which can most easily become the object of the distrust and enmity of the majority—the Negroes, the Jews, the foreign-born, to mention only the most obvious. Yet, paradoxically enough, the enemies of the free market—the Socialists and Communists—have been recruited in disproportionate measure from these groups. Instead of recognizing that the existence of the market has protected them from the attitudes of their fellow countrymen, they mistakenly attribute the residual discrimination to the market.

II
The Role of Government in a Free Society

A common objection to totalitarian societies is that they regard the end as justifying the means. Taken literally, this objection is clearly illogical. If the end does not justify the means, what does? But this easy answer does not dispose of the objection; it simply shows that the objection is not well put. To deny that the end justifies the means is indirectly to assert that the end in question is not the ultimate end, that the ultimate end is itself the use of the proper means. Desirable or not, any end that can be attained only by the use of bad means must give way to the more basic end of the use of acceptable means.

To the liberal, the appropriate means are free discussion and voluntary cooperation, which implies that any form of coercion is inappropriate. The ideal is unanimity among responsible individuals achieved on the basis of free and full discussion. This is another way of expressing the goal of freedom emphasized in the preceding chapter.

From this standpoint, the role of the market, as already noted, is that it permits unanimity without conformity; that it is a system of effectively proportional representation. On the other hand, the characteristic feature of action through explicitly political channels is that it tends to require or to enforce substantial conformity. The typical issue must be decided "yes" or "no"; at most, provision can be made for a fairly limited number of alternatives. Even the use of proportional representation in its explicitly political form does not alter this conclusion. The number of separate groups that can in fact be represented is narrowly limited, enormously so by comparison with the proportional representation of the market. More important, the fact that the final outcome generally must be a law applicable to all groups, rather than separate legislative enactments for each "party" represented, means that proportional representation in its political version, far from permitting unanimity without conformity, tends toward ineffectiveness and fragmentation. It thereby operates to destroy any consensus on which unanimity with conformity can rest.

There are clearly some matters with respect to which effective proportional representation is impossible. I cannot get the amount of national defense I want and you, a different amount. With respect to such indivisible matters we can discuss, and argue, and vote. But having decided, we must conform. It is precisely the existence of such indivisible matters—protection of the individual and the nation from coercion are clearly the most basic—that prevents exclusive reliance on individual action through the market. If we are to use some of our resources for such indivisible items, we must employ political channels to reconcile differences.

The use of political channels, while inevitable, tends to strain the social cohesion essential for a stable society. The strain is least if agreement for joint action need be reached on a limited range of issues on which people in any event have common views. Every extension of the range of issues for which explicit agreement is sought strains further the delicate threads that hold society together. If it goes so far as to touch an issue on which men feel deeply yet differently, it may well disrupt the society. Fundamental differences in basic values can seldom if ever be resolved at the ballot box; ultimately they can only be decided, though not resolved, by conflict. The religious and civil wars of history are a bloody testament to this judgment.

The widespread use of the market reduces the strain on the social fabric by rendering conformity unnecessary with respect to any activities it encompasses. The wider the range of activities covered by the market, the fewer are the issues on which explicitly political decisions are required and hence on which it is necessary to achieve agreement. In turn, the fewer the issues on which agreement is necessary, the greater is the likelihood of getting agreement while maintaining a free society.

Unanimity is, of course, an ideal. In practice, we can afford neither the time nor the effort that would be required to achieve complete unanimity on every issue. We must perforce accept something less. We are thus led to accept majority rule in one form or another as an expedient. That majority rule is an expedient rather than itself a basic principle is clearly shown by the fact that our willingness to resort to majority rule, and the size of the majority we require, themselves depend on the seriousness of the issue involved. If the matter is of little moment and the minority has no strong feelings about being overruled, a bare plurality will suffice. On the other hand, if the minority feels strongly about the issue involved, even a bare majority will not do. Few of us would be willing to have issues of free speech, for example, decided by a bare majority. Our legal structure is full of such distinctions among kinds of issues that require different kinds of majorities. At the extreme are those issues embodied in the Constitution. These are the principles that are so important that we are willing to make minimal concessions to expediency. Something like essential consensus was achieved initially in accepting them, and we require something like essential consensus for a change in them.

The self-denying ordinance to refrain from majority rule on certain kinds of issues that is embodied in our Constitution and in similar written or unwritten constitutions elsewhere, and the specific provisions in these constitutions or their equivalents prohibiting coercion of individuals, are themselves to be regarded as reached by free discussion and as reflecting essential unanimity about means.

I turn now to consider more specifically, though still in very broad terms, what the areas are that cannot be handled through the market at all, or can be handled only at so great a cost that the use of political channels may be preferable.

Government as Rule-Maker and Umpire

It is important to distinguish the day-to-day activities of people from the general customary and legal framework within which these take place. The day-to-day activities are like the actions of the participants in a game when they are playing it; the framework, like the rules of the game they play. And just as a good game requires acceptance by the players both of the rules and of the umpire to interpret and enforce them, so a good society requires that its members agree on the general conditions that will govern relations among them, on some means of arbitrating different interpretations of these conditions, and on some device for enforcing compliance with the generally accepted rules. As in games, so also in society, most of the general conditions are the unintended outcome of custom, accepted unthinkingly. At most, we consider explicitly only minor modifications in them, though the cumulative effect of a series of minor modifications may be a drastic alteration in the character of the game or of the society. In both games and society also, no set of rules can prevail unless most participants most of the time conform to them without external sanctions; unless that is, there is a broad underlying social consensus. But we cannot rely on custom or on this consensus alone to interpret and to enforce the rules; we need an umpire. These then are the basic roles of government in a free society: to provide a means whereby we can modify the rules, to mediate differences among us on the meaning of the rules, and to enforce compliance with the rules on the part of those few who would otherwise not play the game.

The need for government in these respects arises because absolute freedom is impossible. However attractive anarchy may be as a philosophy, it is not feasible in a world of imperfect men. Men's freedoms can conflict, and when they do, one man's freedom must be limited to preserve another's—as a Supreme Court Justice once put it, "My freedom to move my fist must be limited by the proximity of your chin."

The major problem in deciding the appropriate activities of government is how to resolve such conflicts among the freedoms of different individuals. In some cases, the answer is easy. There is little difficulty in attaining near unanimity to the proposition that one man's freedom to murder his neighbor must be sacrificed to preserve the freedom of the other man to live. In other cases, the answer is difficult. In the economic area, a major problem arises in respect of the conflict between freedom to combine and freedom to compete. What meaning is to be attributed to "free" as modifying "enterprise"? In the United States, "free" has been understood to mean that anyone is free to set up an enterprise, which means that existing enterprises are not free to keep out competitors except by selling a better product at the same price or the same product at a lower price. In the continental tradition, on the other hand, the meaning has generally been that enterprises are free to do what they want, including the fixing of prices, division of markets, and the adoption of other techniques to keep out potential competitors. Perhaps the most difficult specific problem in this area arises with respect to combinations among laborers, where the problem of freedom to combine and freedom to compete is particularly acute.

A still more basic economic area in which the answer is both difficult and important is the definition of property rights. The notion of property, as it has developed over centuries and as it is embodied in our legal codes, has become so much a part of us that we tend to take it for granted, and fail to recognize the extent to which just what constitutes property and what rights the owner-ship of property confers are complex social creations rather than self-evident propositions. Does my having title to land, for exam-ple, and my freedom to use my property as I wish, permit me to deny to someone else the right to fly over my land in his airplane? Or does his right to use his airplane take precedence? Or does this depend on how high he flies? Or how much noise he makes? Does voluntary exchange require that he pay me for the privilege of flying over my land? Or that I must pay him to refrain from flying over it? The mere mention of royalties, copyrights, patents; shares of stock in corporations; riparian rights, and the like, may perhaps emphasize the role of generally accepted social rules in the very definition of property. It may suggest also that, in many cases, the existence of a well specified and generally accepted definition of property is far more important than just what the definition is.

Another economic area that raises particularly difficult prob-lems is the monetary system. Government responsibility for the monetary system has long been recognized. It is explicitly provided for in the constitutional provision which gives Congress the power "to coin money, regulate the value thereof, and of foreign coin." There is probably no other area of economic activity with respect to which government action has been so uniformly accepted. This habitual and by now almost unthinking acceptance of governmental responsibility makes thorough understanding of the grounds for such responsibility all the more necessary, since it enhances the danger that the scope of government will spread from activities that are, to those that are not, appropriate in a free society, from providing a monetary framework to determining the allocation of resources among individuals.

In summary, the organization of economic activity through voluntary exchange presumes that we have provided, through government, for the maintenance of law and order to prevent coercion of one individual by another, the enforcement of contracts voluntarily entered into, the definition of the meaning of property rights, the interpretation and enforcement of such rights, and the provision of a monetary framework.

Action through Government on Grounds of Technical Monopoly and Neighborhood Effects

The role of government just considered is to do something that the market cannot do for itself, namely, to determine, arbitrate, and enforce the rules of the game. We may also want to do through government some things that might conceivably be done through the market but that technical or similar conditions render it difficult to do in that way. These all reduce to cases in which strictly voluntary exchange is either exceedingly costly or practically impossible. There are two general classes of such cases: monopoly and similar market imperfections, and neighborhood effects.

Exchange is truly voluntary only when nearly equivalent alternatives exist. Monopoly implies the absence of alternatives and thereby inhibits effective freedom of exchange. In practice, monopoly frequently, if not generally, arises from government supports or from collusive agreements among individuals. With respect to these, the problem is either to avoid governmental fostering of monopoly or to stimulate the effective enforcement of rules such as those embodied in our anti-trust laws. However, monopoly may also arise because it is technically efficient to have a single producer or enterprise. I venture to suggest that such cases are more limited than is supposed but they unquestionably do arise. A simple example is perhaps the provision of telephone services within a community. I shall refer to such cases as "technical" monopoly.

When technical conditions make a monopoly the natural outcome of competitive market forces, there are only three alternatives that seem available: private monopoly, public monopoly, or public regulation. All three are bad so we must choose among evils. Henry Simons, observing public regulation of monopoly in the United States, found the results so distasteful that he concluded public monopoly would be a lesser evil. Walter Eucken, a noted German liberal, observing a public monopoly in German railroads, found the results so distasteful that he concluded public regulation would be a lesser evil. Having learned from both, I reluctantly conclude that, if tolerable, private monopoly may be the least of all evils.

If society were static so that the conditions which give rise to a technical monopoly were sure to remain, I would have little confidence in this solution. In a rapidly changing society, however, the conditions making for technical monopoly frequently change and I suspect that both public regulation and public monopoly are likely to be less responsive to such changes in conditions, to be less readily capable of elimination, than private monopoly.

Railroads in the United States are an excellent example. A large degree of monopoly in railroads was perhaps inevitable on technical grounds in the nineteenth century. This was the justification for the Interstate Commerce Commission. But conditions have changed. The emergence of road and air transport has reduced the monopoly element in railroads to negligible proportions. Yet we have not eliminated the ICC. On the contrary, the ICC, which started out as an agency to protect the public from exploitation by the railroads, has become an agency to protect railroads from competition by trucks and other means of transport, and more recently even to protect existing truck companies from competition by new entrants. Similarly, in England, when the railroads were nationalized, trucking was at first brought into the state monopoly. If railroads had never been subjected to regulation in the United States, it is nearly certain that by now transportation, including railroads, would be a highly competitive industry with little or no remaining monopoly elements.

The choice between the evils of private monopoly, public monopoly, and public regulation cannot, however, be made once and for all, independently of the factual circumstances. If the technical monopoly is of a service or commodity that is regarded as essential and if its monopoly power is sizable, even the short-run effects of private unregulated monopoly may not be tolerable, and either public regulation or ownership may be a lesser evil.

Technical monopoly may on occasion justify a *de facto* public monopoly. It cannot by itself justify a public monopoly achieved by making it illegal for anyone else to compete. For example, there is no way to justify our present public monopoly of the post office. It may be argued that the carrying of mail is a technical monopoly and that a government monopoly is the least of evils. Along these lines, one could perhaps justify a government post office but not the present law, which makes it illegal for anybody else to carry mail. If the delivery of mail is a technical monopoly, no one will be able to succeed in competition with the government. If it is not, there is no reason why the government should be engaged in it. The only way to find out is to leave other people free to enter.

The historical reason why we have a post office monopoly is because the Pony Express did such a good job of carrying the mail across the continent that, when the government introduced transcontinental service, it couldn't compete effectively and lost money. The result was a law making it illegal for anybody else to carry the mail. That is why the Adams Express Company is an investment trust today instead of an operating company. I conjecture that if entry into the mail-carrying business were open to all, there would be a large number of firms entering it and this archaic industry would become revolutionized in short order.

A second general class of cases in which strictly voluntary exchange is impossible arises when actions of individuals have effects on other individuals for which it is not feasible to charge or recompense them. This is the problem of "neighborhood effects." An obvious example is the pollution of a stream. The man who pollutes a stream is in effect forcing others to exchange good water for bad. These others might be willing to make the exchange at a price. But it is not feasible for them, acting individually, to avoid the exchange or to enforce appropriate compensation.

A less obvious example is the provision of highways. In this case, it is technically possible to identify and hence charge individuals for their use of the roads and so to have private operation. However, for general access roads, involving many points of entry and exit, the costs of collection would be extremely high if a charge were to be made for the specific services received by each individual, because of the necessity of establishing toll booths or the equivalent at all entrances. The gasoline tax is a much cheaper method of charging individuals roughly in proportion to their use of the roads. This method, however, is one in which the particular payment cannot be identified closely with the particular use. Hence, it is hardly feasible to have private enterprise provide the service and collect the charge without establishing extensive private monopoly.

These considerations do not apply to long-distance turnpikes with a high density of traffic and limited access. For these, the costs of collection are small and in many cases are now being paid, and there are often numerous alternatives, so that there is no serious monopoly problem. Hence, there is every reason why these should be privately owned and operated. If so owned and operated, the enterprise running the highway should receive the gasoline taxes paid on account of travel on it.

Parks are an interesting example because they illustrate the difference between cases that can and cases that cannot be justified by neighborhood effects, and because almost everyone at first sight regards the conduct of national parks as obviously a valid function of government. In fact, however, neighborhood effects may justify a city park; they do not justify a national park, like Yellowstone National Park or the Grand Canyon. What is the fundamental difference between the two? For the city park, it is extremely difficult to identify the people who benefit from it and to charge them for the benefits which they receive. If there is a park in the middle of the city, the houses on all sides get the benefit of the open space, and people who walk through it or by it also benefit. To maintain toll collectors at the gates or to impose annual charges per window overlooking the park would be very expensive and difficult. The entrances to a national park like Yellowstone, on the other hand, are few; most of the people who come stay for a considerable period of time and it is perfectly feasible to set up toll gates and collect admission charges. This is indeed now done, though the charges do not cover the whole costs. If the public wants this kind of an activity enough to pay for it, private enterprises will have every incentive to provide such parks. And, of course, there are many private enterprises of this nature now in existence. I cannot myself conjure up any neighborhood effects or important monopoly effects that would justify governmental activity in this area.

Considerations like those I have treated under the heading of neighborhood effects have been used to rationalize almost every conceivable intervention. In many instances, however, this rationalization is special pleading rather than a legitimate application of the concept of neighborhood effects. Neighborhood effects cut both ways. They can be a reason for limiting the activities of government as well as for expanding them. Neighborhood effects impede voluntary exchange because it is difficult to identify the effects on third parties and to measure their magnitude; but this difficulty is present in governmental activity as well. It is hard to know when neighborhood effects are sufficiently large to justify particular costs in overcoming them and even harder to distribute the costs in an appropriate fashion. Consequently, when government engages in activities to overcome neighborhood effects, it will in part introduce an additional set of neighborhood effects by failing to charge or to compensate individuals properly. Whether the original or the new neighborhood effects are the more serious can only be judged by the facts of the individual case, and even then, only very approximately. Furthermore, the use of government to overcome neighborhood effects itself has an extremely important neighborhood effect which is unrelated to the particular occasion for government action. Every act of government intervention limits the area of individual freedom directly and threatens the preservation of freedom indirectly for reasons elaborated in the first chapter.

Our principles offer no hard and fast line how far it is appropriate to use government to accomplish jointly what is difficult or impossible for us to accomplish separately through strictly voluntary exchange. In any particular case of proposed intervention, we must make up a balance sheet, listing separately the advantages and disadvantages. Our principles tell us what items to put on the one side and what items on the other and they give us some basis for attaching importance to the different items. In particular, we shall always want to enter on the liability side of any proposed government intervention, its neighborhood effect in threatening freedom, and give this effect considerable weight. Just how much weight to give to it, as to other items, depends upon the circumstances. If, for example, existing government intervention is minor, we shall attach a smaller weight to the negative effects of additional government intervention. This is an important reason why many earlier liberals, like Henry Simons, writing at a time when government was small by today's standards, were willing to have government undertake activities that today's liberals would not accept now that government has become so overgrown.

Action Through Government on Paternalistic Grounds

Freedom is a tenable objective only for responsible individuals. We do not believe in freedom for madmen or children. The necessity of drawing a line between responsible individuals and others is inescapable, yet it means that there is an essential ambiguity in our ultimate objective of freedom. Paternalism is inescapable for those whom we designate as not responsible.

The clearest case, perhaps, is that of madmen. We are willing neither to permit them freedom nor to shoot them. It would be nice if we could rely on voluntary activities of individuals to house and care for the madmen. But I think we cannot rule out the possibility that such charitable activities will be inadequate, if only because of the neighborhood effect involved in the fact that I benefit if another man contributes to the care of the insane. For this reason, we may be willing to arrange for their care through government.

Children offer a more difficult case. The ultimate operative unit in our society is the family, not the individual. Yet the acceptance of the family as the unit rests in considerable part on expediency rather than principle. We believe that parents are generally best able to protect their children and to provide for their development into responsible individuals for whom freedom is appropriate. But we do not believe in the freedom of parents to do what they will with other people. The children are responsible individuals in embryo, and a believer in freedom believes in protecting their ultimate rights.

To put this in a different and what may seem a more callous way, children are at one and the same time consumer goods and potentially responsible members of society. The freedom of individuals to use their economic resources as they want includes the freedom to use them to have children—to buy, as it were, the services of children as a particular form of consumption. But once this choice is exercised, the children have a value in and of themselves and have a freedom of their own that is not simply an extension of the freedom of the parents.

The paternalistic ground for governmental activity is in many ways the most troublesome to a liberal; for it involves the acceptance of a principle—that some shall decide for others—which he finds objectionable in most applications and which he rightly regards as a hallmark of his chief intellectual opponents, the proponents of collectivism in one or another of its guises, whether it be communism, socialism, or a welfare state. Yet there is no use pretending that problems are simpler than in fact they are. There is no avoiding the need for some measure of paternalism. As Dicey wrote in 1914 about an act for the protection of mental defectives, "The Mental Deficiency Act is the first step along a path on which no sane man can decline to enter, but which if too far pursued, will bring statesmen across difficulties hard to meet without considerable interference with individual liberty." There is no formula that can tell us where to stop. We must rely on our fallible judgement and, having reached a judgement, on our ability to persuade our fellow men that it is a correct judgment, or their ability to persuade us to modify our views. We must put our faith, here as elsewhere, in a consensus reached by imperfect and biased men through free discussion and trial and error.

Conclusion

A government which maintained law and order, defined property rights, served as a means whereby we could modify property rights and other rules of the economic game, adjudicated disputes about the interpretation of the rules, enforced contracts, promoted competition, provided a monetary framework, engaged in activities to counter technical monopolies and to overcome neighborhood effects widely regarded as sufficiently important to justify government intervention, and which supplemented private charity and the private family in protecting the irresponsible, whether madman or child—such government would clearly have important functions to perform. The consistent liberal is not an anarchist.

Yet it is also true that such a government would have clearly limited functions and would refrain from a host of activities that are now undertaken by federal and state governments in the United States, and their counterparts in other Western countries. Succeeding chapters will deal in some detail with some of these activities, and a few have been discussed above, but it may help to give a sense of proportion about the role that a liberal would assign government simply to list in closing this chapter, some activities currently undertaken by government in the U.S., that cannot, so far as I can see, validly be justified in terms of the principles outlined above:

1. Parity price support programs for agriculture.
2. Tariffs on imports or restrictions on exports, such as current oil import quotas, sugar quotas, etc.
3. Governmental control of output, such as through the farm program, or through prorationing of oil as is done by the Texas Railroad Commission.
4. Rent control, such as is still practiced in New York, or more general price and wage controls such as were imposed during and just after World War II.
5. Legal minimum wage rates, or legal maximum prices, such as the legal maximum of zero on the rate of interest that can be paid on demand deposits by commercial banks, or the legally fixed maximum rates that can be paid on savings and time deposits.
6. Detailed regulation of industries, such as the regulation of transportation by the Interstate Commerce Commission. This had some justification on technical monopoly grounds when initially introduced for railroads; it has none now for any means of transport. Another example is detailed regulation of banking.
7. A similar example, but one which deserves special mention because of its implicit censorship and violation of free speech, is the control of radio and television by the Federal Communications Commission.
8. Present social security programs, especially the old-age and retirement programs compelling people in effect (a) to spend a specified fraction of their income on the purchase of retirement annuity, (b) to buy the annuity from a publicly operated enterprise.
9. Licensure provisions in various cities and states which restrict particular enterprises or occupations or professions to people who have a license, where the license is more than a receipt for a tax which anyone who wishes to enter the activity may pay.
10. So-called "public-housing" and the host of other subsidy programs directed at fostering residential construction such as FHA

and VA guarantee of mortgage, and the like.

11. Conscription to man the military services in peacetime. The appropriate free market arrangement is volunteer military forces; which is to say, hiring men to serve. There is no justification for not paying whatever price is necessary to attract the required number of men. Present arrangements are inequitable and arbitrary, seriously interfere with the freedom of young men to shape their lives, and probably are even more costly than the market alternative. (Universal military training to provide a reserve for war time is a different problem and may be justified on liberal grounds.)

12. National parks, as noted above.

13. The legal prohibition on the carrying of mail for profit.

14. Publicly owned and operated toll roads, as noted above.

This list is far from comprehensive.

The Heritage Foundation Collection, 1990

CHAPTER 5

Frank S. Meyer

Commentary by Edwin J. Feulner Jr. (1991)

There is nothing wrong with conformity to true values and nothing right about conformity to false ones.

— Frank S. Meyer

Although Frank Meyer probably never stepped in a boxing ring, he was by nature a fighter. An acute thinker, persuasive lecturer, gifted writer, and master debater, he was a man of the right who specialized in intellectual combat.

Sharp-eyed, quick-tongued, and clear-headed, he combined the mental speed and agility of the bantamweight with the endurance and consistency of the welterweight. But he also had the dogged courage of the heavyweight boxer and his willingness to challenge all comers. He was above all a man of principle and as such he fought gladly for what he believed in—if necessary against overwhelming opposition. During his years as a Communist, he had learned the secret of brave men—that it is not the odds but the fighter's will that makes the difference. And in Frank

Meyer, opponents met a man whose will had been tempered to steel.

Barry Goldwater's observation that "Extremism in the defense of liberty is no vice and … moderation in the pursuit of justice is no virtue" could well have been Frank Meyer's theme song. "Don't Worry; Be Happy" certainly would not have figured in his political hymnal. Frank did worry—he worried about the decadence of modern civilization and the corrosive influence of socialism and the corrupting effect of welfare and the deficiencies of contemporary education. He worried about misspelled words and slovenly writing, about "Skinnerite behavioralism" and "sodden Freudianisms," about "empty Sartrean existentialism" and the "rock-pot-sex morass of the 'youth culture.'" But most of all, he worried about communism. He worried that Western leaders failed to understand the full horror of Marxist-Leninism and that when they understood it, they often lacked the courage and the will to fight it.

His own understanding that communism was inimical to man and to all that he holds dear was hard won. Frank knew that this ideology had the power to seduce fine minds and idealistic spirits because he had fallen under its sway himself—escaping only with great difficulty after fourteen years as a Communist. From his time as an operative and a teacher in the Party, Meyer learned first-hand that communism was a godless religion bent on the destruction of man and on the idolatrous enthronement of the totalitarian state. Moreover, he saw clearly that the only principled response to this soul-killing ideology was to fight it everywhere relentlessly until the battle was won. "There can be no question," he wrote, "of our own moral obligation to resist, to counterattack, to destroy, this powerful and proclaimed enemy of man and God." To the objection that such resistance might cost lives, he replied, "the preservation of human life … is an end far lower than the defense of freedom and right and truth."

As a moralist and a teacher, as much as a debater and reviewer, Frank Meyer made a lasting contribution to conservatism—a contribution conditioned by his adoption of Marxist-Leninism, his rejection of the "total hideousness of Communism," and his fervent embrace of conservatism. The life of this man of principle began on May 9, 1909, in Newark, New Jersey. Born to Jack Meyer and his wife Helene Straus, both of German-Jewish extraction, Frank, an only child, was unusually precocious. After attending Newark Academy, he enrolled at Princeton in the fall of 1926, where he stayed only two years, before heading off to Oxford University's Balliol College, from which he graduated in 1930. While there, he fell under the sway of communism, which gave him, he later recalled, "a vision of the correlation of all aspects of experience ... the certainty that an answer could be found to every meaningful question and that everything which did not fit could be dismissed as meaningless, unreal, [a feeling accompanied by] the lifting of doubt and anxiety."

Eventually rising to become a member of the "cadre," men who have been transformed "into the ideal type of Communist," Meyer held responsible posts in the Party both in Britain and in the United States. Studying first at the London School of Economics, from 1932 to 1934, and then later at the University of Chicago, from 1934 to 1938, gave him access to members of the intelligentsia and other possible recruits for the "cadre." Despite his apparent submission to the will of the Party, he nonetheless brooked its ire by enlisting in the U.S. Army during the Second World War.

Thus separated from "the all-pervasive pressure of the Communist movement," he began to recognize the true nature of Marxist-Leninism, as well as the value of what it was trying to destroy. Reading Friedrich von Hayek's *Road to Serfdom* further helped Meyer see that the collectivist state steals man's freedom and warps his soul. The final breaking point, however, came only in 1945, when Earl Browder was ousted as the head of the American Communist Party and Stalin decided to pursue international revolutionary aims abroad—even after the war had ended.

Despite Meyer's increasing awareness of communism's evil nature, he found breaking with it "mentally and spiritually agonizing." Comparing his experience to "a dark night of the soul," he described having to "fight back to the acceptance of the glorious human fate of living with mystery." After recanting, however, Frank devoted the rest of his life to spreading the alarm. He worked ceaselessly to unmask Marxist-Leninism as an intellectually spurious, politically corrupt, morally degenerate ideology and to show how liberalism often, through either willful or inadvertent misunderstanding, paved the way for its world conquest. His life and his work, the charm of his personality and his formidable erudition were all bent to the task of winning hearts and changing minds. Enlightening the ignorant, goading the weary, and inspiring the reluctant, he led the charge to the barricades.

He was a brave man—brave enough to recognize his own mistake and repent it; compassionate enough to warn others away from it; and fearless enough to try to coax those already ensnared by communism out of it. He had nothing but scorn for those who said one couldn't turn back the clock or who cited the march of progress to disguise their own pusillanimity. In one of my favorite Meyerian passages, he remarks, "'Forward-looking' has a brave fine sound. Who wants to be stigmatized as 'backward-looking,' singled out as a counsellor of retreat?" "And yet," he observes, "what virtue is there in going forward when the road has been found to lead to disaster?" "Is not true courage," Meyer asks, "the willingness to turn back, to retrace one's steps as far as need be until the point is reached where the false turning occurred? Mountain climbers, explorers, the most intrepid of men, do no less when their boldness is coupled with the wisdom that transmutes boldness into courage."

Indeed, in rejecting communism, Meyer turned back the clock in his own life and recognized that if the West were to survive, it had to defeat the perfidious doctrine that the future belonged to communism. He believed that history could be reversed and that the West would win and freedom reign triumphant, but only, as he wrote, "if we cease to cower before … our enemies and assert again, proudly and resolutely, the truths of our heritage."

When in 1955, he helped to found *National Review* as one of its senior editors, Meyer proudly and resolutely asserted these truths against the "murk of Liberal double-talk," "the philosophical miasma of the Establishment," and "the horror of Communism." In his regular column, "Principles and Heresies," he took aim at these enormities, articulating a consistent conservative position on everything from nuclear war to student riots. Writing brilliantly, with panache and substance, he and the other editors gave conservatives of my generation a voice and a direction.

Meyer not only articulated the faith and led the fight, he also organized the faithful. Writing, speaking, and instructing, he defined for a whole generation what conservatism was and built a consensus on which future conservatives could build. In addition to his columns for *National Review* and occasional pieces for *Modern Age* (for which he served as an editorial advisor), he wrote two books that advanced conservatism on separate fronts. In *The Moulding of Communists: The Training of the Communist Cadre* (1961), he described how members of the Party's elite are formed, vividly illustrating that the West could make no common cause with such men. The following year, he published *In Defense of Freedom*, in which he argued that without freedom from coercion, man can be neither good nor evil, for he lacks the power to choose virtue or vice. This slim volume, which Meyer considered his most important book, laid the groundwork for the major argument to which he devoted the last ten years of his life: that libertarians and traditionalists, often unbeknownst to them, share a common conservatism, although they emphasize different aspects of the tradition that they have both inherited.

With the publication of *What Is Conservatism?* in 1964, he further advanced this argument by bringing together for the first time in one book twelve divergent views of conservatism—ranging from those of Russell Kirk to those of F. A. Hayek. Meyer, who contributed the introduction and conclusion, as well as "Freedom, Tradition, Conservatism," used these writers' reflections to illustrate that conservatives shared a basic consensus much like that of "the men who founded the Republic and conceived the Constitution." He summarized this consensus as: belief in an objective moral order; agreement that the human person is the proper focus of political and social thought; conviction that the power of the state should be limited; support of "the spirit of the Constitution as originally conceived"; and a shared devotion to Western civilization, coupled with the will to defend it from inimical ideologies.

Finally, in 1969, three years before his death from lung cancer at sixty-two, Meyer published *The Conservative Mainstream*, a collection of columns, book reviews and essays written over a period of fifteen years, covering everything from Khrushchev's meeting with Eisenhower ("The President of the United States has grasped the hand of the jailer of all the Russians") to the student LSD craze (a result of "the jellyfish sloppiness of mind and body which characterize ... avante garde youth"). These pieces—taken together— trace the evolution not only of one conservative, but of conservatism itself from its fledgling days in the mid 1950s to its emergence as a major political force on the eve of the 1970s.

Gifted writer though he was, Frank did not promote conservatism only through the written word. He was also a tireless lecturer and an inveterate organizer. He advised the Young Americans for Freedom, helped to found New York State's Conservative Party and the American Conservative Union, served as a founder and the vice president of the Philadelphia Society and as a director of the U.S. Chess Federation, to say nothing of his membership in the American Political Science Association and the American Legion.

Perhaps he affected people most, though, in the good old-fashioned way—in person, in visits, and on the telephone (his night-time marathon calls were legendary). For a decade and a half, a host of young men found their way to Elsie and Frank Meyer's white house atop Ohayo Mountain far above the town of Woodstock, New York. Many who came there seeking wisdom will remember arriving in the late afternoon (Frank usually slept until

5:30 pm, breakfasted at dusk, and dined at nearly midnight) to find a comfortable, old house filled with books. William F. Buckley Jr. once estimated that there were twenty thousand of them—so many that C. H. Simonds, a frequent guest, once quipped that the Meyers were "insulated with the wisdom of the West." And there amidst all the wisdom lived one of the West's great defenders, ever on the lookout for encroaching barbarians.

A small man with a gray crewcut and piercing, deep-set eyes, often wearing a turtleneck, Frank Meyer was constantly in motion—pacing as he thought and talked, reciting English poetry by the yard and spouting Shakespeare—whole soliloquies at a time. Likeable, animated, outgoing, and pleasantly argumentative, he talked about everything from gardening and baseball to chess and the classics, frequently touching on such favorite topics as Abraham Lincoln's un-American characteristics or the dangers of federally mandated Zip codes. Conversations typically lasted all night, as Frank, fortified by cigarettes and scotch, willingly turned any subject into a debate—as Hugh Kenner once said, "Frank could have ideologized the Big Dipper." Even so, when his guests headed home as the morning star rose in the sky, I doubt, judging from my own experience, that they ever left anything less than exhilarated.

It was, I think, a Friday afternoon in October 1964, when Don Lipsett and I drove from Philadelphia to the Meyers' home in Woodstock (five years before it became famous for other reasons). Frank and Elsie warmly welcomed the National Field Director of the Intercollegiate Studies Institute (Lipsett) and the graduate student at the University of Pennsylvania's Wharton School.

We had a good, but simple meal and started talking after dinner. The Meyer household was a jumble of books—stacks, racks, pieces of books. Clearly, the volumes that Frank received as book review editor of *National Review* didn't end up remaindered at the Strand Book Shop in Manhattan. Instead, they careened in perilous stacks up and down the stairs at the Meyers's charming farm house.

After several hours of intense discussion, I was ready for bed, but not Frank Meyer, who was the first "night person" I had ever met. Between Frank and Don, a perennial insomniac, I was made to feel the odd man out—so, it was a case of staying up until 5:30 am, when we finally retired for the "night." I was woozy for the next week, but that weekend stands out in my memory as one of the intellectual high points of my early education in the conservative movement.

In "Freedom, Tradition, Conservatism," first published in *Modern Age* in 1960, Frank Meyer achieved an intellectual *tour de force*, which redefined the course of modern conservatism. Arguing that libertarian and traditionalist "streams of thought" could be united in "a single ... broad conservative political theory," he shows that they share a common tradition and "are arrayed against a common enemy." He emphasizes that the libertarian's stress on freedom and on the individual, as well as the traditionalist's emphasis on value, virtue, and order, both grow out of Western civilization's implicit acceptance of an objective moral order, the pre-eminence of the person and the necessity of his freedom to act as a moral agent. These two perspectives, he argues, are not only complementary and interdependent, but they also presuppose each other, for the moral order that the traditionalist values so highly would be meaningless if man were not free to embrace it, and conversely, the freedom of the individual alone would be, as Meyer comments, "a meaningless excitation," if that liberty were not ordered to a higher good.

Although libertarians and traditionalists both attacked Meyer for this "fusionist" position when the essay was first published, it has become widely accepted in the conservative movement. Today, when conservatives are sometimes tempted to go their pluralistic ways, it is salutary to be reminded of the common heritage we share and the common goals we cherish. Moreover, it is encouraging to note that virtually all the great modern conservative theorists implicitly accept the "fusionist" view that Meyer so ably articulates.

Since the death of communism, I have often thought of Frank Meyer. How he would have rejoiced to witness what we have seen—oranges for sale in Bucharest, a playwright the freely elected president in Prague, Mindszenty's body repatriated to a free Hungary, private property in what used to be East Germany, and free enterprise in Poland. But most of all he would have delighted in the changes in Russia: public prayer in Red Square, Muscovite metro stops stripped of the names of Bolshevik "heroes," the word "comrade" banished from the lips of children.

Frank would have rejoiced not only in the triumph of freedom, but also in the way that it has happened—with whole societies— one man, one heart, one spirit at a time refusing to acquiesce in iniquity, refusing to be the commissar's creature—for Frank Meyer always believed in the inviolability of man's free will, in the crucial importance of each individual, and in the unlimited potentiality of each person to do good.

The events of our times confirm the message that Frank Meyer never tired of telling: that a small band of men armed with truth, virtue, and courage can defeat a corrupt, idolatrous empire and give birth to a civilization. As Stephen Tonsor has said, when the history of conservatism is written, Frank Meyer will deserve "a most important place in it"—a place ensured by his "cool mind" and "impassioned heart"—the stuff of which great men are made.

Frank S. Meyer

Freedom, Tradition, Conservatism

The intellectual bankruptcy of the collectivist Liberalism which has dominated American thought for the past half century becomes every day more obvious.

The imagination, the verve, the spiritual passion that once characterized it in its days of movement towards power have long since been replaced by a tired repetition of slogans empty of content and sustained only by the weight and inertia of bureaucratic power.

Power, Liberalism still has beyond doubt; but power has only the next to the last word in the affairs of men—not the last word. Power is wielded by men, controlled by men, divided by men, limited by men, as they are guided and inspired by their intellectual and spiritual understanding. There may be a gap of years, of decades, between the onset of the impotence of a false world view, and the decay and defeat of the power structure which has arisen upon the foundations of that world view. But its defeat is, given time, the necessary result of the re-emergence of truth in the consciousness of those who are concerned with matters of the intellect, with matters of the spirit, of those who—though they may have little control over material power at the moment—determine the foundations of the future.

The last half dozen years have seen an intellectual revolt, unparalleled in a century, against the concepts upon which Liberal

From Frank S. Meyer, *What Is Conservatism?* (1964).

collectivism is based. It is ironic, although not historically unprecedented, that such a burst of creative energy on the intellectual level
should occur simultaneously with a continuing spread of the
influence of Liberalism in the practical political sphere, to the point
where it has now captured the decisive positions of power in the
Republican as well as in the Democratic party. But ironic or not, it
is the case. For the first time in modern America a whole school of
thought has consciously challenged the very foundations of collectivist Liberalism; two intellectually serious journals, *Modern Age*
and *National Review,* have established themselves integrally in the
life of the nation; and an increasing number of the newer generation of undergraduates, graduate students, and young instructors
in the universities openly range themselves against the prevailing
Liberal orthodoxy. Most important, perhaps, an intense and
far-reaching discussion has been taking place among the enemies
of Liberalism on the meaning and matter of their position in the
circumstances of mid-twentieth-century America.

It is to this discussion that I want to address myself, with the
hope of helping to clarify some of the issues which divide coun-
sels and hinder the growth of intellectual understanding among
the opponents of collectivism. Semantic difficulties are added to
substantive difficulties in any such discussion, and I ask the indul-
gence of my readers in accepting the word "conservative" as an
over-all term to include the two streams of thought that in practice
unite to oppose the reigning ideology of collectivist Liberalism.
I believe that those two streams of thought, although they are
sometimes presented as mutually incompatible, can in reality be
united within a single broad conservative political theory, since
they have their roots in a common tradition and are arrayed
against a common enemy. Their opposition, which takes many
forms, is essentially a division between those who abstract from
the corpus of Western belief its stress upon freedom and upon the
innate importance of the individual person (what we may call the
"libertarian" position) and those who, drawing upon the same

source, stress value and virtue and order (what we may call the "traditionalist" position).

But the source from which both draw, the continuing consciousness of Western civilization, has been specifically distinguished by its ability to hold these apparently opposed ends in balance and tension, and in fact the two positions which confront each other today in American conservative discourse both implicitly accept, to a large degree, the ends of the other. Without the implicit acceptance of an absolute ground of value, the pre-eminence of the person as criterion of political and social thought and action has no philosophical foundation, and freedom would be only a meaningless excitation and could never become the serious goal of a serious politics. On the other hand, the belief in virtue as the end of men's being implicitly recognizes the necessity of freedom to choose that end; otherwise, virtue could be no more than a conditioned tropism. And the raising of order to the rank of an end overshadowing and subordinating the individual person would make of order not what the traditionalist conservative means by it, but the rule of totalitarian authority, inhuman and subhuman.

On neither side is there a purposeful, philosophically founded rejection of the ends the other side proclaims. Rather, each side emphasizes so strongly the aspect of the great tradition of the West which it sees as decisive that distortion sets in. The place of its goals in the total tradition of the West is lost sight of, and the complementary interdependence of freedom and virtue, of the individual person and political order, is forgotten.

Nevertheless, although these contrary emphases in conservative thought can and do pull away from each other when the proponents of either forsake one side of their common heritage of belief in virtue as man's proper end *and* his freedom under God as the condition of the achievement of that end, their opposition is not irreconcilable, precisely because they do in fact jointly possess that very heritage. Extremists on one side may be undisturbed by the danger of the recrudescence of authoritarian status society if only it would enforce the doctrines in which they believe. Extremists on the other side may care little what becomes of ultimate values if only political and economic individualism prevails. But both extremes are self-defeating: truth withers when freedom dies, however righteous the authority that kills it; and free individualism uninformed by moral value rots at its core and soon brings about conditions that pave the way for surrender to tyranny.

Such extremes, however, are not the necessary outcome of a dialectic between doctrines which emphasize opposite sides of the same truth. Indeed, a dialectic between different emphases based upon the same fundamental understanding is the mode by which finite men have achieved much of the wisdom contained in tradition. Such a dialectic is in the highest degree necessary today between the libertarians and the traditionalists among conservatives. It cannot fail to achieve results of the greatest significance, if only the protagonists, in pressing that aspect of the truth which each regards as decisive, keep constantly in their consciousness other and complementary aspects of the same truth.

The tendency to establish false antitheses obstructing fruitful confrontation arises in part from an inherent dilemma of conservatism in a revolutionary era, such as ours. There is a real contradiction between the deep piety of the conservative spirit towards tradition, prescription, the preservation of the fiber of society (what has been called "natural conservatism") and the more reasoned, consciously principled, militant conservatism which becomes necessary when the fibers of society have been rudely torn apart, when deleterious revolutionary principles ride high, and restoration, not preservation, is the order of the day. For what the conservative is committed to conserve is not simply whatever happen to be the established conditions of a few years or a few decades, but the consensus of his civilization, of his country, as that consensus over the centuries has reflected truth derived from the very constitution of being. We are today historically in a situation created by thirty years of slow and insidious revolution at home and a half century of violent open revolution abroad. To conserve the true and the good under these circumstances is to restore an understanding (and a social structure reflecting that understanding) which has been all but buried; it is not to preserve the transient customs and prescriptions of the present.

It is here that the dilemma of conservatism affects our present doctrinal discussion. The need in our circumstances for the most vigorous use of reason to combat the collectivist, scientistic, amoral wave of the present tends to induce in the libertarian an apotheosis of reason and the neglect of tradition and prescription (which he identifies with the prevailing prescriptions of the present). The traditionalist, suspecting in this libertarian tendency the same fever to impose upon men an abstract speculative ideology that has characterized the revolution of our time—as well as the French Revolution and its spiritual forebears—tends to recoil and in his turn to press a one-sided position. Too often he confounds reason and principle with "demon ideology." Rather than justly insisting upon the limits of reason—the finite bounds of the purview of any one man or any one generation, and the responsibility to employ reason in the context of continuing tradition—he seems sometimes to turn his back on reason altogether and to place the claims of custom and prescription in irreconcilable opposition to it.

Both attitudes obscure the truth; both vitiate the value of the dialectic. The history of the West has been a history of reason operating within tradition. The balance has been tenuous, the tension at times has tightened till it was spiritually almost unbearable; but out of this balance and tension the glory of the West has been created. To claim exclusive sovereignty for either component, reason or tradition, is to smirch that glory and cripple the potentialities of conservatism in its struggle against the Liberal collectivist Leviathan.

Abstract reason, functioning in a vacuum of tradition, can indeed give birth to an arid and distorting ideology. But, in a revolutionary age, the qualities of natural conservatism by themselves can lead only to the enthronement of the prevailing power of the revolution.

Natural conservatism is a legitimate human characteristic, and in settled times it is conducive to good. It represents the universal human tendency to hold by the accustomed, to maintain enlisting modes of life. In settled times it can enlist in healthy tension with the other equally natural human characteristic, the dynamic impulse to break beyond accepted limits in the deepening of truth and the heightening of value. But this is only possible before the fibers of society have been loosened, before the "cake of custom" has been broken. Then these two human tendencies can be held in just proportion, since men of all conditions believe, each at the level of his understanding, in the same transcendent Ground of truth and value. But when, through whatever cause, this unity in tension is riven, when the dynamic takes off into thin air, breaking its tension with the perpetual rhythms of life—in short, when a revolutionary force shatters the unity and balance of civilization—then conservatism must be of another sort if it is to fulfill its responsibility. It is not and cannot be limited to that uncritical acceptance, that uncomplicated reverence, which is the essence of natural conservatism. The world of idea and symbol and image has been turned topsy-turvy; the life stream of civilization has been cut off and dispersed.

This is our situation. What is required of us is a *conscious* conservatism, a clearly principled restatement in new circumstances of philosophical and political truth. This conscious conservatism cannot be a simple piety, although in a deep sense it must have piety towards the constitution of being. Nevertheless in its consciousness it necessarily reflects a reaction to the rude break the revolution has made in the continuity of human wisdom. It is called forth by a sense of the loss which that cutting off has created. It cannot now be identical with the natural conservatism towards which it yearns. The world in which it enlists is the revolutionary world. To accept that, to conserve that, would be to accept and conserve the very denial of man's long-developed understanding, the very destruction of achieved truth, which are the essence of the revolution.

Nor can the conscious conservatism required of us appeal simply and uncomplicatedly to the past. The past has had many aspects, all held in measured suspension. But the revolution has destroyed that suspension, that tradition; the delicate fabric can never be re-created in the identical form; its integral character has been destroyed. The conscious conservatism of a revolutionary or post-revolutionary era faces problems inconceivable to the natural conservatism of a pre-revolutionary time. The modes of thought of natural conservatism are not by themselves adequate to the tasks of a time like this. Today's conservatism cannot simply affirm. It must select and adjudge. It is conservative because in its selection and in its judgment it bases itself upon the accumulated wisdom of mankind over millenia, because it accepts the limits upon the irresponsible play of untrammeled reason which the unchanging values exhibited by that wisdom dictate. But it is, it has to be, not acceptance of what lies before it in the contemporary world, but challenge. In an era like ours the enlisting regime in philosophical thought, as in political and social actuality, is fundamentally wrong. To accept is to be not conservative, but acquiescent to revolution.

Situations of this nature have arisen again and again in the history of civilization; and each time the great renewers have been those who were able to recover true principle out of the wreck of their heritage. They were guided by reason—reason mediated, it is true, by prudence, but in the first instance reason. Like Socrates, Plato, Aristotle, confronting the chaos in the body politic and in the minds of men created by the overweening pride of the Athenian *demos*, we do not live in the happy age of a natural conservatism. We cannot simply revere; we cannot uncritically follow tradition, for the tradition presented to us is rapidly becoming—thanks to the prevailing intellectual climate, thanks to the schools, thanks to the outpourings of all the agencies that mold opinion and belief—the tradition of a positivism scornful of truth and virtue, the tradition of the collective, the tradition of the untrammeled state.

The conservative today, like the conscious conservative of all revolutionary eras, cannot escape the necessity and the duty to bring reason to bear upon the problems that confront him. He has to separate the true from the false, applying basic principle to the task of cutting through the tangled mass of confusion and falsehood; he has the responsibility of establishing in new circumstances forms of thought and institutional arrangements which will express the truth of the great tradition of the West. Respectful though he is of the wisdom of the past and reverent towards precedent and prescription, the tasks he faces can only be carried out with the aid of reason, the faculty which enables us to distinguish principle and thus to separate the true from the false.

The projection of a sharp antithesis between reason and tradition distorts the true harmony which enlists between them and blocks the development of conservative thought. There is no real antagonism. Conservatism to continue to develop today must embrace both: reason operating within tradition: neither ideological *hubris* abstractly creating Utopian blueprints, ignoring the accumulated wisdom of mankind, nor blind dependence upon that wisdom to answer automatically the questions posed to our generation and demanding our own expenditure of our own mind and spirit.

Closely related to the false antithesis between reason and tradition that distorts the dialogue between the libertarian emphasis and the traditionalist emphasis among conservatives is our historical inheritance of the nineteenth-century European struggle between classical liberalism and a conservatism that was too often rigidly authoritarian. Granted there is much in classical liberalism that conservatives must reject—its philosophical foundations, its tendency towards Utopian constructions, its disregard (explicitly, though by no means implicitly) of tradition; granted it is the source of much that is responsible for the plight of the twentieth century; but its championship of freedom and its development of political and economic theories directed towards the assurance of freedom have contributed to our heritage concepts which we need to conserve and develop, as

surely as we need to reject the utilitarian ethics and the secular progressivism that classical liberalism has also passed on to us.

Nineteenth-century conservatism, with all its understanding of
the pre-eminence of virtue and value, for all its piety towards the
continuing tradition of mankind, was far too cavalier to the claims
of freedom, far too ready to subordinate the individual person to
the authority of state or society.

The conservative today is the inheritor of the best in both these
tragically bifurcated branches of the Western tradition. But the division lingers on and adds to the difficulties of conservative discourse.
The traditionalist, although in practice he fights alongside the libertarian against the collectivist Leviathan state of the twentieth century, tends to reject the political and economic theories of freedom
which flow from classical liberalism in his reaction against its
unsound metaphysics. He discards the true with the false, creating
unnecessary obstacles to the mutual dialogue in which he is engaged
with his libertarian *alter ego*. The libertarian, suffering from the
mixed heritage of the nineteenth-century champions of liberty, reacts
against the traditionalist's emphasis upon precedent and continuity
out of antipathy to the authoritarianism with which that emphasis
has been associated, although in actuality he stands firmly for
continuity and tradition against the rising revolutionary wave of
collectivism and statism.

We are victims here of an inherent tragedy in the history of classical liberalism. As it developed the economic and political doctrines of limited state power, the free-market economy, and the
freedom of the individual person, it sapped, by its utilitarianism,
the foundations of belief in an organic moral order. But the only
possible basis of respect for the integrity of the individual person
and for the overriding value of his freedom is belief in an organic
moral order. Without such a belief, no doctrine of political and
economic liberty can stand.

Furthermore, when such a belief is not universally accepted, a
free society, even if it could exist, would become licentious war of

all against all. Political freedom, failing a broad acceptance of the personal obligation to duty and to charity, is never viable. Deprived of an understanding of the philosophical foundations of freedom and exposed to the ravening of conscienceless marauders, men forget that they are fully men only to the degree that they are free to choose their destiny, and they turn to whatever fallacy promises them welfare and order.

The classical liberal as philosopher dug away the foundations of the economic and political doctrines of classical liberalism. But however much he may thereby have contributed to our misfortunes, he himself continued to live on the inherited moral capital of centuries of Christendom. His philosophical doctrines attacked the foundations of conscience, but he himself was still a man of conscience. As Christopher Dawson has said: "The old liberalism, with all its shortcomings, had its roots deep in the soul of Western and Christian culture." With those roots as yet unsevered, the classical liberal was able to develop the theories of political and economic freedom which are part of the conservative heritage today.

The misunderstandings between libertarian and traditionalist are to a considerable degree the result of a failure to understand the differing levels on which classical liberal doctrines are valid and invalid. Although the classical liberal forgot—and the contemporary libertarian conservative sometimes tends to forget—that in the *moral* realm freedom is only a means whereby men can pursue their proper end, which is virtue, he did understand that in the *political* realm freedom is the primary end. If, with Acton, we "take the establishment of liberty for the realization of moral duties to be the end of civil society," the traditionalist conservative of today, living in an age when liberty is the last thought of our political mentors, has little cause to reject the contributions to the understanding of liberty of the classical liberals, however corrupted their understanding of the ends of liberty. Their error lay largely in the confusion of the temporal with the transcendent. They could not distinguish between the *authoritarianism* with which men and institutions suppress the freedom of men, and the *authority* of God and truth.

On the other hand, the same error in reverse vitiated the thought of nineteenth-century conservatives. They respected the authority of God and of truth as conveyed in tradition, but too often they imbued the authoritarianism of men and institutions with the sacred aura of divine authority. They gave way to the temptation to make of tradition, which in its rightful role serves as a guide to the operation of reason, a weapon with which to suppress reason.

It is true that from their understanding of the basis of men's moral existence, from their reverence for the continuity and precedent that ties the present to the past, contemporary conservatism has inherited elements vital to its very existence. Yet we can no more make of the great conservative minds of the nineteenth century unerring guides to be blindly followed than we can condemn out of hand their classical liberal opponents. Sound though they were on the essentials of man's being, on his destiny to virtue and his responsibility to seek it, on his duty in the moral order, they failed too often to realize that the *political* condition of moral fulfillment is freedom from coercion. Signally they failed to recognize the decisive danger in a union of political and economic power, a danger becoming daily greater before their eyes as science and technology created apace immense aggregates of economic energy. Aware, as the classical liberals were not, of the reality of original sin, they forgot that its effects are never more virulent than when men wield unlimited power. Looking to the state to promote virtue, they forgot that the power of the state rests in the hands of men as subject to the effects of original sin as those they govern. They could not, or would not, see a truth the classical liberals understood: if to the power naturally inherent in the state, to defend its citizens from violence, domestic and foreign, and to administer justice, there is added a positive power over economic and social energy, the temptation to tyranny becomes irresistible, and the political conditions of freedom wither.

The tendency of the traditionalist conservative to insist that the crystallization of a conservative outlook today requires only that we carry on the principles of those who called themselves conservatives in the nineteenth century oversimplifies and confuses the problem. That the conservative is one who preserves tradition does not mean that his task is imitation and repetition of what others have done before. Certainly in ultimate terms, upon the basic issue of human destiny, truths have been given us that we cannot improve upon, that we can only convey and make real in the context of our time. Here indeed the conservatives of the nineteenth century played a heroic part, in preserving in the teeth of the overwhelming tendency of the era the age-old image of man as a creature of transcendent destiny.

In the political and economic realm, however, these truths establish only the foundation for an understanding of the end of civil society and the function of the state. That end, to guarantee freedom, so that men may uncoercedly pursue virtue, can be achieved in different circumstances by different means. To the clarification of what these means are in specific circumstances, the conservative must apply his reason. The technological circumstances of the twentieth century demand above all the breaking up of power and the separation of centers of power within the economy itself, within the state itself, and between the state and the economy. Power of a magnitude never before dreamed of by men has been brought into being. While separation of power has always been essential to a good society, if those who possess it are to be preserved from corruption and those who do not are to be safeguarded from coercion, this has become a fateful necessity under the conditions of modern technology. To the analysis of this decisive problem and to the development of political and economic solutions of it, classical liberalism contributed mightily. If we reject that heritage, we should be casting away some of the most powerful among our weapons against socialism, Communism, and collectivist Liberalism. The traditionalist who would have us do so because of the philosophical errors of classical liberalism, like the libertarian who rejects tradition because it has sometimes been associated with authoritarianism, seriously weakens the development of conservative doctrine.

The historical fact is—and it adds to the complexity of our problems—that the great tradition of the West has come to us through the nineteenth century, split, bifurcated, so that we must draw not only upon those who called themselves conservatives in that century but also upon those who called themselves liberals. The economists of the liberal British tradition, from Adam Smith through and beyond the vilified Manchesterians, like the Austrian economists from Menger and Böhm-Bawerk to Mises and Hayek, analyzed the conditions of industrial society and established the principles upon which the colossal power that it produces can be developed for the use of man without nurturing a monstrous Leviathan. Without their mighty intellectual endeavor, we should be disarmed before the collectivist economics of Marx, Keynes, and Galbraith. And in the sphere of political theory, who has surpassed the nineteenth-century liberals in their prophetic understanding of the looming dangers of the all-powerful state? Conservatives today can reject neither side of their nineteenth-century heritage; they must draw upon both.

Differences of emphasis between libertarian and traditionalist cannot be avoided and should not be regretted. Conservatism has no monolithic party line. Our task is to overcome the nineteenth-century bifurcation of the Western tradition in fruitful dialogue, not to perpetuate it by refusing to understand the breadth and complexity of our heritage, out of a narrow historicism that unearths outworn party emblems.

I am well aware that what I have been saying can be criticized as eclecticism and attacked as an effort to smother principle. But it is not the laying aside of clear belief, either by the libertarian conservative or by the traditionalist conservative, in order to present a front against contemporary collectivist Liberalism, that is here conceived. Rather it is the deepening of the beliefs which each holds through the development of their implications in a dialectic free of distorting narrowness. That deepening—and the development of a common conservative doctrine, comprehending both emphases—cannot be achieved in a surface manner by blinking differences or blurring intellectual distinctions with grandiose phraseology. It can only be achieved by hard-fought dialectic in which both sides recognize not only that they have a common enemy, but also that, despite all differences, they hold a common heritage.

As Americans, indeed, we have a great tradition to draw upon, in which the division, the bifurcation, of European thought between the emphasis on virtue and value and order and the emphasis on freedom and the integrity of the individual person was overcome, and a harmonious unity of the tensed poles of Western thought was achieved in political theory and practice as never before or since. The men who created the Republic, who framed the Constitution and produced that monument of political wisdom, *The Federalist Papers,* comprised among them as great a conflict of emphasis as any in contemporary American conservatism. Washington, Franklin, Jefferson, Hamilton, Adams, Jay, Mason, Madison—among them there enlisted immense differences on the claims of the individual person and the claims of order, on the relation of virtue to freedom. But their dialectic was conducted within a continuing awareness of their joint heritage. Out of that dialectic they created a political theory and a political structure based upon the understanding that, while truth and virtue are metaphysical and moral ends, the freedom to seek them is the political condition of those ends—and that a social structure which keeps power divided is the indispensable means to this political end. The debate from which our American institutions arose is a fitting model for our debate.

That debate will the more rapidly and the more profoundly develop the energy and the fruitfulness and the eventual understanding that are intellectually inherent in the opposed emphases, if we constantly keep in mind the vision of life against which we are jointly engaged in fateful combat: the Liberal collectivist body of dogma that has pervaded the consciousness and shaped the actions of the decisive and articulate sections of society over the past half century or more.

In opposition to this image of man as neither free nor inspired by a transcendent destiny, the differences between libertarian and traditionalist are thrown into their true perspective: differences of emphasis, not of underlying opposition. In the light of it, libertarian and traditionalist, as they deepen their understanding in a commonly based dialogue, can maintain a common front and a common struggle. The desecration of the image of man, the attack alike upon his freedom and his transcendent dignity, provide common cause in the immediate struggle. As with our ancestors who laid the foundations of the Republic, the challenge to our common faith inspires us, without surrendering our differences of stress, to create a fundamental unity of doctrine within which libertarian and traditionalist, respecting each other, can mutually vindicate the true nature of man, free and responsible, against the arid, mechanistic, collectivist denial of man's nature which transitorily prevails.

Courtesy of Ludwig von Mises Institute

CHAPTER 6

Ludwig von Mises

Commentary by Edwin J. Feulner Jr. (1998)

First and finest critic of socialism, tireless teacher and "dean" of the Austrian school of economics, Ludwig von Mises was the symbol of another era: a time when "liberalism" meant strength and confidence in defense of liberty; a graceful age of Viennese wit, courtesy and humanity, and of coffeehouse discussions of economics running far into the night. That era was ended by despotic dreamers—Nazis and Communists—but its memories and ideals were carried to America and renewed through the tenacity of an exceptional scholar. Because of his obstinate honesty, Mises risked irrelevance in his own profession; now, he is recognized as one of the most influential economic theorists of the century. And his life stands as a reminder of days, not long ago, when faith in freedom had to be underwritten with physical and intellectual courage. He was, according to William Henry Chamberlin, "a true St. George fighting the dragon of collectivism."

In 1940, when Mises was nearly 60 years old, he and his wife Margit became exiles from the forces of tyranny he had predicted and opposed. Just ahead of Hitler's armies, they made their way across France and Spain to Lisbon, and then to the United States.

Mises's library and personal papers had been confiscated by the Nazis. He was not fluent in English. He was impoverished, with no prospect of a job. His economic masterwork, published two years before, had gone unread and unnoticed in the chaos of the times. The couple moved five times in the first year between hotels and apartments. Later Mises wrote:

> It is a matter of temperament how we shape our lives in the knowledge of an inescapable catastrophe. In high school I had chosen the verse by Virgil as my motto: *Tu ne cede malis sed contra audentior ito* ("Do not yield to the bad, but always oppose it with courage").[1] In the darkest hours of the war, I recalled this dictum. Again and again I faced situations from which rational deliberations could find no escape. But then something unexpected occurred that brought deliverance. I would not lose courage. Even now I would do everything an economist could do. I would not tire of professing what I knew to be right.

Fifty years after this low point of liberty, when collectivism was on the march throughout the world, former Soviet economist Yuri N. Maltsev would contend: "Mises was right and Lenin was wrong. That is the great lesson of the 20th century." Ronald Reagan would provide this tribute: "He rekindled the flames of liberty." Once dismissed as a relic, Mises has been revealed as a prophet. And the Austrian school of free-market economics he defended and embodied, once on the verge of extinction, has become one of the most vital traditions of American conservatism.

Long after his death, Margit was asked to describe her husband. "Foremost," she said, "he was a fighter." And the weapon he employed was logical rigor, honed to a sharp edge. His objective was to draw lines, not soften them. His teaching method represented the triumph of candor over diplomacy, of consistency over compromise.

---

1. The passage is found in Book VI of *The Aeneid.*

While some found this "stern," Professor Ralph Raico observes:

> The totality and enduring intensity of Mises's battle could only be
> fueled from a profound inner sense of the truth and supreme value
> of the ideas for which he was struggling.

But former students also recall his wit, accessibility, and courtly manners. Scholars in Mises's celebrated seminars were told,
"Don't be afraid to speak up. Remember, whatever you say about
the subject and however wrong it might be, the same thing has
already been said by some eminent economist." He was never without a jacket, even in the most oppressive heat. He seldom turned
down an invitation from any group willing to listen, arguing that
economics was the proper study of every person. Friedrich von
Hayek said of his mentor:

> I came to know him mainly as a tremendously efficient executive,
> the kind of man who, as was said of John Stuart Mill, because he
> does a normal day's work in two hours, always has a clear desk
> and time to talk about anything. I came to know him as one of the
> best educated and informed men I have ever known." And he com-
> bined all this, Hayek observes elsewhere, with an "exasperating
> tendency of proving to have been right.

Ludwig von Mises was born in the Austro-Hungarian Empire
on September 29, 1881, his father an engineer and his mother from
a prominent, politically connected family. He made his fame in
Europe, beginning in 1909 and continuing for 25 years, as an economist at the Vienna Chamber of Commerce, which gave official
advice to the government, like an American cabinet department.
Mises was known as an inflation fighter, helping to end Austria's
hyperinflation after World War I while avoiding total economic collapse (unlike in Germany). He also played a major role in preventing Austria from going Communist in 1918 and 1919, convincing

its Marxist leader, in marathon late-night discussions, to back away from the Bolshevik model. It was a task of persuasion, he later recalled, in which he had little help. "Everyone was so convinced of the inevitability of the coming of Bolshevism that they were intent merely on securing for themselves a favorable position in the new order." But his successful efforts earned Mises little credit, and Austrian Socialists exacted revenge by blocking the possibility of a paid university professorship.

Mises saw both socialism and National Socialism of the Nazi variety as "etatism," defined as "the trend toward government control of business," which he also called "the great pervasive evil of the modern world." "The main issue," he argued, "is whether or not man should give away freedom, private initiative and individual responsibility and surrender to the guardianship of a gigantic apparatus of compulsion and coercion, the socialist state." But the tide of collectivism was strong, turning whole nations into prisons.

> For sixteen years, I fought a battle in the Chamber in which I won nothing more than a mere delay of the catastrophe. I made heavy personal sacrifices though I always foresaw that success would be denied me. But I do not regret that I attempted the impossible. I could not do otherwise. I fought because I could do no other.

But perhaps Mises's greatest achievement in the period between the wars was not as an advisor to government, but as teacher and mentor to a small group of intellectuals. Mises sponsored an informal seminar, without grades or papers, that met every other Friday evening from 7 to 10, followed by dinner at an Italian restaurant and discussion over coffee at the Cafe Kunstler until the wee hours of the morning. Over time, it became one of Europe's most prestigious forums for the exchange of economic ideas, attracting thinkers such as Hayek, Eric Voegelin, Oskar Morgenstern, and Gottfried von Haberler.

We formed neither school, congregation, nor sect. We helped each other more through contradiction than agreement ... Each one worked by himself, as befits a thinker. And yet each one of us labored for the circle, seeking no compensation other than simple recognition, not the applause of his friends. There was greatness in this unpretentious exchange of ideas; in it we all found happiness and satisfaction.

Mises's seminar influenced a generation of economists and scholars.

In 1934, Mises left the world he had known and became a refugee, first in Switzerland, then in the United States, part of a great migration of European thinkers. During this period, in 1938, he proposed to Margit, a successful, beautiful actress. "If you want a rich man," he told her, "don't marry me. I am writing about money, but will never have much of my own." But the proposal was accepted. "What impressed me were his beautiful, clear blue eyes," she recalled, "always concentrated on the person to whom he talked, never shifting away." In the United States, he faced the central problem of his professional life: the refusal of academic economists—largely Keynesians who viewed him as a throwback— to offer him a paid teaching position. But he found friends and sponsors like journalist Henry Hazlitt and businessman Lawrence Fertig, who later became a stalwart supporter of The Heritage Foundation.

Finally, he was made a visiting professor at New York University, teaching one course a term, though the school's dean urged students not to take his "right-wing, reactionary classes." It was a Spartan existence. Mises and his wife were able to scrape together enough money to buy one season ticket to the opera and alternated to see the productions. But beginning in 1949, like he did in Vienna, he started teaching a seminar, which he continued for another 20 years.

Says Richard Cornuelle,

When I joined Mises's seminar, it was meeting twice a week in the late evening in a low-ceilinged cellar room, as befitted an underground movement, in the shadow of Trinity Church in lower Manhattan. We were usually about a dozen. Mises arrived last, always on the stroke of the appointed hour, impeccably dressed. He took a single page of notes in German from a small envelope, grasped the edge of the table with his palms flat on the top and his thumbs under, and spoke without interruption for an hour and a half, in a kind of accented chant as if he were reciting scripture from memory ... We sensed we were in the presence of a towering and uncommonly disciplined intelligence, martyred and misunderstood ... We would, except for the practical difficulties, have carved our notes in stone.

The same year his American seminar began, Yale University Press published Mises's *Human Action*, a nearly 1,000-page summary of his approach to economics and social science which compares, in scope and depth, with Marx's *Capital* and Keynes's *General Theory*. "*Human Action* is, in short, at once the most uncompromising and the most rigorously reasoned statement of the case for capitalism that has yet appeared," argued Hazlitt. For Murray Rothbard, it is "one of the finest products of the human mind in our century." Surprisingly, it became an alternate selection of the Book of the Month Club and eventually was published in Chinese, Italian, Spanish, French, and Japanese. Typically, *The New York Times Book Review* attacked Yale University Press for even agreeing to publish it.

In 1947, Mises helped found the Mont Pelerin Society, an international group of free market scholars and economists. He saw friends and associates, influenced by his ideas, become economic advisers to the president of Italy, to Charles de Gaulle in France and to Ludwig Erhard in Germany. And, at the end of his long life, after

25 books and over 250 scholarly articles, Mises found a measure of overdue recognition. His most prominent protégé, Friedrich von Hayek, received the Nobel Prize for economics in 1974, the year after Mises died, providing an exclamation point for the revival of Austrian economics.

"When the history of twentieth century thought is written," says George Roche of Hillsdale College, "Ludwig von Mises will in all probability be recognized as the greatest economist of our age."

Mises is celebrated as an enemy of inflationary credit, which, he argued, results in bad investments and causes the booms and busts of the business cycle. He was a strong defender of the gold standard, to "make the determination of money's purchasing power independent of the changing ambitions and doctrines of political parties and pressure groups." And he is remembered for several groundbreaking contributions to conservative, or classical liberal, thought.

First, in the 1920s, at the high point of socialism's intellectual appeal, Mises subjected it to its first, full-scale economic critique. His 1922 book *Socialism* contended that a socialist system, in the end, could not make rational economic decisions, since the only way to determine if resources in an economy are used efficiently is the calculation of profit and loss. Should more cars be produced? Should another factory be built? Without a price system, such choices are arbitrary. This, Mises says, is "the essential vice" of socialism. "In abolishing economic calculation," he predicted, "the general adoption of socialism would result in complete chaos and the disintegration of social cooperation under the division of labor." "Without economic calculation," he continues, "there can be no economy. Hence, in a socialist state wherein the pursuit of economic calculation is impossible, there can be—in our sense of the term— no economy whatsoever."

Mises, at first, was alone in this stand. But, concerning Mises's *Socialism,* Hayek recalled: "To none of us young men who read the book when it appeared was the world ever the same again." Not only he, but William Roepke in Germany and Lionel Robbins in England were profoundly influenced. And an embarrassing legacy of ruined economies around the world, of course, has justified Mises's precise and prescient warnings.

SECOND, MISES LATER EXTENDED his critique to "mixed"economies, where government intervention is substantial but something short of socialism. "In the terminology of American politics it is often referred to as the middle-of-the-road policy," says Mises. But this approach, he argues, is not sustainable in the long run, since these interventions are generally counterproductive. Rothbard summarizes his argument:

> Mises arrived at a general law that, whenever the government intervened in the economy to solve a problem, it invariably ended, not in solving the original problem, but also in creating one of two others, each of which then seemed to cry out for further government intervention.

So governments:

> face a choice: either repeal the original intervention, or go on to new ones. In this way, government intervention is an unstable system, leading logically either back to *laissez-faire* or on to full socialism.

It is an insight that explains much about the sorcerer's apprentice character of public policy, spawning an endless series of failed fixes.

Third, and perhaps most important, Mises rejected the kind of social science that reduced human beings to physical objects, summarized in statistics and studied like specimens. This type of behaviorism, he argues, seeks to investigate reflexes and instincts, automatisms and unconscious reactions. But it has told us nothing about reflexes that have built cathedrals, railroads and fortresses, the instincts that have produced philosophies, poems and legal systems, the automatisms that have resulted in the growth and decline of empires.

Mises's impatience with "quantitative economics" was based on a very practical concern—that the approach is an invitation to social engineering. The behaviorist:

> proposes to operate the 'human Ford' the way the operator drives his car. He acts as if he owned humanity and were called upon to control and to shape it according to his own design.

Mises's approach is more humanistic, in the best sense of that term. Human action, he argues, is based on individual values and ideas, reason and will, which cannot be adequately summarized or predicted by quantitative laws. "The basic notion of economics," he counters, is "the choosing and acting individual." And both economists and government must show humility before these unique choices and actions, informed by subjective values. People are agents of their destiny, not numbers on a chart, and the shape of the economy must be determined by their complex decisions—based on the mutual benefits of exchange—not by bureaucratic fiat. Mises, in short, rejects any approach to economics or social science that elevates experts by minimizing men.

Mises's influence on Hayek and Wilhelm Roepke, along with other neoclassical economists, places him at the source of a great river running through our times. Milton Friedman declared that no one has done more to promote free markets in this country than Mises. And even moral traditionalists like Russell Kirk understood the magnitude of his contribution, despite reservations about his libertarianism. As a young sergeant in the Chemical Warfare Service, Kirk read both Mises and Hayek, writing a friend that the

Vienna of Freud "also has its great school of economists of a very different and much sounder mind."

"Liberty and Property" was first delivered as a lecture at Princeton University, in October 1958, at the ninth meeting of the Mont Pelerin Society. And while mastering *Human Action* may be a challenge (though well worth the effort), this short essay shows Mises at his most lucid and persuasive, demonstrating what Hayek called his "gift" for "clear and plain language." Here Mises recognizes the profound humanistic achievements of capitalism, which is not "simply mass production, but mass production to satisfy the needs of the masses." It represents a shift in power, from landowners to consumers, who become "the real boss." This raises their standard of living, but it also gives minorities the security and confidence that makes dissent possible. Capitalism is a friend of both prosperity and pluralism. But socialism "substitutes the sovereignty of a dictator, or committee of dictators, for the sovereignty of the consumers." While government is necessary, and not itself evil, it always involves coercion. And its reach must always be tested by a commitment to individualism, "the distinctive principle of Western social philosophy."

My first encounter with the works of Ludwig von Mises occurred when I was a graduate student at the London School of Economics in the mid 1960s. Both *Socialism* and *Human Action* were my companions for many hours in the Reading Room and around the common room. The bloom of socialist planning was still in vogue, although how it could be after Mises's refutation was beyond me.

My one meeting with the Professor occurred in New York City on September 3, 1968. I was awestruck at the opportunity to ask him to inscribe my copies of his great works and then to pose one or two tentative questions. His kindly response and patient explanation belied the rigor of his laser-sharp intellect.

At a tribute to Ludwig von Mises, Fredrick von Hayek said these words:

You have shown an undaunted courage even when you stood alone. You have shown a relentless consistency and persistence in your thought even when it led to unpopularity and isolation. You have for long not found the recognition from the official organization of science which was your due ... But you have been more fortunate than most other sponsors of unpopular causes. You knew that the ideas for which you had so long fought alone or with little support would be victorious. The torch which you have lighted has become the guide for a new movement of freedom which is gathering strength every day.

And that movement, of which we are all a part, would do well to remember, especially at this time of year, Ludwig von Mises's creed: "Do not yield to the bad, but always oppose it with courage."

Ludwig von Mises

Liberty and Property

A t the end of the eighteenth century there prevailed two
notions of liberty, each of them very different from what
we have in mind today in referring to liberty and freedom.
The first of these conceptions was purely academic and without
any application to the conduct of political affairs. It was an idea
derived from the books of the ancient authors, the study of which
was then the sum and substance of higher education. In the eyes of
these Greek and Roman writers, freedom was not something that
had to be granted to all men. It was a privilege of the minority, to be
withheld from the majority. What the Greeks called democracy was,
in the light of present-day terminology, not what Lincoln called government by the people, but oligarchy, the sovereignty of full-right citizens in a community in which the masses were meteques or slaves.
Even this rather limited freedom after the fourth century before Christ
was not dealt with by the philosophers, historians, and orators as a
practical constitutional institution. As they saw it, it was a feature of
the past irretrievably lost. They bemoaned the passing of this golden
age, but they did not know any method of returning to it.

The second notion of liberty was no less oligarchic, although it
was not inspired by any literary reminiscences. It was the ambition

Originally delivered as a lecture at Princeton University, October 1958, at the ninth meeting of the Mont
Pelerin Society.

of the landed aristocracy, and sometimes also of urban patricians, to preserve their privileges against the rising power of royal absolutism. In most parts of continental Europe, the princes remained victorious in these conflicts. Only in England and in the Netherlands did the gentry and the urban patricians succeed in defeating the dynasties. But what they won was not freedom for all, but only freedom for an elite, for a minority of the people.

We must not condemn as hypocrites the men who in those ages praised liberty, while they preserved the legal disabilities of the many, even serfdom and slavery. They were faced with a problem which they did not know how to solve satisfactorily. The traditional system of production was too narrow for a continually rising population. The number of people for whom there was, in a full sense of term, no room left by the pre-capitalistic methods of agriculture and artisanship was increasing. These supernumeraries were starving paupers. They were a menace to the preservation of the existing order of society and, for a long time, nobody could think of another order, a state of affairs, that would feed all of these poor wretches. There could not be any question of granting them full civil rights, still less of giving them a share in the conduct of affairs of state. The only expedient the rulers knew was to keep them quiet by resorting to force.

II

The pre-capitalistic system of production was restrictive. Its historical basis was military conquest. The victorious kings had given the land to their paladins. These aristocrats were lords in the literal meaning of the word, as they did not depend on the patronage of consumers buying or abstaining from buying on a market. On the other hand, they themselves were the main customers of the processing industries which, under the guild system, were organized on a corporative scheme. This scheme was opposed to innovation. It forbade deviation from the traditional methods of production. The number of people for whom there were jobs even in agriculture or in the arts and crafts was limited. Under these conditions, many a man, to use the words of Malthus, had to discover that "at nature's mighty feast there is no vacant cover for him" and that "she tells him to be gone."[1] But some of these outcasts nevertheless managed to survive, begot children, and made the number of the destitute grow hopelessly more and more.

But then came capitalism. It is customary to see the radical innovations that capitalism brought about in the substitution of the mechanical factory for the more primitive and less efficient methods of the artisans' shops. This is a rather superficial view. The characteristic feature of capitalism that distinguishes it from pre-capitalistic methods of production was its new principle of marketing. Capitalism is not simply mass production, but mass production to satisfy the needs of the masses. The arts and crafts of the good old days had catered almost exclusively to the wants of the well-to-do. But the factories produced cheap goods for the many. All that the early factories turned out was designed to serve the masses, the same strata that worked in the factories. They served them either by supplying them directly or indirectly by exporting and thus providing for them foreign food and raw materials. This principle of marketing was the signature of early capitalism as it is of present-day capitalism. The employees themselves are the customers consuming the much greater part of all goods produced. They are the sovereign customers who are "always right." Their buying or abstention from buying determines what has to be produced, in what quantity, and of what quality. In buying what suits them best they make some enterprises profit and expand and make other enterprises lose money and shrink. Thereby they are continually shifting control of the factors of production into the hands of those businessmen who are the most successful in filling their wants. Under capitalism private property of the factors of production is a social function. The entrepreneurs, capitalists, and land owners are

---

1 Malthus, *An Essay on the Principle of Population*, 2nd ed., London 1803, p. 531.

mandatories, as it were, of the consumers, and their mandate is revocable. In order to be rich, it is not sufficient to have once saved and accumulated capital. It is necessary to invest it again and again in those lines in which it best fills the wants of the consumers. The market process is a daily repeated plebiscite, and it ejects inevitably from the ranks of profitable people those who do not employ their property according to the orders given by the public. Big business, the target of fanatical hatred on the part of all contemporary governments and self-styled intellectuals, acquires and preserves bigness only because it works for the masses. The plants that cater to the luxuries of the few never attain big size.

The shortcoming of nineteenth-century historians and politicians was that they failed to realize that the workers were the main consumers of the products of industry. In their view, the wage earner was a man toiling for the sole benefit of parasitic leisure class. They labored under the delusion that the factories had impaired the lot of the manual workers. If they had paid any attention to statistics they would easily have discovered the fallaciousness of their opinion. Infant mortality dropped, the average length of life was prolonged, the population multiplied, and the average common man enjoyed amenities of which even the well-to-do of earlier ages did not dream.

However this unprecedented enrichment of the masses was merely a by-product of the Industrial Revolution. Its main achievement was the transfer of economic supremacy from the owners of land to the totality of the population. The common man was no longer a drudge who had to be satisfied with the crumbs that fell from the tables of the rich. The three pariah castes which were characteristic of the pre-capitalistic ages—the slaves, the serfs, and those people whom patristic and scholastic authors as well as British legislation from the sixteenth to the nineteenth centuries referred to as the poor—disappeared. Their scions became, in this new setting of business, not only free workers, but also customers. This radical change was reflected in the emphasis laid by business on markets. What business needs first of all is markets and again markets. This was the watch-word of capitalistic enterprise. Markets, that means patron, buyers, consumers. There is under capitalism one way to wealth: to serve the consumers better and cheaper than other people do.

Within the shop and factory the owner—or in the corporations, the representative of the share-holders, the president—is the boss. But this mastership is merely apparent and conditional. It is subject to the supremacy of the consumer. The consumer is king, is the real boss, and the manufacturer is done for if he does not outstrip his competitors in best serving the consumers.

It was this great economic transformation that changed the face of the world. It very soon transferred political power from the hands of a privileged minority into the hands of the people. Adult franchise followed in the wake of industrial enfranchisement. The common man, to whom the market process had given the power to choose the entrepreneur and capitalists, acquired the analogous power in the field of government. He became a voter.

It has been observed by eminent economists, I think first by the late Frank A. Fetter, that the market is a democracy in which every penny gives a right to vote. It would more correct to say that representative government by the people is an attempt to arrange constitutional affairs according to the model of the market, but this design can never be fully achieved. In the political field it is always the will of the majority that prevails, and the minorities must yield to it. But business caters not only to the desires of the majority. It serves also minorities, provided they are not so insignificant in number as to become negligible. The garment industry produces clothes not only for normal people, but also for the stout, and the publishing trade publishes not only westerns and detective stories for the crowd, but also books for discriminating readers.

There is a second important difference. In the political sphere, there is no means for an individual or a small group of individuals to disobey the will of the majority. But in the intellectual field private property makes rebellion possible. The rebel has to pay a price for his independence; there are in this universe no prizes that can be won without sacrifices. But if a man is willing to pay the price, he is free to deviate from the ruling orthodoxy or neo-orthodoxy. What would conditions have been in the socialist commonwealth for heretics like Kierkegaard, Schopenhauer, Veblen, or Freud? For Monet, Courbet, Walt Whitman, Rilke, or Kafka? In all ages, pioneers of new ways of thinking and acting could work only because private property made contempt of the majority's ways possible. Only a few of these separatists were themselves economically independent enough to defy the government into the opinions of the majority. But they found in the climate of the free economy among the public people prepared to aid and support them. What would Marx have done without his patron, the manufacturer Friedrich Engels?

III

What vitiates entirely the socialists' economic critique of capitalism is their failure to grasp the sovereignty of the consumers in the market economy. They see only hierarchical organization of the various enterprises and plans, and are at a loss to realize that the profit system forces business to serve the consumers. In their dealings with their employers, the unions proceed as if only malice and greed were to prevent what they call management from paying higher wage rates. Their shortsightedness does not see anything beyond the doors of the factory. They and their henchmen talk about the concentration of economic power, and do not realize that economic power is ultimately vested in the hands of the buying public of which the employees themselves form the immense majority. Their inability to comprehend things as they are is reflected in such inappropriate metaphors as industrial kingdom and dukedoms. They are too dull to see the difference between a sovereign king or duke who could be dispossessed only by a more powerful conqueror and a "chocolate king" who forfeits his "kingdom" as soon as the customers prefer to patronize another supplier.

This distortion is at the bottom of all socialist plans. If any of the socialist chiefs had tried to earn his living by selling hot dogs, he would have learned something about the sovereignty of the customers. But they were professional revolutionaries and their only job was to kindle civil war. Lenin's ideal was to build a nation's production effort according to the model of the post office, an outfit that does not depend on the consumers, because its deficits are covered by the compulsory collection of taxes. "The whole of society," he said, was to "become one office and one factory."[2] He did see that the very character of the office and the factory is entirely changed when it is alone in the world and no longer grants to people the opportunity to choose among the products and services of various enterprises. Because his blindness made it impossible for him to see the role the market and the consumers play under capitalism, he could not see the difference between freedom and slavery. Because in his eyes the workers were only workers and not also customers, he believed they were already slaves under capitalism, and that one did not change their status when nationalizing all plants and shops. Socialism substitutes the sovereignty of a dictator, or committee of dictators, for the sovereignty of the consumers. Along with the economic sovereignty of the citizens disappears also their political sovereignty. To the unique production plan that annuls any planning on the part of the consumers corresponds in the constitutional sphere the one party principle that deprives the citizens of any opportunity to plan the course of public affairs. Freedom is indivisible. He who has not the faculty to choose among various brands of canned food or soap is also deprived of the power to choose between various political parties and programs and to elect the office-holders. He is no longer a man; he become a pawn in the hands of the supreme social engineer. Even his freedom to rear progeny will be taken away by eugenics.

---

2 Lenin, *State and Revolution*, International Publishers, New York, s.d., p. 84.

Of course, the socialist leaders occasionally assure us that dictatorial tyranny is to last only for the period of transition from capitalism and representative government to the socialist millennium in which everybody's wants and wishes will be fully satisfied.[3] Once the socialist regime is "sufficiently secure to risk criticism," Miss Joan Robinson, the eminent representative of the British neo-Cambridge school, is kind enough to promise us, "even independent philharmonic societies" will be allowed to exist.[4] Thus the liquidation of all dissenters is the condition that will bring us what the communists call freedom. From this point of view we may also understand what another distinguished Englishmen, Mr. J. G. Crowther, had in mind when he praised inquisition as "beneficial to science when it protects a rising class."[5] The meaning of all this is clear. When all people meekly bow to a dictator, there will no longer be any dissenters left for liquidation. Caligula, Torquemada, Robespierre would have agreed with this solution.

The socialists have engineered a semantic revolution in converting the meaning of terms into their opposite. In the vocabulary of their Newspeak, as George Orwell called it, there is a term "the one-party principle." Now etymologically party is derived from the noun part. The brotherless part is no longer different from its antonym, the whole; it is identical with it. A brotherless party is not a party, and the one-party principle is in fact a no-party principle. It is a suppression of any kind of opposition. Freedom implies the right to choose between assent and dissent. But in Newspeak it means the duty to assent unconditionally and the strict interdiction of dissent. This reversal of the traditional connotation of all words of the political terminology is not merely a peculiarity of the language of the Russian Communists and their Fascist and Nazi disciples. The social

---

3 Marx, *Sur Kritik des Sozialdemokratischen Programms von Gotha,* 1875 (ed. by Kreibich), Reichenberg 1920, p. 23).

4 Joan Robinson, *Private Enterprise and Public Control* (published for the Association for Education in Citizenship by the English Universities Press Ltd., s.d.) pp. 13–14.

5 J.G. Crowther, *Social Relations of Science,* London 1941, p. 333.

order that in abolishing private property deprives the consumers of their autonomy and independence, and thereby subjects every man to the arbitrary discretion of the central planning board, could not win the support of the masses if were not to camouflage its main character. The socialist would have never duped the voters if they had openly told them that their ultimate end is to cast them into bondage. For exoteric use they were forced to pay lip service to the traditional appreciation of liberty.

IV

It was different in the esoteric discussions among the inner circles of the great conspiracy. There the initiated did not dissemble their intentions concerning liberty. Liberty was, in their opinion, certainly a good feature in the past in the frame of bourgeois society because it provided them with the opportunity to embark on their schemes. But once socialism has triumphed, there is no longer any need for free thought and autonomous action on the part of individuals. Any further change can only be a deviation from the perfect state that mankind has attained in reaching the bliss of socialism. Under such conditions, it would be simply lunacy to tolerate dissent.

Liberty, says the Bolshevist, is a bourgeois prejudice. The common man does not have any ideas of his own, he does not write books, does not hatch heresies and does not invent new methods of production. He just wants to enjoy life. He has no use for the class interests of the intellectuals who make a living as professional dissenters and innovators.

This is certainly the most arrogant disdain of the plain citizen ever devised. There is no need to argue this point. For the question is not whether or not the common man can himself take advantage of the liberty to think, to speak and to write books. The question is whether or not the sluggish routinist profits from the freedom granted to those who eclipse him in intelligence and will power. The common man may look with indifference and even contempt upon the dealings of better people. But he is delighted to enjoy all the benefits which the endeavors of the innovators put at his disposal. He has no comprehension of what in his eyes is merely inane hair-splitting. But as soon as these thought and theories are utilized by enterprising businessmen for satisfying some his latent wishes, he hurries to acquire the new products. The common man is without doubt the main beneficiary of all the accomplishments of modern science and technology.

It is true, a man of average intellectual abilities has no chance to rise to the rank of a captain of industry. But the sovereignty that the market assigns to him in economic affairs stimulates technologists and promoters to convert to his use all the achievements of scientific research. Only people whose intellectual horizon does not extend beyond the internal organization of the factory and who do not realize what makes the businessmen run, fail to notice this fact.

The admirers of the Soviet system tell us again and again that freedom is not the supreme good. It is "not worth having," if it implies poverty. To sacrifice it in order to attain wealth for the masses, is in their eyes fully justified. But for a few unruly individualists who cannot adjust themselves to the ways of regular fellows, all people in Russia are perfectly happy. We may leave it undecided whether this happiness was also shared by the millions of Ukrainian peasants who died from starvation, by the inmates of the forced labor camps, and by the Marxian leaders who were purged. But we cannot pass over the fact that the standard of living was incomparably higher in the free countries of the West than in the communist East. In giving away liberty as the price to be paid for the acquisition of prosperity, the Russians made a poor bargain. They now have neither the one nor the other.

V

Romantic philosophy labored under the illusion that in the early ages of history the individual was free and that the course of historical evolution deprived him of his primordial liberty. As Jean

Jacques Rousseau saw it, nature accorded men freedom and society enslaved him. In fact, primeval man was at the mercy of every
fellow who was stronger and therefore could snatch away from him
the scarce means of subsistence. There is in nature nothing to which
the name of liberty could be given. The concept of freedom always
refers to social relations between men. True, society cannot realize
the illusory concept of the individual's absolute independence. Within society everyone depends on what other people are prepared to
contribute to his well-being in return for his own contribution to
their well-being. Society is essentially the mutual exchange of services. As far as individuals have the opportunity to choose, they are
free; if they are forced by violence or threat of violence to surrender to the terms of an exchange, no matter how they feel about it,
they lack freedom. The slave is unfree precisely because the master
assigns him his tasks and determines what he has to receive if he
fulfills it.

As regards the social apparatus of repression and coercion, the
government, there cannot be any question of freedom. Government
is essentially the negation of liberty. It is the recourse to violence or
threat of violence in order to make all people obey the orders of the
government, whether they like it or not. As far as the government's
jurisdiction extends, there is coercion, not freedom. Government is
a necessary institution, the means to make the social system of cooperation work smoothly without being disturbed by violent acts on
the part of gangsters whether of domestic or of foreign origin. Government is not, as some people like to say, a necessary evil; it is not
an evil, but a means, the only means available to make peaceful
human coexistence possible. But it is the opposite of liberty. It is
beating, imprisoning, hanging. Whatever a government does is ultimately supported by the actions of armed constables. If the government operates a school or a hospital, the funds required are
collected by taxes, i.e., by payments exacted from the citizens.

If we take into account the fact that, as human nature is, there
can neither be civilization nor peace without the functioning of the

government apparatus of violent action, we may call government the most beneficial human institution. But the fact remains that government is repression, not freedom. Freedom is to be found only in the sphere in which government does not interfere. Liberty is always freedom from the government. It is the restriction of the government's interference. It prevails only in the fields in which the citizens have the opportunity to choose the way in which they want to proceed. Civil rights are the statutes that precisely circumscribe the sphere in which the men conducting the affairs of state are permitted to restrict the individuals' freedom to act.

The ultimate end that men aim at by establishing government is to make possible the operation of a definite system of social cooperation under the principle of the division of labor. If the social system which people want to have is socialism (communism, planning) there is no sphere of freedom left. All citizens are in every regard subject to orders of the government. The state is a total state; the regime is totalitarian. The government alone plans and forces everybody to behave according with this unique plan.

In the market economy the individuals are free to choose the way in which they want to integrate themselves into the frame of social cooperation. As far as the sphere of market exchange extends, there is spontaneous action on the part of individuals. Under this system that is called laissez-faire, and which Ferdinand Lassalle dubbed as the nightwatchman state, there is freedom because there is a field in which individuals are free to plan for themselves.

The socialists must admit there cannot be any freedom under a socialist system. But they try to obliterate the difference between the servile state and economic freedom by denying that there is any freedom in the mutual exchange of commodities and services in the market. Every market exchange is, in the words of a school of pro-socialist lawyers, "a coercion over other people's liberty." There is, in their eyes, no difference worth mentioning between a man's paying a tax or a fine imposed by a magistrate, or his buying a newspaper or admission to a movie. In each of these cases the man is subject to governing power. He's not free, for, as Professor Hale says, a man's freedom means "the absence of any obstacle to his use of material goods."[6] This means: I am not free, because a woman who has knitted a sweater, perhaps as a birthday present for her husband, puts an obstacle to my using it. I myself am restricting all other people's freedom because I object their using my toothbrush. In doing this, according to this doctrine, I am exercising private governing power, which is analogous to public government power, the powers that the government exercises in imprisoning a man in Sing Sing.

Those expounding this amazing doctrine consistently conclude that liberty is nowhere to be found. They assert that what they call economic pressures do not essentially differ from the pressures the masters practice with regard to their slaves. They reject what they call private governmental power, but they don't object to the restriction of liberty by public government power. They want to concentrate all that they call restrictions of liberty in the hands of the government. They attack the institution of private property and the laws that, as they say, stand "ready to enforce property rights—that is, to deny liberty to anyone to act in a way which violates them."[7]

A generation ago all housewives prepared soup by proceeding in accordance with the recipes that they had got from their mothers or from a cook book. Today many housewives prefer to buy a canned soup, to warm it and to serve it to their family. But, say our learned doctors, the canning corporation is in a position to restrict the housewife's freedom because in asking a price for the tin can, it puts an obstacle to her use of it. People who did not enjoy the privilege of being tutored by these eminent teachers would say that the canned product was turned out by the cannery, and that the corporation in producing it removed the greatest obstacle to a consumer's getting and using a can, viz., its nonexistence. The mere

---

6 Robert L. Hale, *Freedom Through Law, Public Control of Private Governing Power,* Columbia University, 1952, pp. 4 ff.

7 *Ibid,* p. 5.

essence of a product cannot gratify anybody without its existence. But they are wrong, say the doctors. The corporation dominates the housewife, it destroys by its excessive concentrated power her individual freedom, and it is the duty of the government to prevent such a gross offense. Corporations, says, under the auspices of the Ford Foundation, another of this group, Professor Berle, must be subjected to the control of the government.[8]

Why does our housewife buy the canned product rather than cling to the methods of her mother and grandmother? No doubt because she thinks this way of acting is more advantageous for her than the traditional custom. Nobody forced her. There were people—they are called jobbers, promoters, capitalists, speculators, stock exchange gamblers—who had the idea of satisfying a latent wish of millions of housewives by investing in the cannery industry. And there are other equally selfish capitalists who, in many hundreds of other corporations, provide consumers with many hundreds of other things. The better a corporation serves the public, the more customers it gets, the bigger it grows. Go into the home of the average American family and you will see for whom the wheels of the machines are turning.

In a free country nobody is prevented from acquiring riches by serving the consumers better than they are served already. What he needs is only brains and hard work. "Modern civilization, nearly all civilization," said Edwin Cannan, the last in a long line of eminent British economists, is "based on the principle of making things pleasant for those who please the market, and unpleasant for those who fail to do so."[9] All this talk about the concentration of economic power is vain. The bigger a corporation is, the more people it serves, the more does it depend on pleasing the consumers, the many, the masses. Economic power, in the market economy, is in the hands of the consumers.

---

8 A. A. Berle, Jr., *Economic Power and the Free Society, a Preliminary Discussion of the Corporation,* The Fund for the Republic, New York, 1954.

9 Edwin Cannan, *An Economist's Protest,* London 1928, pp. VI ff.

Capitalistic business is not perseverance in the once attained state of production. It is rather ceaseless innovation, daily repeated attempts to improve the provision of the consumers by new, better and cheaper products. Any actual state of production activities is merely transitory. There prevails incessantly the tendency to supplant what is already achieved by something that serves the consumers better. There is consequently under capitalism a continuous circulation of elites. What characterizes the men whom one calls the captains of industry is ability to contrive new ideas and to put them to work. However big a corporation must be, it is doomed as soon as it does not succeed in adjusting itself daily anew to the best possible methods of serving the consumers. But the politicians and other would-be reformers see only the structure of industry as it exists today. They think that they are clever enough to snatch from business control of the plants as they are today, and to manage them by sticking to already established routine. While the ambitious newcomer, who will be the tycoon of tomorrow, is already preparing plans for things unheard of before, all they have in mind is to conduct affairs along tracks already beaten. There is no record of an industrial innovation contrived and put into practice by bureaucrats. If one does not want to plunge into stagnation, a free hand must be left to those today unknown men who have the ingenuity to lead mankind forward on the way to more and more satisfactory conditions. This is the main problem of a nation's economic organization.

Private property of the material factors of production is not a restriction of the freedom of all other people to choose what suits them best. It is, on the contrary, the means that assigns to the common man, in his capacity as a buyer, supremacy in all economic affairs. It is the means to stimulate a nation's most enterprising men to exert themselves to the best of their abilities in the service of all of the people.

VI

However, one does not exhaustively describe the sweeping changes that capitalism brought about in the conditions of the common man if one merely deals with the supremacy he enjoys in the market as a consumer and in the affairs of state as a voter and with the unprecedented improvement of his standard of living. No less important is the fact that capitalism has made it possible for him to save, to accumulate capital and to invest it. The gulf that in the pre-capitalistic status and caste society separated the owners of property from the penniless poor has been narrowed down. In older ages the journeyman had such a low pay that he could hardly lay by something and, if he nevertheless did so, he could only keep his savings by hoarding and hiding a few coins. Under capitalism his competence makes saving possible, and there are institutions that enable him to invest his funds in business. A not inconsiderable amount of the capital employed in American industries is the counterpart of the savings of employees. In acquiring savings deposits, insurance policies, bonds and also common stock, wage earners and salaried people are themselves earning interest and dividends and thereby in the terminology of Marxism, are exploiters. The common man is directly interested in the flowering of business not only as a consumer and as an employee, but also as an investor. There prevails a tendency to efface to some extent the once sharp difference between those who own factors of production and those who do not. But, of course, this trend can only develop where the market economy is not sabotaged by allegedly social policies. The Welfare State with its methods of easy money, credit expansion and undisguised inflation continually takes bites out of all claims payable in units of the nation's legal tender. The self-styled champions of the common man are still guided by the obsolete idea that a policy that favors the debtors at the expense of the creditors is very beneficial to the majority of the people. Their inability to comprehend the essential characteristics of the market economy manifests itself also in their failure to see the obvious fact that those whom they feign to aid are creditors in their capacity as savers, policy holders, and owner of bonds.

VII

The distinctive principle of Western social philosophy is individualism. It aims at the creation of a sphere in which the individual is free to think, to choose, and to act without being restrained by the interference of the social apparatus of coercion and oppression, the State. All the spiritual and material achievements of Western civilization were the result of the operation of this idea of liberty.

The doctrine and the policies of individualism and of capitalism, its application to economic matters, do not need any apologists or propagandists. The achievements speak for themselves.

The case for capitalism and private property rests, apart from other considerations, also upon the incomparable efficiency of its productive effort. It is this efficiency that makes it possible for capitalistic business to support a rapidly increasing population at a continually improving standard of living. The resulting progressive prosperity of the masses creates a social environment in which the exceptionally gifted individuals are free to give to their fellow citizens all they are able to give. The social system of private property and limited government is the only system that tends to debarbarize all those who have the innate capacity to acquire personal culture.

It is a gratuitous pastime to belittle the material achievements of capitalism by observing that there are things that are more essential for mankind than bigger and speedier motorcars, and homes are equipped with central heating, air conditioning, refrigerators, washing machines, and television sets. There certainly are such higher and nobler pursuits. But they are higher and nobler precisely because they cannot be aspired to by any external effort, but require the individual's personal determination and exertion. Those levelling this reproach against capitalism display a rather crude and materialistic view in assuming that moral and spiritual culture could be built either by the government or by the organization of production activities. All that these external factors can achieve in this regard is to bring about an environment and a competence which offers the individuals the opportunity to work at their own personal perfection and edification. It is not the fault of capitalism that the masses prefer a boxing match to a performance of Sophocles' *Antigone*, jazz music to Beethoven symphonies, and comics to poetry. But is certain that while precapitalistic conditions as they still prevail in the much greater part of the world makes these good things accessible only to a small minority of people, capitalism gives to the many a favorable chance of striving after them.

From whatever angle one may look at capitalism there is no reason to lament the passing of the allegedly good old days. Still less is it justified to long for the totalitarian utopias, whether of Nazi or the Soviet type.

We are inaugurating tonight the ninth meeting of the Mont Pelerin Society. It is fitting to remember on this occasion that meetings of this kind in which opinions opposed to those of the majority of our contemporaries and to those of their governments are advanced are possible only in the climate of liberty and freedom that is the most precious mark of Western civilization. Let us hope that this right to dissent will never disappear.

Courtesy of Intercollegiate Studies Institute

CHAPTER 7

Robert Nisbet

Commentary by Edwin J. Feulner (2003)

Although liberalism appeared to be the dominant political philosophy in America in the post-World War II period, it was already beginning to decline. In contrast, the pivotal years between 1950 and 1953 produced a series of brilliant books that exerted a profound influence on American conservatism and the course of American politics. They included William F. Buckley Jr.'s searing polemic *God and Man at Yale*, Eric Voegelin's magisterial *The New Science of Politics*, Russell Kirk's masterwork, *The Conservative Mind*, and a classic of sociology that has been in print for fifty years—Robert Nisbet's *The Quest for Community*.

Robert Nisbet's thesis (drawing on Edmund Burke and Alexis de Tocqueville) was that the emergence of the sovereign political state was "the greatest single influence upon social organizations in the modern West." The West's history since the Middle Ages was in fact the story of the decline of "intermediate associations" between the individual and the state. However, the deterioration of such institutions as the family, the church, and the neighborhood had not, as many intellectuals had predicted, liberated man. Instead, it had produced isolation, alienation, and despair. But the simple fact is that, in the words of historian George Nash, man cannot live in "Hobbesian isolation."

"The quest for community will not be denied," Nisbet maintained, "for it springs from some of the powerful needs of human nature—needs for a clear sense of cultural purpose, membership, status, and continuity." Seeking to consolidate its power, the modern totalitarian state sought to satisfy these needs and, tragically, succeeded in many instances.

"The single most impressive fact in the twentieth century in Western society," Nisbet said, "was the fateful combination of the widespread quest for community ... and the apparatus of political power" wielded by the totalitarian state. Not only did the centralized state perform more "efficiently" the social functions of the traditional smaller communities, it promised to alleviate the isolation and loneliness of the individual. In the promise of unity and belonging, Nisbet said, "lies much of the magic of totalitarian mystery, appeal and authority."

The totalitarian state depended upon two devices to coax the individual into a new "national community"—the intoxicating spirit of war and the equally intoxicating rhetoric of a charismatic leader. Thus was created, according to Nisbet, the total political state of the twentieth century. Such a state, the author William A. Schambra stated, did not always manifest itself in the "brutal repression or naked terror of Soviet or Nazi totalitarianism." It often appeared as the benevolent provider of the material needs of its citizens and the antidote to the unbearable sense of isolation—that is, as the modern welfare state created and nurtured in America by the Progressives from Woodrow Wilson to Franklin D. Roosevelt.

But for all its seeming benevolence, Nisbet insisted, the national political community, "centralized and omnicompetent," remained the most profound threat to freedom in human history. "Total political centralization," he said, "can lead only to social and cultural death." To live in freedom, man must break the bonds between himself and the state through a revitalization of intermediate associations such as the family, the church and the neighborhood, the "little platoons" of life about which Burke spoke so eloquently.

The desire for community, Nisbet also insisted, could not be satisfied by individualism which overlooked the fact that its ideals were unattainable except in a community. Individualists, said Nisbet, failed the recognize the close dependence of their thought on "the subtle, infinitely complex lines of habit, tradition, and social relationship."

What was needed was neither centralized authority nor unrestrained individualism but a middle way—prudent planning that contented itself with "the setting of human life, not human life itself." Echoing F. A. Hayek in *The Road to Serfdom*, Nisbet said that planning for masses of individuals was not only "a hopeless exercise" but likely to produce that "combination of externally contrived goals and unconditional power" that is "the substance of tyranny and the path to annihilation of personality." Echoing the fusionist philosophy of Frank Meyer, Nisbet stated that man's social needs could only be fulfilled "with the groups and associations that we are given in experience," along with "the prime conditions of individual integrity and autonomy."

When *The Quest for Community* appeared in 1953, American liberals dismissed its message because they were wed to the idea of a national community while conservatives of a libertarian bent paid it scant attention because they favored an individualism that was, however, of little use against a totalitarian state. But Russell Kirk and other traditional conservatives praised *The Quest* warmly, and Nisbet received congratulatory letters from, among others, T. S. Eliot and Reinhold Niebuhr. Then and later, Nisbet acknowledged his deep debt to Kirk's *The Conservative Mind,* which, he said, "gave scholarly and timely pedigree to conservatism in England and the United States, demonstrating the key role of Burke in both countries."

In time, *The Quest for Community* became a widely quoted classic, and the author has been recognized as "the most prominent and influential conservative sociologist in postwar America."

Robert Nisbet was born in Los Angeles, California, on September 30, 1913, and grew up in the small oil town of Maricopa. Wherever they lived—Santa Cruz, San Luis Obispo—education was a constant of the Nisbet family. Robert enrolled at the University of California-Berkeley in 1932 and except when he was in the Army during World War II remained there for the next twenty-one years, as undergraduate, graduate student, and faculty member. He studied under the cultural historian Frederick J. Teggart, who was "almost evangelical" in his discussions of "the built-in conflict between family and state in the history of mankind," and under Max Radin, an expert on Roman law.

By his own admission, Nisbet began as an ardent undergraduate supporter of the New Deal, but by the late 1930s, his support had turned to alienation. It seemed to Nisbet that the New Deal had immersed itself in "an impossible combination of political centralization and of administrative bureaucracy." It was upon his return to Berkeley after the war, wrote his biographer, Brad Lowell Stone, that Nisbet first probed the works of his "two greatest intellectual heroes," Burke and Tocqueville, who strengthened his belief in the critical role of intermediate associations. Nisbet came to believe that "it is the family, not the individual, that is the real molecule of society, the key link of the social chain of being." And as regards society and the state, society is both prior to the state and far more important.

Always a person of high energy, Nisbet accepted an appointment in 1953—the same year as the publication of *The Quest for Community*—as dean of a new liberal arts college established by the University of California-Riverside. He spent the next ten years in administration, except for one "splendid, invigorating" year as a visiting professor at the University of Bologna in Italy. Having rediscovered the joy of teaching at Bologna, Nisbet left administration in 1963 and returned to Riverside where in addition to his classes he wrote five books on sociology and education over the next eight years, including *The Degradation of Academic Dogma:*

The University in America 1945–1970. Nisbet left California for the University of Arizona, but found the intellectual atmosphere there less stimulating than he had hoped and accepted in 1974 the Albert Schweitzer Chair of the Humanities at Columbia University. Among his friends on and off campus in New York were the renowned educator Jacques Barzun and the father of neoconservatism, Irving Kristol.

In an autobiographical introduction to *The Making of Modern Society*, Nisbet said that he hoped he would die over his typewriter, and he almost did. During his years at Columbia, he continued to write prolifically, publishing, for example, the highly regarded work, *Twilight of Authority.* He argued therein that although the full flowering of the welfare state occurred in the last four decades, its roots were in World War I and Woodrow Wilson. According to Nisbet, Wilson's "political, economic, social and intellectual reorganization of America in the short period 1917–1919 is one of the most extraordinary feats in the long history of war and polity." Within these few months, Nisbet wrote, Wilson "transformed traditional, decentralized, regional and localist America into a war state that at its height permeated every aspect of life."

Having vowed to leave the academy before growing indifferent to the demands of teaching, Nisbet retired from teaching in 1978 (at age 65) and moved to Washington, D.C., where he joined the American Enterprise Institute as resident scholar and then adjunct scholar. But he still had much to say, publishing six more books—including *The Present Age: Progress and Anarchy in Modern America*—until his death in 1996, just short of his eighty-third birthday. With Richard Weaver, he argued that "everything vital in history reduces itself ultimately to ideas, which are the motive forces ... Man is what he thinks the transcending moral values are in his life and in the lives of those around him."

Robert Nisbet received many honors and awards throughout his life, including the Award of Merit from Italy, the Ingersoll Award for Scholarly Letters, and the 1988 Jefferson Lectureship, one of the most prestigious academic awards in the nation. Within and without the United States, biographer Stone summed up, Nisbet is recognized as "one of the most original and influential American social theorists of his generation." Although he published several works deserving of study and acclamation, his reputation rests most securely on *The Quest for Community.*

We are fortunate to have Robert Nisbet's mature reflections on his most enduring work (written forty years after publication) and how he came to be a self-described conservative. Although he did not think of *The Quest for Community* as "a conservative treatise," he wrote, he was not taken aback by its identification as such. He himself had become increasingly conservative by the early 1950s, influenced by the "ascent to conservatism" of such individuals as Malcolm Muggeridge in Great Britain and the "spectacular conversions" of once fervid Marxists like Arthur Koestler in the West. Nisbet also noted the signal influence of F. A. Hayek, whom he called "the morning star of America's oncoming conservatism," and works like Richard Weaver's *Ideas Have Consequences,* which drew "surprisingly good reviews even in the liberal press."

Contributing significantly to the conservative renaissance of the 1950s, he said, was the restoration to proper intellectual status of Alexis de Tocqueville and Edmund Burke. Over faculty club lunch tables, he recalled, he heard Tocqueville referred to as often as Marx—"what a thrill!" Burke enjoyed a restoration nearly as dramatic, "thanks in very considerable part to Kirk's *The Conservative Mind.*" Nisbet admitted that he wrote *The Quest* "with the feeling that both Burke and Tocqueville were near at hand." Paraphrasing Burke, he remarked that "society is a partnership of the dead, the living, and the unborn."

Nisbet's conservatism was reinforced by the ever-increasing pervasiveness of government. It seemed, he said, "as if centralization and bureaucracy have lives of their own, independent of the convictions of the occupants of the White House and Congress." He once wrote that "efforts to reduce the state are like nothing so much as chipmunks trying to bring down a giant redwood." Despite the best intentions of even so committed a conservative as Ronald Reagan, he said, the pattern continued into the 1990s "with this malign difference:" more and more were heard the magic words, "National Community." It should be the prime business of any serious conservative group, Nisbet said sternly, "to expose the fraudulence of such a phrase as 'national community.'"

The offer of "individualism" as the logical alternative to national community, Nisbet stated in 1993 as he had in 1953, was misconceived. It was not "lone individuals" who developed America from one coast to the other. It was groups of every kind—neighborhoods, extended families, and voluntary associations—that built the schools, churches, and other community enterprises.

A nation, stated Nisbet, needed a strong government, local and central, because there were "necessities in our lives," like national defense, which required government. But it was also the function of government "to shore up, to reinforce, and otherwise nurture the natural communities in society." Conservative groups, he concluded, therefore had a double task: to work "tirelessly" toward the diminution of the centralized, omnicompetent, and unitary state with its ever-soaring debt and deficit; and to protect and nurture where necessary the varied groups and associations which formed "the true building blocks of the social order."

Nisbet was quite specific, Brad Lowell Stone pointed out, as to what he meant by communities. They are human groups that spring up to fill perennial human needs and to solve problems. Communities are built around some *function*. They have a transcending purpose based on ideals or *dogma*. They are characterized by *authority*, not by power. They are *hierarchical*. They display *solidarity*. They have a strong sense of *honor*. They seek to place themselves at some distance from the surrounding world.

"The Contexts of Democracy" is the penultimate chapter of *The Quest for Community* and reaffirms the central theme of the work—the major objective of political democracy should be to harmonize and make effective the "varied group allegiances which exist in society," not sterilize them in the interest of a centralized political community. Nisbet traces the origins of the unitary state to the latter part of the eighteenth century and to such thinkers as Rousseau. It is "the widening appeal of the collectivist, unitary ideal of democracy" within conditions of social dislocation and moral alienation, he says, "that makes the problem of power so ominous in the Western democracies."

He quotes Tocqueville on the dangers of enslaving men "in the minor details of life" and Jefferson's shrewd observation that a state with the power to do things *for* people has the power to do things *to* them. He says that mass warfare has contributed profoundly to the development of the unitary state. He notes two other supports of the collectivist view of democracy—the desire for unity, in the face of discord, and the faith, "derived from ancient, medieval, and modern ideas of change," in historical necessity. He argues that the appeal of Marxism is due, in part, to Marx's argument that socialism was a stage of society "that must develop dialectically out of the *significant* present."

Popular sovereignty, Nisbet argues, is not enough to assure liberal democracy. A single-minded concentration upon the individual as the sole unit of society is not sufficient for the preservation of freedom. Freedom, he insists, thrives in cultural diversity, in local and regional differentiation, in pluralism and, above all—acknowledging the wisdom of the Founding Fathers—"in the diversification of power."

Nisbet dissects the accelerating power of the bureaucratic state, quoting David Lilienthal, the first head of the heralded Tennessee Valley Authority, that administrative decentralization is absolutely indispensable to modern democracies "if they are not to become victims of the creeping totalitarianism inherent in administrative monopoly and centralization." Nisbet notes the interdependent relationship of big government, big business, and big labor in modern America and asserts that decentralization in these great associations is just as necessary as in the political state.

Robert Nisbet ends with what seems at first reading to be a wildly provocative statement: "what we need above all else in this age is a new philosophy of *laissez-faire*." But he quickly makes clear that he is not advocating the creation of a new mass of unrelated individuals but a vast complex of associations that would comprise individuals, families, clubs, trade unions, colleges, and professions. We need, he says, a *laissez-faire* "in which the basic unit will be the social group."

Certainly, he concedes, autonomy and freedom of personal choice are indispensable to a genuinely free society, but they can only be maintained under the conditions in which liberal democracy thrives—diversity of culture, plurality of associations, and divisions of authority.

Robert Nisbet

The Contexts of Democracy

D efinitions of democracy are as varied as the interests of persons and generations. Democracy is made identical with intellectual freedom, with economic justice, with social welfare, with tolerance, with piety, moral integrity, the dignity of man, and general civilized decency. As a word, democracy has come to be a kind of terminological catch-all for the historic virtues of civilization even as the word totalitarianism has become a catch-all for its evils. But the understanding of political democracy, its excellences and capacities, is served no better by this indiscriminating approach than is the understanding of totalitarianism.

Democracy may be associated with any and all of the virtues listed above, but it is, fundamentally, a theory and structure of *political power*. The historical root of democracy, as distinguished from liberalism which is historically a theory of *immunity* from power, is the proposition that the legitimacy of all political power arises from, and only from, the consent of the governed, the *people*. Lincoln's famous definition of democracy as government of, by, and for the people cannot be improved upon either as a moral ideal or as a historical description. And it is as right and as institutionally relevant today as it was in Lincoln's day.

From Robert Nisbet, *The Quest for Community* (1990).

But with respect to the "people," as with the "individual," everything depends upon the practical, cultural contexts in which we choose to regard the people. The "people," no less than the "individual," is an abstraction, subject not merely to varying verbal uses but also to historically changing political demands and moral imperatives.

We may regard the people as simply a numerical aggregate of individuals regarded for political and administrative purposes as discrete and socially separated, an aggregate given form and meaning only by the nature of the State and its laws. Or, alternatively, we may regard the people as indistinguishable from a culture, its members as inseparable from the families, unions, churches, professions, and traditions that actually compose a culture.

The differences between the two ways of considering the people is vast, and it is decisive in any political theory of democracy. The "will of the people" is one thing, substantively, when it is conceived in purely political terms as arising from a vast aggregate of socially separated, politically integrated *individuals*. It is something very different when it is conceived in terms of the social unities and cultural traditions in which political, like all other, judgments are actually formed and reinforced.

In the first view of the people, a conception of political democracy must inevitably rest heavily upon the State and its formal agencies of function and control. Units of administration become, necessarily, atomistic individuals, conceived abstractly and divorced from the cultural contexts. When the people are regarded in this way, the principal problem of democratic theory and administration becomes not the larger problem of distribution of function and authority in *society* but, rather, the discovery of means by which the human being is brought ever closer to the people *in their political wholeness* and, in practical terms, to the formal administrative structure of the State. By omitting reference to the other authority-wielding and need-gratifying associations in society, by focusing on the abstract political mass, this view of the people becomes administratively committed at the outset to a potentially totalitarian view of the State.

But if we take the second view of the people, the State emerges as but *one* of the associations of man's existence. Equally important to a democratic theory founded on this perspective is the whole plurality of other associations in society. The intermediary associations and the spontaneous social groups which compose society, rather than atomized political particles, become the prime units of theoretical and practical consideration. The major objective of political democracy becomes that of making harmonious and effective the varied group allegiances which exist in society, not sterilizing them in the interest of a monistic political community.

Historically, we find both conceptions of the people in the writings of democratic philosophers and statesmen. But it is the second, the pluralist, conception that is more relevant to the actual history of democracy, especially in the United States, England, the Scandinavian countries, and Switzerland. And, as I shall emphasize in this chapter, it is the reaffirmation of this conception that seems to me absolutely indispensable to the success of liberal democracy at the present time.

It would be naïve, however, to fail to see the powerful influence that is now exerted everywhere by the first, the unitary, view of the people and democracy. It is highly important that we examine this unitary tradition of democracy, for the difference between it and the pluralist tradition may well determine our effort to maintain liberal democracy under the pressure of the powerful quest for community in the present age.

II

The unitary view of democracy, like the ideology of the political community with which it is so closely allied, arose in France during the latter part of the eighteenth century. As a theory it was constructed in light of prevailing rationalist conceptions of man and society, and as an attack upon the still largely feudal social structure. It was based foremost upon the premise that the authorities and responsibilities wielded historically by kings, nobles, and churchmen belonged by nature to the people and should, as a matter of practical policy, be transferred to the people. But the French rationalists used the term people in a way that was remarkably abstract and as divorced from circumstance as some of their other terms.

The image of the people that governed the minds of men like Rousseau and Condorcet and was to spread in revolutionary fashion throughout the world in the nineteenth century was an image derived not from history or experience but from the same kind of conceptualization that had produced the fateful conception of the General Will. Just as the "real" will of the people was distinguished by Rousseau and his disciples from the attitudes and beliefs actually held at any given time by the people, so, in this rationalist view, the "people" had to be distinguished from the actual plurality of persons which experience revealed. If right government was to be made a reality by the rationalists, the "people" had to be separated from existing institutions and beliefs and brought into the single association of the people's State.

Just as the rationalist made the realization of individuality contingent upon the individual's release from his primary contexts of association, so he made the realization of the "people's will" dependent on the release of the whole people—abstractly regarded—from traditional institutions and authorities. And just as the rationalist conceptually endowed the individual with social instincts and drives independent of any social organization, so he endowed the people itself with a natural harmony and stability that would give it all the necessary requisites of persistence and continuity. What we may notice in the case of the rationalist's construct of the people, as in his construct of the individual, is the unconscious transfer of virtues, stabilities, and motivations from a *historical social organization* to an entity regarded as naturally independent of all historical change and social pressure.

Here, of course, the philosophy of Progress was marvelously comforting. For the very essence of the idea of secular progress was its premise that history is inherently organizational in direction, leading always, and without the need of man's guiding hand, to ever higher conditions of civilization. The consequences of institutional dislocation, of the ruthless separating of the people from cherished values and memberships, could be disregarded. History would supply its own correctives. It was only necessary to be certain that the *obstacles* to progress—classes, religious institutions, family solidarities, gilds, and so forth—were removed.

Inevitably the principal strategy of unitary democracy came to be fixed, like the strategies of nationalism and military socialism, in terms of the sterilization of old social loyalties, the emancipation of the people from local and regional authorities, and the construction of a scene in which the individual would be the sole unit, and the State the sole association, of society. Hence, the rising stress on large-scale bureaucracy: to provide new agencies representative of the *whole* people for the discharge of powers and responsibilities formerly resident in classes, parishes, and families. Hence, the increasing administrative centralization of society: to reduce in number and influence the intermediate social authorities. Hence the growing stress upon standardization: to increase the number of cultural qualities shared by the people as a whole and to diminish those shared only by fractions of the population. Hence, also, the drive toward political collectivism: to bring into full light that pre-existent harmony which the rationalists never doubted made a natural unity of the people.

State and individual were the two elements of the unitary theory of democracy. The abstract individual was conceived as the sole bearer of rights and responsibilities. The State, conceived in the image of people who lay incorruptible beneath the superstructure of society, would be the area of fraternity and secular rehabilitation. All that lay between these two elements—gilds, churches, professions, classes, unions of all kinds—were suspect for their fettering influence upon the individual and their divisive consequences to the people's State.

This, in its essentials, is the unitary tradition of democracy. It is, despite its exalted motives, almost indistinguishable from the ideology of the absolute political community. This is the tradition that provides so much of the historic relation between democracy and nationalism, between democracy and collectivism, between democracy and that whole tendency toward cultural standardization which has periodically alienated some of the most liberal of minds. This is the tradition that offers so many of the catchwords and deceptive slogans of contemporary Communism in its typical forms of the "People's States." This is the tradition that led Proudhon to define democracy, bitterly, as the State magnified to the nth power, and Tocqueville to see in it, for all his reluctant admiration for democracy, the seeds of despotism greater than anything before provided by history.

In its most impressive form, this tradition of unitary, collectivist democracy was largely confined, in the nineteenth century, to France and Germany, and to areas that came under their political and cultural influence. The long tradition of Roman law, with its unitary legal premises, the profound influence of the French Revolution, and the growing attraction of the centralized Napoleonic Code provided in these countries a highly propitious set of circumstances for the development of the unitary conception of democracy.

From the Continent, however, the ideas of unitary democracy and centralized administration have spread widely during the past half-century. Beginning in the last part of the nineteenth century these ideas took root in the United States and England, fed by the soil of nationalism which, in the United States, had been enriched by the Civil War, and given increasing relevance by the social callousness of the new business class. Given the mounting evils of the new industrialism, the appearance of new structures of economic power beyond anything seen before, and the widening incidence of economic insecurity, the techniques of administrative centralization were tempting indeed to men of good will. As against the possibilities of redress and security inherent in voluntary association, in the church, and in the local community, those of the State seemed not merely greater but infinitely more swift in possible attainment. Increasingly, American liberalism became committed to the State as the major area of social rehabilitation and to administrative centralization as the means. Imperceptibly the historic emphasis upon localism was succeeded by nationalism, pluralism by monism, and decentralization by centralization.

Today, it is the widening appeal of the collectivist, unitary ideal of democracy, set in conditions of social dislocation and moral alienation, stimulated by the demands of mass warfare, that makes the problem of power so ominous in the Western democracies.

III

We may see in the administrative techniques of unitary democracy certain justifications of a historical nature. Given a society overpowered by inherited traditions, traditions manifestly inimical to both technical advancement and human rights; given a society that is nearly stationary from the hold of ecclesiastical, class, or kinship ties, and overrich to the point of chaos in local and regional diversity, the techniques of administrative uniformity and centralization can have a pragmatic value that is unquestionable. Such, in considerable degree, was the European society of the eighteenth century. Such, in even larger degree, is the society of, say, contemporary India.

Plainly, however, we are not, in the United States, living in that kind of society. Ours is a society characterized increasingly, as we have seen, by the sterilization of group differences—local, class, regional, and associative—which lie outside the administrative framework of the State. And ours is a State society characterized by ever-rising centralization of function and authority. Both characteristics—social atomization and political centralization—are the unmistakable attributes of the beginnings of mass society. And because of these social and political realities the requirements of liberal democracy are profoundly different from what they were a century or two ago.

The principal problems of liberal democracy today arise from what Philip Selznick has so aptly called the "institutional vulnerability" of our society.[1]

This is a vulnerability reflected in the diminished moral appeal of those primary centers of cultural allegiance within which the larger ends of liberal society take on binding meaning. It is reflected in the relative ease with which totalitarian strategies penetrate the normal cultural enclosures of institutional life.

"The decay of parliaments," G. D. H. Cole has written, "has accompanied the democratization of electorates not because democracy is wrong, but because we have allowed the growth of huge political organizations to be accompanied by the atrophy of smaller ones, on which alone they can be securely built."[2]

While we seek constantly to make democracy more secure in the world by diplomatic agreements and national security legislation, we do not often remind ourselves that the most powerful resources of democracy lie in the cultural allegiances of citizens, and that these *allegiances* are nourished psychologically in the smaller, internal areas of family, local community, and association.

These are the areas that contain the images of the larger society, the areas within which human beings are able to define, and render meaningful, democratic values. When the small areas of association become sterile psychologically, as the result of loss of institutional significance, we find ourselves resorting to ever-increasing dosages of indoctrination from above, an indoctrination that often becomes totalitarian in significance. We find ourselves with a society that suffers increasingly from, to use the expressive words of Lamennais, apoplexy at the center and anemia at the extremities. To be sure, liberals strive earnestly to maintain the rights and equalities of individuals before the rising structure of legislative and executive political power. They appeal to the courts, but not even

---

1. "Institutional Vulnerability in Mass Society," *The American Journal of Sociology* (January 1951).
2. "Leviathon and Little Groups," *The Aryan Path* (October 1941).

the American judicial system can remain for very long untouched by the drive toward political uniformity and centralization. They appeal to the rights of man but, except in a religious sense which few liberals take seriously, there are no rights of man that do not proceed from the society in which human beings live. In any event, it is the liberal concentration of interest upon the *individual,* rather than upon the associations in which the individual exists, that serves, paradoxical as it may seem, to intensify the processes that lead straight to increased governmental power.

"More and more is it clear," wrote J. N. Figgis in 1911, "that the mere individual's freedom against an omnipotent State may be no better than slavery; more and more is it evident that the real question of freedom in our day is the freedom of the smaller unions to live within the whole."[3]

The prophetic quality of these words will not be lost upon even the most insensitive observer of our period. It has surely become obvious that the greatest single internal problem that liberal democracy faces is the preservation of a culture rich in diversity, in clear alternatives—and this is a cultural problem that cannot be separated from the preservation of the social groups and associations within which all culture is nourished and developed.

Individual *versus* State is as false an antithesis today as it ever was. The State grows on what it gives to the individual as it does on what it takes from competing social relationships—family, labor union, profession, local community, and church.

And the individual cannot but find a kind of vicarious strength in what is granted to the State. For is he not himself a part of the State? Is he not a fraction of the sovereign? And is he not but adding to his political status as citizen what he subtracts from his economic, religious, and cultural statuses in society?

He is; and in this fractional political majesty the individual finds not only compensation for the frustrations and insecurities to

---

3. *Churches in the Modern State* (London, 1913), p. 51–52.

which he is heir in mass society but also the intoxicating sense of collective freedom.

To find the essence of freedom in the fact of the ultimate political sovereignty of the people, in the existence of mass electorates, in the individual's constitutionally guaranteed participation every two or four years in the election of his public servants, is tempting in the modern world. For it is supported by the premise, so alluring to the reformer and the disinherited alike, that political power, however great and far-reaching it may be, if it is but continuously and sensitively in touch with mass wish and acquiescence, ceases to be power in the ordinary sense. It becomes collective self-determination, collective freedom. Power becomes, in this view, marvelously neutralized and immaterialized.

"Our contemporaries," Tocqueville observed a century ago, "are constantly excited by two conflicting passions: they want to be led and they wish to remain free. As they cannot destroy either the one or the other of these contrary propensities, they strive to satisfy them both at once. They devise a sole, tutelary, and all-powerful form of government elected by the people. They combine the principle of centralization and that of popular sovereignty; this gives them respite: they console themselves for being in tutelage by the reflection that they have chosen their own guardians. Every man allows himself to be in leading strings, because he sees that it is not a person or class of persons, but the people at large who hold the end of the chain.

"I admit that by this means room is left for the intervention of individuals in the more important affairs: but it is not the less suppressed in the smaller and more private ones. It must not be forgotten that it is especially dangerous to enslave men in the minor details of life. For my own part, I should be inclined to think freedom less necessary in the great things than in the little ones, if it were possible to be secure of the one without possessing the other."[4]

---

4. *Democracy in America*, Reeve translation edited by Pillips Bradley (New York, 1945) vol. 2, p. 319–20.

It is especially dangerous to enslave men in the minor details of life. Could any insight be more relevant to the contemporary problem of power in Western society? Too often in our intellectual defenses of freedom, in our sermons and manifestos for democracy, we have fixed attention only on the more obvious historical threats to popular freedoms: kings, military dictators, popes, and financial titans. We have tended to miss the subtler but infinitely more potent threats bound up with diminution of authorities and allegiances in the smaller areas of association and with the centralization and standardization of power that takes place in the name of, and on behalf of, the *people.*

Here, of course, it is always persuasive to argue that modern increases in the administrative authority of the State have been generally associated with the enhancement of mass welfare. But this is no answer to the problem of power. As Jefferson shrewdly pointed out, the State with the power to do things *for* people has the power to do things *to* them. In plain fact the latter power increases almost geometrically in proportion to the former.

Nor is it the answer to the problem of power to argue that political power in the democracies is achieved in the name of the people and through actions of representatives of the people. For we have learned from European experience that it is not primarily the source of power that is at issue but the nature of the power and the degree of unity and unconditionality which it holds over human beings.

The collective political power of the people has increased enormously during the past century. So have available means of political participation by the common man: the referendum, the direct primary, the recall, the continuous abolition of restrictions on voting, and other even more direct means of participation. Yet, along with these increases in popular democracy, it must be observed that there has been a general leveling of local, regional, and associative differences, a nationalization of culture and taste, a collectivization of mind, and a continuous increase in the real powers of government over management, labor, education, religion, and social welfare. Democracy, far from heightening human autonomy and cultural freedom, seems rather to have aided in the process of mechanization that has weakened them. It must be repeated again, however, that this is not the inevitable consequence of the democratic ideal of power vested residually in the people. It is the consequence of the systems of public administration which we have grafted onto the democratic ideal.

IV

In this development of unitary democracy, of bureaucratic centralization, contemporary mass warfare has, of course, a profoundly contributory significance. "War is the health of the State," Randolph Bourne once declared. It is the health of the State as it is the disease, or rather the starvation, of other areas of social function and authority. Everything we observed earlier in this book with respect to the community-making properties of mass warfare in the contemporary world is deeply relevant to the administrative problem of liberal democracy. Even Tocqueville, with all his fear of centralization, was moved to write: "I do not deny that a centralized social power may be able to execute great undertakings with facility in a given time and on a particular point. This is especially true of war, in which success depends much more on the means of transferring all the resources of a nation to one single point than on the extent of those resources. Hence it is chiefly in war that nations desire, and frequently need, to increases the powers of the central government. All men of military genius are fond of centralization, which increase their strength; and all men of centralizing genius are fond of war which compels nations to combine all their powers in the hands of the government."[5]

It is precisely this military imperative of governmental centralization that makes continued warfare, or preparation for war, have so deadly an effect on all other institutions in society. For it is

---

5. Op. cit. vol. 2, p. 300–301.

difficult to perform the administrative measures necessary to political and military centralization without drawing in drastic fashion from the functions, the authorities, and the allegiances that normally fall to such institutions as religion, profession, labor union, school, and local community. Quite apart from direct administrative action, the sheer brilliance of the fires of war has the effect of making dim all of the other lights of culture. The normal incentives of family, occupation, education, and recreation—already so weakened as the result of processes embedded in modern history—become singularly unattractive and irrelevant compared with the intoxicating incentives that arise from war and its now unlimited psychological demands. Given the quickening effects of war on social dislocation and cultural sterilization, it is not strange that the State should become, in time of war, the major refuge of men. Democracy cannot but become ever more unitary, omnicompetent, centralized.

To the imperatives of modern war must be added two other supports of the unitary, collectivist view of democracy. These are two intellectual perspectives, idols of the mind, as Francis Bacon might have called them. The first is the veneration, nurtured by countless centuries of discord, for *unity*. The second is the seemingly ineradicable faith, derived from ancient, medieval, and modern ideas of change, in *historical necessity*.

With respect to the first, it is hard to avoid the fact that unity has had, historically, a symbolic appeal greater than any possessed by the values of plurality and diversity. From the earliest Greek metaphysicians down to the present, the greatest single objective of philosophy has been that of converting plurality into unity, "chaos" into intellectual order. Mind itself has been interpreted in terms that suggest monistic sovereignty by so many philosophers. The deep religious appeal of unity in experience, the craving of all human beings for an inner sense of order, and the age-old rationalist desire to transmute the flux and diversity of experience into symmetrical schemes of meaning have all, in one way or another, contributed to the modern veneration for unity and uniformity in society.

The worship of unity offers no problems so long as it is confined to areas of aesthetics, religion, and metaphysics. But when transferred, under the stress of social dislocations, to the area of politics, it frequently becomes sinister. For then it tends to become absorbed, as an ideal, by existent structures of administrative power. The philosophical quest for unity and certainty becomes, as it were, a kind of apologetics for political standardization and centralization. It is assumed that the spiritual unity which every human being inwardly prizes can be achieved only by an environment made ever more uniform institutionally. In the present age, certainly, he who cries Unity will inevitably have more listeners than he who cries, so irrelevantly it must seem, Plurality and Diversity.

The second intellectual perspective reinforcing the unitary view of democracy is that of historical necessity. The tendency of the human mind to convert the empirical order of changes and events in history into a logical, *necessary* order gives strong support to the view that centralization and political collectivism are somehow in the ordained direction of the future even as they have been the apparent logical development of the past.

The greatest intellectual and moral offense the modern intellectual can be found guilty of is that of seeming to think or act outside what is commonly held to be the linear progress of civilization. It is not the deviation from opinions of others that is censured. Nor is it deviation from established morality, religious or secular. Among modern intellectuals the cardinal sin is that of failing to remain on the locomotive of history, to use Lenin's expressive phrase. This is the most damnable of all offenses in the modern rational mentality. Ordinary heresies, defections, and moral obliquities may be excused, but not the offense of being willfully outside the presumed course of historical realization. In practical terms, we are dealing with a habit of mind that seizes selectively upon *certain* aspects of the present age, e.g. political omnicompetence and administrative centralization, and invests these not just with the ordinary attributes of goodness or rightness, but with that far greater virtue of *necessity*.

We tend thus to subordinate our planning to an imaginary course of evolution in society. In the perspective of Progress the data of the past are necessarily ruled out of practical consideration for present planning purposes simply because, within this perspective, the past can only be likened to the infancy or youth of an organism that is now in maturity and looking toward endless intensification of maturity. History is conceived as a continuous movement, a flow, a unified process, a development, with a beginning, a middle, and a logical, ethical end. This process is regarded as inherently *selective*, always pushing what is good to the chronological front. The evil in an age is held to be no more than persistences or outcroppings of the past. Social philosophy and social planning that do not accept the "necessity" of modern changes are consequently damned as utopian or nostalgic.

The supremacy of Marxism in the modern history of socialism comes in large part from the tactical success Marx and Engels had in investing the ethical ideal of socialism with historical necessity. Other socialists had held up their ideal as something to be described in detail, planned for, and worked for. When Marx scorned such efforts as being utopian and unhistorical and insisted that the future must develop inexorably out of the present, he not only prevented any further consideration of what he contemptuously called "kitchen recipes" but also placed the ideal of socialism firmly in the context of existent trends toward national collectivism and administrative centralization. For Marx, socialism was a stage of society that must develop dialectically out of the *significant* present. Pluralism, localism, voluntary association—all of these to Marx were mere survivals of medievalism. What was *real* in the present was industrialism, collectivism, and administration centralization.

What is true of Marxian socialism has been true of a great deal of modern political and economic philosophy. As Martin Buber[6]

---

6. *Paths in Utopia* (London, 1949).

has recently reminded us, the intellectual's dread of utopianism and his pious desire to be historically "realistic" have led him generally to an all too willing subordination of moral categories to the presumed "direction" of history.

The modern facts of political mechanism, centralization, and collectivism are seen in the perspective of inevitable development in modern history. They seem to be the very direction of history itself. Present differences of political opinion hence usually resolve themselves into differences about who shall guide this developing reality and how little or how much should be administered it in the way of fuel. Any sharp alternative has the disadvantage of running up against the widely flung facts of uniformity and centralization, and the additional disadvantage of seeming to be filiated with historical conditions of the past which give it a manifestly "unprogressive" character.

The imperatives of war, the veneration of unity and uniformity, and the faith in historical necessity, with its corollary of irreversible historical processes—these, then are the most powerful supports for the unitary perspective of democracy at the present time. Given these, together with the constant diminution in the significance of the non-political areas of kinship, religion, and other forms of association, the task of centralization and omnicompetence is not too difficult even in the presence of liberal values. Given these conditions and perspectives, the transition from liberal democracy to totalitarianism will not seem too arduous or unpleasant. It will indeed be scarcely noticed, save by the "utopians," the "reactionaries," and similar eccentrics.

V

Admittedly, there is a degree of unity without which any culture, like any musical composition, would become chaotic. And there is indeed a degree of centralization of authority apart from which no structure—political government, church, or labor union—could operate. So much is true. Yet, given the society in which we now live, it is difficult not to conclude that the requirements of liberal democracy are very different from those which seemed so necessary to men of good will a century ago.

The problem of freedom and authority can no longer be given even the semblance of solution by appeals to the talisman of popular sovereignty. For, despite the unquestioned moral rightness of the proposition that all legitimate political power must flow from the people, we are living in an age in which *all* forms of government, totalitarianism as well as liberal democracy, seek to root their authority in the soil of popular acquiescence. The greatest discovery in nineteenth-century politics, as we have seen, was the principle that the real power of a State may actually be enhanced, not diminished, by widening its base to include the whole of a population. The exploitation of this revolutionary principle of power reaches its highest development in the total State where no effort is spared to drive the functions and symbols of political authority as deeply as possible into the minds and wills of all the people, thus making State power a part of human personality, a projection of the self.

POPULAR SOVEREIGNTY, THEN, is not enough. As a moral principle it must remain our point of departure, but if democracy is to remain liberal democracy, if it is not to become transmuted into the State of the masses, with its power converted into a monolith, we must face the crucial problems of the relation of political authority to all the other forms of authority in society. The reinforcement of these and their constitutional relationship to the political authority of the State become, in the present century, the major problem of democracy. Because of our single-minded concentration upon the individual as the sole unit of society and upon the State as the sole source of legitimate power, we have tended to overlook the fact that freedom thrives in cultural diversity, in local and regional differentiation, in associative pluralism, and above all, in the *diversification of power.*[7]

---

7. Works that have stressed the crucial role of associative pluralism and diversification of social power in the structure of liberal democracy are, unhappily, not numerous. It is a pleasure however to mention the writings of such men as Ernest Barker, A. D. Lindsay, John Dewey, R. M. MacIver, Lewis Mumford, Sidney Hook, and Frank Tannenbaum.

Basically, all of these are reducible, I believe, to the single massive problem of the relation of political government to the plurality of cultural associations which form the intermediate authorities of society. These are many: religious, economic, professional, local, recreational, academic, and so forth. Each of them is a structure, often large, of authorities and functions. Each of them is an organization of human purposes and allegiances related to some distinctive institutional end. Each of them is, apart from the checks provided by the existence of other and competing forms of association, potentially omnicompetent in its relation to its members. And whether it is the economic corporation, the huge labor union, or the profession, each offers, in its own way, innumerable problems of freedom and control in society. There is no unalterable guarantee of freedom in any one of them.

Nevertheless, it is the continued existence of this array of intermediate powers in society, of this plurality of "private sovereignties," that constitutes, above anything else, the greatest single barrier to the conversion of democracy from its liberal form to its totalitarian form. It is the fact of *diversity* of appeal that is foremost in this social constitution. Apart from its setting in a competitive framework, any one of these large-scale intermediate authorities is capable of expanding its own control over members to a point that exceeds the requirements of freedom. But the most notable characteristic of this whole array of social authorities in European history has been the ceaseless competition for human allegiance that goes on among them.

VI

Historically, there are to be seen in Western society recurrent waves of intermediate association.[8] In the eleventh and twelfth centuries arose the gilds, the communes, the universities, and all the other fellowships of interest and belief which, taken together, pro-

---

8. It is unfortunate that no single, systematic historical study of intermediate association exists. The nearest approximation is the massive study done by Otto von Gierke three-quarters of a century ago in Germany, but, except for the fragments translated by F. W. Maitland and Ernest Barker, this work is virtually inaccessible and, in any event, it was written from a point of view that killed much of the work's substance.

vided so much of man's protection from the vicissitudes of fortune and the despotism of kings, popes, and feudal lords. The rise of the sovereign national State, as we have seen, weakened or destroyed many of these. Doctrines of political monism and legal individualism became dominant. But these notwithstanding, we are struck by a renewed efflorescence of social and cultural associations in Western society in the seventeenth century, particularly in England—new organized professions, learned societies, and scientific associations. These have proved among the most powerful supports of cultural diversity and freedom in modern Western Europe. They were weakened in France by the Revolution, as were almost all forms of autonomous association, but in England they proved resistant to administrative centralization and Utilitarian individualism alike.

In the nineteenth century we see another great wave of association rolling over large areas of the Western world. Trade unions, benevolent societies, cooperatives, and mutual aid associations of all kinds arose spontaneously, in Europe and the United States, to meet the problems of individual security and freedom that had been created by the spread of national centralization and by the burgeoning factory system. In these associations, lying intermediate to man and the State, to the worker and market society, lay the promise of both security and freedom—security within the solidarity of associations founded in response to genuine needs; freedom arising from the very diversity of association and from the relative autonomy these associations had with respect to central systems of law and administration. These were the associations that Tocqueville saw, during his visit to the United States, as the real protections of personal liberty, the actual supports of parliamentary or representative government, and the major barriers to the peculiar and oppressive despotism he found latent in the democratic State.

Modern liberalism unfortunately has tended on the whole to step from the cherished individual of the nineteenth century to the myth of the all-benign State in the twentieth. While it has seldom been intolerant of intermediate associations, it has made little effort to formulate a theory of liberal democracy that includes them, that makes them indispensable to free, representative government. In general, modern democratic thought has settled single-mindedly upon the same elements that are crucial to the political community: the abstract individual and the State.

Yet, any careful historical examination reveals the roots political democracy has had in practice in social groups and cultural communities. Man does not live merely as one of a vast aggregate of arithmetically equal, socially undifferentiated, individuals. He does not live his life merely in terms of the procedures and techniques of the administrative State—not, at least, in a free society. As a concrete *person* he is inseparable from the plurality of social allegiances and memberships which characterize his social organization and from the diversities of belief and habit which form a culture.

Most of the tendencies in contemporary society toward the erosion of cultural differences and the standardization of cultural tastes, beliefs, and activities, which are so often charged, mistakenly, against technology and science, are the product, actually, of a centralization of authority and function and a desiccation of local and cultural associations.

The great cultural ages of the past were, almost invariably, ages of social diversity, of small, independent communities and towns, of distinct regions, of small associations which jealously guarded their unique identities and roles. In the competition and rivalry of these, as Bertrand Russell has pointed out,[9] lay the conditions of cultural energy and diversity which gave imperishable works to the world. Culturally, there is little to hope for from a world based increasingly upon mass relationships and upon the sterilization of intermediate associations.

Nor is there much to hope for in the way of freedom. "Who says liberty, says association," declared Lamennais in the early nineteenth century, and he was echoed a generation later by Proudhon: "Multiply your associations and be free."

Only through its intermediate relationships and authorities has any State ever achieved the balance between organization and personal freedom that is the condition of a creative and enduring culture. These relationships begin with the family and with the small informal social groups which spring up around common interests and cultural needs. Their number extends to the larger associations of society, to the churches, business associations, labor unions, universities, and professions. They are the real sources of liberal democracy.

The weakening of these groups reflects not only growing spiritual isolation but increasing State power. To feel alone—does this not breed a desire for association in Leviathan? The individual who has been by one force or another wrenched from social belonging is thrown back upon himself; he becomes the willing prey of those who would manipulate him as the atom citizen in the political and economic realms. Given nothing but his own resources to stand on, what can be his defenses against the powerful propaganda of those who control the principal means of communication in society? The recent history of Western Europe should remind us that a sense of the past, even more than a hope of the future, is the basis of the will to resist; and a sense of the past presupposes cultural continuities within associations which have deep moral appeal.

Only in their social interdependences are men given to resist the tyranny that always threatens to arise out of any political government, democratic or other. Where the individual stands alone in the face of the State he is helpless. "Despotism," wrote Tocqueville, "is never more secure of continuance than when it can keep men asunder; and all its influence is commonly exerted for that purpose." The desire for freedom arises only out of men's reverence for exterior and competing values. Genuine freedom is not based upon the negative psychology of release. Its roots are in positive acts of dedication to ends and values. Freedom presupposes the autonomous existence of values that men wish to be free to follow and live up

---

9. *Authority and the Individual* (London, 1949) p. 59.

to. Such values are social in the precise sense that they arise out of, and are nurtured by, the voluntary associations which men form.

VII

But neither social values nor autonomous social relationships can thrive apart from their possession of meaningful functions and authorities. We end this chapter on the theme with which it began: the centrality of the problem of power, its distribution in society, and its control. Man may be a social animal, but he does not devote himself in any serious way to groups and associations that are no longer clearly related to the larger structure of function and authority in society.

What has been so apparent in the modern history of the family will be no less apparent in the future histories of profession, university, labor union, and all other forms of association in our culture. Deprive these entities of their distinctive functions through increasing nationalization of service and welfare, divest them of the authorities over their members through increasing centralization of political power in society, and these associations, like the extended family, the church, and the local community, must shrink immeasurably in their potential contributions to culture.

Modern philosophies of freedom have tended to emphasize, as we have seen, either the individual's *release* from power of every kind—generally, through an appeal to natural rights—or the individual's *participation* in some single structure of authority like the General Will, which replaces all other structures.

But from the point of view of the real, the historical roots of liberal democracy, freedom has rested neither upon release nor upon collectivization but upon the *diversification* and the decentralization of power in society. In the division of authority and the multiplication of its sources lie the most enduring conditions of freedom. "The only safeguard against power," warned Montesquieu, "is rival power." He was echoed by Lord Acton more than a century later, who declared that "Liberty depends upon the division of power."

Freedom, it has been well said, lies in the interstices of authority. This is indeed, I believe, the real reconciliation of the demands of order and the demands of freedom. Authority, any society, any association, must have. It is simply the structure of the association. But the sole possibility of personal freedom and cultural autonomy lies in the maintenance of a plurality of authorities in any society. Each of these may be tight enough as an individual system to provide a context of security for its members. So long as there are other and competing authorities, so long as man has even the theoretical possibility of removing himself from any that for him has grown oppressive and of placing himself within the framework of some other associative authority, it cannot be said that his freedom has suffered.

It is in these terms, I think, that the role of political government becomes clear in the democracies. Not to sterilize the normal authorities of associations, as does the total State through a pre-emption of function, a deprivation of authority, and a monopolization of allegiance, but to reinforce these associations, to provide, administratively, a means whereby the normal competition of group differences is held within bounds and an environment of law within which no single authority, religious or economic, shall attain a repressive and monopolistic influence—this is the role of government in a democracy.

In what Frank Tannenbaum has well termed "the balance of institutional power" lie the possibilities for a harmonization of personal freedom and associative authority. "The road to social peace," Mr. Tannenbaum writes, "is the balance of the social institutions, and a wise statesman would strengthen those institutions that seemed to be losing ground, even if he were not addicted to them; for the only way to peace in this world of fallible human nature is to keep all human institutions strong, but none too strong; relatively weak, but not so weak as to despair of their survival. *It is only thus that peaceful irritation and strife, so essential to social and individual sanity, can be maintained.*"[10]

How can the power of the State or that of any large-scale association be limited if there do not exist authorities that are always in competition? No one can doubt that there are by now many areas of function which must come under the exclusive jurisdiction of the State. No longer can one doubt that, in modern society, mundane power over human beings will lie in the State itself. And it has become obvious that a politically planned society is, in one degree or another, absolutely essential. These points are not in question.

What is crucially important is not the residual location of power in society. Rather it is the formal administration of that power and the relation between formal public administration of political power and the administrations of the various other forms of power in society—religious, economic, educational, and the like. The philosophy of administrative centralization had its origin at a time when the extrication of the State's power from other powers in society—mostly feudal in nature—was a matter of burning importance. But this problem now belongs in the dustbin of history. There is no other institution that can seriously challenge the sovereignty of the State in the contemporary world.

Unfortunately, our philosophy of administration has not, on the whole, kept pace with the history of sovereignty. We have at the present time only the beginnings of a theory of administration to do justice to the psychological complexities of personality and culture which contemporary social science has discovered. Modern public administration has been too generally dominated by the nineteenth-century rationalist's conception of society as a vast aggregate of unconnected political particles.

It is easy—too easy—to plan for abstract aggregates of *individuals*, regarded for planning purposes as so many arithmetically equal units composed of identical drives and needs. It is far more difficult to plan for, to legislate for, *persons* who live not in simple economic or political perspectives but in complex associative and

10. "The Balance of Power in Society," *Political Science Quarterly* (December 1946) p. 501. Italics mine.

normative systems that are the product of tradition and custom. But planning blind to the autonomous groups and traditional values of a society is a planning likely to be effectuated by an administration that seeks to obliterate, for purposes of rational simplicity, these groups and values.

A distinction has grown up in the literature of applied anthropology relevant to the needs of public administration in contemporary democracies. It is the distinction between direct and indirect rule. In indirect administration every effort is made by colonial administrators to work with and through traditional relationships and lines of authority in native cultures. In direct administration, on the other hand, such relationships and authorities are disregarded, supplanted by new and more "rational" administrative relationships and powers. Not a few of the tragedies connected with Western administration of native cultures in so many areas of the world have come from the well-meaning efforts of administrators, steeped in the intellectual resources of Western political rationalism, to minister directly to the supposed life needs of natives.

Similar tragedies of "direct" administration fill the social histories of Western nations themselves. Under the spur of unitary democracy and through rationalist techniques of administrative centralization, planners and reformers have systematically disregarded local and regional cultures and the traditional social relationships and values of ethnic minorities, and have planned instead from abstract values and assumed "needs," and through channels created by fiat.

It has been one of the deficiencies of much public administration in Western democracies that little distinction has been made between the demands of sovereignty and the possibilities of governmental administration. Sovereignty, we may agree with every major political philosopher since Bodin, is unitary, absolute, and imprescriptible. This is as true in democracy as in any other type of government. No other conception of State authority has been feasible since the breakup of the medieval synthesis. In power the contemporary State is, and must be, *sui generis*. Not all the semantic analyses of misguided pluralists or the adjurations of moralists will change this fact.

But the centrality of sovereignty does not lead logically to the centralization of administration in public affairs. Because the theory and practice of modern administration arose at a time when sovereignty itself was struggling for supremacy against inherited structures of feudal power, it was perhaps inevitable that early conceptions of governmental administration should have been based upon the example of military government. But the residual power of the State is today no longer seriously questioned. The political relationship is as central as was the relationship of the Church in the thirteenth century. Decentralization of administration is not merely feasible technically; it is a prime necessity of free culture.

David Lilienthal is an eloquent public servant who has discovered from practical experience that administrative decentralization is absolutely indispensable to modern democracies if they are not to become victims of the creeping totalitarianism inherent in administrative monopoly and centralization. The Tennessee Valley Authority is itself a magnificent illustration of the basic compatibility between democratic government and administrative decentralization. With all allowance for its errors and for the impatience of certain disciples of centralization, TVA demonstrates that central planning is not inconsistent with local and associative autonomies. We readily admit that planning in terms of aggregates of abstract individuals, conceived in the image of Economic Man, is much easier than planning in terms of existent families, professional associations, labor unions, churches, and regions. But such planning is the surest avenue to an eventual sterilization of the moral appeal of these unities. And from the decline of these and similar associations can come only the cultural atomization that leads to irresistible power.

Planning that dispenses with the autonomous, traditional values of a population can be effectuated only by a system of administration that is eventually forced to liquidate these values. For these will then constitute forces of distraction, even of subversion, to the abstract ends of planning.

The assumption that centralized power must carry with it centralized administration was tenable only in a day when the range of governmental activities was limited. It is no longer tenable. As government, in its expanding range of functions, comes ever closer to the primary spheres of man's existence, the need is intensified for a theory of public administration alive to the fact that the necessary roots of democracy are in the decisions and responsibilities of the people diversified in regions, communities, and associations.

"Centralization in administration," David Lilienthal has written, "promotes remote and absentee control, and thereby increasingly denies to the individual the opportunity to make decisions and to carry those responsibilities by which human personality is nourished and developed. I find it impossible to comprehend how democracy can be a living reality if people are remote from their government and in their daily lives are not made a part of it, or if the control and direction of making a living—in industry, farming, the distribution of goods—is far removed from the stream of life and from the local community. 'Centralization' is no mere technical matter of 'management,' of 'bigness versus smallness.' We are dealing here with those deep urgencies of the human spirit which are embodied in the faith we call 'democracy.'"[11]

VIII

We cannot be reminded too often that the stifling effects of centralization upon society are as evident in large-scale private industry as they are in political government. Big government and big business have developed together in Western society, and each has depended on the other. To these two has been added more recently a third force in society—big labor. In all three spheres, and,

---

11. T.V.A.: *Democracy on the March* (New York, 1944), p. 139.

for that matter in our universities, charities, and various other activities, there is a strong tendency to organize administration in terms of the ideas of power inherited from the seventeenth and eighteenth centuries.

But there is a point beyond which centralized administration cannot go if the meaning and urgency of the ends of any association are to be kept alive in the minds of the individuals who comprise the association. Bertrand Russell has recently written: "In a highly organized world, personal initiative connected with a group must be confined to a few unless the group is small. If you are a member of a small committee you may reasonably hope to influence its decisions. In national politics, where you are one of some twenty million voters, your influence is infinitesimal unless you are exceptional or occupy an exceptional position. You have, it is true, a twenty-millionth share in the government of others, but only a twenty-millionth share in the government of yourself. You are therefore much more conscious of being governed than of governing. The government becomes in your thoughts a remote and largely malevolent 'they,' not a set of men whom you, in concert with others who share your opinions, have chosen to carry out your wishes. Your individual feeling about politics, in these circumstances, is not that intended to be brought about by democracy, but much more nearly what it would be under a dictatorship."[12]

It will be recognized at once that planning and administration in terms of decentralization, localism, and associative autonomy is far more difficult than administration carried on under the myth of territorial masses of discrete individual atoms. Not only does it go against the tendency of the whole history of modern economic, educational, and political administration, but, on its own terms, it raises problems of organization that are immense. "It is obvious," Karl Mannheim wrote, "that the modern nature of social techniques puts a premium on centralization, but this is only true if our sole

---

12. Op. cit. p. 98.

criterion is to be technical efficiency. If, for various reasons, chiefly those concerned with the maintenance of personality, we deliberately wish to decentralize certain activities within certain limits, we can do so."[13]

What Lewis Mumford has written in *The Culture of Cities* is eloquent and irrefutable. "We need, in every part of the city, units in which intelligent and cooperative behavior can take the place of mass regulations, mass decisions, mass actions, imposed by ever remoter leaders and administrators. Small groups: small classes: small communities: institutions framed to the human scale, are essential to purposive behavior in modern society. Very stupidly we have overlooked the way in which large units limit opportunity all along the line: not merely by physical friction of space, or the burden of a vast mechanical and administrative overhead, but also by diminishing opportunities for people with special capacities. Thus Sir Raymond Unwin has pointed out that twenty communities with a population of fifty thousand people would not merely be more adequately governed, probably, than one city that contained a million: it would, for example, give an opportunity for twenty mayors or city managers, against one in the big center. This rule holds true in every other part of society. We demand the impossible in the way of direction and specialized service from a few people, and we fail to demand the possible from those who are better equipped to handle adequately a smaller job. With our overgrown institutions, overgrown colleges, overgrown corporations, overgrown cities, is it any wonder that we easily become the victims of propaganda machines, routineers, and dictators?"[14]

The passage from Mr. Mumford's book makes it plain that the necessity of decentralization is by no means confined to the structure of the political State, great as the need there may be. Decentralization is just as necessary in the operation of the other great associations of modern society—the industrial corporation, the

---

13. *Man and Society in an Age of Reconstruction* (New York, 1940) p. 319.

labor union, the large church, the profession, and the great university. More than a little of the diminution in the psychological and cultural influence of these associations in recent times results from their failure to remain responsive to the small areas of association and collectivization we see in politics. The fault lies in the common failure to unite the broad purposes of the larger associations with the small, informal relationships composing them.

THE LABOR UNION, THE LEGAL or medical association, or the church will become as centralized and as remote as the national State itself unless these great organizations are rooted in the smaller relationships which give meaning to the ends of the large associations. To conceive of a great labor union, industrial enterprise, or church as an association of *individual* members is but to intensify the processes of atomization which such associations can and should counteract. No large association will remain an object of personal allegiance, no matter how crucial its goals may be, unless it is constantly sensitive to the existence of the informal but potent relationships of which it is really composed. It has surely become evident by this time that the most successful and allegiance-evoking business enterprises and cultural associations in modern life are those that regard themselves as associations of *groups*, not of raw individuals. To recognize the existence of informal social relationships, to keep central purposes constantly alive in these small groups, and to work toward the increased spontaneity and autonomy of these groups is, I believe, the cardinal responsibility of the great private association.

Only thus will the large formal associations remain important agencies of order and freedom in democracy. Only thus will they succeed in arresting and banishing the augmenting processes of insecurity and moral isolation which now paralyze individual wills and strike at the roots of stable culture.

---

14. *The Culture of Cities* (New York, 1938), p. 475–6.

There is a vast difference between the type of planning—whether in the large State, industry, or the school—that seeks to enmesh the individual in a custodial network of detailed rules for his security and society's stability, and the type of planning that is concerned with the creation of a political and economic *context* within which the spontaneous associations of men are the primary sources of freedom and order. The latter type of planning is compatible with competition, diversity, rivalry, and the normative conflicts that are necessary to cultural creativity. The former type is not.

IX

I cannot help thinking that what we need above all else in this age is a new philosophy of *laissez faire*. The old *laissez faire* failed because it was based on erroneous premises regarding human behavior. As a theory it failed because it mistook for ineradicable characteristics of individuals qualities that were in fact inseparable from social groups. As a policy it failed because its atomistic propositions were inevitably unavailing against the reality of enlarging masses of insecure individuals. Far from proving a check upon the growth of the omnicompetent State, the old *laissez faire* actually accelerated this growth. Its indifference to every form of community and association left the State as the sole area of reform and security.

We need a *laissez faire* that will hold fast to the ends of autonomy and freedom of choice; one that will begin not with the imaginary, abstract individual but with the personalities of human beings as they are actually given to us in association. "What we actually see in the world is not on the one hand the State, and on the other, a mass of unrelated individuals; but a vast complex of gathered unions, in which alone we find individuals, families, clubs, trade unions, colleges, professions, and so forth."[15]

To create the conditions within which autonomous *individuals* could prosper, could be emancipated from the binding ties of kinship,

---

15. J. N. Figgis, *Studies in Political Thought from Gerson to Grotius*, second edition (Cambridge, 1923) p. 70.

class, and community, was the objective of the older *laissez faire*. To create conditions within which *autonomous groups* may prosper must be, I believe, the prime objective of the new *laissez faire*.

I use the word create advisedly. We should not suppose that the *laissez faire* individualism of the middle nineteenth century was the simple heritage of nature, the mere untrammeled emergence of drives and motivations with which man is naturally endowed. *Laissez faire,* as the economic historian, Polanyi, among others, has emphasized, was *brought* into existence.[16]

It was brought into existence by the planned destruction of old customs, associations, villages and other securities; by the force of the State throwing the weight of its fast-developing administrative system in favor of new economic elements of the population. And it was brought into existence, hardly less, by reigning systems of economic, political, and psychological thought, systems which neglected altogether the social and cultural unities and settled single-mindedly on the abstract individual as the proper unit of speculation and planning. What we need at the present time is the knowledge and administrative skill to create a *laissez faire* in which the basic unit will be the social group.

The liberal values of autonomy and freedom of personal choice are indispensable to a genuinely free society, but we shall achieve and maintain these only by vesting them in the conditions in which liberal democracy will thrive—diversity of culture, plurality of association, and division of authority.

16. *The Great Transformation* (New York, 1944) passim.

PART TWO

Witnesses

CHAPTER 8

Midge Decter

Commentary by Edwin J. Feulner Jr. (1995)

Scourge of feminist dogma, puncturer of liberal pretensions, diviner of social trends, essayist of uncommon power, and advocate for the free world, Midge Decter is the first lady of neoconservatism and one of the most influential social critics of our times. Her restless energy and moral clarity have placed her at the center of controversies from the battle of the sexes to the balance of world power. Midge Decter is a New York intellectual of impeccable credentials who turned her back on the trendy moral anarchy of New York intellectualism. Knowing the methods and motivations of the liberal literati, she has consistently defeated them in their own backyard.

Her "overriding conviction," says Thomas Edwards of the *New York Times,* is that "our anxious interest in the New, the fashions, movements and 'revolutions' that keep demanding radical alterations in ourselves and our expectations, is socially and personally destructive." That is a fine definition of conservatism—neo- or otherwise. Midge Decter expounds this conviction with a self-assured candor that is as endearing to her friends as it is infuriating to her opponents.

On affirmative action: "The core of affirmative action, and its presumption of guilt, is a lot of baloney. And it has created this truculent sense of grievance on the part of middle-class American women who live better than 99 percent of all women on the Earth."

On single mothers: "If we are talking about thirteen and fourteen year olds, the answer is to stop sleeping around ... What is needed is not a new government program, but a new ethos—one in which these little girls will be encouraged to keep their knees together until they grow up and find husbands."

On black anti-Semitism: "Minister Farrakhan and his imitators claim to be offering a new kind of strength and discipline to their flocks, but they are in fact merely rearranging the terms of servitude: Get off drugs, and get yourself a substitute dependency on hatred ... In other words, the Jews as methadone."

Midge Decter's high-impact prose has earned the respect even of those she skewers. One critic refers to her "resourceful, carefully modulated prose and shrewd talent for scoring debating points." Another concludes that Decter "has a way of forcing unwelcome issues. To differ with her is always an exercise in critical thinking."

Midge Decter has had a career of great influence in otherwise liberal institutions, including a stint as executive editor at *Harper's.* It is difficult, but pleasing, to imagine the culture shock that must have resulted. At *Harper's,* she recounts, the office was taken over by a gang of young Libbies. While one was truly competent, the others "were always carrying on, handing around articles—Have you read this?—and instantly all the young men got terrorized and started walking on eggs. Finally I got up and said, 'Okay, if there's going to be lib in this office, nobody's allowed to cry anymore.'"

Though she was born on July 25, 1927, in St. Paul, Minnesota, Midge Decter's ambitions always centered on New York. After leaving the University of Minnesota in her first year and "working through a series of girlish fantasies—I wanted to die on the barricades in Palestine"—she arrived in Manhattan a nineteen-year-old with no job and few prospects. The job she found was as an office

assistant at *Commentary,* then a liberal magazine: "One semester
of typing in high school saved my life."

At *Commentary* she proved a talent for writing and thinking
beyond her typing skills and began a series of contributions to that
publication which has lasted forty-four years. It was here she also
met a young writer named Norman Podhoretz, who courted and
married her, establishing a conservative husband and wife team
rivaled in influence only by Irving Kristol and Gertrude Himmelfarb.

For both Decter and Podhoretz, the 1960s were a decisive
decade. Midge Decter considered herself a liberal anti-Communist.
She opposed the Vietnam War, but then had the eye-opening experience of meeting other intellectuals who also opposed it. "I thought
that the war was imprudent. They thought the United States was
like Nazi Germany."

At the same time, Decter was also questioning the outcome of
the sexual and social revolutions of the 1960s. "I found that the
funny stuff I played around with was actually dangerous to my children. I saw their friends dropping like flies. I got scared."

By the end of the decade, "I had broken with all that." Decter
believes that cultural leftism and foreign policy leftism are part of
the same intellectual trend. Both reject that the United States is "a
just and good society." Her disillusionment with liberalism added
a persuasive voice to the growing neoconservative movement—
former liberals like Kristol, Podhoretz, Peter Berger, and Michael
Novak, who were discovering the bankruptcy of modern American
liberal thought. As a group they were uniquely qualified to engage
their former allies. "We were better able to fight the left," says
Decter. "We know them better."

In the late 1960s, Midge Decter became executive editor at
Harper's, where she worked with a stable of writers including David
Halberstam and Norman Mailer. In 1974, she was offered a posi-
tion as senior editor at Basic Books. "I knew nothing about book
publication. I did not even know the language they were using. But
I knew one thing. I had to get my hands on Thomas Sowell and

George Gilder." It turns out this was enough. Decter fought hard
to get Gilder's *Wealth and Poverty* a first printing of five thousand
books. It became Basic's first bestseller in a decade and President
Reagan's favorite bedside reading.

In addition to raising four children, Midge Decter has written a
series of landmark articles in *Commentary, Esquire, Partisan
Review, Harper's, Newsweek,* and *Policy Review.* She has been the
Executive Director of the Committee for the Free World, a fellow
at the Institute on Religion and Public Life, a member of the advisory board of Radio Martí, and a member of The Heritage Foundation Board of Trustees since 1981.

Midge Decter has made at least three major contributions to the
development of conservatism in America: an insightful, timely critique of feminism; a resolute defense of democracy against tyranny; and a keen understanding of those commitments which unite
every element of the conservative movement.

Decter argues that radical feminism is not a demand for freedom,
but a form of escape from freedom. "Freedom is only freedom. It's
not happiness. It gives you a tremendous amount of responsibility."
But feminism does not embrace the anxious burden of this responsibility; it tries to evade it with talk of victimization and demands
for special treatment. "This mass litany of complaints … is the
biggest put-down of women in the century. They say they're hand-
icapped, crippled, and can't compete with men because the culture
has twisted their minds. It's just not so. The movement wants
women to set no value on themselves, to ask for handouts and
special treatment."

Quotas in particular symbolize this trend. "They're expressions
of self-hate. You have a woman hired as part of a quota, both the
employer and this woman herself will have contempt for her
achievement." "In all major areas of their lives—work, sex, marriage and motherhood—women must now create arrangements that
will help them evade all adult responsibility," she concludes.

Decter's argument extends beyond a critique of feminism to a
defense of family. "Making a family has come to be seen as mere-

ly another of life's options." The women's movement depicts marriage as enslavement. The environmental movement says that human population is destroying the earth. The result is a pervasive "anti-natalism" which complicates the essential work of families. "It is more difficult to lean against a social wind than to protect oneself from a hurricane."

The family is not something to be sentimentalized. There is simply no adequate alternative, but "This doesn't mean we have to praise Aunt Sophie." "Suddenly we have to say, 'The family is good.' Come on, the family is a pain ... But they are necessary and better than the alternative. To revere motherhood is just the obverse of vilifying it. It isn't glorious and it isn't torture. It just is what it is. Most women find life incomplete without it, so it becomes a necessity."

The basic problem, as Decter sees it, is that we can no longer accept our basic natures as men and women. "We are completely at home with the complexities of technology and completely at sea with our own natures as human beings." "Our inability to live any longer in a natural, unthinking relation to what is the very ground of our being is the symptom as well as the source of a very serious social dislocation."

Midge Decter has also been a clear, consistent voice for American values and American strength in the conduct of American foreign policy, a topic she calls "my particular interest." In the 1970s, she had been a vocal critic of Nixon's détente and of Carter's appeasement of Brezhnev. In 1980, she left Basic Books to found the Committee for the Free World.

At the time, there was clearly a need for an organization of pro-Western intellectuals who saw the Soviet system as a real threat to our basic freedoms. The Congress for Cultural Freedom, with similar aims, had folded much earlier when its CIA funding was revealed. Decter decided that the Committee for the Free World would take no government funds under any circumstances.

In 1981, the Committee issued a tough manifesto and gathered a select group of influential supporters. "Over the years," Decter says, "we had no money but made a lot of noise." In particular, the

Committee criticized lopsided arms control treaties and supported anti-Communist movements such as the Contras in Nicaragua.

With the end of the Cold War, the Committee for the Free World declared victory and voluntarily disbanded, having done much to ensure the conditions of its own demise. But Decter continues to speak out on America's place in the world, calling for a new strategic doctrine to guide our actions. "I for one am prepared to say that such a doctrine, when it arrives, will bear a powerful resemblance to something called 'Pax Americana' ... Pax Americana will not be some dark imperialist conspiracy; the further we carry the force of American political culture and spread the influence of American political institutions, the better place the world will be. Russians know that, Ukrainians know that, Poles know that. Why don't we know it? Once again, the main job of convincing people about the legitimacy of American aims will be here at home—and that job is up to us."

Finally, Midge Decter has became a bridge between the various strains of conservatism. Soviet communism was once the enemy which united the modern conservative movement. With its collapse, can that unity be preserved? It is a question Decter asked in 1990: "Are we a group of friends, a family? Or are we a long, sour marriage held together for the kids and now facing an empty nest?"

Decter concludes we are a family, but with a different set of challenges. The challenge of "smug, lazy, ignorant misreporting" by the media. The challenge of enlightened education that leaves children in the dark. The challenge of a cultural elite that is actively undermining the idea of culture. The challenge of racism, cultivated by affirmative action and multiculturalism.

All these challenges are expressions of a "culture war" which calls attention to the "moral component of our domestic discontents." Ronald Reagan's victory, Decter says, was "not so much a wish for radical new policies as an open declaration of war over the culture. And a culture war, as the liberals understood far better than did their conservative opponents, is a war to the death. For a culture war is not a battle over policy, though policy in many cases gives it expression; it is rather a battle about matters of the spirit."

She sees common ground for conservatives in a basic question: "Are all Americans to be paid the minimal respect owing to a free people of being appropriately rewarded or penalized for their actual conduct?" On this common ground the old divisions among conservatives increasingly make no sense. For example, Decter questions the continued usefulness of the word neoconservative. There isn't neoconservatism any more. It is not new. It is just conservatism. It is a point made by the liberal writer Sidney Blumenthal. "The neoconservatives may breed conservatives, who have never known the joy of disillusionment, but not neoconservatives. Generational experience cannot be replicated."

In the early 1980s, Midge Decter gave a landmark speech titled, "Is the West in Danger?" in which she refers to a news photograph of a college student at an antiwar protest. He carried a sign reading: "Nothing is worth dying for." Midge's response is worth quoting in full:

> We desperately do not wish for him to die. But his announcement on that placard is an announcement about more than the draft, more than nuclear weapons, more than war. He who says there is nothing worth dying for says there is nothing worth living for.
>
> We, as a society, have some measure of responsibility for the message on that placard, for the fact that a young American—the healthiest, luckiest, most tenderly treated young man in history ... we have a responsibility for the fact he could find nothing of value save his own skin: neither mother, nor father, nor kith, nor kin, nor country, nor God ... Until we take it upon ourselves to make that boy a free man—both: free and a man, the continued survival of our freedom as a nation will not be assured.

That, in part, is the subject of this essay. How did the children of the 1960s—the most privileged children in the most privileged society in history—grow up to repudiate the values that made our personal and corporate success possible in the first place? How did they become so grossly self-regarding and so "incapable of facing, tolerating or withstanding difficulties of any kind?"

Midge Decter finds fault in her own post-war generation, which hoped to spare their children the hardships they knew. In the process, they became permissive and indulgent. "We refused to assume ... one of the central obligations of parenthood: to make ourselves the final authority on good and bad, right and wrong, and to take the consequences of what might turn out to be a life-time battle." An enlightened, liberal society raised its children to believe that everything was possible and nothing was necessary. "At home they were taught much about life, except that they would one day be assuming responsibility for their own. In school, they were taught much about the world, except that it was a place in which they would one day have to make a living."

In a review of *Liberal Parents, Radical Children,* from which "A Letter to the Young" is taken, Sara Sanborn wrote in 1975 that it was too early to judge the future of a generation only in its twenties. It is not too early now. Its representatives have gone on to become professors, pundits, politicians, and even a president. And they carry all the baggage of their era.

This essay is not so much about today's children, often more conservative than their parents, but about yesterday's children— Baby Boomers who will carry the banner of bankrupt liberal thought into the twenty-first century. Midge Decter calls the Clintons part of the "postwar spawn in America who grew to adulthood believing themselves to be uniquely endowed with superior qualities of heart and mind." "They took the election of 1992 to mean that they—whether in government or in some other sector of society—had at last been put into power, and on that happy account the country would now be made over and made new in their own sensitive, idealistic, and altogether wonderful image." But it is clearly arrogance without accomplishment—the elitism of a failed elite.

Yet, though the focus of this essay is the "destructive generation" of the 1960s, there is much timeless wisdom here as well.
Decter is talking about the obligations that every generation owes
to the next. She is teaching a lesson about the most fundamental
conservative act: passing character to children. Decter warns of a
"charade of trivial freedoms" and argues that standards are the
"training ground and proving ground for true independence." Her
"Letter to the Young" is an affirmation of the conservative belief
that preserving a civilization depends on the cultivation of moral
discipline among children, "the long, slow slogging effort that is
the only route to genuine maturity of mind and feeling."

I first met Midge Decter in 1979 at my office in the old Heritage
Foundation building on Stanton Park. Her common sense and practical approach had a certain street smarts that, in many respects,
was the opposite of a Buckley "born to mingle with the elites," or
a Kirk "born to be an intellectual hermit in the splendid isolation
of Mecosta." She ties her insights to the concrete realities of life—
motherhood, marriage, striving, and hoping—and argues without
illusions and without fear.

Her lectures at Heritage Board meetings and seminars are eagerly awaited. But the contribution for which I am particularly grateful is more private. Over the years, she has given me the benefit of
her advice on how rifts between conservatives could be healed. I
vividly remember a series of meetings early in the 1980s in which
the neoconservatives and the New Right came together to see if they
could understand one another. It was Midge who made that effort
work. And it has been Midge who has bridged chasms on many
other occasions.

In her running battle with utopian liberalism, Midge Decter for
a generation has given intellectual force to the evolving conservative
orthodoxy on a variety of issues and, more importantly, principles:
from social policy to foreign policy. And all of us are left with a better understanding of the role a truly free and liberated woman can
play in the conservative movement and in American society.

In her 1994 Erasmus Lecture, Midge Decter outlined two essential conservative beliefs. The first is "the taking of responsibility for what one does and what one is." The second is a belief in God. "For Jews the real questions are not, does He exist, and if so, who is He, but rather only, what is it that He wants of us? He has, to be sure, answered this question, not only in his Scripture but in the very constitution of our natures: to choose life, to be fruitful and multiply, and to walk in his ways."

This truth is much more than political, but it is not less than political. "It requires one to renounce the arrogant rejection of God's world that many liberals, particularly young ones, call by the name of idealism." It also brings together people who once imagined they had little in common. "The rediscovery of God … was for most of us more like a long climb up a steep hill than a flash of lightning. And among other things it was to bring us into a new and largely unfamiliar community of conservative fellows. It would be hard to say who was more surprised, nonplused and possibly to some extent also amused, by this new association, the old conservatives or their new neoconservative allies."

These thoughts occurred to her, she recalls, on a visit to Jerusalem in a moment of reflection overlooking its ancient skyline. As a child in St. Paul, she had been disturbed by the anti-Semitic taunts of young boys from a Catholic school named Nativity. In that Jerusalem evening, she saw something with great clarity. "I understood with my senses instead of merely with my head how truly dependent on one another Jews and Christians really are—in a world in which they are both so dangerously surrounded by barbarians, Christian and Jewish barbarians among them. The little girl from St. Paul has come a long way and so, I keep hoping and believing, have at least some of the boys from Nativity."

Midge Decter

A Letter to the Young

MY DEAR CHILDREN,
    I salute you this way despite the fact that as the world has always reckoned these things you are no longer entitled to be called children. Most of you are in your twenties by now, some perhaps even in your thirties. Some of you have children of your own. Yet you are still our children not only in terms of the technical definition of a generation but because we are still so far from having closed our parental accounts with you. We are still so far, that is, from having completed that *rite de passage* after which, having imparted to you the ways of our tribe, we feel free to invite you to join the company of its fully accredited adult members.

I am not so foolish as to suppose that you will be moved or even particularly beguiled by the idea that this is most of all being addressed to you. For one thing, you do not in general appear to be very easily moved and certainly not very readily beguiled, or so anyway has been the experience of those of us who encounter you daily. For another thing, there have by now been so many books addressed to you, directly and indirectly—addressed to you, written for you, written by you, written about you: nothing in your after all rather brief lives, it seems, has gone unnoted, unrecorded,

---

From Midge Decter, *Liberal Parents, Radical Children* (1975). The ornament on p. 248 indicates the deletion of two paragraphs, as specified by the author.

or unspoken. So you have no doubt, and with considerable justice, come more or less routinely to expect that you should be at the center of the concern of people like me.

I am a member of what must be called America's professional, or enlightened, liberal middle class. Though you were once taken to represent the whole of your age group, it is no longer a secret that perhaps the most celebrated youth in history—you, variously known as "our young people," "the kids," or simply "the young"— are none other than the offspring, both literally and figuratively, of this class. Not all of us, to be sure, are professionals. Some of us are businessmen, or the employees of businessmen, some the employees of government, and some ladies and gentlemen of leisure. Yet it is as certain that we are members of a common group—social critics have taken to calling us, usefully if not precisely, the "new class"—as that you are our children. You indeed, and our common property in you, are the primary means by which we make known our connection to one another. You all recognize this, of course, at least unconsciously (unconsciously is the only way most Americans in any case permit themselves to know what they truly know about class). Thus you would have little reason to take in any way but perfectly for granted my preoccupation with you.

Nor do I suppose that you will do much more than nod, hopefully politely, at the announcement that the book which is being addressed to you is not only about yourselves but in equal measure about the conduct of your parents. You have long been in the habit of explaining yourselves by reference to your parents; in fact, you tend to think about them and speak of them all the time—more often, I think, and in a more intimate connection to your own attitudes and behavior, than any young people before you.

❦

Now, you would assuredly have your comforters, both among your contemporaries and among mine, who would absolve you of the need for paying serious attention to me. "She is generalizing," they might say. "She speaks of no one. She has no data, no studies, no documentation to bear her out." This is the inevitable peril for anyone who seeks to discuss the world through the medium of his or her own senses. It is doubly the peril for anyone who seeks to say that the evidence of his or her own senses is at odds with all the things most piously and popularly being said. Still, I ask you to consider: if the studies, the data, the expert opinions had succeeded in illuminating what has been going on with you, our "young people," over the past decade or so, why would we all feel—as we all undeniably do—that there is still everything left to say? Why would what I have called the pious and popular explanations of our condition not long ago have satisfied our need to understand it? Why would we, in contemplation of ourselves, still be so indefatigably cheerless—you perhaps even more than I? I submit that the desperate desire of so many people to talk about themselves, to describe what they really feel—a desire for which the members of your generation have given possibly even more evidence than the members of mine—grows precisely out of a tacit acknowledgment that we have failed as a community, parents and children, to find a truthful and satisfying general description of ourselves. The solemn theories we have latched onto about you, whether they be political, ideological, or psychological theories, have not illuminated our problem. Nor have the voluminous accounts that you have so far given of yourselves.

I would caution you generally, in fact, about accepting any further counsel from those who would seek to absolve you of what might be considered difficult or unpleasant tasks, tempting as such counsel might be. Your would-be comforters, those who have so loudly and for so long professed to be your friends, have deceived you. They have deceived you not only about the nature of the world in which you have recently attained to adulthood but about their relation to you as well. Most of them have rushed to make a blanket allowance for you without even bothering to understand the nature of the behavior they have been so passionately intent on tolerating. In other words, they may have praised, but they have not really respected, you.

Take the case of your professors. They told you, they told themselves, they told the rest of us, that you were the brightest, most gifted generation they or the world had ever seen. We should have been delighted. Why, then, were we not? For we were not—not you, not we, and least of all those who made the claim. You were surely bright and gifted—that was plain to see—but you seemed so infernally content to remain exactly as you were, so passive and resisting in the face of all the exciting possibility that the world around you ought to have represented to you. You were bright and gifted, but you were also taking yourselves out of school in numbers, and under circumstances, that first bewildered and then alarmed us.

The answer, we were told, was that you were too good to suffer all the uninspired, dreary, conventional impositions being made upon your minds and spirits. Your professors said that your indictment of your studies, and particularly of the institutions in which you were pursuing them, was a just one. It was your very wisdom, they proclaimed, which had brought you to make the indictment in the first place. Moreover, they hurried to abet you, those of you who managed to remain in school, in your demand to be taught only that which would reflect and deepen your own sense of yourselves.

Yet still you did not prosper—nor did we, nor did they. For as it happens, your indictment of your studies was *not* a just one. Nor could it have accounted for the malaise that you as students were suffering from. In any case, what your admiring professors did not tell you was that your attitude to the university was helping to reflect and deepen *their* sense of *them*selves. In your challenge to the value of their work they found the echo of some profound bad conscience, some need to be disburdened of an unfulfilled responsibility to you. Thus the comfort of their self-abasing tolerance was cold comfort indeed. And what in the end—one may well ask—did it avail you?

Or take another case, in some ways a more important and interesting one: that of all the journalists and critics and commentators who spent the better part of a decade discussing you. They told you, they told themselves, they told the rest of us, that you were the most idealistic generation they or the world had ever seen. Everything about you, everything you did, was ascribed to an unprecedented new accession of idealistic zeal. You were the "constituency of conscience," no longer willing, like your corrupt and self-serving elders, to countenance injustice. Some of these critics and commentators said you were actually a new breed of people, the result of a strange and wonderful new stage in social evolution. You had come, they told us, to lead our society out of evil—the evil of a rampant, heedless materialism that was threatening to infect the whole world with a frenzied quest for ever and ever greater wealth, up to the point of extinguishing even life itself. You had come also— it was really the same mission—to bring peace. At any cost, it was said, you were determined to bring to an end the mindless violence, lust, and greed that had sickened Western society through the long centuries of its ascent into technological splendor and spiritual squalor.

You as the exemplars of this new selflessness, and we as your parents—not to mention the entire society that was about to be so redeemed—should have been deeply gratified: you, for the recognition of your high motives, rarely extended to those engaged in working a noble transformation, and we, for the simple fact that we had sired you. What we all felt, however, was not gratification but anxiety—a peculiar and unremitting sensation of distress. For if you were out to remake the world, you seemed on the other hand to be unsuited for its most rudimentary forms of challenge. You were hanging out in gangs, obedient to group consensus down to the last detail of dress and manner, on the basis of an agreement whose first principle was that neither the strength nor the duration of anyone's fellow feeling should be put to any sort of stringent test. Your philosophy of existence called for a level of private demand coupled with a regimen of self-scrutiny and self-expression such as, when acted upon, threatened fairly to blot out the very materiality

of others; and you were taking yourselves off into rural or urban—
or simply psychic—wildernesses where you sometimes could not
even literally be found, let alone followed. And above all, you
seemed to find it difficult if not impossible to touch the world at
just those tangents where its real work was being done and its real
decisions being made.

The answer, we were told, was that you were too sensitive and
caring, too much in tune with a higher order of values, to allow
yourselves to be dragged into the terms of our brutish common existence. It was your very superiority, said the critics and commentators, your very refusal to tolerate the cruelty and inhumanity of the
acquisitive life which had brought you to turn your backs on it.
What the pundits did not tell you was that their passionate advocacy of your attitudes was the material with which they themselves
were attempting to forge a powerful and well-paid position in the
world. Your hanging back from the contest, in other words, had
become the stuff of their own determined effort to win it. No wonder they beatified you: and no wonder your anxiety persisted.

Finally, there was our deception, your parents' deception, of you,
the most kindly meant but cruelest deception of all. We told you,
we told ourselves, and we told one another, that the so-called new
style of life you were inventing for yourselves was some kind of
great adventure in freedom. However we responded to it, whether
with approval, anger, or anguished tears, we consented to call your
expression of attitude toward us and toward the world we were
offering you by the name of rebellion. You were indeed speaking
in the language of rebellion and making certain of its gestures. But
if you were, as you liked to put it, busily intent on "doing your own
thing," you were also continuing to allow us to pay your bills. No
matter how high or far you flew, beneath you always you and we
together had seen to it that our parental net would be stretching—
a financial net, a physical, and above all, an emotional one. The
truth is that your freedom, your rebellion, even your new
"life-styles" were based on a fiction, the kind of fiction that gets

constructed between people who are, for their own separate reasons, engaged in denying the facts. We wrung our hands in the fictional pose of those abandoned, and continued to write out our checks and proffer the abundance of our homes and hands, no questions asked.

It may not have seemed to you that we were praising or comforting you, but there was great flattery in our treatment of you nonetheless, flattery of you and flattery of ourselves. We flattered you in agreeing to call every manifestation of disorderliness on your part, no matter how aimless or short-lived, a symptom of your stern rebelliousness; and we flattered ourselves with the notion that we were doing our very utmost to behave magnanimously.

Such, my dear children, was the admiration and encouragement of you that resounded through the American air of the 1960s. Who can be surprised that it has cheered you or benefited you so little? If there is any consolation to you in such a thought, it has cheered and benefited your parents even less.

Here we are, then. You are now full-grown, your lives becoming more and more fixed; and we have reached the point where it is no longer any use to deny to ourselves that we are middle aged. And we are, all of us, left with a truly terrible need to understand why life became what it did for you.

It is of course a platitude lying heavy on the public tongue that people need to understand themselves and one another. We chant this platitude daily in our country, like a salute to the flag, and, I expect, are about as deeply touched by it. I say that the members of my generation need to understand what has happened to our children over the past decade, and that the members of your generation, if you are to make satisfactory lives for yourselves, need to understand it even more, and as I write the words, I can almost hear the cadences of boredom in which by now they march into the mind. How can I impress upon you—so impervious behind all your strategies of retreat and passive knowingness—the present urgency of the need I am referring to?

I invite you to look long and well into the faces of your mothers and fathers. You will see there the feigned control of people who have long been whistling in the dark and whose lips are now fixed in a pucker from behind which no further sound can issue. From one end of this country to the other, in each of the comfortable suburbs and fashionable neighborhoods that have been settled by the members of the "new class," are to be found people of my age huddling together from time to time in a great common bewilderment. What, finally, they are asking one another—and in the asking, creating the first basic vocabulary of an honest community language—has gone wrong with the children? No disputes, public or private, no ideological schisms interrupt the almost telepathic flow of gestures, signals, shrugs, sighs through which the parents of The Young are able to communicate to one another the harrowing tales of their disappointment and worry for the future.

Two women, barely acquainted, meet over some luncheon table. "How is your son X or your daughter Y?" one of them, in an ordinary effort at polite conversation, asks the other. With the reply, My son is in San Francisco, or perhaps it will be, My son is in Arizona, or My daughter has left school, or has returned to school, or has returned home and is thinking about what she might do—with whatever reply might be forthcoming, the two women will suddenly have come upon a common ground of empathy and interest. They may share nothing else, but between them now—with regard to what was once the most intimate but has become the most readily available of subjects—there has collected a whole unspoken but highly meaningful set of references. One of these women is telling the other what the other might, with only a minor adjustment of details, in turn be telling her: the children, having had every advantage pressed upon them, having suffered no hardship, beloved, encouraged, supported, sympathized with, heaped with largesse both of the pocketbook and of the spirit, the children yet cannot find themselves. The children are not, for some reason—may God please tell them what it is—in good shape.

A group of husbands and wives, old friends, spend an evening together. They have no need to ask one another the kind of polite questions asked by the women at lunch. On the contrary, they attempt to shut out the subject of children, for they have come together for a bit of fun. And in any case, they already know the answers. So-and-so's boy, he who once made his parents the envy of all the rest, handsome, healthy, gifted, well-mannered, winner of a scholarship to Harvard, languishes now in a hospital where the therapists feel that in another few months he might attempt a few simple tasks and ultimately—for the prognosis is good—even hold down a job, provided it is not of the sort to make him feel too challenged or tense. Another of the sons of this group has lately sent a postcard to his sister announcing that he has taken up photography and that as soon as he gets some work he plans to buy himself a piece of land and build himself a house on it. Yet another—his parents should, they know, be grateful by comparison with some others, and are frequently troubled with the realization that they do not feel so—is in business; he has organized some friends into a firm of handymen and movers and, rather to his astonishment and theirs, the firm is prospering. So-and-so's elder daughter is living, unmarried, with a divorced man and looking after his two adolescent children, while the younger has just set off in pursuit of her third—or is it her fourth?—postgraduate degree. Someone else's daughter, who lives at home, has taken and lost or abandoned five jobs within two years and now finds that she wishes to work only part-time so that she might paint. Still another, who is married and the mother of two small children, has discovered a marriage encounter group. She and her husband, she says, wish to broaden the range of their relationship, and they believe that everyone, including their parents, ought to do the same. One couple in this group have a son in Sweden, whence he exiled himself to avoid the draft. He writes to them weekly, demanding that they find some way to secure him an unconditional amnesty, for he wishes to return home; under no circumstances, he underscores, will he agree to submit himself to a term of compensatory public service. His younger brother has decided to give up farming in Vermont and enter law school. His parents, people of rather modest circumstances, are delighted to "lend" him the $15,000 that will enable him to devote himself to his studies and at the same time provide for his wife and young baby; they have mailed him the proceeds of the re-mortgage on their house and vacillate wildly between relief and the irrepressible gnawing fear that he may not, even yet, remain content. The sister of those two, a schoolteacher, participant in a long series of painfully inconclusive love affairs, has taken to spending all her free time on various projects for raising her consciousness to a full perception of the injustices that have been wreaked upon her. She has grown surly, neglects her appearance, and is in an odd new way touchy and difficult to get along with.

As you know better than anyone, these are not extraordinary cases, these women at lunch, these couples gathered for an evening's recreation, unable *not* to talk about their children and at the same time wishing to use only the barest signals: X has left home, or variously X has returned home, sufficing by now to invoke a whole rich vocabulary of anxiety and bewilderment; X is looking for work or X has found work or X is returning to school or X has gone to Europe or India or Israel sufficing by now to speak volumes, nay entire bookshelves, of incomprehension at the turn things have taken. You know better than anyone, of course, that such gatherings and exchanges are taking place from one end of this country to another, from Los Angeles to St. Louis to Minneapolis, Cleveland, Boston, Washington, and by all means New Jersey, Connecticut, and New York. For they are taking place in the homes and communities in which you have grown up, and they are taking place about you, or at least about a good many of the people you know.

Fundamentally, the question your parents have not dared address in so many words, either to themselves or to their friends— and yet cannot any longer keep hidden behind some false front of approving good cheer or resigned hopes for the future—is the question that must surely, at two o'clock in the morning, be growing upon some of you as well. It is, Why have you, the children, found it so hard to take your rightful place in the world? Just that. Why have your parents' hopes for you come to seem so impossible of attainment?

Some of their expectations were, to be sure, exalted indeed. As children of this peculiar enlightened class, you were expected one day to be manning a more than proportional share of the positions of power and prestige in this society: you were to be its executives, its professionals, its artists and intellectuals, among its business and political leaders, you were to think its influential thoughts, tend its major institutions, and reap its highest rewards. It was at least partly to this end that we brought you up, that we attended so assiduously to your education, that we saw to the cultivation of every last drop of your talents, that we gave you to believe there would be no let or hindrance to the forward, upward motion into which we had set you going from the day of your birth. I don't believe that this was actually a conscious intention for most of us. We did not—anyway, most of us did not for most of the time—tell ourselves of these expectations in so many words. Yet they were unmistakably what we had in mind.

But on the other hand, not all our expectations were of this nature. Beneath these throbbing ambitions were all the ordinary—if you will, mundane—hopes that all parents harbor for their children: that you would grow up, come into your own, and with all due happiness and high spirit carry forward the normal human business of mating, home-building, and reproducing—replacing us, in other words, in the eternal human cycle. And it is here that we find ourselves to be most uneasy both for you and about you.

Of course, you would see, or would claim to see, in this concern of ours for you merely another confirmation of the leading attitude of the youth culture: that we are incapable of perceiving and accepting you as you are. It has after all been a major assertion of the songs you sing, the books you read and write, the films you devour, that we are too bound up in our timid, sickly assumptions about life to open ourselves to the range of the new human possibility that you have engendered. And for a long time, as I have said, we ourselves tried to believe in your explanation for our feelings. We permitted ourselves to be soothed and distracted by the idea that we were in the presence of a revolution, that you were not, as you might have seemed, displaying an incapacity to get on with your lives in an orderly fashion but rather that you were creating a new kind of order alien to and superseding our own.

Were you dropping out of school or otherwise refusing the blandishments of prosperity, security, and privilege? That was because you were attempting to fulfill a need, quite murderously neglected by us and our society, to return to the sources of natural being. Did you appear, from our point of view at first quite mysteriously, to be turning your backs on the kind of striving for excellence in all things for which you had been so unstintingly and expensively brought up? That was because you were engaged in transcending the mean competitiveness to which everyone in America had mindlessly been made hostage and were moving on to a new plane of gentleness and fraternal feeling. Did you seem to be getting dangerously attached to the use of drugs? That was because you were seeking to intensify the quality of experience, because—unlike us, hypocritically engaged in our own use of alcohol and drugs to still the mind and deaden the emotions—you were daring to recover the passional and sensory world so long denied to Western man. Did your initiation into sex seem to us curiously uneventful and haphazard, without moment or weight? That was because you were freeing yourselves from our own crippling obsessions with sex and restoring the whole process to its proper, inconsequent, exuberant animal function.

Such were the things we told one another, and tried to tell ourselves, about you for a long time. They were popular things to say; to speak otherwise branded us not only as enemies of the young but as enemies of all things virtuous in the liberal culture of which the youth revolution had become a cornerstone. They were also, I have pointed out, self-flattering things to say, putting us as they did squarely on your side and as such, on the side of all things new, daring, and open to the future. Above all, however, these ideas about you protected us, if only temporarily, from the sense of failure that had come to stalk us by day and by night.

Well some of us may continue to say them to one another—though fewer every day—but none of us says them any longer to himself. And you? Some of you are still prone to go on as before declaiming your superiority to the meannesses and the hypocrisies of the achieving society, and your sensitive refusal to have a hand in its crushing of the human spirit (although those of you who speak this way are doing so less noisily than you once did). But what are you truly, in the privacy of genuine self-confrontation, saying to yourselves?

You are adults now—or should be—no longer in process of formation or unfolding, no longer *in potentia* but fully here. Thus there are things to be observed about your generation on which the count is already in, things that can no longer be denied by us and that are the real and hard ground from which you must now proceed.

You will surely think that I speak harshly—if not worse. Though you have made a great point of how you have experienced hostility from us, I do not in fact think that you are actually prepared for the possibility that any parent of yours might discuss your behavior in simple moral terms. In social terms, yes, and psychological ones, certainly—psychology has been the main medium of all our communications—but there has been little in the history of our relations over the past two or three decades to give rise to the idea that ordinary judgments of morality might one day be directed from our side to yours instead of the other way around.

As it happens, my purpose here is not to preach but to *describe*. Nor do I mean to describe you alone. I shall also be describing us. One need subscribe to no school of thought beyond that of the plainest common sense to be aware that the behavior of the

members of my class and generation as parents has had the greatest bearing on your behavior as our children. Yet the things that
we, all of us, stand on the brink of recognizing about your generation are inescapably entailed in moral questions.

The first thing to be observed about you, then, is that taken all
together, you are more than usually incapable of facing, tolerating,
or withstanding difficulty of any kind. From the time of your earliest childhood you have stood in a relation to the world that can
only be characterized as a refusal to be tested. This refusal was
announced, sometimes literally, sometimes cloaked in the assertions
of a higher creativity, in your schools. It shaped your attitude to
play, to sports, to sex, to the reading of difficult books and the clarification of difficult ideas, to the assumption of serious roles within your families and communities, and to the consideration of
possibilities for your future. It lent enormous impact to your experience of drugs, whose greatest seduction for you lay in their power
to create the sensation of well-being with little or no effort on your
part. Later, when you were either in or out of college, this refusal
took on all the convenient coloration of ideology. The idea that the
system was evil, and engaged in an evil war, provided cover for a
number of your far deeper impulses to retreat from, or to circum-
vent, the demand that you take on distasteful tasks—whether it be
to endure a bit of necessary boredom, or to serve in the army, or to
overcome the anxieties of normal ambition. The word most frequently on your lips, in the days when you were said to be mounting your relentless campaign against evil, was "hassle." To be
hassled meant to be subjected to difficulty of, from your point of
view, an incomprehensible as well as intolerable sort. And everything, you assured us over and over again, everything we had either
to offer or to impose upon you was a "hassle."

In the city where I live, which is New York, there are certain
interesting ways in which a number of you have latterly taken to
making your living: you are pushcart vendors, taxi drivers, keep-
ers of small neighborhood shops that deal in such commodities as

dirty comic books and handmade candies, you are housepainters, housecleaners, and movers of furniture. Let us leave aside the larger social significance of this—in American history, at least, unprecedented—voluntary downward mobility. In purely personal terms, all these unexpected occupations of yours have one large feature in common: they are the work of private, and largely unregulated, entrepreneurs—full of their own kind of woe, you have no doubt learned, but free of all that patient overcoming and hard-won new attainment that attend the conquest of a professional career. And they are free, most of all, from any judgments that would be meaningful to *you* as judgments of success or failure. Customers may irritate, and unpaid bills oppress you, as they do any private entrepreneurs; but there hangs over you no shadow of the requirement that you measure, ever so minutely and carefully, the distance of your progression from yesterday to today. In the pushcart—many-layered symbol!—is bodied forth the notion that you might, if sufficiently displeased, simply move on to some new stand.

The second thing to be observed about you is that you are, again taken as a whole, more than usually self-regarding. No one who has dealt with you, neither parent, nor teacher, nor political leader, nor even one of the countless panderers to or profiteers from your cyclonically shifting appetites, can have failed to notice the serenity—the sublime, unconscious, unblinking assurance—with which you accept their attentions to you. A thinker, or a book, with ideas to impart that you do not already understand and agree with is immediately dubbed "boring" or "irrelevant" and must immediately thereby forfeit all claims upon you. For some reason, it seems never to occur to you that a failure to comprehend, to appreciate, to grasp a subtlety not already present in your own considerations might be a failure of your own. (In this respect, you very closely resemble that middle-American philistine known to my generation as Babbitt, superiority to whom has been a prime tenet of your, as well as our, self-definition.) What is more important, no member of the so-called adult community appears to have been deemed by you too imposing, too intimidating, or merely too plain busy to be the recipient of those endless discourses upon yourselves by which you make known certain delicate daily calibrations of the state of your feeling. The thought that some attitude or experience of your own might be less formed, less distilled in the twin refineries of time and intellection, less valid, than those of your elders, even those of your elders whom you have elected to call master, seems never to have crossed your minds. Thus, the entire world of thought and art comes to you filtered through a single supreme category of judgment: has it succeeded, or has it failed, by your own lights to move you? To use your own parlance for this category of judgment, does it or does it not "turn you on"? Anyone or anything that leaves you unsatisfied in the way of private, self-generating response is remanded to obscurity. On the other hand, anyone or anything that touches or confirms what you already think and feel, no matter how lacking in any other virtue, is automatically important. Do you find yourselves peculiarly touched, say, by the songs of Bob Dylan? Well, then, he is among the great poets of the ages. Do you have a taste for movies in which the sound track has assumed equal significance with the images? Well, then, the true art-form of the age has been discovered. Are you disinclined to do certain kinds of work? Well, then, the very nature and organization of society is due for a complete overhaul. In short, you, and only you, are the ultimate measure of all that you survey.

And the third thing to be observed about you—it is really in some sense a concomitant of the first two—is that you are more than usually dependent, more than usually lacking in the capacity to stand your ground without reference, whether positive or negative, to your parents. So many of your special claims on this society are claims not on the distribution of its power but on the extension of its tolerance; what you so frequently seem to demand is not that the established community make way for you but that it approve of you. Take the case of your conduct with respect to sex. You have, you say, created a revolution in sexual behavior, particularly adolescent sexual behavior. But this revolution is not something you have done, it is something you have requested your parents and schools and other parietal authorities to do for you. It is in the apartments that we have rented for you, in the dormitories that we have sexually integrated for you, and in the climate of toleration that we have surrounded you with that you have pursued, in all passive supplication, your alleged revolution.

Or to state the case in the obverse, take the fashions in dress and personal habit that were so recently rife among you. Being children of the aspiring middle and upper-middle class, you had been raised by your parents with the expectation that you would be well dressed, therefore you dressed yourselves in rags. (Indeed, a little-noted feature of your sartorial fashion is how often it has been a kind of half-grown version of the games of "dress-up" played by little children in their mommies' and daddies' cast-off finery.) You were raised with the expectation that you would be clean and healthy, after the privileged condition of the class into which you were born, therefore you cultivated the gaudiest show of slovenliness and the most unmistakable signs of sickliness. You were raised on the premise that you would be prompt and energetic and reasonably prudent, and mindful of your manners, therefore you compounded a group style based on nothing so much as a certain weary, breathless vagueness and incompetence—enriched by the display of a deep, albeit soft-spoken, disrespect for the sensibilities and concerns of others. That the key to this entire assertion of style lay in an exact reverse translation of what your parents had taken for granted on your behalf is only one mark of how necessary we were in all your efforts to define yourselves, with the main issue for you so obviously being not "what in my own mature opinion will be best for me?" but "what will *they* think or how will *they* feel in the face of this present conduct of mine?"

Another mark of how necessary we were to your self-definition—only apparently a contradictory one—is that withal, you were never so adamant, never so energetic, never so articulate as in your

demands that we lend our assent to it. Not for nothing did you call
the collective products of your search for group style and group
meaning by the name of "the counterculture." For it was a search
that utterly depended on, and was positively defined by, that which
it opposed. We had little cause to wonder that sooner or later so
many of you, having had one sort of fling or another out there in
the wide world, would return home to us, either from time to time
for a brief sojourn or for what in some cases has seemed to have
become by now a permanent stay. Where but at home were you to
find the true nourishment for your illusory sense of adventure? In
overcoming us, it seems, has lain your major, perhaps your only,
possibility for tasting the joys of triumph.

In any case, whatever you are lately in a mood to say to yourselves, it is such thoughts about you that inform and focus our own
new mood as parents. Yet surely if a whole generation of our grown
children have been left with such a great deal to undo in themselves
before they can take on what we all know, deep down, to be the
essential requirements of membership in the adult tribe—surely in
such a case no one's shortcomings and failures are better reflected
than our own. If you have a low tolerance for difficulty, that is
because we were afflicted with a kind of cosmic hubris which led
us to imagine that we were bringing up children as all our
ancestors on earth before us had not had the wisdom or purity of
heart to do. In the life we promised ourselves to give you there
would be no pain we had not the power to assuage, no heartache
we had not come upon the correct means to deal with, and no challenges that could not be met voluntarily and full of joy. There can
have been no more arrant disrespecters of the past, of the sorrows
of the past and its accumulated wisdoms, than we members of the
enlightened liberal community. And in nothing can our assurance
of being superior to our own parents—wiser, kinder, healthier of
mind and outlook, cleverer, more perceptive, and in better control
of the dark side of our natures—have played a more crucial role
than in the theories and practices which we brought to the task of

parenthood. So we imagined, and taught you to believe, that pain and heartache and fear were to be banished from your lives.

If you are self-regarding, this is because we refused to stand for ourselves, for both the propriety and hard-earned value of our own sense of life. Our contentions with you were based on appeal, not on authority. Believing you to be a new phenomenon among mankind—children raised exclusively on a principle of love, love unvaryingly acted out on our side and freely and voluntarily offered on yours—we enthroned you as such. We found our role more attractive this way, more suited to our self-image of enlightenment, and—though we would have died on the rack before confessing—far easier to play. In other words, we refused to assume, partly on ideological grounds but partly also, I think, on esthetic grounds, one of the central obligations of parenthood: to make ourselves the final authority on good and bad, right and wrong, and to take the consequences of what might turn out to be a lifelong battle. It might sound a paradoxical thing to say—for surely never has a generation of children occupied more sheer hours of parental time—but the truth is that we neglected you. We allowed you a charade of trivial freedoms in order to avoid making those impositions on you that are in the end both the training ground and proving ground for true independence. We pronounced you strong when you were still weak in order to avoid the struggles with you that would have fed your true strength. We proclaimed you sound when you were foolish in order to avoid taking part in the long, slow, slogging effort that is the only route to genuine maturity of mind and feeling. Thus, it was no small anomaly of your growing up that while you were the most indulged generation, you were also in many ways the most abandoned to your own meager devices by those into whose safekeeping you had been given.

CHAPTER 9

Albert Jay Nock

Commentary by Edwin J. Feulner Jr. (1990)

lbert Jay Nock was a great American individualist. Brilliant,
eccentric, witty, and critical, he was a man of passionate
dislikes and intense loyalties. Inspiring as well as infuriating, he was nothing if not provocative. A libertarian who denounced
any encroachment on freedom, whether from the left or the right,
Nock saw himself as a "spiritual Robin Hood," a man of principle
fighting the State and all of its works.

But the State was not his only opponent. Armed with formidable learning, wry wit, and impeccable prose, he regularly contended with giants. No mean polemicist, he was a one-man munitions
factory, firing off salvos against the modern period, the Middle
Ages, institutionalized religion, and Western civilization.

Nor did he scruple to stalk smaller game: he excoriated American society, culture, business, and education; and roundly criticized
mass man, modern women, European governments, the World
Wars, politicians in general and diplomats in particular. He even
went on record against dogs—whom he called "natural-born New
Dealer[s]," and, for good measure, added that he had a "horror"
of children. No wonder that Nock's obituary in the *New York*

Times, published in August of 1945, remarked that the only things known to have escaped his censure were "classical literature, beer, wine, [and] Chinese food"!

This ironical summation, however, is not quite fair. He was also enamored of baseball, billiards, and tennis, and throughout his life, remained a great admirer of modern and classical languages, smart people, attractive women, foreign travel and well-written prose. The list could be further extended to include the America of his childhood, his parents, the countryside around nineteenth-century Brooklyn where he grew up, the English language, the American dictionary, and the Bible. But no list would be complete if it did not also record his enduring admiration for the man from Monticello, Thomas Jefferson; the frontier humorist Artemus Ward; the Victorian critic Matthew Arnold; the sixteenth-century French writer François Rabelais; the nineteenth-century British philosopher Herbert Spencer; and the American theorist of the single tax, Henry George.

Despite his many enthusiasms, Nock was, as Clifton Fadiman wrote in the *New Yorker,* "a highly civilized man who does not like our civilization." Even his many admirers, like the critic Jacques Barzun, recognized that Nock belonged to "the great American tradition of the judicious eccentric" who is out of step with his times.

Considering himself the quintessential outsider, Nock christened his autobiography *Memoirs of a Superfluous Man.* In this book, which many consider his finest work, he explained why he thought he was superfluous: "I knew I had nothing to contribute to our society that it would care to accept," for "the only contribution it would care for was something that might fall in with its doctrine of economism, and I had nothing of that sort to offer." Consequently, he contended, he was like "a man who had landed in Greenland with a cargo of straw hats. There was nothing wrong with Greenland or with the straw hats ... but there was not the faintest chance of a market for his line of goods."

As is so often the case, however, his self-deprecation is somewhat disingenuous. A well-read literary critic himself, he clearly expected his title to remind readers of Turgenev's *Diary of a Super-fluous Man,* the story of a refined intellectual who cannot fully use his gifts because society is both unworthy of and oblivious to his talents. Thus, the title of Nock's *Memoirs,* which suggests modest self-assessment, really indicts the society that fails to appreciate and use the talents of its most gifted members. Moreover, he clearly saw himself playing the same role as the "superfluous man" in Russian literature who, although unappreciated, acts as a reproach to society and goads its other gifted members into action.

Nock certainly played this role in the modern conservative movement, exerting considerable influence on many of its leading figures. During the Second World War, Robert Nisbet read and "practically memorized" Nock's *Memoirs,* and at the same time, Russell Kirk began to correspond with him. Earlier still, William Buckley fell under Nock's influence during the latter's frequent visits to the Buckleys' home in Connecticut. Nock also influenced Frank Chodorov, who later founded *Analysis,* an "individualistic publication," interpreting "events and trends in the light of Nock's philosophy." Chodorov and others then went on to reestablish the *Freeman* (the name of the magazine Nock had founded and edited from 1920-1924) and, still later, helped to establish the Intercollegiate Society of Individualists, which subsequently became the Intercollegiate Studies Institute. Clearly, as Robert Crunden has observed, Nock's "real place is in a select gallery of American nonconformists whose legacy is their ability to irritate men into thought."

Nock's thought also continues to animate—if not irritate—the enthusiastic members of the Nockian Society, founded over thirty years ago in Irvington, New York, by a group of clergymen interested in theology and economics. The Society, which has no officers, dues, or meetings, aids its members, according to Edmund Opitz, one of the founders, by staying out of their way and by pursuing "a policy of salutary neglect." Today, interest in Nock is on the rise. The Nockian Society has reprinted several of his books. Liberty Press and Regnery Gateway have reprinted others.

What accounts for this resurgent interest? What were Nock's characteristics as a man, thinker, and writer that enabled him to exert such influence on the conservative movement, to win philosophical allies, and to garner the admiration of the Nockians who still meet in his memory half a century after his death? Clearly, he had more to offer than his detractors suggest. He was no mere misanthrope who slipped too easily into the shoes of the classical curmudgeon or donned too readily the boxing gloves of the in-house iconoclast. His sympathies were not so narrow, his views so grim, or his reactions so disinterested as he sometimes suggested. A charming, cultivated man who admired Rabelais's irrepressible humor and Thomas Jefferson's "Tory manners," Nock was not above a certain amount of self misrepresentation—especially if he could err on the side of urbanity, nonchalance, and indifference. His stoicism cost him much more than he acknowledged and his cantankerousness resulted more from outraged idealism than from a basically querulous temperament.

Born in 1870 in Scranton, Pennsylvania, to a mother of French Huguenot descent and to an Episcopalian minister descended from Methodist ironworkers, Nock was, from the beginning, an unusual person. An only child who, he records, was never read to, sung to, or given toys, he taught himself to read by gazing at an upside-down piece of the *New York Herald* stuck in a cracked basement window of his father's rectory. This accomplishment—learning to read wrong-side-up and backwards while still a toddler—provides a good metaphor for his later life. Precocious, independent, self-reliant, gifted, nonconformist and skeptical, Albert not only read the signs of the times differently from his contemporaries, but he also deciphered them earlier and from a distinctly different point of view. It hardly seems accidental that he, who as an adult was often called anachronistic, was "greatly taken with ... pictures of prehistoric creatures." Nor, in the light of his later erudition, is it surprising that young Albert's favorite book was the dictionary, "quite literally," his *Memoirs* record, "my bosom friend," for, as he confides, "I lugged it about, clasped to my breast with both hands."

By the age of eight, Nock had moved on to Latin and Greek under his father's tutelage, but surprisingly he did not go to school until he was fourteen. A few years later, in 1897, he enrolled at St. Stephen's (which became Bard College) from which he graduated in 1892, after studying the "grand old curriculum"—including Latin, Greek, logic, mathematics, and history, with forays into French, philosophy, astronomy, Hebrew, and chemistry.

After graduating, Nock played semi-professional baseball and studied theology at divinity school before being ordained an Episcopal minister in 1897. He spent the next twelve years at parishes in Pennsylvania, Virginia, and Michigan, and during this time, married and had two children, but his *Memoirs* mention neither them nor his life as a minister.

Leaving his wife, family, and ministry in 1909, he moved to New York, where he wrote for *American Magazine,* a muckraking journal that also employed the famous Ida Tarbell and Lincoln Steffens. After four years as a journalist, Nock appears to have gone to Europe as the personal representative of William Jennings Bryan, but the nature of his mission is unclear. A fervent pacifist, Nock campaigned hard for Woodrow Wilson, only to be thoroughly disillusioned by the role Wilson played during and after the war.

Nock's disillusionment with Wilson and with the war, which he attributed to duplicitous diplomacy, nationalistic imperialism, and avaricious businessmen, signaled the end of his flirtation with liberalism. "We cannot help remembering," he wrote in 1923, "that this was a liberal's war, a liberal's peace, and that the present state of things is the consummation of a ... long ... extensive, and extremely costly experiment with liberalism in political power."

Utterly disenchanted with the progressivist agenda, he concluded that "The political liberal is the most dangerous person in the world to be entrusted with power." Abandoning his belief in the perfectability of man, he relinquished the Jeffersonian optimism that he had cherished. Although he retained a life-long love for the America of his childhood, he believed that his fellow Americans were becoming more and more "Neolithic," that the State was increasingly intrusive and that big business and crass materialism were "rebarbarizing" country and citizens alike.

After the war, he founded the famous *Freeman* magazine, considered by many to be America's most impressive venture in literary journalism. From 1920 to 1924, he edited and wrote a wide variety of essays, addressing everything from feminism and education to taxation and morals. After the magazine went out of business, Nock again set sail for Europe, where, over the next two decades, he did some of his best writing. Although he derided biographies as catering to the public's "prurient" interest, he wrote three himself (on Jefferson, Artemus Ward, and François Rabelais), as well as his own *Memoirs*.

Such seeming inconsistencies exemplify Nock's contradictory character. A cosmopolitan isolationist, a classical scholar who played professional baseball, an ordained minister who had little use for organized religion, an editor and writer who detested newspapers and compared journalism to prostitution, he was an enigma—even to his friends. He was also, despite his apparent pessimism, an idealist. At first glance, this seems highly unlikely. After all, he was a man who believed that most people should not receive a college education, who insisted that widespread literacy had lowered literary standards; universal suffrage had constricted freedom; and State charity had corrupted its recipients.

Only an idealist, however, could have written "Isaiah's Job." First published in 1936, this witty article tells the story of the prophet Isaiah whom God called during the reign of King Uzziah, about 740 BC, to prophesy to His people. As Nock puts it, the Lord said, "Tell them what is wrong and why, and what is going to happen unless they have a change of heart and straighten up. Don't mince matters. Make it clear that they are positively down to their last chance. Give it to them good and strong, and keep on giving it to them."

Understandably, Isaiah becomes apprehensive when the Lord adds, "I suppose I ... ought to tell you that it won't do any good. The official class and ... intelligentsia will turn up their noses at you, and the masses will not ... listen ... and you will probably be lucky if you get out with your life." When Isaiah asks why he should bother to prophesy if no one will listen, the Lord replies: "you do not get the point. There is a Remnant ... that you know nothing about. They are obscure, unorganized, inarticulate.... They need to be encouraged ... because when everything has gone completely to the dogs, they are the ones who will come back and build up a new society, and meanwhile your preaching will reassure them and keep them hanging on. Your job is to take care of the Remnant, so be off now and set about it."

The concept of the Remnant is, of course, very much alive at The Heritage Foundation. Like Isaiah, we knew from the beginning that ours was an important mission. Although, like him, we sometimes wondered whether anyone was listening, we always believed that if we proclaimed the truth, someone, somewhere, would hear it and that our message would make a difference.

When Heritage first opened its doors in 1973, in a suite of rented offices with a handful of employees operating on a shoestring budget, we could not foresee how great a difference our "prophesying" would make. Nor could we have guessed that by reiterating the truths in which we believed we would help to sow the seeds of freedom that would tear down walls of oppression world-wide. Traveling in Asia, Eastern Europe, and Russia, members of our Board, my colleagues at Heritage, and I have repeatedly been amazed by how the convictions that we share—a belief in free enterprise, representative government, and the fundamental dignity of man—have united us with members of the Remnant world-wide and have played a crucial role in encouraging them to fight for freedom.

Whenever I have encountered the truths that we Americans hold to be self-evident in corners of the globe where one would least expect to find them, I have been grateful that someone, somewhere, took a leap of faith and preached to a Remnant he could not see. I have frequently been amazed, heartened, and, frankly, humbled to see how a pamphlet that we at Heritage have published, a talk we have sponsored, or research we have funded has borne fruit far afield—often in the face of great odds.

Such encounters underline a point that "Isaiah's Job" makes most forcefully—those who hear the truth incur a debt to proclaim it. While re-reading Nock's essay, I recalled with gratitude my own debt to Leonard Read (who first gave it to me in 1963 at a seminar conducted by the Foundation for Economic Education) and to Edmund Opitz who spoke so eloquently about the Remnant's duty to society. But my debt to Nock was incurred earlier still when ISI first introduced me to his idea that right thinking could transform society.

This approach raises our sights above mere political victories or losses. Both of these are temporary, but the permanent things in which we believe are based on underlying principles that do not change.

The most fundamental of these permanent things is the conviction—central to "Isaiah's Job"—that one must do the right thing regardless of the cost. No defense of freedom is possible without prophets who, despite the starkest circumstances, proclaim the truth and a Remnant that hears and acts on it.

"Isaiah's Job" reminds us that even when the shadows lengthen and the forces of darkness prepare for victory, there is always such a prophet and such a Remnant waiting in the wings. In this sense, "never despair" is the synopsized version of Nock's essay—a message that seems strange on the lips of an avowed pessimist. But then, Nock was also a realist. He knew that one man armed with the truth could change the world and that the Remnant could redirect the course of history.

It is worthwhile to remember that Isaiah has had the last laugh—his mission has been vindicated and his prophecy fulfilled. Perhaps most astonishing of all, his message—originally intended for a tiny elite—has gone out to all the world. That is surely success—even according to the stringent standards of Albert Jay Nock!

Albert Jay Nock

Isaiah's Job

O ne evening last autumn I sat long hours with a European acquaintance while he expounded a politico-economic doctrine which seemed sound as a nut, and in which I could find no defect. At the end he said with great earnestness, "I have a mission to the masses. I feel that I am called to get the ear of the people. I shall devote the rest of my life to spreading my doctrine far and wide among the populace. What do you think?"

An embarrassing question in any case, and doubly so under the circumstances, because my acquaintance is a very learned man, one of the three or four really first-class minds that Europe produced in his generation, and naturally I, as one of the unlearned, was inclined to regard his lightest word with reverence amounting to awe. Still, I reflected, even the greatest mind cannot possibly know everything, and I was pretty sure he had not had my opportunities for observing the masses of mankind, and that therefore I probably knew them better than he did. So I mustered courage to say that he had no such mission and would do well to get the idea out of his head at once; he would find that the masses would not care two pins for his doctrine, and still less for himself, since in such circumstances the popular favourite is generally some Barabbas. I even went so far as to say (he is a Jew) that his idea seemed to show that

From Albert Jay Nock, *Free Speech and Plain Language* (1937).

he was not very well up on his own native literature. He smiled at my jest, and asked what I meant by it; and I referred him to the story of the prophet Isaiah.

It occurred to me then that this story is much worth recalling just now when so many wise men and soothsayers appear to be burdened with a message to the masses. Dr. Townsend has a message, Father Coughlin has one, Mr. Upton Sinclair, Mr. Lippmann, Mr. Chase and the planned-economy brethren, Mr. Tugwell and the New Dealers, Mr. Smith and the Liberty Leaguers—the list is endless. I cannot remember a time when so many energumens were so variously proclaiming the Word to the multitude and telling them what they must do to be saved. This being so, it occurred to me, as I say, that the story of Isaiah might have something in it to steady and compose the human spirit until this tyranny of windiness be overpast. I shall paraphrase the story in our common speech, since it has to be pieced out from various sources; and inasmuch as respectable scholars have thought fit to put out a whole new version of the Bible in the American vernacular, I shall take shelter behind them, if need be, against the charge of dealing irreverently with the Sacred Scriptures.

The prophet's career began at the end of King Uzziah's reign, say about 740 BC. This reign was uncommonly long, almost half a century, and apparently prosperous. It was one of those prosperous reigns, however, like the reign of Marcus Aurelius at Rome, or the administration of Eubulus at Athens, or of Mr. Coolidge at Washington, where at the end the prosperity suddenly peters out, and things go by the board with a resounding crash. In the year of Uzziah's death, the Lord commissioned the prophet to go out and warn the people of the wrath to come. "Tell them what a worthless lot they are," He said. "Tell them what is wrong, and why, and what is going to happen unless they have a change of heart and straighten up. Don't mince matters. Make it clear that they are positively down to their last chance. Give it to them good and strong, and keep on giving it to them. I suppose perhaps I ought to tell you," He added, "that it won't do any good. The official class and their intelligentsia will turn up their noses at you, and the masses will not even listen. They will all keep on in their own ways until they carry everything down to destruction, and you will probably be lucky if you get out with your life."

Isaiah had been very willing to take on the job; in fact, he had asked for it; but this prospect put a new face on the situation. It raised the obvious question why, if all that were so, if the enterprise were to be a failure from the start, was there any sense in starting it? "Ah," the Lord said, "you do not get the point. There is a Remnant there that you know nothing about. They are obscure, unorganized, inarticulate, each one rubbing along as best he can. They need to be encouraged and braced up, because when everything has gone completely to the dogs, they are the ones who will come back and build up a new society, and meanwhile your preaching will reassure them and keep them hanging on. Your job is to take care of the Remnant, so be off now and set about it."

II

Apparently, then, if the Lord's word is good for anything—I do not offer any opinion about that—the only element in Judaean society that was particularly worth bothering about was the Remnant. Isaiah seems finally to have got it through his head that this was the case; that nothing was to be expected from the masses, but that if anything substantial were ever to be done in Judaea, the Remnant would have to do it. This is a very striking and suggestive idea; but before going on to explore it, we need to be quite clear about our terms. What do we mean by the masses, and what by the Remnant?

As the word *masses* is commonly used, it suggests agglomerations of poor and unprivileged people, labouring people, proletarians, and it means nothing like that; it means simply the majority. The massman is one who has neither the force of intellect to apprehend the principles issuing in what we know as the humane life, nor the force of character to adhere to those principles steadily and strictly as laws of conduct; and because such people make up the great, the overwhelming majority of mankind, they are called collectively *the masses*. The line of differentiation between the masses and the Remnant is set invariably by quality, not by circumstance. The Remnant are those who by force of intellect are able to apprehend these principles, and by force of character are able, at least measurably, to cleave to them; the masses are those who are unable to do either.

The picture which Isaiah presents of the Judaean masses is most unfavourable. In his view the mass-man, be he high or be he lowly, rich or poor, prince or pauper, gets off very badly. He appears as not only weak-minded and weak-willed, but as by consequence knavish, arrogant, grasping, dissipated, unprincipled, unscrupulous. The mass-woman also gets off badly, as sharing all the mass-man's untoward qualities, and contributing a few of her own in the way of vanity and laziness, extravagance and foible. The list of luxury-products [1] that she patronized is interesting; it calls to mind the women's page of a Sunday newspaper in 1928, or the display set forth [2] in one of our professedly "smart" periodicals. In another place Isaiah even recalls the affectations that we used to know by the name of the "flapper gait" and the "debutante slouch." It may be fair to discount Isaiah's vivacity a little for prophetic fervour; after all, since his real job was not to convert the masses but to brace and reassure the Remnant, he probably felt that he might lay it on indiscriminately and as thick as he liked—in fact, that he was expected to do so. But even so, the Judaean mass-man must have been a most objectionable individual, and the mass-woman utterly odious.

If the modern spirit, whatever that may be, is disinclined towards taking the Lord's word at its face value (as I hear is the case), we may observe that Isaiah's testimony to the character of the masses

---

1 Isaiah 3:18-23.

2 Ibid., 3:16

has strong collateral support from respectable Gentile authority. Plato lived into the administration of Eubulus, when Athens was at the peak of its great jazz-and-paper era, and he speaks of the Athenian masses with all Isaiah's fervency, even comparing them to a herd of ravenous wild beasts. Curiously, too, he applies Isaiah's own word *remnant* to the worthier portion of Athenian society; "there is but a very small *remnant,*" he says, of those who possess a saving force of intellect and force of character—too small, precisely as in Judaea, to be of any avail against the ignorant and vicious preponderance of the masses.

But Isaiah was a preacher and Plato a philosopher; and we tend to regard preachers and philosophers rather as passive observers of the drama of life than as active participants. Hence in a matter of this kind their judgment might be suspected of being a little uncompromising, a little acrid, or as the French say, *saugrenu*. We may therefore bring forward another witness who was preeminently a man of affairs, and whose judgment cannot lie under this suspicion. Marcus Aurelius was ruler of the greatest of empires, and in that capacity he not only had the Roman mass-man under observation, but he had him on his hands twenty-four hours a day for eighteen years. What he did not know about him was not worth knowing, and what he thought of him is abundantly attested on almost every page of the little book of jottings which he scribbled offhand from day to day, and which he meant for no eye but his own ever to see.

This view of the masses is the one that we find prevailing at large among the ancient authorities whose writings have come down to us. In the eighteenth century, however, certain European philosophers spread the notion that the mass-man, in his natural state, is not at all the kind of person that earlier authorities made him out to be, but on the contrary, that he is a worthy object of interest. His untowardness is the effect of environment, an effect for which "society" is somehow responsible. If only his environment permitted him to live according to his best lights, he would undoubtedly show himself to be quite a fellow; and the best way to secure a more favourable environment for him would be to let him arrange it for himself. The French Revolution acted powerfully as a springboard for this idea, projecting its influence in all directions throughout Europe.

On this side of the ocean a whole new continent stood ready for a large-scale experiment with this theory. It afforded every conceivable resource whereby the masses might develop a civilization made in their own likeness and after their own image. There was no force of tradition to disturb them in their preponderance, or to check them in a thoroughgoing disparagement of the Remnant. Immense natural wealth, unquestioned predominance, virtual isolation, freedom from external interference and the fear of it, and, finally, a century and a half of time—such are the advantages which the mass-man has had in bringing forth a civilization which should set the earlier preachers and philosophers at naught in their belief that nothing substantial can be expected from the masses, but only from the Remnant.

His success is unimpressive. On the evidence so far presented one must say, I think, that the mass-man's conception of what life has to offer, and his choice of what to ask from life, seem now to be pretty well what they were in the times of Isaiah and Plato; and so too seem the catastrophic social conflicts and convulsions in which his views of life and his demands on life involve him. I do not wish to dwell on this, however, but merely to observe that the monstrously inflated importance of the masses has apparently put all thought of a possible mission to the Remnant out of the modern prophet's head. This is obviously quite as it should be, provided that the earlier preachers and philosophers were actually wrong, and that all final hope of the human race is actually centered in the masses. If, on the other hand, it should turn out that the Lord and Isaiah and Plato and Marcus Aurelius were right in their estimate of the relative social value of the masses and the Remnant, the case is somewhat different. Moreover, since with everything in their favour the masses have so far given such an extremely discouraging account of themselves, it would seem that the question at issue between these two bodies of opinion might most profitably be reopened.

III

But without following up this suggestion, I wish only, as I said, to remark the fact that as things now stand Isaiah's job seems rather to go begging. Everyone with a message nowadays is like my venerable European friend, eager to take it to the masses. His first, last and only thought is of mass-acceptance and mass-approval. His great care is to put his doctrine in such shape as will capture the masses' attention and interest. This attitude towards the masses is so exclusive, so devout, that one is reminded of the troglodytic monster described by Plato, and the assiduous crowd at the entrance to its cave, trying obsequiously to placate it and win its favour, trying to interpret its inarticulate noises, trying to find out what it wants, and eagerly offering it all sorts of things that they think might strike its fancy.

The main trouble with all this is its reaction upon the mission itself. It necessitates an opportunist sophistication of one's doctrine which profoundly alters its character and reduces it to a mere placebo. If, say, you are a preacher, you wish to attract as large a congregation as you can, which means an appeal to the masses, and this in turn means adapting the terms of your message to the order of intellect and character that the masses exhibit. If you are an educator, say with a college on your hands, you wish to get as many students as possible, and you whittle down your requirements accordingly. If a writer, you aim at getting many readers; if a publisher, many purchasers; if a philosopher, many disciples; if a reformer, many converts; if a musician, many auditors; and so on. But as we see on all sides, in the realization of these several desires the prophetic message is so heavily adulterated with trivialities in every instance that its effect on the masses is merely to harden them in their sins; and meanwhile the Remnant, aware of this adulteration and of the desires that prompt it, turn their backs on the prophet and will have nothing to do with him or his message.

Isaiah, on the other hand, worked under no such disabilities. He preached to the masses only in the sense that he preached publicly. Anyone who liked might listen; anyone who liked might pass by. He knew that the Remnant would listen; and knowing also that nothing was to be expected of the masses under any circumstances, he made no specific appeal to them, did not accommodate his message to their measure in any way, and did not care two straws whether they heeded it or not. As a modern publisher might put it, he was not worrying about circulation or about advertising. Hence, with all such obsessions quite out of the way, he was in a position to do his level best, without fear or favour, and answerable only to his august Boss.

If a prophet were not too particular about making money out of his mission or getting a dubious sort of notoriety out of it, the foregoing considerations would lead one to say that serving the Remnant looks like a good job. An assignment that you can really put your back into, and do your best without thinking about results, is a real job; whereas serving the masses is at best only half a job, considering the inexorable conditions that the masses impose upon their servants. They ask you to give them what they want, they insist upon it, and will take nothing else; and following their whims, their irrational changes of fancy, their hot and cold fits, is a tedious business, to say nothing of the fact that what they want at any time makes very little call on one's resources of prophecy. The Remnant, on the other hand, want only the best you have, whatever that may be. Give them that, and they are satisfied and you have nothing more to worry about. The prophet of the American masses must aim consciously at the lowest common denominator of intellect, taste and character among 120,000,000 people; and this is a distressing task. The prophet of the Remnant, on the contrary, is in the enviable position of Papa Haydn in the household of Prince Esterhazy. All Haydn had to do was to keep forking out the very best music he knew how to produce, knowing it would be understood and appreciated by those for whom he produced it, and caring not a button what anyone else thought of it; and that makes a good job.

In a sense, nevertheless, as I have said, it is not a rewarding job. If you can touch the fancy of the masses, and have the sagacity to keep always one jump ahead of their vagaries and vacillations, you can get good returns in money from serving the masses, and good returns also in a mouth-to-ear type of notoriety:

Digito monstrari et dicier, Hic est!

We all know innumerable politicians, journalists, dramatists, novelists and the like, who have done extremely well by themselves in these ways. Taking care of the Remnant, on the contrary, holds little promise of any such rewards. A prophet of the Remnant will not grow purse-proud on the financial returns from his work, nor is it likely that he will get any great renown out of it. Isaiah's case was exceptional to this second rule, and there are others, but not many.

It may be thought, then, that while taking care of the Remnant is no doubt a good job, it is not an especially interesting job, because it is as a rule so poorly paid. I have my doubts about this. There are other compensations to be got out of a job besides money and notoriety, and some of them seem substantial enough to be attractive. Many jobs which do not pay well are yet profoundly interesting, as, for instance, the job of the research-student in the sciences is said to be; and the job of looking after the Remnant seems to me, as I have surveyed it for many years from my seat in the grandstand, to be as interesting as any that can be found in the world.

IV

What chiefly makes it so, I think, is that in any given society the Remnant are always so largely an unknown quantity. You do not know, and will never know, more than two things about them. You can be sure of those—dead sure, as our phrase is—but you will never be able to make even a respectable guess at anything else. You do not know and will never know who the Remnant are, or where they are, or how many of them there are, or what they are doing or will do. Two things you know, and no more: first, that they exist; second, that they will find you. Except for these two certainties, working for the Remnant means working in impenetrable darkness; and this, I should say, is just the condition calculated most effectively to pique the interest of any prophet who is properly gifted with the imagination, insight and intellectual curiosity necessary to a successful pursuit of his trade.

The fascination and the despair of the historian, as he looks back upon Isaiah's Jewry, upon Plato's Athens, or upon Rome of the Antonines, is the hope of discovering and laying bare the substratum of right thinking and well-doing which he knows must have existed somewhere in those societies because no kind of collective life can possibly go on without it. He finds tantalizing intimations of it here and there in many places, as in the Greek Anthology, in the scrapbook of Aulus Gellius, in the poems of Ausonius, and in the brief and touching tribute *Bene merenti* bestowed upon the unknown occupants of Roman tombs. But these are vague and fragmentary; they lead him nowhere in his search for some kind of measure of this substratum, but merely testify to what he already knew a priori, that the substratum did somewhere exist. Where it was, how substantial it was, what its power of self-assertion and resistance was—of all this they tell him nothing.

Concerning all this, too, the prophet of the present knows precisely as much and as little as the historian of the future; and that, I repeat, is what makes his job seem to me so profoundly interesting. One of the most suggestive episodes recounted in the Bible is that of a prophet's attempt—the only attempt of the kind on record, I believe—to count up the Remnant. Elijah had fled from persecution into the desert, where the Lord presently overhauled him and asked what he was doing so far away from his job. He said that he was running away, not because he was a coward, but because all the Remnant had been killed off except himself. He had got away only by the skin of his teeth, and, he being now all the Remnant there was, if he were killed the True Faith would go flat. The Lord replied that he need not worry about that, for even without him the True Faith could probably manage to squeeze along somehow, if it had to; "and as for your figures on the Remnant," He said, "I don't mind telling you that there are seven thousand of them back there in Israel whom it seems you have not heard of, but you may take My word for it that there they are."

Similarly, when the historian of two thousand years hence, or two hundred years, looks over the available testimony to the quality of our civilization and tries to get any kind of clear, competent evidence concerning the substratum of right thinking and well-doing which he knows must have been here, he will have a devil of a time finding it. When he has assembled all he can get and has made even a minimum allowance for speciousness, vagueness, and confusion of motive, he will sadly acknowledge that his net result is simply nothing. A Remnant were here, building a substratum, like coral insects—so much he knows—but he will find nothing to put him on the track of who and where and how many they were, and what their work was like.

At that time probably the population of Israel could not have run to much more than a million or so; and a Remnant of seven thousand out of a million is a highly encouraging percentage for any prophet. With seven thousand of the boys on his side, there was no great reason for Elijah to feel lonesome; and incidentally that would be something for the modern prophet of the Remnant to think of when he has a touch of the blues. But the main point is that if Elijah the Prophet could not make a closer guess on the number of the Remnant than he made when he missed it by seven thousand, anyone else who tackled the problem would only waste his time.

The other certainty which the prophet of the Remnant may always have is that the Remnant will find him. He may rely on that with absolute assurance. They will find him without his doing anything about it; in fact, if he tries to do anything about it, he is pretty sure to put them off. He does not need to advertise for them, or resort to any schemes of publicity to get their attention. If he is a preacher or a public speaker, for example, he may be quite indifferent to going on show at receptions, getting his picture printed in the newspapers, or furnishing autobiographical material for publication on the side of "human interest." If a writer, he need not make a point of attending any pink teas, autographing books at wholesale, or entering into any specious freemasonry with reviewers. All this and much more of the same order lies in the regular and necessary routine laid down for the prophet of the masses; it is, and must be, part of the great general technique of getting the mass-man's ear—or, as our vigorous and excellent publicist, Mr. H. L. Mencken, puts it, the technique of boob-bumping. The prophet of the Remnant is not bound to this technique. He may be quite sure that the Remnant will make their own way to him without any adventitious aids; and not only so, but if they find him employing such aids, as I said, it is ten to one that they will smell a rat in them and will sheer off.

The certainty that the Remnant will find him, however, leaves the prophet as much in the dark as ever, as helpless as ever in the matter of putting any estimate of any kind upon the Remnant, for, as appears in the case of Elijah, he remains ignorant of who they are that have found him, or where they are, or how many. They do not write in and tell him about it, after the manner of those who admire the vedettes of Hollywood nor yet do they seek him out and attach themselves to his person. They are not that kind. They take his message much as drivers take the directions on a roadside signboard; that is, with very little thought about the signboard, beyond being gratefully glad that it happened to be there, but with very serious thought about the directions.

This impersonal attitude of the Remnant wonderfully enhances the interest of the imaginative prophet's job. Once in a while, just about often enough to keep his intellectual curiosity in good working order, he will quite accidentally come upon some distinct reflection of his own message in an unsuspected quarter; and this enables him to entertain himself in his leisure moments with agreeable speculations about the course his message may have taken in reaching that particular quarter, and about what came of it after it got there. Most interesting of all are those instances, if one could only run them down (but one may always speculate about them), where the recipient himself no longer knows where or when or from whom he got the message; or even where, as sometimes happens, he has forgotten that he got it anywhere, and imagines that it is all a self-sprung idea of his own.

Such instances as these are probably not infrequent, for, without presuming to enroll ourselves among the Remnant, we can all no doubt remember having found ourselves suddenly under the influence of an idea, the source of which we cannot possibly identify. "It came to us afterward," as we say; that is, we are aware of it only after it has shot up full-grown in our minds, leaving us quite ignorant of how and when and by what agency it was planted there and left to germinate. It seems highly probable that the prophet's message often takes some such course with the Remnant.

If, for example, you are a writer or a speaker or a preacher, you put forth an idea which lodges in the *Unbewusstsein* of a casual member of the Remnant, and sticks fast there. For some time it is inert; then it begins to fret and fester until presently it invades the man's conscious mind and, as one might say, corrupts it. Meanwhile he has quite forgotten how he came by the idea in the first instance, and even perhaps thinks he has invented it; and in those circumstances the most interesting thing of all is that you never know what the pressure of that idea will make him do.

V

For these reasons it appears to me that Isaiah's job is not only good but also extremely interesting; and especially so at the present time when nobody is doing it. If I were young and had the notion of embarking in the prophetical line, I would certainly take up this branch of the business; and therefore I have no hesitation about recommending it as a career for anyone in that position. It offers an open Weld, no competition; our civilization so completely neglects and disallows the Remnant that anyone going in with an eye single to their service might pretty well count on getting all the trade there is.

Even assuming that there is some social salvage to be screened out of the masses, even assuming that the testimony of history to their social value is a little too sweeping, that it depresses hopelessness a little too far, one must yet perceive, I think, that the masses have prophets enough and to spare. Even admitting in the teeth of history that hope of the human race may not be quite exclusively centered in the Remnant, one must perceive that they have social value enough to entitle them to some measure of prophetic encouragement and consolation, and that our civilization allows them none whatever. Every prophetic voice is addressed to the masses, and to them alone; the voice of the pulpit, the voice of education, the voice of politics, of literature, drama, journalism—all these are directed towards the masses exclusively, and they marshal the masses in the way that they are going.

One might suggest, therefore, that aspiring prophetical talent may well turn to another Weld. *Sat patriae Priamoque datum*— whatever obligation of the kind may be due the masses is already monstrously overpaid. So long as the masses are taking up the tabernacle of Moloch and Chium, their images, and following the star of their god Buncombe, they will have no lack of prophets to point the way that leadeth to the More Abundant Life; and hence a few of those who feel the prophetic afflatus might do better to apply themselves to serving the Remnant. It is a good job, an interesting job, much more interesting than serving the masses; and moreover it is the only job in our whole civilization, as far as I know, that offers a virgin Weld.

The Heritage Foundation Collection, 1989

Chapter 10

Whittaker Chambers

Commentary by Edwin J. Feulner Jr. (1986)

T hough born in the twentieth century, Whittaker Chambers was brought up in a world and in a way that seem surprisingly remote from our own. Raised on Long Island, when it was dotted with quaint villages, in a genteel household that revered Pre-Raphaelite art, he hardly seems a representative man of our time—much less one of its heroes. What was heroic, one might ask, in running away from home, writing a "blasphemous" play, dropping out of college, joining the Communist Party, serving in its underground, and actively attempting to infiltrate and undermine the American government? Where was there heroism in the life of a man who was later called "a self-confessed liar, spy, and traitor"? How did an individual who described himself as "a short, squat, solitary figure, trudging through ... halls of public buildings" become a hero? He did it in the hardest way possible: by publicly, painfully, poignantly "witnessing"—describing his seduction by communism, his repudiation of this false ideology, and his eventual conversion to belief in the West, in Freedom, and in God.

In *Witness*, Chambers's autobiography, he heroically chronicles his pilgrimage from darkness to light, from confusion to wisdom, from faith in the preeminence of man to belief in the sovereignty of God. *Witness* is the work of a prophet in the ancient sense: one who gives what he believes is a divinely inspired explanation of man's plight and warns what will happen if society does not change radically.

In "A Letter to My Children," which originally appeared as the foreword to *Witness*, Whittaker Chambers identifies the two great faiths of the twentieth century as Communism and Freedom; explains his role in "witnessing" against one and for the other; and describes what leads men to Communism. More important, he shows what leads some of them to repudiate this philosophy, and what specifically caused him to reject it. His chilling words before the House Committee on Un-American Activities vividly record why he "broke" with communism: "I repudiated Marx's doctrines and Lenin's tactics," because, he said, "[e]xperience and the record had convinced me that Communism is a form of totalitarianism" and "that its triumph means slavery to men whenever they fall under its sway, and spiritual night to the human mind and soul."

"A Letter to My Children," however, does not only warn against the creeping shadows of this "spiritual night," but also evokes the intense light generated by the faith, family, and freedom that enabled Whittaker Chambers to testify against the darkness that had threatened to engulf him. He recalls for his children the ten happy years that they shared between his break with the Communist Party and his public denunciation of still active Communists guilty of espionage against the Government of the United States. Finally, he offers himself as a guide to his children and to the children of all men, offering to lead them through the dark places where he has been, where "in shadow things uncoil and slither away" up into the light where pain is transcended by wisdom.

Chambers wisely recognizes that communism's terrible strength derives from its identity as a religion and its horrors result from its identity as a false religion. In fact, as he points out, communism is man's "second oldest faith," first instituted in response to the serpent's promise "Ye shall be as gods." Chambers's witness shows the fraudulence of this promise and testifies to his own faith in Western civilization—risking his life to defend it. He believes that the fate of the West will depend upon his witness and that of others, and that they will determine "whether all mankind is to become Communist, whether the whole world is to become free, or whether in the struggle, civilization as we know it is to be completely destroyed or completely changed."

Whittaker Chambers writes not only to alert modern man to the irreconcilable conflict between Communism and Freedom and to urge him to take up the battle, but also to remind him of the consequences of its possible loss. He also writes to warn those caught in the snare of Communism that one night they will hear, as he did, the screams of souls in agony, the screams of the faceless victims of a religion that considers terror an "instrument of policy." Beyond this, he writes so that others may profit from his sacrifice and suffering, so that some lasting victory may be won as a result of them, so that from his passion some resurrection will be wrought— for himself, for his children, and for the West.

Otherwise, his "witness"—one might even say his "martyrdom," for "martyr" is the Greek word for witness—would be in vain. For him, that would be the intolerable possibility—that his children and others should come to the Place of Skulls unenlightened by the tragedy which he has seen, no wiser from the agony through which he has passed. Not to be able to distinguish the thieves on that bleak hill from Him who stole life from death would be, for Whittaker Chambers, the greatest desolation.

Witness is important not only because it records one man's journey from darkness to light, but also because Chambers clearly recognizes that Communism and Freedom are the two irreconcilable forces of our time. He is keenly aware that one must vanquish the other and that all of human history will depend on which is victorious. He recognized that communism is the central fact of the first half of the twentieth century and urgently asks: how can we make the restoration of freedom the central fact of the second half?

Much has been made of his sobering statement, when he left communism, that he thought he was leaving "the winning side for the losing side." Although he added, "it is better to die on the losing side than to live under Communism," his words are profoundly disquieting. Did he really believe that communism would inevitably triumph? Did he really think that his own testimony for God, for Freedom, and for the inherent rights of man were in vain? Did he really consider his own wrenching witness a merely futile gesture? One of Chambers's good friends, Ralph de Toledano, answered that question definitively: "Let me tell you a little secret. When he said that he was on the losing side, I do not think he really believed it."

Although Chambers ends "A Letter to My Children" with an evocation of Golgotha, he begins *Witness* with an allusion to Lazarus and a description of his own "impossible return" from the soul-killing depths of Communism. He hoped that he would be able to make this "impossible return" because, as Malraux said of him, he had not returned from Hell empty-handed. He had brought with him the ability to see and to rejoice in the light. As a result of his travail in the depths, he could see the heights—and beyond.

Therefore, we salute not only the courage and the vision, but especially the hope of Whittaker Chambers.

Whittaker Chambers

A Letter to My Children

Beloved children, I am sitting in the kitchen of the little house at Medfield, our second farm which is cut off by the ridge and a quarter-mile across the Welds from our home place, where you are. I am writing a book. In it I am speaking to you. But I am also speaking to the world. To both I owe an accounting.

It is a terrible book. It is terrible in what it tells about men. If anything, it is more terrible in what it tells about the world in which you live. It is about what the world calls the Hiss-Chambers Case, or even more simply, the Hiss Case. It is about a spy case. All the props of an espionage case are there—foreign agents, household traitors, stolen documents, microfilm, furtive meetings, secret hideaways, phony names, an informer, investigations, trials, official justice.

But if the Hiss Case were only this, it would not be worth my writing about or your reading about. It would be another fat folder in the sad files of the police, another crime drama in which the props would be mistaken for the play (as many people have consistently mistaken them). It would not be what alone gave it meaning, what the mass of men and women instinctively sensed it to be, often without quite knowing why. It would not be what, at the very beginning, I was moved to call it: "a tragedy of history."

From Whittaker Chambers, *Witness* (1952).

For it was more than human tragedy. Much more than Alger Hiss or Whittaker Chambers was on trial in the trials of Alger Hiss. Two faiths were on trial. Human societies, like human beings, live by faith and die when faith dies. At issue in the Hiss Case was the question whether this sick society, which we call Western civilization, could in its extremity still cast up a man whose faith in it was so great that he would voluntarily abandon those things which men hold good, including life, to defend it. At issue was the question whether this man's faith could prevail against a man whose equal faith it was that this society is sick beyond saving, and that mercy itself pleads for its swift extinction and replacement by another. At issue was the question whether, in the desperately divided society, there still remained the will to recognize the issues in time to offset the immense rally of public power to distort and pervert the facts.

At heart, the Great Case was this critical conflict of faiths; that is why it was a great case. On a scale personal enough to be felt by all, but big enough to be symbolic, the two irreconcilable faiths of our time—Communism and Freedom—came to grips in the persons of two conscious and resolute men. Indeed, it would have been hard, in a world still only dimly aware of what the conflict is about, to find two other men who knew so clearly. Both had been schooled in the same view of history (the Marxist view). Both were trained by the same party in the same selfless, semi-soldierly discipline. Neither would nor could yield without betraying, not himself, but his faith; and the different character of these faiths was shown by the different conduct of the two men toward each other throughout the struggle. For, with dark certitude, both knew, almost from the beginning, that the Great Case could end only in the destruction of one or both of the contending figures, just as the history of our times (both men had been taught) can end only in the destruction of one or both of the contending forces.

But this destruction is not the tragedy. The nature of tragedy is itself misunderstood. Part of the world supposes that the tragedy in the Hiss Case lies in the acts of disloyalty revealed. Part believes that the tragedy lies in the fact that an able, intelligent man, Alger Hiss, was cut short in the course of a brilliant public career. Some find it tragic that Whittaker Chambers, of his own will, gave up a $30,000-a-year job and a secure future to haunt for the rest of his days the ruins of his life. These are shocking facts, criminal facts, disturbing facts: they are not tragic.

Crime, violence, infamy are not tragedy. Tragedy occurs when a human soul awakes and seeks, in suffering and pain, to free itself from crime, violence, infamy, even at the cost of life. The struggle is the tragedy—not defeat or death. That is why the spectacle of tragedy has always filled men, not with despair, but with a sense of hope and exaltation. That is why this terrible book is also a book of hope. For it is about the struggle of the human soul—of more than one human soul. It is in this sense that the Hiss Case is a tragedy. This is its meaning beyond the headlines, the revelations, the shame and suffering of the people involved. But this tragedy will have been for nothing unless men understand it rightly, and from it the world takes hope and heart to begin its own tragic struggle with the evil that besets it from within and from without, unless it faces the fact that the world, the whole world, is sick unto death and that, among other things, this Case has turned a finger of fierce light into the suddenly opened and reeking body of our time.

My children, as long as you live, the shadow of the Hiss Case will brush you. In every pair of eyes that rests on you, you will see pass, like a cloud passing behind a woods in winter, the memory of your father—dissembled in friendly eyes, lurking in unfriendly eyes. Sometimes you will wonder which is harder to bear: friendly forgiveness or forthright hate. In time, therefore, when the sum of your experience of life gives you authority, you will ask yourselves the question: What was my father?

I will give you an answer: I was a witness. I do not mean a witness for the Government or against Alger Hiss and the others. Nor do I mean the short, squat, solitary figure, trudging through the impersonal halls of public buildings to testify before Congressional committees, grand juries, loyalty boards, courts of law. A man is not primarily a witness *against* something. That is only incidental to the fact that he is a witness *for* something. A witness, in the sense that I am using the word, is a man whose life and faith are so completely one that when the challenge comes to step out and testify for his faith, he does so, disregarding all risks, accepting all consequences.

One day in the great jury room of the Grand Jury of the Southern District of New York, a juror leaned forward slightly and asked me: "Mr. Chambers, what does it mean to be a Communist?" I hesitated for a moment, trying to find the simplest, most direct way to convey the heart of this complex experience to men and women to whom the very fact of the experience was all but incomprehensible. Then I said:

"When I was a Communist, I had three heroes. One was a Russian. One was a Pole. One was a German Jew.

"The Pole was Felix Djerjinsky. He was ascetic, highly sensitive, intelligent. He was a Communist. After the Russian Revolution, he became head of the Tcheka and organizer of the Red Terror. As a young man, Djerjinsky had been a political prisoner in the Paviak Prison in Warsaw. There he insisted on being given the task of cleaning the latrines of the other prisoners. For he held that the most developed member of any community must take upon himself the lowliest tasks as an example to those who are less developed. That is one thing that it meant to be a Communist.

"The German Jew was Eugen Leviné. He was a Communist. During the Bavarian Soviet Republic in 1919, Leviné was the organizer of the Workers and Soldiers Soviets. When the Bavarian Soviet Republic was crushed, Leviné was captured and court-martialed. The court-martial told him: 'You are under sentence of death.' Leviné answered: 'We Communists are always under sentence of death.' That is another thing that it meant to be a Communist.

"The Russian was not a Communist. He was a pre-Communist revolutionist named Kalyaev. (I should have said Sazonov.) He was arrested for a minor part in the assassination of the Tsarist prime minister, von Plehve. He was sent into Siberian exile to one of the worst prison camps, where the political prisoners were flogged. Kalyaev sought some way to protest this outrage to the world. The means were few, but at last he found a way. In protest against the flogging of other men, Kalyaev drenched himself in kerosene, set himself on fire and burned himself to death. That also is what it meant to be a Communist."

That also is what it means to be a witness.

But a man may also be an involuntary witness. I do not know any way to explain why God's grace touches a man who seems unworthy of it. But neither do I know any other way to explain how a man like myself—tarnished by life, unprepossessing, not brave—could prevail so far against the powers of the world arrayed almost solidly against him, to destroy him and defeat his truth. In this sense, I am an involuntary witness to God's grace and to the fortifying power of faith.

It was my fate to be in turn a witness to each of the two great faiths of our time. And so we come to the terrible word, Communism. My very dear children, nothing in all these pages will be written so much for you, though it is so unlike anything you would want to read. In nothing shall I be so much a witness, in no way am I so much called upon to fulfill my task, as in trying to make clear to you (and to the world) the true nature of Communism and the source of its power, which was the cause of my ordeal as a man, and remains the historic ordeal of the world in the 20th century. For in this century, within the next decades, will be decided for generations whether all mankind is to become Communist, whether the whole world is to become free, or whether, in the struggle, civilization as we know it is to be completely destroyed or completely changed. It is our fate to live upon that turning point in history.

The world has reached that turning point by the steep stages of crisis mounting for generations. The turning point is the next to the last step. It was reached in blood, sweat, tears, havoc and death in World War II. The chief fruit of the First World War was the

Russian Revolution and the rise of Communism as a national power. The chief fruit of the Second World War was our arrival at the next to the last step of the crisis with the rise of Communism as a world power. History is likely to say that these were the only decisive results of the world wars.

The last war simplified the balance of political forces in the world by reducing them to two. For the first time, it made the power of the Communist sector of mankind (embodied in the Soviet Union) roughly equal to the power of the free sector of mankind (embodied in the United States). It made the collision of these powers all but inevitable. For the world wars did not end the crisis. They raised its tensions to a new pitch. They raised the crisis to a new stage. All the politics of our time, including the politics of war, will be the politics of this crisis.

Few men are so dull that they do not know that the crisis exists and that it threatens their lives at every point. It is popular to call it a social crisis. It is in fact a total crisis—religious, moral, intellectual, social, political, economic. It is popular to call it a crisis of the Western world. It is in fact a crisis of the whole world. Communism, which claims to be a solution of the crisis, is itself a symptom and an irritant of the crisis.

In part, the crisis results from the impact of science and technology upon mankind which, neither socially nor morally, has caught up with the problems posed by that impact. In part, it is caused by men's efforts to solve those problems. World wars are the military expression of the crisis. Worldwide depressions are its economic expression. Universal desperation is its spiritual climate. This is the climate of Communism. Communism in our time can no more be considered apart from the crisis than a fever can be acted upon apart from an infected body.

I see in Communism the focus of the concentrated evil of our time. You will ask: Why, then, do men become Communists? How did it happen that you, our gentle and loved father, were once a Communist? Were you simply stupid? No, I was not stupid. Were you morally depraved? No, I was not morally depraved. Indeed, educated men become Communists chiefly for moral reasons. Did you not know that the crimes and horrors of Communism are inherent in Communism? Yes, I knew that fact. Then why did you become a Communist? It would help more to ask: How did it happen that this movement, once a mere muttering of political outcasts, became this immense force that now contests the mastery of mankind? Even when all the chances and mistakes of history are allowed for, the answer must be: Communism makes some profound appeal to the human mind. You will not find out what it is by calling Communism names. That will not help much to explain why Communism whose horrors, on a scale unparalleled in history, are now public knowledge, still recruits its thousands and holds its millions—among them some of the best minds alive. Look at Klaus Fuchs, standing in the London dock, quiet, doomed, destroyed, and say whether it is possible to answer in that way the simple question: Why?

First, let me try to say what Communism is not. It is not simply a vicious plot hatched by wicked men in a sub-cellar. It is not just the writings of Marx and Lenin, dialectical materialism, the Politburo, the labor theory of value, the theory of the general strike, the Red Army, secret police, labor camps, underground conspiracy, the dictatorship of the proletariat, the technique of the coup d'état. It is not even those chanting, bannered millions that stream periodically, like disorganized armies, through the heart of the world's capitals: Moscow, New York, Tokyo, Paris, Rome. These are expressions of Communism, but they are not what Communism is about.

In the Hiss trials, where Communism was a haunting specter, but which did little or nothing to explain Communism, Communists were assumed to be criminals, pariahs, clandestine men who lead double lives under false names, travel on false passports, deny traditional religion, morality, the sanctity of oaths, preach violence and practice treason. These things are true about Communists, but they are not what Communism is about.

The revolutionary heart of Communism is not the theatrical appeal: "Workers of the world, unite. You have nothing to lose but your chains. You have a world to gain." It is a simple statement of

Karl Marx, further simplified for handy use: "Philosophers have explained the world; it is necessary to change the world." Communists are bound together by no secret oath. The tie that binds them across the frontiers of nations, across barriers of language and differences of class and education, in defiance of religion, morality, truth, law, honor, the weaknesses of the body and the irresolution of the mind, even unto death, is a simple conviction: It is necessary to change the world. Their power, whose nature baffles the rest of the world, because in a large measure the rest of the world has lost that power, is the power to hold convictions and to act on them. It is the same power that moves mountains; it is also an unfailing power to move men. Communists are that part of mankind which has recovered the power to live or die—to bear witness—for its faith. And it is a simple, rational faith that inspires men to live or die for it.

It is not new. It is, in fact, man's second oldest faith. Its promise was whispered in the first days of the Creation under the Tree of the Knowledge of Good and Evil: "Ye shall be as gods." It is the great alternative faith of mankind. Like all great faiths, its force derives from a simple vision. Other ages have had great visions. They have always been different versions of the same vision: the vision of God and man's relationship to God. The Communist vision is the vision of Man without God.

It is the vision of man's mind displacing God as the creative intelligence of the world. It is the vision of man's liberated mind, by the sole force of its rational intelligence, redirecting man's destiny and reorganizing man's life and the world. It is the vision of man, once more the central figure of the Creation, not because God made man in His image, but because man's mind makes him the most intelligent of the animals. Copernicus and his successors displaced man as the central fact of the universe by proving that the earth was not the central star of the universe. Communism restores man to his sovereignty by the simple method of denying God.

The vision is a challenge and implies a threat. It challenges man to prove by his acts that he is the masterwork of the Creation—by making thought and act one. It challenges him to prove it by using the force of his rational mind to end the bloody meaninglessness of man's history—by giving it purpose and a plan. It challenges him to prove it by reducing the meaningless chaos of nature, by imposing on it his rational will to order, abundance, security, peace. It is the vision of materialism. But it threatens, if man's mind is unequal to the problems of man's progress, that he will sink back into savagery (the A and the H bombs have raised the issue in explosive forms), until nature replaces him with a more intelligent form of life.

It is an intensely practical vision. The tools to turn it into reality are at hand—science and technology, whose traditional method, the rigorous exclusion of all supernatural factors in solving problems, has contributed to the intellectual climate in which the vision flourishes, just as they have contributed to the crisis in which Communism thrives. For the vision is shared by millions who are not Communists (they are part of Communism's secret strength). Its first commandment is found, not in the *Communist Manifesto,* but in the first sentence of the physics primer: "All of the progress of mankind to date results from the making of careful measurements." But Communism, for the first time in history, has made this vision the faith of a great modern political movement.

Hence the Communist Party is quite justified in calling itself the most revolutionary party in history. It has posed in practical form the most revolutionary question in history: God or Man? It has taken the logical next step which three hundred years of rationalism hesitated to take, and said what millions of modern minds think, but do not dare or care to say: If man's mind is the decisive force in the world, what need is there for God? Henceforth man's mind is man's fate.

This vision *is* the Communist revolution, which, like all great revolutions, occurs in man's mind before it takes form in man's acts. Insurrection and conspiracy are merely methods of realizing the vision; they are merely part of the politics of Communism. Without its vision, they, like Communism, would have no meaning and could not rally a parcel of pickpockets. Communism does not summon men to crime or to utopia, as its easy critics like to think. On the plane of faith, it summons mankind to turn its vision into practical reality. On the plane of action, it summons men to struggle against the inertia of the past which, embodied in social, political and economic forms, Communism claims, is blocking the will of mankind to make its next great forward stride. It summons men to overcome the crisis, which, Communism claims, is in effect a crisis of rending frustration, with the world, unable to stand still, but unwilling to go forward along the road that the logic of a technological civilization points out—Communism.

This is Communism's moral sanction, which is twofold. Its vision points the way to the future; its faith labors to turn the future into present reality. It says to every man who joins it: the vision is a practical problem of history; the way to achieve it is a practical problem of politics, which is the present tense of history. Have you the moral strength to take upon yourself the crimes of history so that man at last may close his chronicle of age-old, senseless suffering, and replace it with purpose and a plan? The answer a man makes to this question is the difference between the Communist and those miscellaneous socialists, liberals, fellow travelers, unclassified progressives and men of good will, all of whom share a similar vision, but do not share the faith because they will not take upon themselves the penalties of the faith. The answer is the root of that sense of moral superiority which makes Communists, though caught in crime, berate their opponents with withering self-righteousness.

The Communist vision has a mighty agitator and a mighty propagandist. They are the crisis. The agitator needs no soapbox. It speaks insistently to the human mind at the point where desperation lurks. The propagandist writes no Communist gibberish. It speaks insistently to the human mind at the point where man's hope and man's energy fuse to fierceness.

The vision inspires. The crisis impels. The workingman is chiefly moved by the crisis. The educated man is chiefly moved by the vision. The workingman, living upon a mean margin of life, can afford few visions—even practical visions. An educated man, peering from the Harvard Yard, or any college campus, upon a world in chaos, finds in the vision the two certainties for which the mind of man tirelessly seeks: a reason to live and a reason to die. No other faith of our time presents them with the same practical intensity. That is why Communism is the central experience of the first half of the 20th century, and may be its final experience—will be, unless the free world, in the agony of its struggle with Communism, overcomes its crisis by discovering, in suffering and pain, a power of faith which will provide man's mind, at the same intensity, with the same two certainties: a reason to live and a reason to die. If it falls, this will be the century of the great social wars. If it succeeds, this will be the century of the great wars of faith.

You will ask: Why, then, do men cease to be Communists? One answer is: Very few do. Thirty years after the Russian Revolution, after the known atrocities, the purges, the revelations, the jolting zigzags of Communist politics, there is only a handful of ex-Communists in the whole world. By ex-Communists I do not mean those who break with Communism over differences of strategy and tactics (like Trotsky) or organization (like Tito). Those are merely quarrels over a road map by people all of whom are in a hurry to get to the same place.

Nor, by ex-Communists, do I mean those thousands who continually drift into the Communist Party and out again. The turnover is vast. These are the spiritual vagrants of our time whose traditional faith has been leached out in the bland climate of rationalism. They are looking for an intellectual night's lodging. They lack the character for Communist faith because they lack the character for any faith. So they drop away, though Communism keeps its hold on them.

By an ex-Communist, I mean a man who knew clearly why he became a Communist, who served Communism devotedly and knew why he served it, who broke with Communism unconditionally and knew why he broke with it. Of these there are very few—an index to the power of the vision and the power of the crisis.

History very largely fixes the patterns of force that make men Communists. Hence one Communist conversion sounds much like another—rather impersonal and repetitious, awesome and tiresome, like long lines of similar people all stolidly waiting to get in to see the same movie. A man's break with Communism is intensely personal. Hence the account of no two breaks is likely to be the same. The reasons that made one Communist break may seem without force to another ex-Communist.

It is a fact that a man can join the Communist Party, can be very active in it for years, without completely understanding the nature of Communism or the political methods that follow inevitably from its vision. One day such incomplete Communists discover that the Communist Party is not what they thought it was. They break with it and turn on it with the rage of an honest dupe, a dupe who has given a part of his life to a swindle. Often they forget that it takes two to make a swindle.

Others remain Communists for years, warmed by the light of its vision, firmly closing their eyes to the crimes and horrors inseparable from its practical politics. One day they have to face the facts. They are appalled at what they have abetted. They spend the rest of their days trying to explain, usually without great success, the dark clue to their complicity. As their understanding of Communism was incomplete and led them to a dead end, their understanding of breaking with it is incomplete and leads them to a dead end. It leads to less than Communism, which was a vision and a faith. The world outside Communism, the world in crisis, lacks a vision and a faith. There is before these ex-Communists absolutely nothing. Behind them is a threat. For they have, in fact, broken not with the vision, but with the politics of the vision. In the name of reason and intelligence, the vision keeps them firmly in its grip—self-divided, paralyzed, powerless to act against it.

Hence the most secret fold of their minds is haunted by a terrifying thought: What if we were wrong? What if our inconstancy is our guilt? That is the fate of those who break without knowing clearly that Communism is wrong because something else is right, because to the challenge: *God or Man?*, they continue to give the answer: *Man*. Their pathos is that not even the Communist ordeal could teach them that man without God is just what Communism said he was: the most intelligent of the animals, that man without God is a beast, never more beastly than when he is most intelligent about his beastliness. "*Er nennt's Vernunft*," says the Devil in Goethe's *Faust*, "*und braucht's allein, nur tierischer als jedes Tier zu sein*"—Man calls it reason and uses it simply to be more beastly than any beast. Not grasping the source of the evil they sincerely hate, such ex-Communists in general make ineffectual witnesses against it. They are witnesses against something; they have ceased to be witnesses for anything.

Yet there is one experience which most sincere ex-Communists share, whether or not they go only part way to the end of the question it poses. The daughter of a former German diplomat in Moscow was trying to explain to me why her father, who, as an enlightened modern man, had been extremely pro-Communist, had become an implacable anti-Communist. It was hard for her because, as an enlightened modern girl, she shared the Communist vision without being a Communist. But she loved her father and the irrationality of his defection embarrassed her. "He was immensely pro-Soviet," she said, "and then—you will laugh at me—but you must not laugh at my father—and then—one night—in Moscow—he heard screams. That's all. Simply one night he heard screams."

A child of Reason and the 20th century, she knew that there is logic of the mind. She did not know that the soul has a logic that may be more compelling than the mind's. She did not know at all that she had swept away the logic of the mind, the logic of history, the logic of politics, the myth of the 20th century, with five annihilating words: one night he heard screams.

What Communist has not heard those screams? They come from husbands torn forever from their wives in midnight arrests. They come, muffled, from the execution cellars of the secret police, from the torture chambers of the Lubianka, from all the citadels of terror now stretching from Berlin to Canton. They come from those freight cars loaded with men, women and children, the enemies of the Communist State, locked in, packed in, left on remote sidings to freeze to death at night in the Russian winter. They come from minds driven mad by the horrors of mass starvation ordered and enforced as a policy of the Communist State. They come from the starved skeletons, worked to death, or flogged to death (as an example to others) in the freezing filth of sub-arctic labor camps. They come from children whose parents are suddenly, inexplicably, taken away from them—parents they will never see again.

What Communist has not heard those screams? Execution, says the Communist code, is the highest measure of social protection. What man can call himself a Communist who has not accepted the fact that Terror is an instrument of policy, right if the vision is right, justified by history, enjoined by the balance of forces in the social wars of this century? Those screams have reached every Communist's mind. Usually they stop there. What judge willingly dwells upon the man the laws compel him to condemn to death—the laws of nations or the laws of history?

But one day the Communist really hears those screams. He is going about his routine party tasks. He is lifting a dripping reel of microfilm from a developing tank. He is justifying to a Communist fraction in a trade union an extremely unwelcome directive of the Central Committee. He is receiving from a trusted superior an order to go to another country and, in a designated hotel, at a designated hour, meet a man whose name he will never know, but who will give him a package whose contents he will never learn. Suddenly, there closes around that Communist a separating silence, and in that silence he hears screams. He hears them for the first time. For they do not merely reach his mind. They pierce beyond. They pierce to his soul. He says to himself: "Those are not the screams of man in agony. Those are the screams of a soul in agony." He hears them for the first time because a soul in extremity has communicated with that which alone can hear it—another human soul.

Why does the Communist ever hear them? Because in the end there persists in every man, however he may deny it, a scrap of soul. The Communist who suffers this singular experience then says to himself: "What is happening to me? I must be sick." If he does not instantly stifle that scrap of soul, he is lost. If he admits it for a moment, he has admitted that there is something greater than Reason, greater than the logic of mind, of politics, of history, of economics, which alone justifies the vision. If the party senses his weakness, and the party is peculiarly cunning at sensing such weakness, it will humiliate him, degrade him, condemn him, expel him. If it can, it will destroy him. And the party will be right. For he has betrayed that which alone justifies its faith—the vision of Almighty Man. He has brushed the only vision that has force against the vision of Almighty Mind. He stands before the fact of God.

The Communist Party is familiar with this experience to which its members are sometimes liable in prison, in illness, in indecision. It is recognized frankly as a sickness. There are ways of treating it— if it is confessed. It is when it is not confessed that the party, sensing a subtle crisis, turns upon it savagely. What ex-Communist has not suffered this experience in one form or another, to one degree or another? What he does about it depends on the individual man. That is why no ex-Communist dare answer for his sad fraternity the question: Why do men break with Communism? He can only answer the question: How did you break with Communism? My answer is: Slowly, reluctantly, in agony.

Yet my break began long before I heard those screams. Perhaps it does for everyone. I do not know how far back it began. Avalanches gather force and crash, unheard, in men as in the mountains. But I date my break from a very casual happening. I was sitting in our apartment on St. Paul Street in Baltimore. It was shortly before we moved to Alger Hiss's apartment in Washington. My daughter was in her high chair. I was watching her eat. She was the most miraculous thing that had ever happened in my life. I liked to watch her even when she smeared porridge on her face or dropped it meditatively on the floor. My eye came to rest on the delicate convolutions of her ear—those intricate, perfect ears. The thought passed through my mind: "No, those ears were not created by any chance coming together of atoms in nature (the Communist view). They could have been created only by immense design." The thought was involuntary and unwanted. I crowded it out of my mind. But I never wholly forgot it or the occasion. I had to crowd it out of my mind. If I had completed it, I should have had to say: Design presupposes God. I did not then know that, at that moment, the finger of God was first laid upon my forehead.

One thing most ex-Communists could agree upon: they broke because they wanted to be free. They do not all mean the same thing by "free." Freedom is a need of the soul, and nothing else. It is in striving toward God that the soul strives continually after a condition of freedom. God alone is the inciter and guarantor of freedom. He is the only guarantor. External freedom is only an aspect of interior freedom. Political freedom, as the Western world has known it, is only a political reading of the Bible. Religion and freedom are indivisible. Without freedom the soul dies. Without the soul there is no justification for freedom. Necessity is the only ultimate justification known to the mind. Hence every sincere break with Communism is a religious experience, though the Communist fails to identify its true nature, though he fails to go to the end of the experience. His break is the political expression of the perpetual need of the soul whose first faint stirring he has felt within him, years, months or days before he breaks. A Communist breaks because he must choose at last between irreconcilable opposites— God or Man, Soul or Mind, Freedom or Communism.

Communism is what happens when, in the name of Mind, men free themselves from God. But its view of God, its knowledge of

God, its experience of God, is what alone gives character to a society or a nation, and meaning to its destiny. Its culture, the voice of this character, is merely that view, knowledge, experience, of God, fixed by its most intense spirits in terms intelligible to the mass of men. There has never been a society or a nation without God. But history is cluttered with the wreckage of nations that became indifferent to God, and died.

The crisis of Communism exists to the degree in which it has failed to free the peoples that it rules from God. Nobody knows this better than the Communist Party of the Soviet Union. The crisis of the Western world exists to the degree in which it is indifferent to God. It exists to the degree in which the Western world actually shares Communism's materialist vision, is so dazzled by the logic of the materialist interpretation of history, politics and economics, that it fails to grasp that, for it, the only possible answer to the Communist challenge: Faith in God or Faith in Man? is the challenge: Faith in God.

Economics is not the central problem of this century. It is a relative problem which can be solved in relative ways. Faith is the central problem of this age. The Western world does not know it, but it already possesses the answer to this problem—but only provided that its faith in God and the freedom He enjoins is as great as Communism's faith in Man.

MY DEAR CHILDREN, before I close this foreword, I want to recall to you briefly the life that we led in the ten years between the time when I broke with Communism and the time when I began to testify—the things we did, worked for, loved, believed in. For it was that happy life, which, on the human side, in part made it possible for me to do later on the things I had to do, or endure the things that happened to me.

Those were the days of the happy little worries, which then seemed so big. We know now that they were the golden days. They will not come again. In those days, our greatest worry was how to meet the payments on the mortgage, how to get the ploughing done in time, how to get health accreditation for our herd, how to get the hay in before the rain. I sometimes took my vacation in hay harvest so that I could help work the load. You two little children used to trample the load, drive the hay truck in the fields when you could barely reach the foot pedals, or drive the tractor that pulled up the loaded harpoons to the mow. At evening, you would break off to help Mother milk while I went on haying. For we came of age on the farm when we decided not to hire barn help, but to run the herd ourselves as a family.

Often the oven-like heat in the comb of the barn and the sweet smell of alfalfa made us sick. Sometimes we fell asleep at the supper table from fatigue. But the hard work was good for us; and you knew only the peace of a home governed by a father and mother whose marriage the years (and an earlier suffering which you could not remember) had deepened into the perfect love that enveloped you.

Mother was a slight, overalled figure forever working for you in the house or beside you in the barns and gardens. Papa was a squat, overalled figure, fat but forceful, who taught John, at nine, the man-size glory of driving the tractor; or sat beside Ellen, at the wheel of the truck, an embodiment of security and power, as we drove loads of cattle through the night. On summer Sundays, you sat between Papa and Mama in the Quaker meetinghouse. Through the open doors, as you tried not to twist and turn in the long silence, you could see the far, blue Maryland hills and hear the redbirds and ground robins in the graveyard behind.

Only Ellen had a vague, troubled recollection of another time and another image of Papa. Then (it was during the years 1938 and 1939), if for any reason she pattered down the hall at night, she would find Papa, with the light on, writing, with a revolver on the table or a gun against the chair. She knew that there were people who wanted to kill Papa and who might try to kidnap her. But a wide sea of sunlight and of time lay between that puzzling recollection and the farm.

The farm was your kingdom, and the world lay far beyond the protecting walls thrown up by work and love. It is true that comic strips were not encouraged, comic books were banned, the radio could be turned on only by permission which was seldom given (or asked), and you saw few movies. But you grew in the presence of eternal wonders. There was the birth of lambs and calves. You remember how once, when I was away and the veterinarian could not come, you saw Mother reach in and turn the calf inside the cow so that it could be born. There was also the death of animals, sometimes violent, sometimes slow and painful—nothing is more constant on a farm than death.

Sometimes, of a spring evening, Papa would hear that distant honking that always makes his scalp tingle, and we would all rush out to see the wild geese, in lines of hundreds, steer up from the southwest, turn over the barn as over a landmark, and head into the north. Or on autumn nights of sudden cold that set the ewes breeding in the orchard, Papa would call you out of the house to stand with him in the now celebrated pumpkin patch and watch the northern lights flicker in electric clouds on the horizon, mount, die down, fade and mount again till they filled the whole northern sky with ghostly light in motion.

Thus, as children, you experienced two of the most important things men ever know—the wonder of life and the wonder of the universe, the wonder of life within the wonder of the universe. More important, you knew them not from books, not from lectures, but simply from living among them. Most important, you knew them with reverence and awe—that reverence and awe that has died out of the modern world and been replaced by man's monkeylike amazement at the cleverness of his own inventive brain.

I have watched greatness touch you in another way. I have seen you sit, uninvited and unforced, listening in complete silence to the third movement of the Ninth Symphony. I thought you understood, as much as children can, when I told you that that music was the moment at which Beethoven finally passed beyond the suffering of his life on earth and reached for the hand of God, as God reaches for the hand of Adam in Michelangelo's vision of the Creation.

And once, in place of a bedtime story, I was reading Shakespeare to John—at his own request, for I never forced such things on you. I came to that passage in which Macbeth, having murdered Duncan, realizes what he has done to his own soul, and asks if all the water in the world can ever wash the blood from his hand, or will it not rather

The multitudinous seas incarnadine?

At that line, John's whole body twitched. I gave great silent thanks to God. For I knew that if, as children, you could thus feel in your souls the reverence and awe for life and the world, which is the ultimate meaning of Beethoven and Shakespeare, as man and woman you could never be satisfied with less. I felt a great faith that sooner or later you would understand what I once told you, not because I expected you to understand it then, but because I hoped that you would remember it later: "True wisdom comes from the overcoming of suffering and sin. All true wisdom is therefore touched with sadness."

If all this sounds unduly solemn, you know that our lives were not; that all of us suffer from an incurable itch to puncture false solemnity. In our daily lives, we were fun-loving and gay. For those who have solemnity in their souls generally have enough of it there, and do not need to force it into their faces.

THEN, ON AUGUST 3, 1948, you learned for the first time that your father had once been a Communist, that he had worked in something called "the underground," that it was shameful, and that for some reason he was in Washington telling the world about it. While he was in the underground, he testified, he had worked with a number of other Communists. One of them was a man with the odd name of Alger Hiss. Later, Alger Hiss denied the allegation. Thus the Great Case began, and with it our lives were changed forever.

Dear children, one autumn twilight, when you were much smaller, I slipped away from you in play and stood for a moment alone in the apple orchard near the barn. Then I heard your two voices, piping together anxiously, calling to me: "Papa! Papa!" from the harvested cornfield. In the years when I was away five days a week in New York, working to pay for the farm, I used to think of you both before I fell asleep at night. And that is how you almost always came to me—voices of beloved children, calling to me from the gathered fields at dusk.

You called to me once again at night in the same orchard. That was a good many years later. A shadow deeper and more chilling than the autumn evening had closed upon us—I mean the Hiss Case. It was the first year of the Case. We had been doing the evening milking together. For us, one of the few happy results of the Case was that at last I could be home with you most of the time (in life these good things usually come too little or too late). I was washing and disinfecting the cows, and putting on and taking off the milkers. You were stripping after me.

In the quiet, there suddenly swept over my mind a clear realization of our true position—obscure, all but friendless people (some of my great friends had already taken refuge in aloofness; the others I had withdrawn from so as not to involve them in my affairs). Against me was an almost solid line-up of the most powerful groups and men in the country, the bitterly hostile reaction of much of the press, the smiling skepticism of much of the public, the venomous calumnies of the Hiss forces, the all but universal failure to understand the real meaning of the Case or my real purpose. A sense of the enormous futility of my effort, and my own inadequacy, drowned me. I felt a physical cold creep through me, settle around my heart and freeze any pulse of hope. The sight of you children, guiltless and defenseless, was more than I could bear. I was alone against the world; my longing was to be left completely alone, or not to be at all. It was that death of the will which Communism, with great cunning, always tries to induce in its victims.

I waited until the last cow was stripped and the last can lifted into the cooler. Then I stole into the upper barn and out into the apple orchard. It was a very dark night. The stars were large and cold. This cold was one with the coldness in myself. The lights of the barn, the house and the neighbors' houses were warm in the windows and on the ground; they were not for me. Then I heard Ellen call me in the barn and John called: "Papa!" Still calling, Ellen went down to the house to see if I were there. I heard John opening gates as he went to the calf barn, and he called me there. With all the longing of my love for you, I wanted to answer. But if I answered, I must come back to the living world. I could not do that.

John began to call me in the cow stable, in the milk house. He went into the dark side of the barn (I heard him slide the door back), into the upper barn, where at night he used to be afraid. He stepped outside in the dark, calling: "Papa! Papa!"—then, frantically, on the verge of tears: "Papa!" I walked over to him. I felt that I was making the most terrible surrender I should have to make on earth. "Papa," he cried and threw his arms around me, "don't ever go away." "No," I said, "no, I won't ever go away." Both of us knew that the words "go away" stood for something else, and that I had given him my promise not to kill myself. Later on, as you will see, I was tempted, in my wretchedness, to break that promise.

MY CHILDREN, when you were little, we used sometimes to go for walks in our pinewoods. In the open fields, you would run along by yourselves. But you used instinctively to give me your hands as we entered those woods, where it was darker, lonelier, and in the stillness our voices sounded loud and frightening. In this book I am again giving you my hands. I am leading you, not through cool pinewoods, but up and up a narrow defile between bare and steep rocks from which in shadow things uncoil and slither away. It will be dark. But, in the end, if I have led you aright, you will make out three crosses, from two of which hang thieves. I will have brought you to Golgotha—the place of skulls. This is the meaning of the journey. Before you understand, I may not be there, my hands may have slipped from yours. It will not matter. For when you understand what you see, you will no longer be children. You will know that life is pain, that each of us hangs always upon the cross of himself. And when you know that this is true of every man, woman and child on earth, you will be wise.

Your Father

CHAPTER 11

Michael Novak

Commentary by Edwin J. Feulner Jr. (1989)

Michael Novak once wrote, "There is probably nothing more difficult for an intellectual of the Left than to risk [his] credentials by radical criticism of the Left," for the "punishment is excommunication." He knew whereof he spoke, for that was the punishment that he not only courted but won. Valuing truth more than his own preconceptions, and the evidence of his senses more than the siren-song of an ideological vision, he boldly repudiated socialism and utterly horrified his erstwhile colleagues by embracing free enterprise.

Novak declared that "socialism makes no sense as an economic theory," asserted that it has not worked well in any of the 110 countries where it has been tried, and pointed out that it has resulted mainly in tyranny and poverty. Furthermore, he observed that capitalism alone recognizes that "the cause of the wealth of nations is the creativity of the human person."

Such a devastating critique of socialism was not easy for Michael Novak to make. He knew that it would enrage many former colleagues, injure some friendships, and close the doors of numerous publications and schools to his writings and speeches. Worst of all, he would be accused of having "sold out" to the denizens of Wall Street, the complacent country club set, the intellectually simplistic, and the morally disingenuous. None of his detractors has, as far as I know, actually accused him, Chinese-style, of being "a running dog of capitalism," but that was the tenor of the charges hurled at him when he unceremoniously "defected."

No one, according to Michael, was more surprised by this gradual change of heart than he. In his contribution to Peter Occhiogrosso's *Once a Catholic*, Novak writes, "I found to my surprise around 1977 that I really could not call myself a socialist. I was afraid to publish this, didn't want to admit it publicly, [and] hesitated to tell anyone (even my wife)." In retrospect, humorously comparing this experience to "coming out of the closet," he comments, "But even when I held up to myself pictures of Sweden, it didn't help." Once he decided to announce his change of allegiance, however, it is typical of him that he did so boldly—declaring his new perspective in the *Washington Post* in an article facetiously entitled "A Closet Capitalist Confesses."

Novak certainly entertained no illusions concerning how what he himself called his "conversion" would be received, for he was keenly aware that "much of [modern] intellectual life consists in positioning oneself, in keeping one's credentials in order, [and] in flattering the beliefs of one's ideological kin, who clap or boo at each presentation." The adulation or disapprobation of the crowd, however, could not capture the imagination of a man who believed that "life is too short to live for less than the truth."

He knew all too well that one eye fixed on the crowd and the other on the truth would result not in double vision, but in no vision at all. "It is extraordinarily difficult," he wrote, "to keep one's eye on the ball, to hit the truth exactly, to knock it out of the park, when one worries about what others will say." But in this simple comment, Michael Novak tips his hand, so to speak. While many other intellectuals are busy fanning the flames of academic conflagrations, positioning themselves in the forefront of the *avant-garde* and watching the crowd's reaction, Novak has his eye on the truth, and is trying to hit an existential home run.

But simply to say that a man is in love with the truth does not explain how he got up to bat in the first place, much less how he decided to change from a left-handed hitter to a right—while still at bat. When Michael first made this "switch," and certainly ever since, many have wondered how a man who once was, as Occhiogrosso observes, "a hero of ... young Catholic liberals" and of "radical students of all denominations" could turn his back on socialism to become one of America's "leading ... apologists for the free enterprise system."

"Errand into the Wilderness," Michael Novak's autobiographical article, first published in *Political Passages*, tells how and why he made such a startling about-face. What happened?

For many years, Novak, to continue our baseball metaphor, appeared to be the quintessential southpaw—with all his "stats" adding up to a "man of the Left," as he liked to think of himself. When he left home at fourteen, it was to begin studies at Notre Dame that would lead to his becoming a Holy Cross priest—one of the Church's most liberal orders. After leaving the seminary twelve years later, but six months before ordination, he headed to New York where he wrote for such progressive magazines as *Commonweal* and *America,* while also penning campaign speeches for "a would-be Democratic congressman for New Jersey."

Shortly thereafter, when he took a leave of absence from Harvard (where Novak later earned an MA in religion), it was to cover the Vatican Council for the *National Catholic Reporter,* a notoriously left-wing paper which delights in pillorying the hierarchy, deriding the Church, and scandalizing the faithful by its *outré* positions on matters of faith and morals. In fact, during this period, Michael's own mother registered her concern about his progressive views by sending him clippings from conservative newspapers that denounced him "in no uncertain terms."

If his liberal credentials had been sterling at Harvard, they soon became golden, when, in 1965, Novak was appointed as the first

Catholic in Stanford's Religion Department and twice voted one of the "two most influential professors." From 1968 to 1973, he taught at the experimental college at SUNY in Old Westbury where liberalism not only reigned, but careened, pirouetted, stomped, stalked, and rampaged all over campus.

Ironically, it was there that Michael first wondered whether putting radical principles into practice was in the best interest of the polity. It was hard, for example, to see the wisdom of conducting class—as one of his colleagues did—under a seminar table in order to demonstrate "a rigorously egalitarian atmosphere." Likewise, it troubled Michael when a professor of political science kicked in the door of the bookstore to protest its being closed during set "bourgeois hours." Even more disturbing were bomb threats against the Novak family in reprisal for any attempt to enforce academic standards. From this grisly experience, Novak learned that "The entire vocabulary of the far left—which sounds the more plausible the less likely it is to be realized—assumes an entirely different significance when a dominant majority begins to act it out and impose it."

Despite his reservations concerning the wisdom of acting on radical principles, Novak was caught up in a whirlwind of political activity in the late sixties and early seventies. In 1967, he covered the "real story" in South Vietnam for the *National Catholic Reporter* flew to Washington, D.C., to protest America's role in the war; remonstrated with the Secretary of Defense, and co-authored *Vietnam: Crisis of Conscience.* Meanwhile, he worked to elect Robert Kennedy, wrote speeches for Sargent Shriver, and campaigned for McGovern. In spite of the increasing acclaim that Novak received as a leading liberal theologian, political theorist, and journalist, he confesses that he was "of two minds" for most of the 1970s." "Philosophically," he explains, "I was slowly turning away from the radical left [but] ... I was [still] painfully eager to maintain my credentials."

As he indicates in "Errand into the Wilderness," three experiences particularly opened his eyes to the true nature of the Left.

Living with "student radicalism" at Old Westbury acquainted him with some of the "pathologies ... [of] the Left"; contemplating "the genocide in Cambodia, the miseries of the 'boat people' from Vietnam, and accounts of life today in South Vietnam," showed him that much in his anti-war writings had been "mistaken"; and the understanding he gained from participating in the congressional and presidential campaigns of 1970, 1972, and 1976 revealed how far the new power elite of the Democratic Party had divorced itself from mainstream Democrats and from the values of the American people. This gap between them, he discovered with a shock, was caused by the Left's "failure to create an adequate moral vision."

In search of an economic theory that would provide such a moral vision, Novak began to investigate capitalism. By 1982, with the publication of *The Spirit of Democratic Capitalism,* he finally recognized that the only test of any political theory lies in its practice. Moreover, he saw that a fair examination of capitalism and socialism must compare the results they achieve rather than weigh some liberal utopian vision against an actual instance of free enterprise. Making such comparisons, he saw that "The socialist economic ideal clearly did not work in practice, not anywhere." He further realized that socialism is also theoretically flawed, for it "is not designed to create new wealth, but only to mobilize envy." Moreover, he recognized that the goal of socialism is all too often self-empowerment and that in Leninism, its most brutal form, it "is about power through ... terror."

Novak's "Errand into the Wilderness" fits in well with the essays in this volume. Like Chambers who was a Communist activist-turned-journalist, like Weaver who began as a liberal academic but became a renowned conservative professor of literature, and like Roepke, once a socialist economist and later a defender of capitalism, Michael Novak has been a socialist journalist, professor, and economic thinker. Unlike them, he has also been a seminarian, novelist, theologian, and political activist. In fact, as James Finn remarks in a tribute to Novak published in *National Review*

(December 31, 1988), the number of activities in which he has engaged and the diversity of writings that he has produced "seem too varied and abundant to be the work of a single person." Indeed, one reviews his achievements with amazement. Novak has published more than twenty books focusing on theology, politics, economics, and culture. A syndicated columnist, visiting professor, frequent lecturer, and resident scholar at the American Enterprise Institute, he has acted as the Head of the U.S. Delegation to the United Nations Human Rights Commission in Geneva; served on the Board for International Broadcasting; numbered among the members of the Presidential Task Force on Economic Justice; and garnered the Templeton Prize for Progress in Religion.

Despite, or perhaps because of this astonishing record of achievement, Michael Novak seems extremely humble. His writing is full of confessions of mistakes, inadequacies, and embarrassments. In "Errand into the Wilderness," he stresses that "Words ... I had written about the American majority complacently drinking beer in front of television ... made shame color my cheeks," for "my literary imagination had been calumnious." Later in the same essay, he admits, "Knowing I was wrong once, I would be glad to be shown again where now I am in error." Elsewhere, he asks poignantly, "But who was I to be anything but grateful to this country that had taken in an impoverished and much oppressed family of former serfs from Slovakia, and that had given me and countless others opportunities unprecedented in history?"

His humility and charity—even in his critiques—are refreshing, but not accidental characteristics. In *Confessions of a Catholic*, Novak praises humility, which he writes, "is itself an extraordinary achievement," but one that is not easily attained. Cultivation of this virtue, Michael stresses, requires "radical truthfulness," a clear view of reality, and association with the virtuous—both in life and in literature, for, "true humility," he emphasizes, "is learned by the experience of excellence." And, according to Novak, such excellence is nowhere more manifest than in the "brilliance of holy lives." Sensitive to the demands of the spiritual economy, he writes, "The world today needs more ... such lives to relieve it from the mediocrity, shallowness and tedium of abundant sensation." In other words, "We need to be awakened to the depths in which the real human drama occurs, the drama of the soul."

The drama of the soul chronicled in "Errand into the Wilderness" stresses Michael Novak's autobiographical journey as a voyage of discovery, a pilgrimage, and a quest. Its very title suggests his discovery of the role that economic exchange plays in life and the way that his understanding of *practical* commerce opened his eyes to the ruse of socialism. The word "errand" also emphasizes the purposefulness of Michael's journey—he may have set out for the wilderness, but he was willing to brave its dangers in exchange for enlightenment and insight. His choice of the term "errand" is especially fitting for an essay that narrates a conversion that occurred as a result of actual travels (to "err" in the archaic sense of the word), and which grew out of mistaken ideas and behavior (to "err" in the modern sense of the term).

In dealing with a man that Pat Moynihan once called "the beatific Michael Novak," I do not think it is fanciful to associate the idea of an "errand in the wilderness" with a quest or even with knight errantry. Of medium height, sturdy build, broad shoulders and deep chest, with a round, Slavic face and a ready smile, Michael does not look like the stereotypical knight errant and certainly does not resemble the famous one of the "woeful countenance." Nonetheless, he has been something of a tilter at windmills and even more a quester, a man seeking that elusive goal, "wisdom in action."

Like the knights of old, he is very much concerned with charity, civility, courtesy, and chivalry, but is also intensely aware of the need to do battle—with oneself and others—in the cause of intellectual and spiritual integrity. Significantly, he dedicated a copy of his *Free Persons and the Common Good* to one of his conservative colleagues with the telltale words: "for ... one of our most battling, glorious knights," words that apply to him as well.

Michael Novak's intrepidity nowhere expresses itself better than in his willingness to forge ahead into unchartered intellectual territory. As he writes in the book cited above, "say that this project is wrongheaded ... or poorly executed, but do not say that it is lacking in intellectual daring." Indeed, "intellectual daring" enables Michael to seek out "the wilderness," confident that he will return with hard-won insights, that his errand will not be in vain and that he will not come back empty-handed.

Michael Novak

Errand into the Wilderness

S ince at least second grade, I have wanted to become a writer. From ages fourteen to twenty-six, I studied for the Roman Catholic priesthood until, six months before ordination, in 1960, I decided not to become a priest. Not long after I first began publishing in earnest, the Second Vatican Council (1962–1965) brought the Catholic Church to more favorable public attention than it had earlier received in America. From about 1967 until 1971, those who knew my writing had reason to describe me as a "progressive, left-of-center Catholic," and even as one who sided with the radical left, over against the "corporate liberalism" (as I then called it) of the mainline left. I liked being thought of in that way. Nonetheless, a left-wing friend described me to her colleagues in 1968 as one whose "temperament is conservative but who thinks himself into left-wing positions." (That taught me a new way of thinking about myself.) Slowly, though, I also thought my way out of left-wing positions.

My first published book was a novel, *The Tiber Was Silver* (1961). I was long uncertain whether I wanted to be a scholar, a novelist, a social critic, or an engaged activist. The French tradition of Mauriac, Sartre, Camus, and others taught me that an intellectual could properly do all four, each in its season. Aristotle

From Michael Novak, *Political Passages: Journeys of Change Through Two Decades 1968–1988* (1988).

counseled that until he is at least fifty, a philosopher should engage in a broad range of activities at first hand. In my own poor way, I have given that a shot, more or less systematically involving myself in and reflecting upon various dimensions of American life.

During the three decades of my adulthood, political and cultural changes have occurred rapidly. "Movements" of many kinds have swept through the consciousness of readers and writers. On these changes swift judgments are often required. Making them, one can often lose old friends. Families—even spouses—have been driven apart by answering them in different ways. Those who were once allies often become, almost overnight, bitterly estranged. Too often these days, dinner parties erupt in loud and angry disagreement. All this happens because new forms of "consciousness"—concerning American "imperialism," détente, feminism, homosexuality, liberation theology, the rebels in Nicaragua—have confronted our generation with a relentless series of fundamental decisions. *What should we think? What should we hope for? What should we do?*

There is a "vulgar Marxist" way of answering these questions. There is a "line." In fact, other progressives often bully one into becoming "sophisticated." (There is in our society a deep, although disguised, hunger for orthodoxy, especially among persons who think of themselves as progressives. Most do not wish to appear to be orthodox, only sophisticated. It is the same thing.) With unprecedented speed, the literate are urged to adapt to new ideas, to new ways of thinking, and to new standards of judgment. Theology is done, again and yet again, "in a new key." I have come to call it *neodoxy:* obedience to the new.

At a certain point, one wants to get off the train; at least, *I* wanted to get off the train. The progressive "line" draws strength from many diverse cultural feeders but always runs in one direction. It is consistent in the disciplines and inhibitions it wishes to destroy, and in which direction it wants to move. (Near the top of the Book of Genesis, for example, we are told, "Man and woman He made them." *That* is one of the differentiations to be destroyed.) The

climate becomes ever more utopian, ever more dreamy. The mildly
Marxist analysis that is the vanguard of left-wing consciousness is
not random or undirected. It is an analysis of a quite distinctive
type. But this is to get too far ahead in the story.

I WROTE SOME YEARS AGO that life is in some equal measure self-
discovery and self-invention. In part we discover—over time and
through much darkness—who we are. In part, through trial and
error, we choose to be who we are; we give ourselves our own identity. In mobile and free societies such as ours, with access to an
almost infinite range of experiences, books, and thoughts, it is not
so easy as it once was to live a life of straight-line logic. Experiences
occur that call into question earlier certitudes. Fresh insights and
new paradigms allow us to break through earlier established hori-
zons, sometimes from heights (or depths) that alter our vision
of the entire landscape round about. In my case, I once had a vision
of political economy that I have since come to discover was
mistaken.

Like many young Catholics and Jews, I had imbibed from an
early age a set of suspicions concerning big business, capitalism,
Marlboro man individualism, and Anglo-Saxon ethnic superiority.
While never seriously tempted to join a socialist party, I rather liked
socialist analyses that attacked the complacency of America. The
anticapitalism of such writers as R. H. Tawney on Protestantism and
the acquisitive instinct appealed to me. One need not be a socialist
or a Marxist to be fairly systematically anticapitalist (and radically
critical of American society). For all practical purposes, though, one
usually becomes thus the ally of socialists and Marxists.

Today, some of my best friends remain far to the left. *Remain*
far to the left? During the past twenty years, by their own admission, they have moved ever farther left. Like me, they are voyagers.
Their voyages in recent years have taken them into three specific
desert fastnesses: that the United States is an imperialist nation
oppressive to people in the Third World; that capitalism is an evil

economic system, propelling imperialism abroad and multiple ills at home; and that the combination of imperialism and capitalism is fed by patriarchy, machismo, and male domination.

Although twenty years ago I was poised to journey into that wilderness myself, such friends now look around to find me not only absent from their caravan but among their nagging critics. Some have expressed hurt. Others find my own change of direction (even though it was not sudden, but protracted; and not secret, but argued out step-by-step in print) puzzling, troubling, and—when they are angry enough to say so—a mark of disloyalty, betrayal, and downright moral corruption. Their own deepening involvement with the left seems to them so correct, so commanded by the evidence, and so morally obligatory that it is truly difficult for them to understand my "defection." They know that their own views are moral. (I once thought so too, but no longer.) They feel themselves impelled by Christian faith and moral obligation. For them, it is a matter of *Saying Yes and Saying No* (the title of a book by one of my closest former colleagues, Robert McAfee Brown). If they say yes, while I say no, it is virtually impossible for them to allow that I am moral, or even to be open to argument that *their* position is immoral.

Around them, socialist experiments crumble. The most publicly uncelebrated fact of the late twentieth century is the death of the socialist idea, especially in economics. (Why, I often wonder, did it take me so long to discover this myself?) The 3 percent of the land allotted to private farming and to market transactions within the USSR yields roughly 33 percent of the foodstuffs that reach the Soviet table, as Secretary General Gorbachev has been obliged to note—and to hold up as the standard for the "new" Soviet economy. Weary of being both socialist and poor, the Chinese have recently turned to private property, markets, and other capitalist techniques, thereby doubling their food production within two short years (an achievement which in a country of one billion citizens carries a certain clout).

Perhaps sensing the ground shift beneath their feet, my old colleagues on the left are most reluctant to enter into debate concerning the empirical record of the ideal they have made central to their moral vision: socialism as a means of liberating the poor. They are unwilling to point to any existing socialist society as the model toward which they aspire, or even to specify the institutions they believe essential to the socialism of their dreams. The dreamier, the better. I think they sense the verdict that history will pronounce upon them, for their tone is increasingly shrill and anxious. They have internalized the neo-Marxist analysis of oppression and dependency. Their paralysis springs from the shame they feel at being Americans. They have the right idea: to help the poor. But they have chosen methods bound to disappoint them. Slowly many will see that.

Not all, though. The older among them are fully grown adults who have formed their views deliberately, and are fully culpable or (as they think) praiseworthy on that account. Many of them believe that capitalism is inherently evil, that business is based on greed, and that Americans ought to live in shame for living as they do. They are alienated grown adults, who think that their alienation is a higher form of virtue, rather than a form of bad faith.

It is not they, then, who are likely to be persuaded through reason and an analysis of cases. They have made their commitment. It is, rather, the younger ones, still open-minded and searching, the questioning and the self-affirming, who know in the depths of their minds that self-hatred, alienation, and resentment are signs of an illness of the spirit, and that a falsely learned alienation is a lie. It is to the latter, not the former, that argument is usefully addressed. The former do not dialogue, I have sadly learned. They excommunicate. There is nothing to fear in that. It is a blessing.

In September 1947, I traveled by train to South Bend, Indiana, to begin my studies—a long course of studies—leading, I hoped, to ordination as a Catholic priest. I will never forget my first sight of the dome of Notre Dame or, once at the heart of the campus, of St. Mary's Lake, still and leaden in the hot late-summer air, and across it on a grassy mound the gray stones of Holy Cross Seminary, which was to be my home for four years. I was then just a few days short of my fourteenth birthday, about to become a high school freshman. I said a prayer of commitment. I would give it my best.

My parents had tried to dissuade me from entering the seminary. My father was in those days a touch anticlerical. "Remember, you're a Novak," he said in our last embrace at the Pittsburgh train station, as if we were of noble lineage. He said one more time, "Don't let them put you on a pedestal." He then talked vividly about how lonely the life of a priest could be; he told me of a priest friend of his who had described how many achingly long evenings he had sat alone at the piano. My father had also described the many symbols—the cassock and collar, the being set apart, the eager deference of the people toward the clergy—that could relentlessly and steadily go to a young man's head. (I do not think now that he was right about that. In this generation, many priests are quite modest; a crisis in self-confidence is apparent now.)

A few weeks earlier, when I was out of earshot, my father had responded to my uncle, who strongly objected to my going to the seminary at such a young age, that I was unusually mature, that he had made his objections known, but that I had thought it out and was determined to go. "Besides," I heard him say, the more I would say no, the more Mike would say yes."

I had long loved getting up early and walking a mile and a half across the iron-squeaking snow to serve the 7:00 am mass, arriving early enough to kneel before the tabernacle in our parish church, with the red sanctuary candle flickering, where no one could observe me. I wasn't certain I would become a priest, but I was perfectly sure that I should try; the call was strong. At last giving up on his objections, my father said: "If you go, give it a good shot; stay at least a full year, don't give up easily. But when you want to come home, we want you here."

One afternoon, he and yet another uncle of mine had watched me play eighth-grade football (we had no league, nor any equipment but what we bought for ourselves). During the first half I scored five touchdowns, until I had to leave with my father. "Pretty good, Mike," Uncle Johnnie said at the car. "He's not well coordinated for this game," my father said matter-of-factly as he closed the car door on the other side. He had never said I should not play football in high school, although the local coach (famous in that area) had already stopped by to watch me play and to encourage me to come and see him. It is odd that part of me accepted my father's assessment of my abilities, although another part of me was exhilarated by the success on the field that I usually experienced.

There was no doubt in my mind, on arrival in South Bend, that I should enter the seminary *then, there*. I was not sure that I would manage to finish all four years in that gray building across the sky-reflecting lake. But I knew it was my inner destiny to try. I knew that if I did not try now, before high school, then football and girls—I was prematurely crazy about girls—would fatefully distract me. Now was the time, Notre Dame was the place. I had tried to enter the Jesuits and had inquired of several other communities. The Jesuits didn't take candidates until after high school, and the Holy Cross Fathers (who run Notre Dame) offered the broadest scope of priestly activities, from teaching and research, through television and journalism, to foreign and domestic missions. My eighth-grade yearbook suggested that I would be an anchorman or journalist (I wrote the prediction myself), but I was uncertain what I wanted to do, and wanted room to experiment. Holy Cross was perfect.

So it turned out to be. I loved my years of study, including Latin, Greek, French, and (much later) Hebrew and Italian. After graduating from high school, I chose to leave the Notre Dame province to join the newer and more pioneering venture of building up the new Stonehill College in Massachusetts. First, though, came a concentrated year of prayer and a more strictly monastic life in the novitiate at North Dartmouth, Massachusetts. The years at

Stonehill were happy and fruitful (to my joy, our seminary team in the intramural football league lost only two games during four years). After graduation, my superiors selected me for study at the Gregorian University in Rome. I had been having doubts about becoming a priest. I wanted to do so many things that I didn't know how I could do them all, bound under obedience. I wanted and needed to be a free lance. But that conflict took a while to become intense.

Over the years, I had almost quit several times. (All one had to do was say the word and go; of the thirty-nine I started with in 1947, I was the last to go; none of the "original class" made it into the priesthood, although of course others who entered along the way did.) But I basically loved the study, the prayer, the atmosphere of charity and learning.

After two years in Rome, in 1958, I finally asked to leave. My superior back in Massachusetts, a marvelous priest (a missionary in Chile and Peru for many years), agreed that I should leave. "Still," he said, "you've put in so many years. Perhaps Rome got you down. Graduate studies in literature here may refresh you. Why don't you be a little more patient, make certain what you're doing, then decide? Either way, I'm with you."

It did seem reasonable to be certain that later I'd have no regrets. For another year and a half, I gave it all I had. Then I knew. Contrary to custom at the time, my superior allowed the whole seminary—in Washington, D.C., at Catholic University—to hold a good-bye party for me. That was a warming gesture. He also gave me money for a suit, my first in twelve years that wasn't clerical black. After a visit with my family, disappointed but supportive, I set off for New York City in January 1960 to make a career as a novelist, with a hundred dollars from my father. I found the garret of my dreams and worked hard.

By the time my first novel was accepted, late in the summer of that year, I had also won a fellowship in philosophy at Harvard. Not knowing better, I had applied only to Harvard and to Yale; Harvard offered more support. After having lived in Manhattan on thirty-five dollars a week, earned by writing, I enjoyed the relative opulence of a Harvard dormitory and regular meals. But Harvard philosophy—heavy on logic and language analysis—was more narrow in its intellectual range than Stonehill or Rome had been, and it seemed to me terribly inadequate to the century of the Holocaust, to the turmoil in Europe (the Hungarian revolution of 1956 had occurred just as I arrived in Rome), and to the spiritual quest many had been experiencing in the late 1950s. *Harper's* asked me to do a piece for a special issue on the universities; it came out as "God in the Colleges," and was later reprinted in several anthologies of the New Left. Its basic theme was that behind the logic and the pragmatism, behind the cloverleaves and the swift, finned automobiles, there was growing a hunger to ask, "Who are we, under the stars, with the wind on our faces?"

IN THE SEMINARY, I used to admire the intellectual leaders of the religious and philosophical left most of all. One of the first models around whom I wished to fashion my own career was the young Michael Harrington, then of the Catholic Worker movement, who used to write in the *Commonweal* well before he became famous for *The Other America*. In the generation following Reinhold Niebuhr and John Bennett, Robert McAfee Brown and Harvey Cox were personal friends. In the mid-1960s, I was invited to serve as the first Roman Catholic on the editorial board of the *Christian Century*, and also on the board of *Christianity and Crisis*, Niebuhr's own journal. And, of course, I cherished my outlets in the *Commonweal* and the *National Catholic Reporter*, the two major lay Catholic journals. (There was a time, the joke went, that no religious magazine of the left could publish without Michael Novak on its board.) Gradually, I could no longer avoid seeming adversarial within these journals because they were moving leftward, while I no longer believed in left-wing visions.

How did that conversion happen? If I had been knocked down from a horse by a blinding light on a single memorable day, it would be easier to say. Instead, it was quite gradual, through examining my own left-wing presuppositions one by one. Underneath this questioning, perhaps, lay a pursuit of self-knowledge, a drive to be faithful to my family and roots, to be myself.

Half of my grandfather's family remained behind in Slovakia when four brothers came to America just before the turn of the century. Part of our family still lives behind the Iron Curtain. Socialism to me was not, therefore, merely an intellectual symbol, but a family matter. Nonetheless, my education was as anticapitalist as that of any other liberal arts major who took seriously the anticapitalist reflections of English literary critics and of most literary giants in America and Britain. As a Catholic, I was perhaps somewhat more Euro-centered than my fellow students in my intellectual interests. I especially loved Albert Camus, but also read a great deal about the worker-priests of France and Catholic Action in Italy. I read the early (anticapitalist) writings of the Christian Democrats; Graham Greene, Heinrich Böll, Alberto Moravia, Ignazio Silone, and others. Following Michael Harrington (although suspicious of the scholasticism of his Marxism), I thought I could be a social democrat or democratic socialist—a democrat in politics, a mild socialist in economics, a blend of conservative and modernist in culture. It seemed there must be a "third way" between oppressive socialism and laissez-faire capitalism, probably something like democracy plus a cooperative economy gently directed in some new way.

It has never been difficult for me to identify with the poor. I was born among them. Johnstown, Pennsylvania, its steel mills strung out for a dozen miles along the valley floors of the Conemaugh and Stony Creek rivers, flanked by steep green hills, was a good place to grow up, among plain, solid people. The countryside is beautiful round about; deer are seen frequently, large bears occasionally, and ring-neck pheasants and rabbits are abundant. I used to marvel at the thick red smoke from the open hearth at Bethlehem steel, and the white-hot ingots brought out in toy-soldier rows to cool. Watching the thick clouds of smoke billow over the hilltops, I felt sorry for the almost naked Indians who once camped upon the Conemaugh, near the point where the two rivers join. (The Point Stadium still sits there, from which Babe Ruth once hit a home run fifteen feet above the 406-foot mark in right field, my father says, and still climbing.) The poor Indians had no industry, no heated homes, no wheels, no iron stoves. I was an admirer of Progress. It did not surprise me later to learn that the Germans sent the Graf Zeppelin over Johnstown, for espionage purposes, in about 1936, when I was three; and I think I faintly remember it. I certainly remember the vast formations of aircraft—especially the P-38s— winging overhead on their way to Europe from 1942 on, and the hulks of tanks, German and American, shipped back to the Johnstown mills for meltdown from the African campaign.

My father had had to leave school during the sixth grade to help support the family. His father had died when a carriage overturned on him at a funeral, when my father was two. His mother, who had been sent to America as a girl of sixteen with a sign "Passaic" around her neck, now supported six children by taking in washing and housecleaning. They lived on Virginia Avenue, which clings to the side of a steep hill above the mills, its narrow frame houses almost two stories higher on the back side than on the street side; you have to see Virginia Avenue to believe it.

One uncle, on my mother's side, went to college, until the bank collapse in 1933 forced him to withdraw. Practically all the men went off to war. My father was all packed and ready for the Navy, when on the day before the train departed a telegram brought word of a new ruling exempting men of his age and number of children (then four). Later, in December 1944, another telegram announced the death of his best friend, Mickey Yuhas, in the Battle of the Bulge. On the same day I was hit by a car while sledding and, the doctor said, came within an inch of having my skull crushed and an eye lost (my head smashed the headlight at its edge, and I went up over the fender). Three weeks later at midnight mass, marching in the choir in the darkened church with a candle in my hand, I was the eleven-year-old whose black eye made people in the pews cover smiles and whisper.

MARRIAGE AND A HONEYMOON in Rome in the fall of 1963, to cover the Second Vatican Council, interrupted my Harvard studies. The stunning new "openness" of the Catholic Church fulfilled many of my seminary dreams of what ought to happen. I was glad to be able to report on it, with all the freedom of a layman but with an insider's knowledge. Lord Acton's account of the First Vatican Council a century earlier was my model. From Stanford, Robert McAfee Brown came to Rome as a Protestant observer; soon enough, he proposed a teaching position at Stanford, where in 1965 I became the first Catholic in the religion department. It was there that my radical phase began.

Stanford in 1965 was just becoming alive with radical politics as Karen (big with our first child) and I arrived. Until early 1967, I was in favor of the Kennedy-Johnson commitment to South Vietnam, for Niebuhrian "realist" and anti-Communist reasons. The cause was just. Gradually, though, I became convinced that the strategy and tactics of the conduct of the war were not likely to lead to success, and began to oppose it on just-war grounds.[1] This measured judgment did not satisfy the left, but did persuade many moderate people. I spent a month in Vietnam during the election period of August 1967, and came back with a sharper grasp of the concrete setting, a deeper appreciation of the complex antagonisms among the Vietnamese, and a confirmation of my modulated—but clearly antiwar—views. I was not, I could not be, an anti-American. "To love one's own country is not a sin," I used to paraphrase Camus. To stop the war was one aim; to negotiate a safe period during which to secure a free and mutual reunification of Vietnam over the long term was another, at once more complex and more honorable.

In the spring of 1968, after campaigning vigorously for Robert Kennedy and being devastated by his murder, I moved back east

---

1. Decisive in my thinking was Theodore Draper's article in *Commentary* in January 1967, which asserted that in December 1964, the North Vietnamese had moved 400 regular troops into South Vietnam—a tiny "invasion," it seemed to me then. We now know that many more troops than that had been coming south and from far earlier.

to the idyllic campus of Old Westbury, the newest branch of the State University of New York. Two things attracted me. First, Old Westbury was to be an experimental college, and educational reform was clearly a coming priority. Second, the president, Harris Wofford, had helped begin the Peace Corps, and his interests in Democratic Party politics and his enthusiasm for whatever he undertook were terribly winning. Given my seminary background, I felt I very much needed more experience of the world, especially in politics. At Old Westbury, we would be in the vanguard of educational reform, and I would learn a lot from the Peace Corps style of Wofford. My expectations were abundantly fulfilled, although as usual not in the way I expected.

So radical were the first hundred students admitted to Old Westbury for its first year in 1968–1969 that, in one survey, all students except one thought electoral politics was a bourgeois fraud and only that one planned to participate at all; he was for Eugene McCarthy. Both Harris and I went to the Chicago convention; that was a searing experience, amid stink bombs and tear gas, ignorant armies clashing by night.

Back on campus, the students soon turned against Harris; there were endless demonstrations, grievances, protests, and bizarre behaviors. The fact that the bookstore was open only during assigned hours was interpreted as "bourgeois"; one of the faculty members smashed the door down with his foot, and students took what they wanted. Another professor, to demonstrate a rigorously egalitarian atmosphere, met his seminar under the large classroom table, all squatting and ducking their heads at egalityrannical levels. Think of this as childish vulgar Marxism; the grown-up version has uncannily repeated itself in every Communist Party victory. At Stanford, the small proportion of radicals were (until violence erupted in the year following my departure) like a little salt sprinkled over a large roast. At Old Westbury, there was little else besides salt, and I very soon rebelled.

Most students wanted total liberty, meaning no standards, no restrictions, no differentiations, no authorities, no requirements.

Against this, a few of us established a second college within the college, which quite deliberately we called the Disciplines College. Assignments, authorities, standards, requirements. We were said by some to be—what else?—fascists.

One of my favorite moments at Old Westbury was an invitation I extended to Herbert Marcuse to hold a seminar. Prussian to his fingertips, Marcuse said no student should feel competent to rebel against a teacher until he had mastered what his teacher knew; until then, revolution must mean discipline. *Delectatio morosa*: Marcuse plunged in the estimation of our most vocal radicals, and I enjoyed their discontent.

The very word "radical," of course, began to make me queasy. The entire vocabulary of the far left—which sounds the more plausible the less likely it is to be realized—assumes an entirely different significance when a dominant majority begins to act it out and to impose it. Some really *do* mean "paranoia is true perception." I began to understand the disbelief that many millions in this century have experienced when totalitarians actually began to put into practice the assault upon "bourgeois standards" that once sounded merely clever and literary. At Old Westbury, some really *did* mean that Shakespeare is "crap" and burned his books to dramatize their feelings. Someone even carefully placed human excrement on a piece of cardboard and put it in the desk drawer of a woman on the faculty. What some didn't like they simply disrupted. Anarchy and tyranny, contempt for disciplined intellect and a fascination with "the ferocious exercise of will"[2] are not so far buried in human consciousness that they cannot easily be released.

All the words of the far left began to sound new chords in my head. Like all words, each of them has an Orwellian double meaning. If one understands them in a decent, bourgeois liberal way, they

---

2. Mussolini used this expression to define the essence of the new type of system in history, totalitarianism. In Mussolini is found the *locus classicus* of the "totalitarian/authoritarian" distinction.

have an attractive sound. (Who can be against freedom or equality?) If one grasps what these same words mean when they are acted out apart from the restraints of checks and balances, and through the coercions of a majority willing to throw tantrums in order to get its way, their true force is to dehumanize those who use them and to imperil any who get in the way. Played in the classic liberal key, words such as "freedom," "equality," "justice," and "the poor" have had a powerful meaning for my family and for many others. (The United States is like a Broadway hit, with immigrants lined up around the block by the millions waiting to get in.) Played in their naked vulgar Marxist key, the same words intend only one thing: a rationale for naked power. Wherever they are around the world, at the fringes of Britain's Labor Party or the German SDP, at feminist caucuses or among the Sandinista *turbas,* extreme leftists do whatever is necessary to get their way. My wife was told our house would be bombed; we took care to keep close track of both our children, then ages three and one.

The hard lessons learned from living in a "total community" with the fervent radicals of Old Westbury, who brooked no opposition and shouted down appeals to reason, were like a vaccination. What Kolakowski wrote of the relation between Marx and the totalitarian USSR might also be said of the relation between the ideas of the serious left and the infantile leftists of Old Westbury: while one could not predict from the words of the former what the latter would make of them, neither was there anything in the former that would prevent the worst from happening. And everything done by the new left could be justified by quoting amply from the old left.

At Stanford, the year after my departure, buildings were bombed. Elsewhere, the radical left turned to kidnappings, bombings, and bank robberies. The decline of the universities was in full swing. Many of my associates who had been hesitant were rapidly now becoming radicalized, just as I was moving in the opposite direction, becoming *de*radicalized. But disaffection with the left is not enough to constitute a true conversion.[3]

IN 1975, AMERICAN INVOLVEMENT in Vietnam ended with an irrational, irresponsible abruptness. The vision of hundreds of thousands of boat people, preyed upon by pirates who raped and looted and murdered, afflicted my conscience. As I read about the sufferings of the Vietnamese people left behind in Vietnam and (still later) of the systematic deceptions practiced by the North Vietnamese upon those of us in the antiwar movement, I dreamt at night of blood on my own hands. The situation in present-day Vietnam is a rebuke to the antiwar movement, as is the continuing expansion of Soviet air and naval power in the South Pacific.

More to the point, as I surveyed the economic record of the socialist nations of Eastern Europe, Asia, Africa, and Cuba, I could find none that I admired, or would choose as a model for the world. The socialist *economic* ideal clearly did not work in practice, not anywhere. Upon sustained reflection, it also became clear to me that its flaw lay not only in its practice, but in its fundamental ideas. Socialism as an economic ideal is not designed to create new wealth, but only to mobilize envy. Idealists say that its aim is to distribute wealth evenly. Realists must observe that socialist elites retain uncommon powers, privileges, and wealth. Socialist idealism is a deception.

The great advantage the socialist ideal brings to an intellectual, however, is difficult to do without. Socialism is essentially a vision for organizing history. Cosmic in its attraction, it offers security and solid footing. Through its gaze, we *know* that capitalist institutions are destined for the dustbin, that to favor freer markets is "ideological," and that the growth of collective power is inevitable in history. Therefore, faced with any event or proposition, one must

---

3. Political conversions are not as deep as religious conversions. Psychologically, as Gordon Allport once observed, they occur on different levels of the psyche. But they are deep enough, since they affect all one's judgment and actions as a citizen. Different visions of political economy embody different senses of reality, different views of human nature, different senses of historical narrative, and quite different forms of self-knowledge.

only analyze whether it furthers the collapse of capitalism or enhances the growth of collective power. If so, it belongs to the future, gains its *truth* from that, and ought to be applauded and supported. If not, we know that it is to be despised as out of date and doomed.

When I ceased relying upon socialist methods of analysis, therefore, I felt a significant inner emptiness. If one is not a card-carrying socialist, but a pragmatic leftist, one can of course employ many forms of socialist and Marxist analysis without being ideologically careful about the full sweep of their logic. Still, losing faith in socialist methods of analysis is like losing an inner compass, a chart, a vision. Fortunately, there fell into my hands, among other writings, some of the essays of Irving Kristol, recalling me to an intellectual tradition I had hitherto avoided: that of the American Framers and that of British and French liberals of the early nineteenth century. I trusted former persons of the left more than conservative intellectuals; the fact that others (soon to be labeled by Michael Harrington "neoconservatives") had doubts and questions similar to mine much strengthened me.

Both as a Slavic Catholic and by temperament, I am partial to thinkers who are somewhat skeptical of a merely geometric logic, of rationalism. I am attracted to thinkers who love the unpredictability of fact, who respect the ambiguity of history, and the concreteness of ethical reasoning and ethical perception—to Aristotle and Aquinas, for example, and to the Whig tradition. I respect those who give due weight to the ethical role of the family, to tradition, to religion, to the tacit wisdom built up through the social experience of the human race. For such reasons, the sheer individualism of some Anglo-American thinkers (from Bentham to Rawls) has always less than satisfied me. But such writers as Adam Smith, Edmund Burke, John Stuart Mill (despite my allergy to his socialist inclinations), Montesquieu, Bastiat, Lord Acton, and John Henry Newman awakened deeply responsive chords in me. When I read Hayek's postscript to *The Constitution of Liberty,* "Why I Am Not a Conservative," I responded as one who finally grasped a way of stating what I am. I belong to what used to be called the Whig tradition; its vision of progress is quite different from that of the "progressives"—a term captured by socialist ways of thought. In offering an alternative to the socialist dream of the future, it has captured the idea of the future. It is more realistic, more likely to work, proven in its successes. In these respects, this vision (for which I would have preferred the name "neoliberal") is a much greater threat to leftists than conservatives have ever been. That is why it infuriates leftists.

MEANWHILE, ON ANOTHER FRONT, another stage in my conversion began in 1970, continued through the process of writing *The Rise of the Unmeltable Ethnics* (1972), and culminated in my efforts on behalf of the McGovern campaign in 1972. In July 1970, just after I had set aside a report in the *New York Times* that Sargent Shriver, recently resigned as ambassador to France, was launching a national campaign to help elect Democrats to Congress, and just after telling my wife that I would love to be involved in that, my telephone rang. It was Mr. Shriver, telling me that he had just finished *The Experience of Nothingness,* and wanted me to write for him in his campaign. Could I come down to Washington? I didn't even shave my long beard.

There followed three splendid months of living with the Shrivers at their home in Rockville, Maryland, and flying out on fascinating campaign trips to some thirty states. We had a marvelous time. I don't think I have ever met a man with so much energy, so much enthusiasm, and such a serious practical interest in philosophical and religious ideas. We had so many good laughs, doing the zany things media campaigns force politicians to do (being pulled by speedboats on inflated tractor-tire inner tubes on a lake in South Dakota, for example), and so many long and happy conversations that those months are a kind of highlight in my memory.

Most of all, though, by election day in the congressional year 1970, I felt I had a far better grasp of the diverse neighborhoods of America than I had ever had before. I had seen at first hand the true significance of ethnicity and localism in American life. On the same day, we once met with black ministers for whom "quotas" mean being brought in; a Jewish women's group for whom "quotas" mean a history of being kept *out;* and an electrician's union (mostly Italian-Catholic) for whom "quotas" mean "they never include us." Political symbols have their own geography. A speechwriter needs to know which words mean what to whom, where, and when. Moreover, I learned to respect the great openness, yearning, generosity, and hope of all those ordinary people that we met along the way, hands rough or smooth, faces beautifully kept or weathered, speech cultivated or rough. Words that I had written about the American majority—complacently drinking beer in front of television—in *Toward a Theology of Radical Politics* now made shame color my cheeks. I met the American people in the flesh; my literary imagination had been calumnious. But this had not been my vision only. In rejecting it, I was rejecting the leftist vision of America (or Amerika), the anti-Americanism so common among my intellectual colleagues.

I noted, too, that the great political commentators often had things wrong. In poor black neighborhoods, we avoided speaking of crime, which we took to be a "code word"; but the local black politicians who spoke before Mr. Shriver attacked crime far more heatedly than anyone I had ever seen on television. In working-class neighborhoods, we often spoke in bars near factories or in union meeting halls that were far better integrated, whites and blacks in obvious camaraderie, than I had ever seen in any other social location. And why not? In major cities such as Philadelphia and Pittsburgh, Cleveland and Gary, Newark and Detroit, the great Democratic politicians such as Jack and Robert Kennedy, Lyndon Johnson and Hubert Humphrey, rang up great majorities among blacks and white ethnics alike. The more highly educated observers,

I learned (most political journalists these days have graduate degrees), were nowadays less in touch with working-class America than I had imagined.

Ed Muskie was my candidate in 1972, but neither he nor his chief speechwriter, Robert Shrum, thought much of my thesis about whites and blacks together in *The Rise of the Unmeltable Ethnics*. Muskie struck me as an admirable man, as quick to irascibility as a Slav ought to be (I know it in myself), and genial and warm, too; but he seemed to think of himself as a Maine Yankee and patrician. In any case, McGovern won the nomination. And the instant Senator Eagleton pulled out, I *knew* Shriver would eventually be nominated for vice president, and began writing his acceptance speech. Without waiting to be invited, I showed up on his doorstep in Rockville the day the decision was announced. Although he already had a team of veteran Kennedy speechwriters hard at work, I labored quietly over my own draft of his acceptance speech. He slowly read all the drafts (unsigned), then accepted mine, and gave it hours later, on television, at the "miniconvention" hastily summoned to present him to the public

There followed some ten or eleven hectic weeks on the Shriver campaign plane. We actually thought the crowds were getting bigger and more supportive toward the end; perhaps they were only compensating for being sorry they would not vote for us. In any case, as I saw more and more "sparklies" and "trendies" operating in the campaign—and heard the media appeals to the "new vote" of the blacks, the young, and women—I felt the Democratic Party changing its allegiance, away from working people and toward the symbol-making class around the universities, the news media, and the industries of culture. Partly as a consequence of their new class allegiances, since 1968 the Democrats have lost all but 21 percent of the electoral votes in the past five presidential elections.

Even before the campaign, I had begun to see that I was caught up in a new form of class warfare. During 1972, I published an essay in *Commentary,* "Needing Niebuhr Again," describing the "new class" of symbol makers who were wresting leadership within the Democratic Party from the labor unions, big-city mayors, and traditional politicians whose electoral base lay among the poor and working classes. This essay occasioned an editorial by Norman Podhoretz, the distinguished editor of *Commentary,* that led to a fresh burst of "new class" criticism chronicled by B. Bruce-Biggs in *The New Class* (1979). The more highly educated, more utopian "lifestyle" liberals were gaining salience throughout society, and the Democratic Party was quickly seduced by their glittery power. There was much evidence of this in the campaign of 1972. Mr. Shriver was greeted with scarcely veiled disdain, I thought, by workers at the gates of the Homestead Steel mills—my own kind of folks, who would normally be with us by upwards of 89 percent. In Joliet, Illinois, on a factory floor where I encountered dozens of Slovak faces that made me think of my cousins in Johnstown, workers did not want to shake McGovern-Shriver hands. Trying to find out why, I met with our "advance person"—a young woman wearing a miniskirt, high white boots, and a see-through blouse, with a large pro-abortion button on her collar. On that factory floor in 1972, the clash of social classes and cultural politics could scarcely have been more discordant.

After the campaign, I gladly joined with other traditional Democrats in founding the Coalition for a Democratic Majority, under the leadership of "Scoop" Jackson, Hubert Humphrey, Pat Moynihan, Tom Foley, and others. Foreign policy most worried me, but so did the efforts by upper-class liberals to separate blacks and Hispanics from white ethnics and from labor, discarding the latter (so blind they were) as reactionary and racist. I had requested a leave of absence from Old Westbury, precisely to campaign against Nixon in 1972 (a promise I had made myself when Humphrey lost in 1968). Fighting for the soul of the Democratic Party, I saw the other side gain control of it.

Now I understand that there were *two* "power elites" in this nation: (1) the "old elite," whose base lies in the business sector, and whose vision of what makes America great looks to her economic and political freedoms, and (2) the "new class," whose base ties in education and the new communications industries, and whose vision of what makes America great is a compassionate (therefore, large) government. (The so-called "Yuppies" of later years are divided between these two elites, trending now one way, now another.) Unknowingly, until now, I had been supporting the politics of the new class, out of an uncritical acceptance of "progressive" ideology. What would happen if I turned against the new class the same intensity of critical fire that I had earlier learned from my education to turn against the old elite? Didn't the new one deserve it more? The imbalance of criticism in the academy and among intellectuals is a scandal. The naked ambition of the new class for power, its self-interest, its lack of self-knowledge, and its moral arrogance are transparent. So are its resentments.

Even though I slowly was becoming deradicalized, the information in my head during these years was very often exclusively derived from writers of the far left. In *Ascent of the Mountain, Flight of the Dove* (1971), for example, I wrote "a huge bureaucracy with an unparalleled budget has grown up around the Department of Defense." Again: "The economic, bureaucratic interests represented by that budget tend to govern the direction not only of American foreign policy but also of American domestic life. They determine what 'the realities' of American life are." The footnotes to such wildly exaggerated passages refer to such authors as Fred J. Cook, *The Warfare State*, Richard J. Barnet, *The Economy of Death*, a book of essays called *American Militarism 1970*, and Seymour Melman, *Pentagon Capitalism*. I had not been educated in the left-wing radical tradition, and I thought of myself here as being open-minded. What I did not do was to submit such partisans to rigorous cross-examination. As a percentage of gross national product, for example, military budgets in 1970 (not far above 5 percent) were a very small tail to be wagging a very large dog. Moreover, the relatively low spending on arms *qua* arms during the 1970s placed the nation in considerable peril, as even Jimmy Carter slowly realized. Far from being "militaristic," the American people were about to secure a long series of years of declining defense budgets. This was to happen just as the Soviets were rapidly expanding theirs. The new thrusts of Soviet expansion and the upsurge of terrorism were a vivid consequence. Less spending brought greater violence, not less.

For most of the 1970s, I was of two minds. Philosophically, I was slowly turning away from the radical left. Informationally, my mind was stuffed with uncritically accepted information from highly partisan sources. Furthermore, I was painfully eager to maintain my credentials on the left. I remembered Maritain writing (in defense of his support of liberal Christian Democratic movements) that he always wished to be "a man of the left." That seemed to me too, at that time, to be the only moral alternative. My *will* to be on the left was stronger than any intellectual reasons I could assemble for being there. What the heart wills the mind for a time finds reasons for. Until, one by one, those reasons turn to ash.

Yet even my first tentative criticisms of the left brought down upon my head passionate assaults, less given to answering my arguments than to questioning my morality. Some reviews of *The Rise of the Unmeltable Ethnics,* which I thought would help inspire the left to a base-broadening realism, were so unfair and so hostile to my person that, on at least one occasion (I was less thick-skinned then), I took to my bed until I could gain composure to get back to work. I had to call upon the intellectual guidance I had established for myself in *The Experience of Nothingness* (1970)—namely, the calm knowledge that one had to be prepared to go forward "with no supports," relying on no one.

Reinhold Niebuhr had taught me to weigh powers, interests, and facts carefully *before* pronouncing moral judgment; so I knew I had to do some long rethinking. About all the left-wing information in my head, I began to ask, Is it actually well founded? No longer relying upon socialist forms of analysis (with their predetermined outcomes), I began to ask, What fair-minded evaluation can be made of capitalism? My first essay on this latter subject suggested that, at the very least, capitalism is among intellectuals "an underpraised and undervalued system." By contrast, I had learned that socialism, although highly praised for its "ideals," is quite disillusioning once the facts about any instances of its practice are examined. I backed into a more positive judgment of capitalism very, very slowly, having to fight against my broadly anticapitalist education.

On the theological side of the question, I found, one has to do most of the work oneself. Perhaps von Mises, Hayek, and others do persuade those who are already liberal (in the classical sense). But for those of us who were taught to think through anticapitalist analysis, such arguments can only be conducted in highly moral terms that present a comparable historical vision. Seven or eight new insights are necessary. It takes time and patience to achieve them. Cardinal Newman was correct: one can drive out a powerful idea only in the light of a still more powerful idea. It took me until 1982, with the completion of *The Spirit of Democratic Capitalism,* to begin to get that intellectually stronger set of ideas in my head. That vision remained critical of flaws in all three systems of American life—political, economic, moral-cultural—but in a systematic way I kept asking, *Compared to what?* At last, I was thinking empirically in a sustained way.

Slowly, I saw that being on the left had been a sort of "bad faith," a learned ideology that was false to my own experience, to that of my family, and indeed to that of millions of families all around the world. I had been teaching myself to debunk the American system, and by means of arguments whose plausibility lay, not in themselves, but in their conformity to a prearranged mental scheme: capitalism is of the past, immoral, and doomed, whereas steps toward a more socialist economy are "progressive," right, and predetermined by history to be victorious. Recently, I have encountered a slogan of the Sandinistas that shockingly expresses the relevant mental scheme, although in terms so gross that they would have repelled me even in my most progressive days: "To learn from the Soviet Union is to advance; to learn from the United States is to retreat." Supply "progressivism" for "Soviet Union," and "capitalism" for "the United States," and that is how I had earlier interpreted history. Reality does not support such blind faith.

The great and liberating interpretive idea, I have come to think, is Jefferson's: "The God who gave us life gave us liberty." Human beings are made in the image of God: creatures of insight and liberty, of intelligence and responsibility. The only social systems worthy of creatures of such gifted dignity are those that allow them to be relentlessly inquiring, creative, and responsible: a free polity, a relatively free economy, and a free moral-cultural order. All systems that secure such individual rights and that are now empirically available have predominantly capitalist economies.[4]

A STORY OF THIS SORT NECESSARILY has two tracks, one consisting of a record of experiences, the other a record of newly acquired insights. During my left wing, or radical, period (1967–1971), bounded by the antiwar movement on the one end and the experience of "radical culture" at Old Westbury on the other, I had become adept at trying to explain my radical ideas in liberal terms. "Liberal" is the cover that most socialist-minded leftists employ to make their ideas seem continuous with those of the pragmatic, mainline left. I had to learn the hard way the discontinuity between "socialist" and "liberal," just as an earlier generation (Sidney Hook, for example) had learned to see the sharp divide between "communist" and "socialist." In that earlier generation, the dividing line had been commitment to democracy. Communists accepted Party discipline and were radically undemocratic. Democratic socialists and social democrats insisted upon the primacy of democracy and free personal inquiry. A generation later, the deplorable economic

---

4. Peter Berger's *The Capitalist Revolution* (Basic Books, 1986) assembles the empirical evidence in an easily accessible way, in the form of fifty falsifiable theses.

record of socialism since World War II is more in evidence; and the dependence of social democracy on capitalist institutions (markets, incentives, private property, and openness) is more transparent. In our generation, the dividing line between liberals and socialists is how much freedom to allow a free economy. "Socialists" (the word has lost much of its practical meaning) tend to favor greater political controls; liberals tend to favor greater economic liberties. At its best, this argument is pragmatic and experimental.

Some years after the fact, I have come to see the role played in my own thought by the gradual acceptance of several key ideas. As a matter of intellectual biography, it seems worthwhile to state a few of them, even without space to argue against the objections my earlier ways of thinking had employed to block them.

Utopianism Versus Realistic Morality

By nature, I tend to be idealistic and wholehearted; to respect ambiguity, irony, and tragedy is a tendency I have always wanted to strengthen in myself. But the discovery of the systematic biases of my own class, the new class, taught me that I must make a still sharper distinction between reasoning about moral ideals and reasoning about political realities. When I was on the left, I found myself looking *down* upon the American people, upon "vulgar" business activities, upon capitalism. I implicitly pictured my friends on the left and myself as more "pure" than all the others. In *Toward A Theology of Radical Politics* (1969), I had unmasked the "Myth of the Pure Protester," the contemporary version of Dostoyevsky's "Myth of the Grand Inquisitor." But it is one thing to detect a mythic structure in one's colleagues, and another to drive it out of one's own habitual practice. The Pure Protester loves his or her own moral purity, sacrificing all else to that. To overcome it, I learned, one has to distinguish more sharply between one's high moral claims and the actual effects of one's ideas and actions on the plain of battle.

To begin with, one must grant that others, too, make high moral claims. One must compare moral claims to moral claims. But one must also examine *what happens in history because of those moral claims*: one must compare *practice* to *practice*. Sometimes those who make high claims bring about results more evil than the results achieved by those whose moral claims have been more cautious. In practice, this meant for me that I must stop having contempt for those (to my right) with whom I was in moral disagreement. And I must take greater responsibility for the actual results of my own moral claims. For example, after the Democratic Convention of 1968, I was so hostile to Hubert Humphrey (because of a disgraceful speech he had made on the war at Stanford that spring) that I wrote in favor of abstaining from voting, even if Richard Nixon won the election. I added that those who followed such an injunction would incur an obligation to work that much harder to defeat Nixon in 1972—which explains my taking an unpaid leave of absence in the fall of 1972 to do so. This was moral purity masked as practical politics. I learned from such an error that I must never again seek moral purity at the expense of responsibility for the results.

As a result, I have striven to conduct argument with those with whom I disagree on two separate levels: to argue against their moral claims, on one level, and to argue against the probable practical consequences of their moral claims, on yet another. One effect of this resolution was to free me from the grip of the moral vision of the left, in the many forms in which I had encountered it. I began to examine its consequences more closely and to experiment with a better vision that might have better consequences. In short, consequences matter.

"Bad Faith"

One of the features of being on the left that most disquieted me was the "bad faith" in which it placed me. In arguing for left-wing positions, I found myself putting down other Americans, trying to shock "the complacent" (as I thought them) and writing of U.S. "militarism" and "imperialism." But who was I to be anything but grateful to this country that had taken in an impoverished and much oppressed family of former serfs from Slovakia, and that had given to me and countless others opportunities unprecedented in history? I had always tempered my radical criticism with explicit patriotism and gratitude, but still, I had conceded far too much to an unwarranted anti-Americanism. The more I examined the neo-Marxist analysis of oppression and dependency, the less tenable it was. Its main substance is emotional, not intellectual. It *begins* with feelings of guilt, awaits no evidence, and includes the final verdict in the method of analysis. Eventually, I could not stomach this bad faith. I understood the anger that union workers felt when they saw privileged university students burning American flags, for which so many in their own families (like Mickey Yuhas) had gladly given their lives. Working people shamed me into abandoning my bad faith.

Future as Truth

The first insinuation of a Marxist-Leninist way of thinking into one's mind is through epistemology: "The tide of history is on the side of revolution." Here is how it happens. The first temptation is to hold that "the correspondence theory of truth" is Aristotelian and old-fashioned. One should not examine claims to truth in the light of empirical evidence. Empiricism is static and reactionary. Instead, one must keep one's eye upon the goal of the future. Truth is what brings the revolution of the future into power. What helps the revolution belongs to the future and is true. What blocks the revolution is reactionary and against the stream of history, so it is false. The dynamic course of history has been scientifically discerned; history is driven forward both by the "contradictions of capitalism" and by the triumphant logic of egalitarianism, the end of alienation, and the common good, i.e., socialism. "To learn from socialism is to advance; to learn from capitalism is to retreat." Only "progressives" grasp the larger picture. Appeals to empirical fact regarding the failures of socialism are signs of bourgeois reasoning. To be a progressive is to be ennobled by an inner vision of a superior truth. It is to belong to a secular religion. If only one holds tightly to that shining vision, the imperfections of the present will be enveloped in the soft light of ideals that drive one onward. How much progress has been made already!

Having long fought against "cheap grace"—having been chastened by my own "dark night of the soul," as suggested in *The Experience of Nothingness* (1970)—I had long since fled from an adolescent Christian faith to an adult one. So I resisted the soft light of socialism. No Robert Heilbroner or Irving Howe "visions" for me. I had Catholicism, a much tougher faith—tested by fire—and had no vacuum in the religious depths of my soul that socialism could possibly fill. If one doesn't need socialism as a religion, then it must stand or fall by its record in historical praxis. One advantage of a capitalist economy, indeed, is that it asks to be judged on no other than empirical and practical grounds. It is asymmetrical with socialism; it offers no comparable "vision."

Thus, as I mentally toured the horizon of the twentieth century, I could see less and less reason for any serious mind to believe—against the overpowering evidence—that actual socialism matches socialist claims. On the contrary, from the USSR to a communist Vietnam, from communist Albania to Cuba, socialism is a human wasteland. As for the "socialism" of Sweden, Israel, and France, many of their own socialists have come to see that what is most vital in such nations is their commitment to democracy, and what are most retardant are the state controls that drag down their market economies. In economics, democratic socialists are democratic capitalists who argue for slightly larger governmental initiatives and controls at the margin. In practice, democratic socialists and social democrats live as parasites upon democratic capitalist systems while claiming to have purer and larger hearts pulsing with "compassion." To some extent (when it works), this is a useful leaven and

I sometimes support them. To a great extent, however, socialist visions serve the interests and ambitions of large segments of the educated class (who in Europe staff government-owned media, universities, and the massive welfare administrative apparatus) and paralyze the poor. In addition, many democratic socialists tend toward an unhealthy preference for the foreign policy of the USSR over that of the USA in virtually every concrete circumstance. Most leftists are ritualistic anti-Stalinists. In practice, however, they nearly always oppose American policy. Sometimes they may be correct; the issue rests with exact judgment, case by case. Underlying ideological support for Cuba and Nicaragua, for example, is an epistemology that holds that socialism will prevail over capitalism, left-wing progressives over right-wing reactionaries, the vision of a shining future over the sad realities of Cuban prisons and fervent Sandinista Leninism. When one's vision is of paradise, the dungeons in which prisoners are tortured cannot be seen.

The Factual Record

Once one sets aside vulgar Marxist epistemology and tries to see the world whole and factual, one is free to judge socialism by its record—and to reexamine capitalism afresh. It is difficult to get socialists to name a socialist experiment on which they rest their case. Their touching faith in each successive project lasts only so long as the full story has not come out—in China before Westerners could freely visit it; in Albania before "socialist youth brigades" from Western Europe came home with shocking tales; in Cuba before Armando Valladares awakened the poets, essayists, and novelists of the outside world.

In Western Europe, socialists in power turn increasingly to capitalist techniques because they work better than socialist techniques. Once socialist economies are submitted to the same rigorous tests as capitalist economies, the jig is up. As an economic idea, socialism has died a thousand deaths by qualification. Markets, incentives, private property, and openness work better in the humble history of fact. Since it is basically an empirically derived set of techniques, one does not have to give capitalism even two cheers; still, in an imperfect world, it wins hands down. Chinese and Soviets pay it the sincerest form of flattery.

What Is Capitalism?

The liberal arts tradition of Britain and the United States owes much to the aristocratic traditions of the distant past, and keeps alive the resentment of aristocrats against the "philistinism" of the rising business class and the *nouveaux riches*. The social sciences are profoundly anti-individual, collectivist in spirit and in method, and often antithetical to the tacit wisdom of tradition and the indirect "spontaneous order" (Hayek) of many traditional social institutions, including markets. Thus, most of us grow up being taught to think ill of capitalists and capitalism. Some reasons are aesthetic. Some are class-based: aristocratic tastes preferred to business-inspired tastes. Some are radical. We may not hold that "property is theft" or fully accept the "labor theory of value," according to which all value derives from labor and any profit not distributed to labor is ill-gained. Nonetheless, socialists such as Tawney have taught us that capitalism is rooted in acquisitiveness, in selfish as opposed to public interests, and in vaguely tainted "profit." There are some on the left who regard capitalism as an essentially evil system that must be replaced. Perhaps a larger number have made peace with capitalism which, though vulgar and disreputable, is a necessary practicality. (Not even Adam Smith held actual businessmen in high regard.)

It took me a long while to recognize in myself just how much of this received wisdom I had uncritically received. Beyond that, there is also a taboo against assessing capitalism seriously and fairly. Within the horizon of progressivism, to approach the morality of capitalism as an open question is regarded as selling out. To render a favorable empirical verdict upon capitalism while recognizing its defects where they undeniably exist makes socialist analysis totter on its foundations. These foundations are mainly anticapitalist, negative rather than positive. (And insofar as they are positive, they are utopian.)

Those who remain attached to socialist methods of analysis, of course, do not give up even when they lose particular arguments.

Progressivism is a closed system. It has an answer to everything. It does not rest upon empirical verification; it does not employ the criterion of falsifiability. It insists upon "vision," upon "perspective," upon "point of view." Once one is within that horizon, nothing can penetrate it. It is reinforced by everything that happens. It is more like a religious faith than like a scientific theory subject to falsification. But it lacks one key constitutive element common to Jewish and Christian religious faith. Jewish and Christian faiths hold each believer personally responsible for the reasonableness of the act of faith; both engage the unbeliever (present within every believer) in argument. The progressive never takes the doubter seriously; to doubt progressivism is considered to be not an intellectual but a moral act. For Jew and Christian, God is truth. For the progressive, history is a tale of irresistible power, to which truth is secondary. Progressives do not argue; they attack the *bona fides* of doubters.

That is why the first battle of the soul in rejecting the progressive horizon is to subject it to tests of empirical falsifiability. Since the first of all moral maxims is to think clearly, this struggle is a moral one. Does truth stand outside of history, as a judge upon it, or within it, as a subject judged by history? Some prefer to be "on the side of" history. Others choose to subject historical movements to the judgment of truth. Castro had Valladares under the thumb of history, naked in an unlit cell; but Valladares clung to a truth beyond the power of history.

Once one begins to examine the historical record of capitalist societies—the paradigm case is the United States—one learns that the received wisdom about the nature of capitalism is erroneous. Far from being theft, private property is (as even Leo XIII said) the necessary condition for individual freedom of action in history. The right to private property supplies the wherewithal for self-determination. This important empirical claim is subject to tests of falsifiability: An order that respects rights to private property is more likely to result in the improvement of nature, the advancing of the common good, superior creativity, and social vitality than any collectivist order. In the practical sphere, the proper question is, *Compared to what?* Compared to traditionalist and socialist orders, the capitalist economic order has empirically shown superior results.

In my first ruminations, following Max Weber, I thought of capitalism as essentially consisting in a regime of private property, markets, incentives, and profits. But all traditional societies (such as Jerusalem in the biblical era, and most Third World regimes today) have had these. Still they were (or are) pre-capitalist. Only slowly did I come to the precise capitalist insight: creativity is more productive than rote labor; therefore, the primary form of *capital* is mind. The cause of the wealth of the nations is mind. Capitalism is not constituted solely by private property, incentives, markets, double-entry bookkeeping, or any other social techniques (though all of these are necessary elements), but rather by a social order favorable to alertness, inventiveness, discovery, and creativity. This means a social order based upon education, research, the freedom to create, and the right to enjoy the fruits of one's own creativity. Thus, all the American steps to protect the rights of citizens to exercise their own practical judgment—i.e., Article 1, Section 8, of the U.S. Constitution, asserting the rights of "authors and inventors"; the Homestead Act; the Land Grant College Act; and an immense national commitment to universal private and public education— were indispensable stages along the road to a civilization that favored invention and discovery more than any other in history. "The first developed nation" owes its development chiefly to the cultivation of intellect, both practical and theoretical.

The Nature of Communism

For intellectuals, the most divisive event of the twentieth century has been the rise of communism. How should communism be judged? For many intellectuals of a generation ago, communism was a profound temptation. Most attributed this to their own idealism, rather than to their lust for power or their envy of the business class. To others today, to seem friendly and unconcerned about the rise of communism seems to be more idealistic than to be anticommunist. Even before the era of Joseph McCarthy, to be anticommunist was thought to represent a failure of idealism, imagination, creative sympathy, and broad-mindedness. Besides, anticommunism seemed vulgar. It represented a middlebrow or lowbrow reflex, worthy perhaps of the *Reader's Digest* but scarcely of the academy. Thus, even today many who have refused to become communists would prefer not to be known as anticommunists—indeed, would prefer to be less anticommunist than anti–anti-communist.

This tendency has effects upon foreign policy debates. Many intellectuals today grasp the failure of the *Marxist* component of Marxism-Leninism—recognize, that is, the rebuff history has given to the nineteenth-century economics of Marx. But many of the same persons continue to accept, perhaps unconsciously, the *Leninist* doctrine that imperialism is the natural expression of capitalism. And they interpret American foreign policy (not Soviet foreign policy) accordingly. American foreign policy in Southeast Asia, in Central America, and elsewhere, they say, is driven by business interests. These consist either of malign multinational corporations or of the military-industrial complex. These accusations are fair enough; but it is only fair to hear the other side of the evidence, not merely to give in to reflexive feelings of guilt. The evidence does not support the accusations. Nonetheless, what is left of Marxism-Leninism is Leninism. The Leninist doctrine of imperialism satisfies deep anti-American longings.

There is no excuse for serious men and women not to have an exact and accurate picture of the power controlled by the Communist Party USSR: in offensive nuclear might and strategic defense against nuclear attack; in naval power on (and under) every ocean surface; in conventional arms massed near the European frontier and along the borders separated from the Persian Gulf solely by Iran; in a covert intelligence force larger and more versatile than any in history; and in a capacity for ideological penetration, both in the West and in the Third World, unrivaled in human history. According to the Brezhnev Doctrine, where communism begins to govern it never surrenders. (The single minor rollback has been Grenada.) By the end of the Carter administration, the boundaries defended by this doctrine had been extended far beyond those of 1945. Nicaragua, ripe as a plum, seems to be next in line. By 1998, if present trends continue, the boundaries protected by the Brezhnev Doctrine are quite likely to be more extensive than they are in 1988.

Pure Leninism is about power, naked power, brutal power, power through terror. To the dictator within a Leninist system, anything is permitted. To appeal to values beyond naked power in the hands of a Leninist vanguard, one must go outside of Leninism. Thus, belief in Marxism-Leninism as a set of substantive doctrines has waned, especially in communist nations. Ironically, though, utopian progressivism, the marshland in which communism incubates, thrives happily in the affluent West among the privileged. The resentments of intellectuals against the business class nourish it far more than any evidence warrants. Meanwhile, the naked military power of the USSR is stronger than that of Adolf Hitler at the peak of his power. And Marxist-Leninist ideology, even in decline, still awakens an echoing resonance among intellectuals that the Nazi ideology, based upon race, never could.

The capacity of Western intellectuals to deny the reality of Soviet power, the scope of Soviet ambition, and the record of Soviet deception is one of the marvels of history. It represents a triumph of intellectual dishonesty and massive self-contempt. To refuse to take part in this "treason of the intellectuals" is said to be troglodytic, reactionary, the work of a cold warrior, bellicose, and a sign of reflexive anticommunism. It is none of these things. It is a refusal to go on being complicit in intellectual dishonesty and self-contempt. An exact and accurate picture must be argued out empirically. So also the strategic response. On concrete matters, honest persons may disagree. But resistance to communism, principled and militarily effective, is morally obligatory.

Openness

How can I explain to myself the attacks upon my own work by former colleagues on the left once I began to move from concentrating my criticism on the right to directing some of it onto the left? Persons who had written that I was brilliant began to find my work—which was far more penetrating than it had been—evidence of a bad character. No doubt, my positions of today have faults, which I would be glad to correct. Virtually never do my critics respond with argument, however. Only seldom have they met the case I have made head-on. Their main advice to their faithful flock is not to read my work. Their technique is ridicule in a falsetto voice; consult the reviews of *The Spirit of Democratic Capitalism* in religious left-wing journals. True, elsewhere the more open among them have accepted several basic points, and this process continues.

Knowing that I was wrong once, I would be glad to be shown again where now I am in error. I fear no arguments from the left. I welcome them eagerly. Having expanded my views before, to meet overpowering evidence, I would gladly do so again. To admit that one has been wrong is, after the first time or two, joyful work, because it demonstrates a willingness to follow inquiry where it leads.

I see, of course, that intellectual conversions, or "raisings of consciousness," still move some persons to the left. The left, given its epistemology, regards such conversions as signs of natural growth. Nonetheless, the numbers of those on the left who are embracing more and more of the "Whig" (realistic, democratic capitalist) analysis is growing yet more rapidly, for sound empirical reasons. In intellectual life, there is no determinism. Honest inquiry has its own power, its own laws, and its own respect for time.

The Ironic Law of Small Differences

It is an odd feature of arguments about political economy, I have found, that small differences in *the balance of judgment* have very large consequences for action. In the world of practice, judgments are necessarily probabilistic. Manichaeism is out. There are almost always *some* reasons for most (but not all) systemic positions. (Hitler's maniacal efforts to eradicate Jews, like Stalin's earlier deliberate starvation of some 8 million Ukrainians, have come as close to pure and massive evil as the world has ever seen.) Thus, consider the judgment that, on balance, the United States is a force for good in the international arena. To interpret that judgment in numerical terms, one person may judge that by 51–49, or 55–45, it is correct; another, by 49–51, or 45–55, the other way. But this relatively small margin of difference between the acceptance and the rejection of that proposition may involve extremely large differences in further judgment and action. One may still wish to make judgments case by case. But one is *likely* to give the benefit of the doubt one-way or the other: thumbs up or thumbs down. History demands action. Playing Hamlet is certain tragedy. Once a judgment is reached (by however small a margin), action must be wholehearted.

Moreover, judgment about political economy evokes high passion. Even if one disagrees with those on the other side of a question for action by only 2 or 5 or 25 percent, still, that difference has the effect that a civil war does in dividing the consciences of even close brothers within a family. At the extreme, killing one another may result (as in the American Civil War; among Vietnamese, Nicaraguans, and others). Far short of that, even in an argument over dinner, passions are likely to rise. The temptation of those on opposite sides to paint each other in extreme colors, to demonize one another, is extremely hard to resist.

In action in history, small differences in the balance of judgment often lead to dramatic, passionate, and life-and-death opposition. To recognize this helps to diminish fanaticism. But it does not alleviate the need to go into opposition. Civility is then an almost heroic achievement. Still, civility remains necessary.

Whether to the left or the right, in any case, those inquirers for whom I have the greatest admiration are willing to continue facing argument, to stay in dialogue, and to rethink things again. Surprisingly, one does not find in life many open minds. There are not multitudes whose drive to question is virtually unrestricted. When you find one whose views are radically different from yours but who is willing to discuss such differences openly and at length, you find a pearl of great price.

WHERE, THEN, AM I TODAY? As before, I remain both a Democrat and a member of the Democratic Party in politics ("republican" in the early American sense, a biblical or civil republican). In culture, I am, as Lord Acton was, that loneliest of breeds, a liberal Catholic; not a conservative one, because Catholicism is a living force, ever ancient and ever new. In economics, I am in favor of the mind-centered, creative, inventive system—in short, capitalism. I have come to see that these are the *three* liberations symbolized by the classic liberal tricolor: liberation from tyranny and torture, through *democracy;* the liberation of conscience, association, and expression, through *pluralism;* and liberation from poverty, through *capitalism.*

No one who holds faith with such commitments, Hayek wrote, is properly to be called a "conservative." For each of these three liberations names a *dynamic* principle as deep as human nature itself, the powerful propeller of history. These are the principles that will be decisive in the future, the principles at the heart of every form of progress. In practical cases, some will favor government intervention, others will favor a freer economy; in an open society, there is ample room for pragmatic argument and closely watched experimentation.

And yet, of course, to hold fast to such principles as these is not to have sprung as innocent and naked as Venus from the sea. It is to stand on principles one's forebears have wrested over centuries from the ambiguities and ironies of human history, and is, in that sense, conservative (a conservative is one who believes that his forebears were at least as intelligent as he). To hold to principles dynamic in their nature and yet ancient and traditional in their gradual elucidation is to be simultaneously a person of the future and of the past, a conservative and a progressive—in short, a Whig. Alas, that name seems no longer to be retrievable. But the principles it signals are everlastingly available, rooted as they are in the natural liberty (and its tendency toward historical progress) that our Creator has endowed in us.

And so I end my story. Having begun life in the bosom of a good family in an out-of-the-way steel town, best known for the tragedies it has endured by flood in 1889, 1936, and 1977; having had an excellent classical education in philosophy, literature, and theology; having from the start declared my intention to create a philosophy of the distinctively American experience; having begun by seeking a "third way" between capitalism and socialism, as a result of the typical anticapitalist biases of the humanities (not least in Catholic thought); having long looked for this "third way" in the direction of socialist thought and radical politics—after all this, during my forties, I came to find the socialist and radical paths destructive of truth, and signs of bad faith. And I came back to rediscover the power of the American idea, "man's best hope" as Jefferson called it in his First Inaugural. I came back, in short, to the tradition of Aristotle, Cicero, and Aquinas; of Madison, Hamilton, Jay, Jefferson, and Lincoln; of Montesquieu, Smith, Burke, and Acton—i.e., to the Whig tradition. Many call me a neoconservative. I prefer neoliberal. Yet the name matters less than the reality: a threefold commitment to democracy, capitalism, and pluralism, whose premise is liberation—from tyranny and torture, from poverty, and from oppression of intellect, art, and conscience. To be where I am, I judge, is a good place to be—for which thanksgiving be to my Creator, merciful to those who wander in the wilderness.

Courtesy of Intercollegiate Studies Institute

CHAPTER 12

Wilhelm Roepke

Commentary by Edwin J. Feulner Jr. (1988)

The existentialists are right about one thing: in life every man faces a moment of truth. How he faces it reveals what kind of man he is and dictates what course he will pursue. For Wilhelm Roepke, the architect of Europe's economic recovery after the Second World War, that moment came in February 1933, when he stood at the grave of his teacher Walter Troeltsch and delivered the eulogy for which he was reported to the Gestapo.

That day, a few hours before the fire that destroyed the Reichstag laid the groundwork for the National Socialists' usurpation of power, Roepke courageously denounced the Nazis' spiritual, intellectual, and social bankruptcy. Couching his language in metaphors drawn from gardening—a hobby he and Troeltsch shared—Roepke observed that the deceased, a professor of religion, "did not fit into our present time, which is on the verge of destroying the garden of culture and reconverting it to the primitive jungle." These words, in which he praised the decorum of a fading civilization and excoriated the vulgarity of the coming regime, earned him exile.

Choosing banishment over appeasement, he committed himself to thirty years as a "fearless fighter" (as Karl Brandt calls him) against immoral ideologies that violate man's nature and rights. In this struggle he courted professional derision and physical danger, but feared only the ignominy of failing to defend his principles.

With the same courage that won him an Iron Cross on the battlefields of Picardy in the Great War, he criticized those who supported leaders, governments, or theories that diminish human dignity and restrict man's freedom.

Although he was both an intellectual and scholar, he was among the first to condemn the *Tat* group, a circle of influential intellectuals who, by vilifying capitalism, facilitated the triumph of the National Socialists. Not content with skirmishes in the halls of academe, Roepke openly lobbied farmers to vote against the Nazis. Ironically, he who embodied the Aryan ideal—a tall, blond, blue-eyed skier and mountain climber—rejected National Socialism and all its works. As a result of his fearless candor, this golden-haired boy became *persona non grata*. At twenty-four he had been acclaimed as the youngest full professor in Germany. Ten years later he became the first professor in the country to elect exile rather than capitulate to Nazi terror.

If anything, exile increased Roepke's moral courage, emboldening him to attack wrong-headedness and intellectual dishonesty wherever he found them. From 1942–1945, his famous trilogy appeared—acutely analyzing current economies, governments and policies, but, more important, suggesting ways to restore harmony and economic prosperity through reliance on the free market. For many in war-torn Europe these volumes—sometimes bought on the black market, smuggled home illegally, and read in secret—offered hope for reconstructing Europe's post-war economy and restoring her civilization.

Banned in Germany, the first in the series, *The Social Crisis of Our Time* (1942), inspired fierce resistance to Nazism. In fact, when the National Socialists took over in Hungary in 1944, they announced, "the time of Röpkeism is over"—as if Roepke himself stood for all dissent. For his own countryman Ludwig Erhard (who later became Germany's first minister of Economic Affairs and later chancellor), reading black market copies of this book, as well as the later two, *Civitas Humana* (1944) and *International Order* (1945), was like drinking "fertile water" in the desert.

After World War II, when many European intellectuals abjured fascism, but still extolled left-wing ideologies, Roepke inveighed tirelessly against the fundamental immorality of all planned economies, denouncing the brutality and bestiality of communism. He argued forcefully against economists who insisted that socialist regimes were the wave of the future. He bravely criticized the New Deal when critics were few, and sang a virtual solo against the popular socialist policies of J. M. Keynes.

Roepke's views were vindicated, however, when at his urging, the German minister of economics, Ludwig Erhard, gambled on a free-market economy against the wishes of virtually all his financial advisers. Astonished at West Germany's incredible post-war recovery, Roepke's adversaries hailed it as a miracle rather than admit it was the logical outcome of free-market policies.

Encouraged by the results that the Germans had achieved, Roepke's friend, Luigi Einaudi, Italy's first president after the war, restored the Italian economy by implementing the measures that the German economist advocated. The French soon followed suit. The result was not only an economic recovery, but the restoration, at least in part, of European society. This recovery and restoration provided the necessary bulwark against the socialization or, worse still, the communization of Europe.

As Roepke recognized, all forms of socialism pose a great threat to man's freedom because they are based on a fundamental misunderstanding of human nature. Indeed, in *A Humane Economy*, he declared, "I reject ... socialism [as] a philosophy which ... places too little emphasis on man, his nature, and his personality." By devaluing man and misperceiving his nature, socialist regimes and collectivist economies were, Roepke believed, inherently repressive. As a result, he argued that they invariably lead to "impoverishment and tyranny," for socialism itself can exist only by "doing something eminently immoral, by compelling people—by force or cunning and deceptions—to act against their own nature."

In contrast, he defended the "intrinsic morality of the market economy" which allows the individual to profit by working for his own welfare and that of his fellow man. "In capitalism," Roepke asserted, "we have a freedom of moral choice, and no one is *forced* to be a scoundrel. But this is precisely what we are forced to be in a collectivist social and economic system." For this reason, he wrote, "I champion an economic order ruled by free prices and markets [for it is] ... the only economic order compatible with human freedom."

This freedom, Roepke argued, was man's God-given birthright, for "I see in man the likeness of God; [so] I am profoundly convinced that it is an appalling sin to reduce man to a means ... and that each man's soul is something unique, irreplaceable, priceless, in comparison with which all other things are as naught."

Roepke was convinced that the failure of the Communists to recognize man's nature and dignity would finally be their undoing. In fact, he confidently predicted as early as 1958 that the Soviet regime "would go the way of all godless effrontery." In those years when Marxism seemed everywhere in the ascendant, he foresaw that it had already begun to decline as "a spiritual and moral world power." In the crushing defeat of the Poles and Hungarians, he read a moral victory—no matter how "much naked force seem[ed] to prevail once more." The Soviets, he believed, had suffered a stunning setback because in the revolts of the Poles and Hungarians "whole peoples" had risen against "the darkest and most dangerous aspect of Communism"—"against the violation of the human soul."

But Roepke warned that the West was by no means exempt from such violations. In fact, he accused the democratic nations of squandering their "spiritual patrimony," in pursuit of a higher standard of living. Ironically, the West's slavish devotion to materialism, he pointed out, decreased the quality of life by making society ever more urban, industrial, and proletarian. This, he was convinced, deprived man of his sense of tradition, principles, and history, and robbed him of his individuality. Roepke claimed that the result was a "cultural catastrophe," a "mass society ... a sandheap of individuals ... depersonalized ... isolated, uprooted, abandoned, and socially disintegrated."

He feared that a society populated by such "spiritual and moral pygmies" could not defeat Marxism because he recognized that "The decisive battle between Communism and the free world will have to be fought ... on the field of spiritual and moral values." "The free world," he warned, "will prevail only if it succeeds in filling the emptiness of the soul with its own values," for communism feeds "more on empty souls than on empty stomachs." Roepke knew that these empty souls could not be filled by consumer goods alone. In a deft paraphrase of the Gospel warning that "man is not fed by bread alone," he observes, "Man simply does not live by radio, automobiles, and refrigerators alone, but by the whole unpurchasable world beyond the market ..., the world of dignity, beauty, power, grace, chivalry, love, and friendship. ..."

Roepke's intense concern for things that go "beyond supply and demand" and his recognition that "Economics ... is a moral science" that deals with "man as a spiritual and moral being" mark him as a philosopher as well as an economist. His realization that "the essential thing ... always lies in the realm of the immeasurable and imponderable" shows him to be a sage as well. But the questions that he asks of every movement and theory—"What happens to man and his soul? What happens to the things which cannot be ... expressed in monetary terms or bought but which are the ultimate conditions of man's happiness and of the fullness and dignity of his life?"—these indicate that he was also a great humanist.

His fascination with these questions—evident in the ten books and more than six hundred articles that Roepke wrote—animates "The Economic Necessity of Freedom," his autobiographical memoir.

In this retrospective account, Roepke, born in 1899, recalls his edenic childhood in Schwarmstedt, Germany, and the shattering of that world by the Great War. For him, life in the trenches and the barbarity of war symbolized the modern condition at its worst: the physical and moral degradation of "mass existence, mass feeding, mass sleep."

Ironically, his hatred of this existence provided Roepke with his life's endeavor: to discover the economic and social conditions that would prevent war, protect individualism, and promote freedom. After originally embracing socialism as the path most likely to lead to these aims, he discovered that Marxism encouraged nationalism, curtailed individual rights, necessitated moral coercion, and dehumanized man. Armed with this awareness, Roepke realized that his "indignation over the war" was really a protest "against the unlimited powers of the state." This, in turn, enabled him to reject socialism because he saw that it meant "accepting the state as Leviathan," which, like the war, "gave endless and irresponsible power to the few and degraded the many."

This realization led Roepke to embrace the free market economy because he believed that it alone encouraged individual freedom and promoted the common good. In the last analysis, however, he recognized that capitalism cannot survive without the support of the moral and spiritual values on which it is based. Indeed, without them, he saw that modern man is stripped of much of his dignity and transformed into *"Homo sapiens consumens*—man-the-consumer—whose myopic vision extends no further than the bottom line. The remedy, Roepke argues, is to abandon "the hopeless effort ... to get along without God" and to stop vaingloriously putting "man, his science, his art, his political contrivances, in God's place."

Along with other essays in this volume, Roepke's "The Economic Necessity of Freedom," offers an autobiographical account of the author's conversion from socialism as a result of his own experiences. This seems particularly fitting, for conservatives are, first and last, individualists who insist that their beliefs—like English common law—be grounded in personal experience and that the abstract give way before the concrete.

Roepke's great strength as an economist was his ability to transcend the limitations of his own field and to recognize that calculations and equations can never yield the sum of all things. In fact, he was the first to admit "The crucial things in economics are about as mathematically intractable as a love letter or a Christmas celebration" because "[t]hey reside in moral and spiritual forces."

These forces, Roepke realized, were in constant contention with the evil influences that threaten the modem world. Moreover, he recognized that the contest between them casts every man in the role of metaphysical economist. Each of us, Roepke insisted, must with alarming regularity answer the great economic question, "What profiteth it a man to gain the whole world if he lose his soul?" A shrewd economist himself, Roepke insisted on warning others against this kind of fraudulent exchange.

Wilhelm Roepke

The Economic Necessity of Freedom

Born in the last days of 1899 on the Lüneburger Heide, where my father was a country doctor, I had the good luck to pass my childhood and earliest youth in the sunset of the long, rosy European day lasting from the Congress of Vienna to 1914. Those whose lives began in our present Arctic night can have no just conception of those times, and to try to summon up their atmosphere makes one feel rather like an Adam telling his sons about the life that had existed before they could have been. That figure is not, of course, applicable to the whole world of my youth, which was hardly everywhere a Paradise, but it is true enough of what I knew or could understand of the world before I became a soldier. The beginnings of 1914 were laid long before my birth, but history does not advance by the orderly route that the notion of "progress" implies; study and reflection may find the present's furthest source, but through the years the stream from it runs a random way, accepting now one tributary and now another, so that many far uplands remained untouched before the gathering waters burst into flood with the First World War.

A man's own life meanders in a similar way, and I know I shall find it hard to indicate all the currents that, hindering or sustaining me, have brought me to the point at which I presently rest. The

From Wilhelm Roepke, "The Economic Necessity of Freedom," *Modern Age*, Summer 1959, pp. 227–336.

names on the way are numerous—Hanover, the neighborhood of Hamburg, the universities of Goettingen, Tuebingen and Marburg, Berlin, Jena, the United States, an Austrian provincial capital, Istanbul, and now Geneva—and the chances that led me to each, though I cannot scrutinize the providence that intended them, seem to me to have some pattern of logic directed toward my own deeper education and understanding of the world in which I have lived. The immeasurably greater flow of history has its logic, too, and my task as an economist has been to explore a delimited portion of it, to decide why it had gone the ways it had, and to apply whatever rules were there discovered to surmising its future course, depending upon whether or not men acknowledged these rules. The smaller region I am now attempting to explore is where my own life and history have been confluent, so I think I can properly begin with the cataclysm by which the next forty years of history were to be determined—the war of 1914.

I belong, then, to the generation of Germans, Englishmen, Frenchmen, and Belgians who in their youth and young manhood went through the horrors of gigantic battles on the plains of France and whose subsequent lives have been shaped by this common experience. At an early and receptive age, there was brutally revealed to me much that in the quiet pre-War dusk had been obscured, and the sights of these times were ever to remain in my mind's eye, the constantly renewed starting points of the thoughts that confirmed in me a violent hatred of war. War I came to see as the expression of a brutal and stupid national pride that fostered the craving for domination and set its approval on collective immorality. Shortly in the course of this revelation, I vowed that if I were to escape from the hell in which it was given to me, I would make my remaining life meaningful by devoting it to the task of preventing the recurrence of this abomination, and I resolved to extend my hand beyond the confines of my nation to any who might be my collaborators in the task. In this I was only typical of many thousands of my contemporaries, who, facing each other on the battle lines, were determined that no one should again find himself forced into their positions.

My adult life began with a crisis of international society, passed into the stage of revolution we call war. To understand the reasons for the crisis, to learn what brought it to the stage of war, and to find if war indeed resolved anything, I determined to become an economist and a sociologist. Like all who are young, much of my curiosity must have been for its own sake, but since from the first my studies were directed toward the prevention of the thing I studied, a moral imperative lay behind them. Looking back on the third of a century that had passed since then—a third of a century that has taken me through two revolutions, the biggest inflation of any time, the spiritual ferment and social confusion of my country, and my own exile—I see that the determining background of my scientific studies has been far less those quiet halls of learning I have known in the Old and the New Worlds than it has been the battlefields of Picardy. The tendency of my thought, I can see from a later vantage point, has always been *international,* seeking to examine the larger relationship between countries, for it was in a crisis of this relationship that my thought began.

If I was typical of those who went through the War in my wish to make sure that it should not happen again, I think I was also typical in the analysis I made of it. We who were under a common obligation to kill one another had a great deal more in common too, and, since all of us on either side were roughly trained along the same lines, our revulsion with war brought us pretty much to a single conclusion. Our personal experience told us that a society capable of such monstrous depravity must be thoroughly rotten. We had been educated just enough to call this society "capitalism." Dumping everything into this concept that seemed to us rightly damnable, we became socialists.

Particularly for a young German of those days, this seemed the obvious path to take, for the political system of which Prussia was the exponent had been supported by every political group except the socialists. Those who wished to make a radical protest against the Prussian system became socialists almost as a matter of course. No one can understand modern socialism as a mass movement who does not see it as a product of the political development that took place in the nineteenth century in Germany after Bismarck had deprived of all influence the liberal and democratic forces that made their appearance on the surface during the unfortunate Revolution of 1848. To the extent that the German bourgeoisie made its peace with Bismarck and his state, social democracy became the gathering point, and the only one, not alone of social revolutionaries but also of those for whom the social was quite secondary to the political revolution. Very few guessed how much Prussian mentality lay hidden in this same socialism, for so long as it was merely a persecuted opposition, kept away from all responsibility, its leaders managed to conceal its inner contradictions.

So, as I have said, the explanation of things we formed in the trenches of the First World War was quite simple. This means war, we told ourselves, the bankruptcy of the entire "system." Our protest against imperialism, militarism, and nationalism was a protest against the prevailing economic and political system, which was a feudal and capitalistic one. The protest and its attendant denial made, the affirmation followed of itself: socialism. None of us was quite clear about the concrete content of our affirmation, and those of whom we expected enlightenment seemed, at bottom, no more certain than we; but this, rather than a discouragement, was a challenge to search further.

And, in fact, we searched; I know that I did. And I think that many of us, after years of confusion, arrived at a point we had hardly expected. We learned that we had gone astray with our very point of departure. In my own case the realization came, as it must have with most others, bit by bit through study and experience. Because the starting point had been the protest against war and nationalism, there followed from it a commitment to liberalism in the sphere of international economic relations; in other words, to free trade. This commitment I myself made, and I have not since departed from it. No more than average insight was needed to see that there was an irreconcilable difference between socialism and international economic liberalism, a difference not to be done away with by the lip-service of individual socialists to free trade.

After all, nobody was immediately working for world socialism. But if socialism could only be achieved within a national frame-work, state boundaries took on a new and primarily economic significance. Did not the simplest logic make it clear that a socialist state, which directed economic life within the nation, could not grant even so much freedom to foreign trade as had the protective tariffs against which we had protested? The deduction was this: there is only one ultimate form of socialism, the national. With that, my generation wanted nothing to do.

Other reflections followed. With recognition of the responsibility of one's own government in causing the war, went a great wariness about the powers of the modern state and, along with this, about the powers of the various pressure groups within the nation. That neither state nor pressure group should again attain the evil eminence it had in the War, the power of one would have to be limited and the other would have to be suppressed. At first, these seemed essential points of a socialist program. But in time it became evident that they were liberal notions, expressed by the great liberal thinkers, and they appeared to be socialist only because the socialists, so long as they were not in power, found them useful. Wherever socialism approached power after the War and exerted influence on government, the tendency was all toward acknowledging the omnicompetence of the state, and, looking at the socialists who held office, what slightest guarantee was there that the propose would be a rule of the wisest and the best? What proof was there that the new despotism would be for the general good when "nationalization" and "planned economy," those two vaunted socialist weapons against monopoly and vested interest, in actual practice led to the strengthening of the pressure groups? And where socialism had entire control, as in Russia, and power increasingly gathered in a single hand, wasn't the situation worse for the mere individual's liberty than in those countries where many private groupings of wealth and power continued to compete side by side?

Doubts of this kind were not merely the result of an abstract enthusiasm for liberty. Life in the army had shown what it meant for the individual to exist as part of an apparatus whose every function assumed lack of freedom and unconditional obedience. The immoralities and discomforts of army life were obvious enough; to make war means to kill and be killed, the exaltation of lying and the fostering of hatred for these purposes, and the destruction, filth, thirst, hunger, and illness that accompanied large-scale killing; but this physical degradation was also accompanied by a spiritual one that worked to the total debasement of human dignity in mass existence, mass feeding, mass sleep—that frightful soldier's life in which a man was never alone and in which he was without resource or appeal against the might (inhuman but wielded by man) that had robbed him of his privacy. Less well organized than the army, civilian life retained a few crevices where privacy could be enjoyed, but there too the notion worked that the fundamental liberties could be abrogated. Looking back on it today, I can see that this life of constraint had its compensations, which lay in the human contacts its very inhumanity enforced; but at the time I saw only its inhumanity and could not have borne it but for the thought of a higher goal—the elimination of this same thing in the future—and the sense of duty in which I had been raised.

I could not then have extolled for you the peculiar virtues of the soldier, for I was profoundly antimilitarist, so longing for civilian life that every leave was a foretaste of paradise. The fact that I and my fellows who were university graduates did not differ in this from our comrades who were proletarians proves that we did not have a sentimental longing for something that the proletariat had long ago forgotten. Leave—the periodic return to the basic freedom of civilian existence—meant as much to the worker as to us of the "professional classes." It is not class prejudice, anxious for outmoded privileges, that speaks out against the lack of freedom in a collectivized, i.e., militarized, system.

The more I looked into it, the more clearly I saw that my indignation over the war was a protest against the unlimited power of the state. The state—this elusive but all-powerful entity that was outside of moral restraints—had led us into the War, and now continued to make us suffer while it intimidated and deceived us. War was simply the rampant essence of the state, collectivity let loose, so was it not absurd to make one's protest against the dominance of man over man take the form of professing collectivism? Not all the pacifist, antimilitarist, and freedom-demanding statements of even the most honest socialists could obscure the fact that socialism, if it was to mean anything at all, meant accepting the state as Leviathan not only for the emergency of war but also for a long time to come.

Any future increase of state power could only bring about an increase of what was now issuing from the unwarranted, but still limited, power of the state, and only the most extreme gullibility could expect deliverance from the evils of militarism by a society that made militarism a permanent institution. Collectivism and war were, in essence, one and the same thing; they both gave endless and irresponsible power to the few and degraded the many. If socialists really were not serious about their collectivism, they were playing a curious and dangerous game in trying to fill their ranks by announcing goals that no one whose final commitment was to freedom could accept.

Thus was marked out a route of inquiry and effort that I continued along for a quarter of a century. The signposts were few and not often clear, and often enough I had to grope my way painstakingly back. Nor was the way itself easy, for at every turn stood the spirit of war, nationalism, Machiavellianism, and international anarchy. As my professional career progressed and I was called to positions of some official importance, I spoke for what reason dictated in the field of political economy, and this meant speaking against most of the groups and policies that prevailed in the field of economics between the wars. It was a struggle against economic nationalism, the groups that supported it, or the particular strategies it employed—a struggle against monopolies, heavy industry, and large-scale farming interests, against the inexcusable inflation, whose engineers obscured what they were doing with fantastic monetary theories, against the aberrations of the policy of protective tariffs, against the final madness of autarky.

To whatever extent my abilities and my office allowed, and wherever I found those with whom to join cause, I sought to mend the torn threads to international trade and to normalize international money and credit relations, to have German reparations considered in their proper aspect and without regard to "patriotism," to aid the re-integration of the vanquished countries into a democratic and peaceful world, and, when the crisis of 1929 broke out, to have adopted an economy that would not end in the blind alley of deflation and autarky. Those of us who spoke thus were a small company, and the degree of our effectiveness is shown in the history of 1918–1939. Forced out of my position by the Nazi regime, I had to emigrate from Germany, and first from Turkey and then from Switzerland could contemplate the flood of political nihilism that swirled over Europe.

It would only be a sort of inverted vanity to say that the Second World War marked the failure of the effort that I had conceived in the trenches of the First World War. I think it more modest to say that in a fashion I succeeded—not, of course, in external accomplishment but in having now learned how the goal may be achieved that my youthful optimism looked toward, though the way there is a far harder one than my youth dreamed. And I think the history of the past thirty-five years proves that my starting-point was a good one. The starting-point was apparently paradoxical: I sided with the socialists in their rejection of capitalism and with the adherents of capitalism in their rejection of socialism. I was to find in time that these two negatives amounted, as two minuses in algebra can be a plus, to a positive. Both rejections were accepted because they were based on certain positive notions about the nature of man and the sort of existence that was fitting to that nature, so that as the inquiry proceeded it always had something concrete and real to refer to and was protected from the tendency of the over-abstract to result in monstrosities when it is brought into the human realm. The third way I have pursued, beginning on it as it were out of the accident of history, has come with good reason to be called "economic humanism."

The accident of history has also required, as I have said, that I should look on economics largely in their international aspect, and in this aspect the operation of economics has again and again shown itself to be a question of order. Order is something continuous; in its true sense, it is a harmony of parts, not a regularity imposed from without. International order can only be a wider projection of the order prevailing within nations, and if today, as in the immediate past, we find ourselves more engaged with the problems of international order, that is because international relations are a screen upon which the internal phenomena of a disintegrating society are thrown and enlarged, making them visible long before they become evident within the various nations. The disturbance of the international order is not only a symptom of the inner malaise; it is also a sort of quack therapy, as is proved by the case of the totalitarian states, which temporarily avert collapse by aggressively diverting the forces of the destruction to the outside.

The years between the wars saw much mistaking of the symptoms for the disease. The international crisis, looked on in isolation, was taken for a regrettable aberration of an otherwise healthy society of nations. So followed the attempts to mend things by improving the charter of the League of Nations, holding world-economy conferences, revising debts, arranging the cooperation of money-issuing banks, repeating the irrefutable arguments for free trade, and the rest of it. August 1939 was terrible proof that profounder measures were needed. The lessons of it are lost if we assume the present international crisis is simply one of a healthy West besieged by forces from without. There remains an internal crisis and the external, the international, one will not be resolved until the two are grasped as a unity and so dealt with.

I think I have demonstrated how I came to see that socialism did not have the cure for our social ills, that indeed socialism was a heresy which aggravated these ills the more men acted on it. The economic "orthodoxy" according to which I adjudged socialism a heresy was historical liberalism, and with this liberalism I am quite willing to take my stand. What such liberalism advocates in the economic realm can be very simply stated. It holds that economic activities are not the proper sphere of any planning, enforcing, and penalizing authority; these activities are better left to the spontaneous cooperation of all individuals through a free market, unregulated prices, and open competition.

But there is more to the matter than the advocacy of a certain economic technique. As an economist, I am supposed to know something about prices, capital interests, costs, and rates of exchange, and all of them supply arguments for free enterprise; but my adherence to free enterprise goes to something deeper than mere technical grounds, and the reason for it lies in those regions where each man's social philosophy is ultimately decided. Socialists and non-socialists are divided by fundamentally different conceptions of life and life's meaning. What we judge man's position in the universe to be will in the end decide whether our highest values are realized in man or in society, and our decision for either the former or the latter will also be the watershed of our political thinking.

Thus my fundamental opposition to socialism is to an ideology that, in spite of all its "liberal" phraseology, gives too little to man, his freedom, and his personality; and too much to society. And my opposition on technical grounds is that socialism, in its enthusiasm for organization, centralization, and efficiency, is committed to means that simply are not compatible with human freedom. Because

I have a very definite concept of man derived from the classic-Christian heritage of Europe in which alone the idea of liberty has anywhere appeared, because that concept makes man the image of God whom it is sinful to use as a means, and because I am convinced that each man is of unique value owning to his relationship to God but is not the god declared by the *hybris* of an atheistic humanism— because of these things, I look on any kind of collectivism with the utmost distrust. And, following from these convictions along the lines of reason, experience, and the testimony of history, I arrive at the conclusion that only a free economy is in accordance with man's freedom and with the political and social structure and the rule of law that safeguard it. Aside from such an economic system (for which I make no claims of automatically perfect functioning), I see no chance of the continued existence of man as he is envisaged in the religious and philosophical traditions of the West. For this reason, I would stand for a free economic order even if it implied material sacrifice and if socialism gave the certain prospect of material increase. It is our undeserved luck that the exact opposite is true.

There is a deep moral reason for the fact that an economy of free enterprise brings about social health and a plenitude of goods, while a socialist economy ends in social disorder and poverty. The "liberal" economic system delivers to useful ends the extraordinary force inherent in individual self-assertion, whereas the socialist economy suppresses this force and wears itself out in the struggle against it. Is the system unethical that permits the individual to strive to advance himself and his neighbor through his own productive achievement? Is the ethical system the one that is organized to suppress this striving? I have very little patience with the moralizing of intellectuals who preach the virtues of the second system, inspired by their ambition to hold commanding places in the vast supervisory machinery such a system entails but too uncritical of themselves to suspect their own *libido dominandi*. It makes virtue appear irrational and places an extravagant demand upon human nature when men in serving virtue in a collectivist economy must act against their own proper interests in ways that, as even the simplest of them can see, do nothing to increase the total wealth. The collectivist state that, in peacetime, supports itself with the patent dishonesties of foreign-exchange control, price ceilings, and confiscatory taxes acts with greater immorality than the individual who violates these regulations to preserve the fruits of his own labor. I cannot believe that it is moral and will make for a better world to muzzle the ox that treadeth out the corn.

The greater error of socialism is its steadfast denial that man's desire to advance himself and his family, and to earn and retain what will provide his family's well-being far beyond the span of his own life, is as much in the natural order as the desire to be identified with the community and serve its further ends. They are both in the natural order, both are intrinsic to humanity, and balanced against each other they prevent the excesses that destroy a fit human existence. To deny the elementary force of self-interest in society is an unrealism that eventually leads to a kind of brutal internal *Realpolitik*. The eccentric morality that confuses the eternal teachings of Christianity with the communism of early Christians expecting the imminent end of all things, and calls private property unchristian and immoral, ends by approving a society in which highly immoral means—lying, propaganda, economic coercion, and naked force—are necessities. An economic order which has to rely on propaganda in the press, in moral tracts, and over the radio and on decorations and threats to make people work and save, and which cannot rely on them to see, as peasants do, the self-evident need for work and saving, is basically unsound and contrary to the natural order. An economic system that presupposes saints and heroes cannot endure. As Gustav Thibon says: "Every social system that makes it necessary for the majority of men, in the ordinary conduct of their lives, to display aristocratic virtues reveals itself to be unhealthy." The welfare state, in its rage for egalitarianism, gives its citizens the status and opportunities of slaves, but calls on them to act like heroes.

In speaking of a balance between the elementary drive of self-interest and the urge of the communal sense, I am of course admitting that the former needs taming and channeling. At the very outset, self-interest becomes family interest, and the "civilizing" restraints this sets upon it are too obvious to need mention. Beyond this, a free market operating within a framework of firm legislation seems about as much as is required in the way of economic organization to confine the acquisitive instinct to socially tolerable forms. But this in itself is not enough. The defender of a "liberal" economy must make plain that the realm of economy in which self-interest develops, constrained by legislation and competition, is not set against but enclosed within the realm in which is developed man's capacity for devotion, his ability to serve ends that do not look to his own immediate betterment. Society as a whole cannot be based on the law of supply and demand, and it is a good conservative conviction that the state is more than a joint-stock company. Men who measure their strengths in the competition of the open market have to be united by a common ethic; otherwise competition degenerates into an internecine struggle. Market economy is not in itself a sufficient basis of society. It must, instead, be lodged in an overall order that not only allows, and is in some measure determined by, supply and demand, free markets and competition, but that also allows the imperfections and hardships of economic freedom to be corrected and helps man to attain an existence in which he is more than the mere economic animal. For such an existence, man must voluntarily accept the community's prior rights as against certain short-term satisfactions of his own, and he must feel that in serving the community he ennobles his own life with the *philia* by which, according to Aristotle, men are united in political societies. Without this, he leads a miserable existence, and he knows it.

The economist, too, has his occupational disease: restricted vision. I speak from experience when I say that it is not easy for him to look beyond his field and modestly admit that the market is not the whole of the world but only a segment of it, important enough, to be sure, but still merely a part of the larger order for which the theologian and the philosopher, not the economist as such, are competent. Here one could quote a variation on the words of Georg Christoph Lichtenberg, the eighteenth-century physicist: "Whoever understands economics only, understands not even them." My own effort has always been to look beyond the fence enclosing the narrow field of my science, for I have learned that it is not to be worked fruitfully without allowing for the highly complex world in which even the simplest economic law must, in the end, operate. In my own passion for synthesis, I do not think I have forgotten that these laws must be allowed to function according to their own nature; but the more I have inquired into their logic and the effects of ignoring it, the more I have seen that their operating toward humanly good ends presupposes an equivalent function of human goodness. Economic laws will not work to our benefit unless they work within a society that admits of the human virtues which issue in true service (not just "service to the customer"), devotion, charity, hospitality, and in the sacrifices which genuine communities demand.

Two things are absolutely fatal for such a society: mass and centralization. Community, fraternity, charity—they are all possible only in the small, easily comprehended circles that are the original patterns of human society, the village community, the community of small and medium-sized towns, etc. These small circles of human warmth and mutual responsibility increasingly give way to mass and centralization, the amorphous agglutination of the big cities and industrial centers with their deracination, mass organization, and anonymous bureaucracy that end in the monster state by which, with the help of police and tax officials, our crumbling society is now actually held together. This society, paradoxically fragmented and amorphous, at the same time crowned with a vast monolithic superstructure whose irrational weight continues the pulverization that must in time bring the whole thing to collapse, I have tried to describe in *The Social Crisis of Our Time*, in *Civitas Humana*, and in *Beyond Supply and Demand*.

The measures needed to avert this collapse immediately suggest themselves—we must decentralize, put down roots again, extract men out of the mass and allow them to live in forms of life and work appropriate to men. To some this seems a romantic and unworldly program, but I know of no alternative to it that does not threaten to aggravate fatally the disease. Because a suggested treatment is distasteful to the very lethargy induced by the illness it is intended to cure, it does not mean it is impractical. In the gravity of our present situation, there are no easy measures that are going to save man, no gently homeopathic doses that will enable him to shake off his symptoms without effort. If man is to be restored to the possibility of simple, natural happiness, it can only be done by putting him once more in a humanly tolerable existence, where, placed in the true community that begins with the family and living in harmony with nature, he can support himself with labor made purposeful by the institution of private property. The almost desperate character of this effort does not testify against its necessity if we wish to save our civilization. In measure as we see how slight are its chances of acceptance and how serious the present situation is, we can see how badly it is needed.

Here, too, lies one of the basic reasons for the crisis of modern democracy, which has gradually degenerated into a centralized mass democracy of Jacobin complexion and stands more urgently in need of those counterweights of which I spoke in my book *Civitas Humana*. Thus we are led to a political view whose conservative ingredients are plainly recognizable in our predilection for natural law, tradition, *Corps intermediaires*, federalism and other defenses against the flood of modern mass democracy. We should harbor no illusions about the fateful road which leads from the Jacobinism of the French Revolution to modem totalitarianism.

If I find some tendencies of liberal thinking compatible with this conservatism, I think I do so in a manner learned from Lord Acton and Jacob Burckhardt, and without being deceived that certain individual and hard-to-define currents of thought which are commonly thrown together under the heading of "liberalism" are not free of elements of moral and spiritual disintegration. They are the currents of modern "progressivism," the type of rationalism and intellectualism that I have identified with "sinistrismo."

I cannot here draw the portrait of the progress-minded modern who, in my reckoning, accounts for so much that is wrong in our world, but I can list a few of the things that attend him: the dissecting intellect, lacking wisdom and even common sense; the radicalism going in short relays from humanitarianism to bestiality; the nihilism of intellectuals who have lost hold of ultimate convictions and values and ceased to be true *clercs;* the relativism tolerating everything, including the most brutal intolerance; the egalitarianism that, presupposing an omnipotent state machinery, leads to extreme inequality in the most important respect, the distribution of power, and unleashes the soul-corroding forces of envy and jealousy; the grimace of an art called modern whose one achievement is to mirror our society's inner disintegration. Who has seen these things needs no extraordinary illumination to know toward what they tend, for the past twenty years have given us enough examples of its ruin and misery; and no one, seeing all that has been the work of men and not of blind forces, can come to any other conclusion than that men must take council with themselves and set their faces toward another way.

Here my thought comes to its deepest layer, resting on the point from which, in the logical order, all men's thinking must proceed, though in actual life they may be years gaining it. The point is one of religious conviction; I will say it in all candor: the nidus of the malady from which our civilization suffers lies in the individual soul and is only to be overcome within the individual soul. For more than a century, we have made the hopeless effort, more and more baldly proclaimed, to get along without God and vaingloriously to put man, his science, his art, his political contrivances, in God's place. I am convinced that the insane futility of this effort, now evident only to a few, will one day break on most men like a tidal wave, and that they will see that self-idolatry has created a situation in which a moral and spiritual creature cannot exist, a situation in which, despite television, pleasure cruises, and air-conditioned modern architecture, man cannot exist at all. It is as though we had wanted to add to the already existing proofs of God's existence, a new and finally convincing one: the universal destruction that follows on assuming God's non-existence.

For the Catholic, secured in his faith, this poses enviably few personal problems. It is a very different matter for those Protestants who consider the Reformation, or, if you wish, the situation it created, one of the greatest calamities in history, but one that, neither in whole nor in part, can be undone. Such a Protestant has difficulties in finding his religious home either in contemporary Protestantism, which in its disruption and lack of orientation is worse than ever before, or in contemporary, post-Reformation Catholicism. For his own part, he can only try, with whatever grace is allowed him, to re-assemble in himself the essential elements of pre-Reformation, undivided Christianity, and in this I think I am one of a company of men whose good will at least is beyond dispute. But it is a most difficult course and so far a lonely one, since there seems little present hope of establishing thus a religious community that goes much beyond a mutual respect for outward forms. If we have to content ourselves with this for the time being, it is more than ever our duty to work untiringly for our own recollection and to stir others from their indifference.

The Heritage Foundation Collection, 1990

CHAPTER 13

Richard M. Weaver

Commentary by Edwin J. Feulner Jr. (1987)

As a scholar, teacher, writer, and most of all, man of integrity, Richard Weaver deserves our attention. Perhaps he deserves it all the more because he is the kind of man our society is quick to overlook. Reserved, professorial, bespectacled, his was a life of hard work, self-sacrifice, and quiet virtue. Living alone in a rented room on the south side of Chicago, sometimes wearing two overcoats against fierce winter winds, this southern gentleman wrote passionately about goodness, beauty, and truth. Often working seven days a week to defend these treasured beliefs, he died in 1963 at age fifty-three, the victim of heart trouble and hard work.

Weaver's life was characterized by the kind of quiet heroism one would expect of a man who believed in chivalry and fought for the restoration of piety. He did not, however, hesitate to act on his ideas. He became an early trustee of the Intercollegiate Studies Institute (ISI) and an editor of *Modern Age*. He contributed to *National Review,* and participated in the University of Chicago's Committee on Social Thought.

Although he died young, Richard Weaver left an impressive legacy. As George Nash points out in *The Conservative Intellectual Movement in America Since 1945,* Weaver has played a central role in American conservatism—a point William F. Buckley Jr. emphasized by entitling one of his own books *Up from Liberalism,* the title of this essay.

Weaver's articles and books have introduced several generations to conservatism; the Intercollegiate Studies Institute's graduate fellowships named after him have enabled many young scholars to study Weaver's ideas, and the Ingersoll Foundation's annual Richard M. Weaver Award for Scholarly Letters encourages senior scholars to examine the ideas that animated his work and to emulate his grace and erudition.

In this autobiographical work, Weaver's "unorthodox defense of orthodoxy" is startlingly evident. How many southerners, scholars, and conservatives would have audaciously compared their own delivery from the snares of liberalism, socialism, and the "maladies of modernism" with Booker T. Washington's release from slavery? How many would have recognized so unerringly that liberalism's promise of freedom ends in servitude?

The most important single fact about "Up from Liberalism" is that it chronicles a conversion. It not only narrates Weaver's move from socialism to conservatism, but also explains that liberalism cannot work because it is "that state of mind before we have made up our mind." As such, socialism is the halfway house for the undecided, "the refuge favored by intellectual cowardice, because the essence of the liberal's position is that he has no position." Thus, Weaver claims, liberalism can provide no basis for societal improvement: "as something to construct with, never!"

The road to Weaver's conversion began in Weaverville, North Carolina, where he was born in 1910. At the age of seventeen he entered the University of Kentucky. At the time, he described himself as a "gloomy, ardent, stupid" collegian making "wayward choices" at a "provincial university" that would have been better had it been "more provincial in the right way."

Foremost among these "wayward choices" was his decision to embrace socialism. Graduating in 1932, when the Great Depression was at its nadir, he joined the American Socialist Party, convinced that those he opposed were "people of ignorance or malevolence."

He discovered, however, that his comrades were also an odd, unendearing group: "academic people,... nondescripts,... eccentrics, novelty-seekers, victims of restlessness ... hopelessly confused about the nature and purpose of socialism." This discovery and the painful realization that he did not like these "dry, insistent people ... of shallow objectives" sowed the seed of his later disillusionment with liberalism.

Graduate studies in literature at Vanderbilt University under John Crowe Ransom and other Southern Agrarians, whom he liked, although he rejected their socioeconomic policies, gave him further pause. Weaver's interest in Ransom's "unorthodox defense of orthodoxy," suggesting that traditional American beliefs were in retreat because of default by their conservative defenders, left Weaver ripe for a change of heart.

The "rampant philistinism" he encountered while teaching at "a large technical college in Texas" set the stage for his "conversion to the poetic and ethical vision of life." The moment of awakening came when he "woke up" to the fact that he had free will and could reject the "worship of false idols." Ironically, this road-to-Damascus experience occurred in the fall of 1939 while he was "driving across the monotonous prairies of Texas to begin [his] third year [of teaching]." "It came to me," he recalls, "like a revelation that I did not *have* to go back to this job ... and ... did not *have* to go on professing the clichés of liberalism."

This realization, the beginning of his emancipation, necessitated reeducation, so he enrolled at the University of Louisiana. He emerged three years later with a doctorate in English—after writing an extensive study of southern culture, later published posthumously as *The Southern Tradition At Bay* (1968).

Believing that "Dangers are always best met on the frontier," Weaver then headed north into the midst of Yankees and liberal academics who—as a group—did not share his reverence for courtesy, conservatism, and Christianity. There, for twenty years at the

University of Chicago, he taught English, specializing in rhetoric.

For him, rhetoric was the discipline of teaching men to know the good, speak and write about it convincingly, and act upon it. To this end, he taught, spoke, and wrote tirelessly—publishing two books that have become classics—*The Ethics of Rhetoric* (1953) and *Ideas Have Consequences* (1948). The former expresses Weaver's belief that language is a divine gift that accurately represents its speakers and their culture. Moreover, he warns that language, by its very nature, is "sermonic," always encouraging its auditors to good or ill. The debasement of words, he insisted, attacked the ideas and realities they represent.

Ideas Have Consequences, his most influential book, occupies a seminal place among modern conservative works for, as Russell Kirk observes, its attack on modern nominalism heralded the revival of conservatism in America. It also expressed Weaver's most deeply held beliefs. Writing immediately after World War II, he claimed that the ills of modernity began in the fourteenth century when, "like Macbeth, Western man made an evil decision" to abandon "belief in transcendentals."

This fateful choice resulted, Weaver wrote, in "the dissolution of the West." He believed that this dissolution expressed itself in the decline of proper sentiment; eradication of rightful distinctions; and obliteration of legitimate hierarchies. This, in turn, led to fragmentation, with specialists knowing more and more about less and less, while individuals, cut off in time, space, and intimacy from their fellows, became increasingly obsessed with egotistic self-realization. Weaver believed that this self-absorption defaced modern work and art, and ruined contemporary lives: "he who is cognizant mainly of self suffers an actual derangement." Such self-absorption, Weaver commented, cuts man off "from the 'real' reality and from ... social harmony."

Despite this situation, our egotism, Weaver maintained, is constantly being fed by what he called the Great Stereopticon, false images of reality purveyed by the media. Designed to increase our "spoiled-child psychology," these images promise us everything for nothing in a "pushbutton existence."

Weaver does not, however, merely wring his hands over the demise of the West. He offers bracing correctives for those who will act on them. What is needed, he asserts, is a return to piety—which he defines as a respectful "attitude toward things which are immeasurably larger and greater than oneself." Without piety, Weaver claims, "man is an insufferably brash, conceited,... frivolous animal." He specifically suggests that man must re-establish the proper attitude toward nature, his fellow man, and the past. For Weaver, this means admitting that we are creatures beset by original sin and that our lives are the arenas in which good and evil contend for souls. Finally, he insists that we must remember the past in order to escape the "stultifying Whig theory of history" with "its bland assumption that every cause which has won deserved to win."

This theory, coupled with "presentism," the belief that nothing but the present counts, filled Weaver with horror. He believed that modernism was itself a pernicious form of provincialism that "declines to look beyond the moment." For him, the present moment was unusually bleak—he called modern man "a moral idiot," evincing "symptoms of mass psychosis" while on a "toboggan slide toward cheapness and vulgarity."

He believed that our only hope was to recognize the madness of the modern age and institute reforms. Those who argued that "you can't turn back the clock," he contended, were guilty not only of "presentism" but also of bad faith, for they implicitly championed time-bound circumstances over timeless truths.

Despite his acute awareness of the pitfalls of "presentism," Weaver falls prey to it himself in one peculiar paragraph in *Up from Liberalism*. He announces that the imbalance between man's technological and spiritual prowess has created an unheard-of instability that can be controlled only by a government that incites the "desire of conquest" or constantly invokes "the national security." He accuses America of taking the second alternative and asserts that modern technology has made war "increasingly total and nihilistic." He then prophesies that the chance of not using atomic bombs, unless they are abolished, is "infinitesimal."

Concentrating exclusively on the situation when he was writing, Weaver himself committed what he called the "fallacy of technology": "the conclusion that because a thing can be done, it must be done." In this he was guilty not so much of a failure of vision as of imagination. In the aftermath of World War II he could not conceive that a technological breakthrough might limit or prevent war. He certainly could not imagine something like the Strategic Defense Initiative reviving a chivalric code which endangers only armed belligerents, while protecting the innocent from harm.

Weaver's lack of insight on this issue is surprising only because he was right so consistently on so many others. His basic premise was that "life and the world are to be cherished" and he regarded reality as his ally. Conservatives, he believed, were, above all, realists who discern both the present and transcendent reality, As such, he considered them uniquely equipped to defend liberty and to reform society.

Although he considered the twentieth century to be an "age of crisis," Weaver did not despair. He believed fervently that "man will prevail over the dark forces of this time" and that "a chief means of his prevailing will be ... persuasive speech in the service of truth." Such speech Richard Weaver gave abundantly. He was convinced that the Word would eventually triumph. For him, Dante's statement that "In His will is our peace" was the "final discovery." He was well aware, however, that such a discovery had to be earned. As he wrote in the postscript on a Christmas card shortly before he died, "There is much to be done."

Richard M. Weaver

Up from Liberalism

There is a saying by William Butler Yeats that a man begins to understand the world by studying the cobwebs in his own corner. My experience has brought home to me the wisdom in this; and since the contemporary ideal seems to run the other way, confronting the youth first with the abstractions of universalism, collectivism, and internationalism, I propose to say something on behalf of the historic and the concrete as elements of an education.

The discovery did not come to me as a free gift, for practically every conviction I now hold I have had to win against the propositional sense and general impetus of most of my formal education. This was owing partly to special circumstances, but mainly, I now believe, to the fact that the United States tends to institutionalize the chaotic and superficial type of education and to impose it with an air of business efficiency. This is not to imply that I was wiser than my generation, for I was filled with the formless aspirations which make such an education look like a good thing, and I fell into most of the pitfalls that were left open. But I hope that a retrospect of twenty-five years, involving much change of opinion, gives some right to pass judgment; and furthermore I wish, in this testament, to discuss education as one of the proven means of doing something about the condition of man.

From Richard M. Weaver, *Life Without Prejudice and Other Essays* (1965).

I was born in the Southern section of the United States, and at the age of seventeen I entered the University of Kentucky. I have more than once recalled how well Charles Peguy's description of himself at the beginning of his career at the *Ecole Normale* fitted me at this time: "gloomy, ardent, stupid." The University of Kentucky was what would be called in Europe a "provincial university," but I have since come to believe that if it had been more provincial in the right way and less sedulously imitative of the dominant American model, it would have offered better fare. Like most of our state-supported universities during the period, it was growing in enrollment and physical plant and losing in character; moreover, it was given to the "elective" system, whereby seventeen-year-old students, often of poor previous training and narrow background, tell the faculty (in effect) what they ought to be taught. After many wayward choices I managed to emerge, at the end of my undergraduate course, with a fair introduction to the history—but not the substance—of literature and philosophy.

The professors who staffed this institution were mostly earnest souls from the Middle Western universities, and many of them— especially those in economics, political science, and philosophy— were, with or without knowing it, social democrats. They read and circulated *The Nation*, the foremost liberal journal of the time; they made sporadic efforts toward organizing liberal or progressive clubs; and of course they reflected their position in their teaching very largely. I had no defenses whatever against their doctrine, and by the time I was in my third year I had been persuaded entirely that the future was with science, liberalism, and equalitarianism, and that all opposed to these trends were people of ignorance or malevolence.

That persuasion was not weakened, I must add, by the fact that my class graduated in May 1932 at almost precisely the time that the Great Depression reached its lowest point on the economic charts. College graduates were taking any sort of job they could get, however menial or unrelated to their preparation, and many, of course, were not getting jobs at all. It seemed then that some sort of political reconstruction was inevitable, and in that year I joined the American Socialist party. My disillusionment with the Left began with this first practical step.

The composition of our small unit of the Socialist party was fairly typical, I have since learned, of socialist organizations throughout the world. There was on the one side a group of academic people—teachers and students—who were intellectually trained and fairly clear in their objectives, but politically inexperienced and temperamentally not adapted to politics. On the other side was about an equal number of town people who cannot be described for the good reason that they were nondescripts. They were eccentrics, novelty-seekers, victims of restlessness; and most of them were hopelessly confused about the nature and purpose of socialism. I remember how shocked I was when a member of this group suggested that we provide at our public rallies one of the "hillbilly bands" which are often used to draw crowds and provide entertainment in Southern political campaigns. This seemed to me entirely out of tone with what we were trying to do. I have since had to realize that the member was far more astute practically than I; the hillbilly music would undoubtedly have fetched more auditors and made more votes than the austere exposition of the country's ills which I thought it the duty of a Socialist to make. But I am sure that the net result would not have been socialism. The two groups did not understand one another, and it is a wonder to me that they worked together as long as they did.

In the course of a membership of about two years, during which I served as secretary of the "local," as it was called, I discovered that although the socialist program had a certain intellectual appeal for me, I could not like the members of the movement as *persons*. They seemed dry, insistent people, of shallow objectives; seeing them often and sharing a common endeavor, moreover, did nothing to remove the disliking. I am afraid that I performed my duties with decreasing enthusiasm, and at the end of the period I had intimations, which

I did not then face, that this was not the kind of thing in which I could find permanent satisfaction.

Meanwhile another experience had occurred which was to turn my thoughts in the same direction. I had gone as a graduate student to Vanderbilt University to pursue an advanced degree in literature. Vanderbilt was another provincial university, but it had developed in the hands of men intelligent enough to see the possibilities that exist in a reflective provincialism. It was at that time the chief seat of the Southern Agrarian school of philosophy and criticism. This was one of the most brilliant groups in the United States, but its members held a position antithetical in almost every point to socialism and other purely economic remedies. By some their program was regarded as mere antiquarianism: by others it was attacked as fascist, since it rejected science and rationalism as the supreme sanctions, accepted large parts of the regional tradition, and even found some justification for social classes. But here, to my great surprise and growing confusion, I found that although I disagreed with these men on matters of social and political doctrine, I liked them all as persons. They seemed to me more humane, more generous, and considerably less dogmatic than those with whom I had been associated under the opposing banner. It began to dawn upon me uneasily that perhaps the right way to judge a movement was by the persons who made it up rather than by its rationalistic perfection and by the promises it held out. Perhaps, after all, the proof of social schemes was meant to be a posteriori rather than a priori. It would be a poor trade to give up a nonrational world in which you liked everybody for a rational one in which you liked nobody. I did not then see it as quite so sharp an issue; but the intellectual maturity and personal charm of the Agrarians were very unsettling to my then-professed allegiance.

Moreover, during my residence at Vanderbilt University I had the great good fortune to study under John Crowe Ransom, a rare teacher of literature and, apart from this and in his own right, a profound psychologist. Of the large number of students who have felt his influence, I doubt whether any could tell how he worked his effects. If one judged solely by outward motions and immediate results, he seemed neither to work very hard at teaching nor to achieve much success. But he had the gift of dropping living seeds into minds. Long after the date of a lecture—a week, a month, a year—you would find some remark of his troubling you with its pregnancy, and you would set about your own reflections upon it, often wishing that you had the master at hand to give another piece of insight. The idea of Ransom's which chiefly took possession of me at this time was that of the "unorthodox defense of orthodoxy," which he had developed in his brilliant book *God Without Thunder*. I began to perceive that many traditional positions in our world had suffered not so much because of inherent defect as because of the stupidity, ineptness, and intellectual sloth of those who for one reason or another were presumed to have their defense in charge.

This was a troubling perception, because the 1930s were a time when nearly all of the traditional American ideologies were in retreat, and I had never suspected that this retreat might be owing to a kind of default. If there was something to be said for them, if their eclipse was due to the failure of their proponents to speak a modern idiom or even to acquire essential knowledge, this constituted at least a challenge to intellectual curiosity. I had tried some of the Leftist solution and had found it not to my taste; it was possible that I had been turned away from the older, more traditional solutions because they wore an antiquarian aspect and insisted upon positions which seemed irrelevancies in the modern context. Actually the passage was not an easy one for me, and I left Vanderbilt University poised between the two alternatives. I had seen virtually nothing of socialism and centralism in practice, and the mass man I had never met; there was also reluctance over giving up a position once publicly espoused, made somewhat greater by a young man's vanity. Nevertheless, I had felt a powerful pull in the direction of the Agrarian ideal of the individual in contact with the rhythms of nature, of the small-property holding, and of the society of pluralistic organization.

I had left the University to take a teaching post in a large technical college in Texas. It has been remarked that in the United States California is the embodiment of materialism and Texas of naturalism. I found the observation true with regard to my part of Texas, where I encountered a rampant philistinism, abetted by technology, large-scale organization, and a complacent acceptance of success as the goal of life. Moreover, I was here forced to see that the lion of applied science and the lamb of the humanities were not going to lie down together in peace, but that the lion was going to devour the lamb unless there was a very stern keeper of order. I feel that my conversion to the poetic and ethical vision of life dates from this contact with its sterile opposite.

I recall very sharply how, in the autumn of 1939, as I was driving one afternoon across the monotonous prairies of Texas to begin my third year in this post, it came to me like a revelation that I did not *have* to go back to this job, which had become distasteful, and that I did not *have* to go on professing the clichés of liberalism, which were becoming meaningless to me. I saw that my opinions had been formed out of a timorous regard for what was supposed to be intellectually respectable, and that I had always been looking over my shoulder to find out what certain others, whose concern with truth I was beginning to believe to be not very intense, were doing or thinking. It is a great experience to wake up at a critical juncture to the fact that one does have a free will, and that giving up the worship of false idols is a quite practicable proceeding.

Anyhow, at the end of that year I chucked the uncongenial job and went off to start my education over, being now arrived at the age of thirty.

In the meantime I had started to study the cobwebs in my own corner, and I began to realize that the type of education which enables one to see into the life of things had been almost entirely omitted from my program. More specifically, I had been reading extensively in the history of the American Civil War, preferring first-hand accounts by those who had actually borne the brunt of it as soldiers and civilians; and I had become especially interested in those who had reached some level of reflectiveness and had tried to offer explanations of what they did or the manner in which they did it. Allen Tate has in one of his poems the line "There is more in killing than commentary." The wisdom of this will be seen also by those who study the killings in which whole nations are the killers and the killed, namely, wars. To put this in a prose statement: the mere commentary of a historian will never get you inside the feeling of a war or any great revolutionary process. For that, one has to read the testimonials of those who participated in it on both sides and in all connections; and often the best insight will appear in the casual remark of an obscure warrior or field nurse or in the effort of some ill-educated person to articulate a feeling.

I once heard of a man who made it a lifetime hobby to study the reasons people in various circumstances gave as to why they felt it necessary to tell a lie. I believe that it is equally worthwhile and perhaps more interesting to study the reasons that people have given for passing from the use of reason to the use of force. At what point does reason tell us that reason is of no more avail? The American Civil War, because it was a civil struggle, with an elaborate ideology on both sides, left a rich store of material on this subject.

From the viewpoint of my general purpose, I had come to believe that one way to achieve the education which leads to understanding and compassion is to take some period of the past and to immerse oneself in it so thoroughly that one could think its thoughts and speak its language. The object would be to take this chapter of vanished experience and learn to know it in three if not four dimensions. That would mean coming to understand why certain actions which in the light of retrospect appear madly irrational appeared at that time the indisputable mandate of reason; why things which had been created with pain and care were cast quickly on the gaming table of war; why men who had sat in the senate chamber and debated with syllogism and enthymeme stepped out of it to buckle on the sword against one another. Almost any book of history will give you the form of such a time, but what will give you the *pressure* of it? That is what I particularly wished to discover.

I am now further convinced that there is something to be said in general for studying the history of a lost cause. Perhaps our education would be more humane in result if everyone were required to gain an intimate acquaintance with some coherent ideal that failed in the effort to maintain itself. It need not be a cause which was settled by war; there are causes in the social, political, and ecclesiastical worlds which would serve very well. But it is good for everyone to ally himself at one time with the defeated and to look at the "progress" of history through the eyes of those who were left behind. I cannot think of a better way to counteract the stultifying "Whig" theory of history, with its bland assumption that every cause which has won has deserved to win, a kind of pragmatic debasement of the older providential theory. The study and appreciation of a lost cause have some effect on turning history into philosophy. In sufficient number of cases to make us humble, we discover good points in the cause which time has erased, just as one often learns more from the slain hero of a tragedy than from some brassy Fortinbras who comes in at the end to announce the victory and proclaim the future disposition of affairs. It would be perverse to say that this is so of every historical defeat, but there is enough analogy to make it a sober consideration. Not only Oxford, therefore, but every university ought to be to some extent "the home of lost causes and impossible loyalties." It ought to preserve the memory of these with a certain discriminating measure of honor, trying to keep alive what was good in them and opposing the pragmatic verdict of the world.

For my part, I spent three years reading the history and literature of the Civil War, with special attention to that of the losing side. The people who emerged were human, all-too-human, but there was still the mystery of the encompassing passion which held them together, and this I have not yet penetrated. But in a dozen various ways I came to recognize myself in the past, which is at least an important piece of self-knowledge.

Toward the end of this inquiry, I published my first article, "The Older Religiousness in the South." It was an attempt to explain why the South, although it was engaged in defending institutions which much of the world was condemning on moral grounds, seemed to exhibit a more intense religiosity than its opponents. It was a first effort toward an unorthodox explanation of an orthodoxy, and it showed me how much more was to be done in historical revision of the kind before the shallow liberal interpretation could be exposed in its inadequacy.

Looking back over this discipline, I feel confident enough of its principle. The aim is to strip aside the clichés of generalization, the slogans which are preserved only because they render service to contemporary institutions, and of course to avoid the drug of economic interpretation. Henry Adams felt an impulse to do something like this amid the hullabaloo of his America, and his inquiry led him—this bloodless, self-questioning descendant of New England Puritans—to ponder the mystery of the Virgin. It seems to me that in some corresponding way the process will compel any honest seeker to see that the lines of social and political force are far more secret than the modern world has any mind to recognize, and that if it does not lead him to some kind of faith, it will lead him safely away from the easy constructions of those who do not wish to understand, beyond grasping what can be turned to serve a practical purpose. Whereas conventional schoolbook history leaves men cocksure and ignorant, this multidimensional kind ought to leave them filled with wonder. Long before, I had been impressed by Schopenhauer's statement that no one can be a philosopher who is not capable at times of looking upon the world as if it were a pageant. This kind of detachment, produced by a suppression of the instinct to be arbitrary, seems to me a requirement for understanding the human condition.

The attempt to contemplate history in all its dimensions and in the fullness of its detail led directly to the conviction that this world of substantial things and substantial events is the very world which the Leftist of our time wishes to see abolished; and such policy now began to appear egotistical and presumptuous. I am disinclined to the view that whatever exists necessarily has a commission to go on existing. On the contrary, I have a strong tendency to side with the bottom dog, or to champion the potential against the actual if the former seems to have some reason behind it; and I am mindful of the saying that God takes delight in bringing great things out of small ones. To this extent I am a reformer or even a subverter. But I feel that situations almost never present themselves in terms so simple. They usually appear in terms like these: we have before us a tremendous creation which is largely inscrutable. Some of the intermediate relationships of cause and effect we can grasp and manipulate, though with these our audacity often outruns good sense and we discover that in trying to achieve one balance we have upset two others. There are, accordingly, two propositions which are hard to deny: we live in a universe which was given to us, in the sense that we did not create it; and, we don't understand very much of it. In the figure once used by a philosopher, we are inhabitants of a fruitful and well-ordered island surrounded by an ocean of ontological mystery. It does not behoove us to presume very far in this situation. It is not a matter of affirming that whatever is, is right; it is a recognition that whatever is there is there with considerable force (inertia even being a respectable form of force) and in a network of relationships which we have only partly deciphered. Therefore, make haste slowly. It is very easy to rush into conceit in thinking about man's relationship to the created universe. Science paved the way for presumption, whether wittingly or not; and those political movements which appeal to science to vindicate their break with the past have often made the presumptuous attitude one of their tenets. I found myself in decreasing sympathy with those social and political doctrines erected upon the concept of a man-dominated universe and more and more inclined to believe with Walt Whitman that "a mouse is miracle enough to stagger sextillions of infidels."

As a further consequence of reflecting upon this problem, I began to see it in theological terms. As I have suggested, "the authority of fact" is a phrase that I am a little uncomfortable with, because it is readily turned, unless one is vigilant, into an idolatry of circumstance, and this is the most unspiritual of all conditions. Nevertheless, there is a way in which "the authority of fact" carries a meaning that we can accept. It merely requires that we see "fact" as signifying what the theological philosophers mean by the word "substance." Now the denial of substance is one of the greatest heresies, and this is where much contemporary radicalism appears in an essentially sinful aspect. The constant warfare which it wages against anything that has *status* in the world, or against all the individual, particular, unique existences of the world which do not fit into a rationalistic pattern, is but a mask for the denial of substance. If one benighted class of men begins by assuming that whatever is, is right, they begin by assuming that whatever is, is wrong. Had we to decide between these two—and I hope to make it clear that I do not think we have to decide thus—the latter would appear more blasphemous than the former because it makes a wholesale condemnation of a creation which is not ours and which exhibits the marks of a creative power that we do not begin to possess. The intent of the radical to defy all substance, or to press it into forms conceived in his mind alone, is thus theologically wrong; it is an aggression by the self which outrages a deep-laid order of things. And it has seeped into every department of our life. In the reports of the successful ascent of Mt. Everest, the British members of the expedition talked of "conquering" the mountain, but the Nepalese guide who was one of the two to reach the summit spoke of a desire to visit the Buddha who lives at the top. The difference between these attitudes is a terrible example of the modern Western mentality, with its metaphysic of progress through aggression.

Here again was an invitation to ponder one of the oldest and deepest of human attitudes, which is generally expressed by the word "piety." The war of the radicals against substance is a direct repudiation of this quality. It is true that a great many instances of sham, in both word and deed, have been associated with this term, so that one runs a danger by bringing it into any modern discussion of ethics and religion. Nevertheless, it seems to me that it signifies an attitude toward things which are immeasurably larger and greater than oneself without which man is an insufferably brash, conceited, and frivolous animal. I do not in truth see how societies are able to hold together without some measure of this ancient but now derided feeling. The high seriousness of this life expresses itself as a kind of *pietas,* or a respect for the tragedy of existence, if nothing else. Piety is another one of those orthodoxies which have broken down because the defenders have not been able to show what is necessary in them. They have erected their defenses on positions quite easily overrun, and the places they could easily have defended they have left unmanned. As long as the term is associated exclusively with the avoidance of foibles and minor vices, there seems no hope of restoring the vital idea for which it stands. But when one shows that the habit of veneration supplies the whole force of social and political cohesion, one hits at its enemies where the blow cannot be ignored.

The realization that piety is a proper and constructive attitude toward certain things helped me to develop what Russell Kirk calls "affection for the proliferating variety and mystery of traditional life." I feel now, in looking over the course of things, that such an attitude has always been in my nature, but that it had been repressed by dogmatic, utilitarian, essentially contumacious doctrines of liberalism and scientism, so that it was for me a kind of recovery of lost power or lost capacity for wonder and enchantment. The recovery has brought a satisfaction which cannot be matched, as far as my experience goes, by anything that liberalism and scientism have to offer.

It is what I feel when I return to the South, as I do each summer. There are numberless ways in which the South disappoints me; but there is something in its sultry languor and in the stubborn humanism of its people, now battling against the encroachments of industrialism—and with so little knowledge of how to battle—which tells me that for better or worse this is my native land. It is often said today that the hope of the world lies in internationalism. That may be true, but it is also true, and true with a prior truth, that there can be no internationalism without a solid, intelligent provincialism. That is so because there is nothing else for internationalism to rest on.

Nevertheless, it is most important, as I have tried to suggest earlier, to draw a line between respect for tradition because it is tradition and respect for it because it expresses a spreading mystery too great for our knowledge to compass. The first is merely an idolatry, or a tribute to circumstance, which has engendered some of the most primitive, narrow, and harmful attitudes which the human race has shown. There is a worship of tradition and circumstance which is all fear, distrust, and feebleness of imagination, and to this the name "reaction" is rightly applied. There can be no hope for good things from an attitude as negative as this. But the other attitude is reverential and creative at the same time; it worships the spirit rather than the graven image; and it allows man to contribute his mite toward helping Providence. Obviously free will would be meaningless if the world were to be left entirely untouched by us. Some things we have to change, but we must avoid changing out of *hubris* and senseless presumption. And always we have to keep in mind what man is supposed to be.

At the same time that the radical is engaged in denying the substance, he is engaged in denying the existence of evil, which is another great heresy. This takes the form today, as we all recognize, of assuming the perfectibility of man, the adequacy of social and political measures for the salvation of the individual person, and all the means of state engineering which are supposed to take the place of the old idea of redemption. Apart from the dilemma that the denial of evil involves us in, it brings into our moral, intellectual, and cultural life a number of destructive fallacies. It brings in, for example, the flattery of the popular will, the idealization of the mediocre, and along with these a spirit of rebelliousness toward anything that involves self-discipline, sustained effort, and service to autonomous ideals. There is abroad in democracies today an idea that to criticize anybody for anything is treasonable, that the weak, the self-indulgent, and the vicious have the same claims toward respect and reward as anybody else, and that if a man chooses to be a beast, he has a sort of natural, inviolable right to be one. As far as I can see, there is no possible way of opposing this idea until we admit the existence of evil and the duty of combating it. Here modem radicalism has failed again to interpret the issue.

It has been said that disillusionment with human nature most often turns the mind toward Christianity. I know that in my period of jejune optimism the concept of original sin seemed something archaically funny. Now, twenty years later, and after the experience of a world war, there is no concept that I regard as expressing a deeper insight into the enigma that is man. Original sin is a parabolical expression of the immemorial tendency of man to do the wrong thing when he knows the right thing. The fact of this tendency everyone should be able to testify to, not only from his observation but also from his personal history. And it is the rock upon which nine-tenths of the socialist formula for universal happiness splits. The Socialists propose to offer man peace and plenty; and they seem not to realize that he may reject both for crime and aggrandizement. He has done so before in both the individual and the national units. It would be more realistic for the reformers to start with the old assumption that the heart of man is desperately wicked and that he needs external help in the form of grace. At least, we cannot build on the quicksand that he is by nature good, for he is not. Whether he has inherited his sin from Adam is perhaps a question for another level of discussion; the plain situation is that he has inherited it, and that it will sink any scheme which is founded on a complacent faith in man's desire always to do the good thing. Nothing can be done if the will is wrong, and the correction of the will is precisely the task which modern radicalism fails to recognize.

It is only realistic to point out that the concept of original sin, if not anti-democratic, is at least a severe restraint upon democracy. Democracy finds it difficult ever to say that man is wrong if he does things in large majorities. Yet even politically this notion has to be rejected; and that is why constitutions and organic laws are created in nearly all representative governments, and are indeed regarded as the prime unifiers of such governments. A constitution is a government's better self, able to rebuke and restrain the baser self when it starts off on a vagary. If the mass of every electorate were wholly right at every period, constitutions would be only curious encumbrances. This means of distinguishing what is right deeply and naturally from what is wrong needs to be carried over also into our individual lives, where it sets a limit on indulgences of the self.

For all these reasons, those who say that evil is but a bad dream or an accident of history or the creation of a few antisocial men are only preparing us for worse disillusionments and disasters. It is necessary to recognize evil as a subtle, pervasive, protean force, capable of undoing plans that promise the fairest success, but also capable of being checked by proper spiritual insight and energy. This makes the problem of improving the individual and society continuous with known human history and not different according to different phases of economic and technological development.

The persistence of the fact of evil was then being underlined for me by the dreadful events of the Second World War. A question was posed in sharp form when the claims of modern and "advanced" civilization were being refuted by the presence of this greatest creator of misery. Wars not only were becoming more frequent, they were also becoming more absolute or more undiscriminating in their ends and means.

The prosecution of the war by the Western allies was to me a progressive disillusionment. My study of the American Civil War had made me acquainted with the principle that as a war continues, the basis of the war changes, but I had not been prepared to see the extent to which the moral aim may deteriorate. My faith in the honesty of our case was shaken by an incident that occurred about the middle of the conflict. The incident is not very well remembered because it concerned chiefly a small country, but what does a small country count for in a world where everything is decided by a Big Four or a Big Three or a Big Something? This was the abandonment of Finland by Britain and the United States, who had previously bucked up her morale and to some extent her strength against the Russian foe. I felt that if Finland could be cheerfully thrown to the wolves in the haste for victory and vengeance, much worse things must be anticipated, and so it has proved. And the Yalta Conference seemed to me at the very time when the newspapers were crowded with the most fantastic tributes and eulogies a piece of political insanity.

In sum, I felt that, thanks to our wonderful press and our Office of War Information and our political leaders, almost nobody in the United States knew what the war was really about. I recall sitting in my office in Ingleside Hall at the University of Chicago one fall morning in 1945 and wondering whether it would not be possible to deduce, from fundamental causes, the fallacies of modern life and thinking that had produced this holocaust and would insure others. In about twenty minutes I jotted down a series of chapter headings, and this was the inception of a book entitled *Ideas Have Consequences*. At first it seemed destined to have only a *succès de scandale,* since it was so out of line with most current thinking on the subject. But many letters I later received from readers convinced me that other minds were tormented by the same questions, and that I had only gone to the point of saying what numerous people were thinking. The kind of opposition it aroused too seemed a confirmation.

It may sound odd, but it is true that the thesis of this book was first suggested by the bygone ideal of chivalry. My reading of history had encouraged the belief that at one time this had been an ideal of considerable restraining power, and that it contained one conception that seems to be absent from all the contemporary remedies for curing war—the conception of something spiritual which stood above war itself and included the two sides in any conflict. I have never had any faith in the notion of ending wars by fighting one war to a victorious and sweeping conclusion. The idea of a "war to end all wars" is worthy only of a mountebank. What such an attempt does in actuality is to scatter the seeds of war more widely, and possibly plant them more deeply. It does not take into account the intransigency of human nature.

The profoundly interesting feature of chivalry was that it offered a plan whereby civilization might contain a war and go on existing as civilization. It did not premise itself upon simplifications which are soon rejected, such as the proposition that "all war is murder." On the contrary, it tried to treat war or human combat as one of the activities of civilization, a dangerous one, to be sure, but one that could be kept under control. War under the code of chivalry might be likened to what the insurance companies call a "friendly fire." It is a useful thing to man as long as it is kept in a furnace or whatever place is intended for it. But a fire which gets out of the place created for it ceases to be friendly; it is a foe and can spread quick and terrible devastation. Thus the warfare controlled, or the war of limited objectives, is the friendly fire; but a war which has unlimited objectives has broken out of control and may, with the weapons now available, be capable of consuming civilization in a holocaust. Hence the problem is: what kind of thing is capable of controlling war, or of keeping it *within* civilization? It would be absurd to claim that chivalry accomplished all that the ideal pointed toward; there were episodes in the age of chivalry which make unpleasant reading. Nevertheless, it was a moderating influence; and it did one thing which makes it appear realistic in comparison with the solutions which are being proposed today. It insisted that even in war, when maximum strain is placed upon the passions, man may not become an absolute killer. In war there are some considerations which must not be crowded out by hatred and fear. This is true because even your foe has some rights, and these rights you must respect although your present course has his destruction in view. This may seem to some too paradoxical, but let us consider it in terms of an analogy. Modern wars have tended increasingly to resemble lynching parties. A lynching party acts in the belief that the guilt of the victim is absolute and unqualified, and that the only thing that matters is to put him to death immediately. Any means will do: beating, pistol fire, a tree and a rope. Of course this idea is contrary to that of juridical procedure. The law never takes the view that a man's guilt is so absolute and so completely known that he is not allowed to say a word in his defense. On the contrary, the most atrocious murderer is given police protection and a trial according to forms of law, with a chance to state his side of the affair.

The law is in such instances upholding an idea similar to that of chivalry, inasmuch as it takes the position that no one—not even an "enemy of society"—can be denied rights entirely. In modern international warfare, however, the idea of a binding agreement such as this is being abandoned rapidly. The object now is to pulverize the enemy completely, men, women, and children being lumped into one common target; it is to reduce a country to "atomic ashes," to recall a frightful phrase which I saw recently in a newspaper. And then, if anything remains, the next step is the unethical one of demanding unconditional surrender. No further analysis should be needed to show that this moves in a direction opposite to that of the chivalric ideal, in that it pulls everything into the madness and destruction of war and leaves nothing, as far as I can see, to help pull even the victor out again.

There are those who maintain that modern technology, when applied to war, makes all such concepts as the one upheld by chivalry simply fantastic. There is no way of restraining a technology, they say, which is so developed that it cannot produce anything short of annihilation once it is turned to destructive ends. Perhaps this cannot be disputed as a fact. Yet if it is a fact, it seems one more proof that we have allowed science to reach a point at which it no longer allows us to be human beings. If we have got ourselves into a position where our only choice is to blow up or be blown up, this circumstance refutes the idea that we have increased the mastery of our lives.

There cannot be any improvement in the world's condition until the human spirit has counterbalanced and more than counterbalanced the hectic brilliance of technological invention. The deadly trap into which the pride of the modern world in technology and invention has led us is not often described in its real nature. It has produced a world condition of unheard-of instability. The only way in which this instability can be overcome even temporarily is through rigid, centralized control of the national life. And the only way that a rigid, centralized control can be maintained is to keep the people living in a mentality of war. One can do this by filling them with desire of conquest, or one can do it by keeping them fearful of a real or imaginary enemy. Then one has a trump card to play on every occasion. If there is any relaxing or any resentment of controls, one has only to invoke "the national security" to silence opposition and even render it disreputable. We in the United States are living under the second of these policies now. The choice appears to lie between chaos and perpetual preparation for war, and the trouble with preparation for war is that it always issues in war. Here again technology steps in to make the dilemma more cruel, since it causes warfare to be increasingly total and nihilistic, and increasingly beyond the power of civilizing influences to absorb. From now on, as Maurice Samuel has pointed out, humanity will be living in the shadow of its own demonic omnipotence, and this is a calamity so great that almost nobody is able to face it. The chance that the world will not use atomic bombs if it goes on making them is infinitesimal.

How this tide is flowing even into the small interstices of our lives may be shown by a small incident. A few years ago there stood on the edge of the campus of the University of Chicago a small cafe. It was a poor affair, without style or pretensions; but here in the afternoons members of the liberal-arts faculties were wont to go for a cup of coffee, to get out of their professional grooves for an hour, to broach ideas and opinions, to be practicing humanists, you might say. Today a monstrous gray structure given to atomic research covers the site: the little cafe is no more; and the amiable *Kaffeeklatsches* no longer take place.

The chief result of what I now think of as my reeducation has been a complete disenchantment with the liberalism that was the first stage of my reflective life. Liberalism is the refuge favored by intellectual cowardice, because the essence of the liberal's position is that he has no position. It may be true, with due qualifications, that in certain transitional phases, where the outline of issues is none too clear, the liberal or uncommitted attitude has its expediency. But as something to construct with, never! It is that state of mind before we have made up our mind. The explanation of why liberalism has been erected into a kind of philosophy in our time is perhaps to be sought in the fact that our world is disintegrating rapidly. It is thereby creating the impression that nothing is permanent but change, and that the very concept of truth is a stumbling block to adaptation as the disintegration goes on.

But even after this concession to the state of affairs, it is easy to see how the liberal's lack of position involves him in contradictions that destroy confidence. He is a defender of individualism and local rights, but let some strong man appear who promises salvation through "leadership," and the liberal becomes indistinguishable from the totalitarian. Hence the totalitarian liberal of our times, a contradiction in terms, but an embodiment in the flesh, and a dire menace to government based upon rights. In times of peace, the liberal is often a shouter for pacifism, but let something he dislikes appear upon the horizon and he is the first to invoke the use of armed force. In education, he believes in the natural goodness of the child and abhors the idea of corporal discipline, but he believes in spanking nations with atomic bombs until their will is broken.

It is frequently said that while our knowledge of the natural world is increasing rapidly, our knowledge of the nature and spirit of man shows no gain, and that most of our troubles arise out of this disproportion. I think that our situation is considerably worse than this figure represents it, for I am of the opinion that our knowledge of the nature and spirit of man is decreasing, and this not relatively but absolutely. No one can study Greek philosophy or medieval Christianity or the other great religions of the world without realizing that these saw man as a creature fearfully and wonderfully made, and that each tried to lead him with appropriate imagination and subtlety. Today, living under the shadow of this demonic technological omnipotence, we are trying to get along by supposing such crudities as economic man, "naturally good" man, and so on. Of course they do not work, and the more they are tried in our context, the nearer we are to catastrophe.

Somehow our education will have to recover the lost vision of the person as a creature of both intellect and will. It will have to bring together into one through its training the thinker and the doer, the dialectician and the rhetorician. Cognition, including the scientific, alone is powerless, and will without cognition is blind and destructive. The work of the future, then, is to overcome the shallow rationalisms and scientisms of the past two centuries and to work toward the reunion of man into a being who will both know and desire what he knows.

The Heritage Foundation Collection, 1990

CHAPTER 14

Ronald W. Reagan

Introduction by Edwin J. Feulner Jr. (1996)

onqueror of communism, sworn enemy of statism, leader
of unshakable conviction and contagious optimism, embodiment and culmination of conservative hopes, Ronald
Reagan is one of history's heroes and the greatest of our great
contemporaries. He transformed conservatism from an intellectual movement into a political revolution—a running revolt that
continues to this day. He exposed the bankruptcy of modern liberalism and proved that true liberty is still a fighting faith. He saw
the momentum of freedom in the sweep of history, and through the
power of his words and the determination of his deeds placed the
last shovel of dirt on the grave of Leninism. In the end, he restored
our confidence in the presidency itself, proving that Jefferson's
"splendid misery" could simply be splendid.

As a leader and a man, Ronald Reagan is much admired, and
sometimes misunderstood. While other presidents seemed overwhelmed or defeated by their duties, he treated the job with his
trademark good humor, stubbornly refusing to view it as a
sleepless hardship. Just before leaving the White House, Reagan
commented that, on returning to California, he would take a long

nap, adding, "Now, come to think of it, things won't be all that much different, after all." Throughout his career he has remained unfailingly genial—a man who always acts, says Peggy Noonan, "as if he's lucky to be with you."

Yet when issues of principle were at stake, Reagan could also show what George Will calls "steel and acid." As Tip O'Neill found on tax cuts, or Mikhail Gorbachev discovered on SDI this kind and genial man could be as inflexible as iron and as immovable as a cliff.

Ronald Reagan is called the "Great Communicator," and with good reason. He has a profound appreciation for the importance of rhetoric. As a youth, he listened intently to President Franklin Roosevelt's fireside chats and even memorized some of FDR's finer passages.

Yet Reagan always placed more emphasis on substance than style. "I never thought it was my style or the words I used that made a difference—it was the content. I wasn't a great communicator, but I communicated great things, and they didn't spring full blown from my brow, they came from the heart of a great nation—from our experience, our wisdom and our belief in the principles that guided us for two centuries."

Ronald Reagan is persuasive because he is so deeply persuaded of these ideas himself. Americans, in the eight years of his presidency, were not fooled by stagecraft (as some critics contend); they were impressed by principle. Unlike some current leaders, who adopt endless visions and revisions, Ronald Reagan followed the cloud and fire of certain permanent convictions. He boiled down politics to its most fundamental level and spoke a plain language of right and wrong. "At the heart of our message should be five simple familiar words. No big economic theories. No sermons on political philosophy. Just five short words: family, work, neighborhood, freedom, peace."

Because these convictions are eternally true, they are also eternally controversial. Our view of the Reagan legacy predicts our entire view of politics. If Reagan was right, liberals will always be wrong. So the argument about his legacy is now and always will be lively and current—a tribute to his continuing influence.

That legacy includes not just conviction, but courage. Seventy days after Reagan entered office, an assassin put a bullet within an inch of his heart. He responded with extraordinary grace and wit, joking with the doctors and reassuring the nation. At 7:15 on the morning after his surgery, he signed a piece of legislation into law. Greeting White House aides the same morning, he said, "Hi, fellas. I know it would be too much to hope that we could skip a staff meeting." Even bitter political opponents were impressed. "The way he's deported himself," commented Mario Cuomo, "has been a moral instruction to my children."

Perhaps most important, in Ronald Reagan's two terms as president, he gave America a transfusion of his own optimism and hope. He diagnosed our nation's worst problem as a loss of "faith in itself." He rejected a historical hypochondria that found the essence of America in its sickness, faults, and failures. These, he believed, were our challenges, not our essence.

Conservatism, in his view, is the recovery of a belief in our nation's unique character and destiny. Reagan proved that conservatives can also be idealists, because our ideals are strong enough to justify our hopes. He restored a soaring sense of the possible and led a revolution of rising confidence and expectations—a revolution that rescued America from defeatism and much of the world from tyranny.

Born in 1911 in Tampico, Illinois, Ronald Reagan had a childhood of poverty and promise. His family was forced by economic need to move several times, but Reagan's athleticism and leadership were quickly evident. Employed as a lifeguard at a riverside beach near Dixon, he saved seventy-seven people from drowning over seven summers. The town erected a plaque in his honor.

After graduating in 1932 from Eureka College, where he was elected class president, Reagan was hired as a sports broadcaster in Des Moines, Iowa, for five dollars a week and bus fare. Gifted with a fine radio voice, "Dutch" Reagan announced Chicago Cubs baseball games and became one of the most successful sportscasters in the Midwest.

In 1937, Reagan accompanied the Cubs to California for spring training and took a Hollywood screen test. Warner Brothers signed him for a two hundred dollar-a-week contract. He got his first major role, in *Love Is on the Air,* because the first leading man who was chosen, whom he resembled, committed suicide. Over the next two decades, Reagan became, in his words, the "Errol Flynn of the B pictures." Considered for the role of Rick Blaine in *Casablanca,* Reagan established his acting reputation in classics such as *Knute Rockne—All American* and *King's Row.* One Hollywood producer described him as a "very good, very professional, and very competent actor, without any confusion about getting artistic." Reagan was president of the Screen Actors guild for five consecutive terms—later becoming the first American president who had been head of a union.

In 1952, he married Nancy Davis at the Little Brown Church in Los Angeles, with William Holden and his wife as attendants. Nancy had worked in Broadway theater and eventually appeared in eleven films. As First Lady she led an anti-drug crusade that helped reduce teen drug use by 50 percent—one of the great social policy successes of recent history. Their marriage has been an inspirational love story—a happy ending in the best tradition of Hollywood. "It's a wonderful thing," comments President Reagan, "to be so proud of the person you love."

Ronald Reagan came to politics relatively late in life. As a young man, he recounts, he was "a near-hopeless, hemophiliac liberal." Beginning with his first vote at twenty-one, he supported FDR four times. He campaigned for Harry Truman in 1948. In 1952, when he was considering a run for the House of Representatives, the Los Angeles County Democratic Central Committee would not endorse him, thinking he was too liberal.

But by the late 1950s, Reagan's thinking began to shift. He had always been firmly anti-Communist. Now he moved toward domestic conservatism as well. "By 1960," he recounts, "I realized the real enemy wasn't big business, it was big government." In 1962, he finally switched his voting registration from Democrat to Republican.

Reagan came to national attention in 1964 during Senator Barry Goldwater's presidential campaign. First in California, then before a national television audience, Reagan gave what has come to be known as "The Speech." William Buckley described it at the time as "a deft and rollicking indictment of overweening government." Its attack on oppressive taxes, regulation, and bureaucracy excited both Republican activists and Republican donors, raising over five million dollars in contributions for Goldwater (then a record sum) and igniting a Reagan-for-governor movement in California.

When Goldwater was defeated, Reagan wrote in *National Review* that conservatism was not routed, only its "false image." And he was determined to correct that distorted image. In 1966, he ran for California governor as a "citizen-politician" promising to cut taxes and spending. The incumbent, Governor Pat Brown, launched an offensive of low blows. Speaking on camera to a small child at one point in the campaign, Brown remarked that Ronald Reagan was an actor and it was an actor who had murdered Abraham Lincoln. Reagan beat Brown soundly and was reelected four years later.

Reagan's political potential was soon undeniable. *Newsweek* magazine reported a joint appearance with Reagan and Robert Kennedy on the topic of Vietnam in 1966: "To those unfamiliar with Reagan's big-league savvy, the ease with which [Reagan] fielded questions about Vietnam may come as a revelation. Political rookie Reagan left old campaigner Kennedy blinking when the session ended." After a Reagan speech in 1967, a correspondent for the *New York Times* concluded, "I've never seen anything like it. I've been covering them since Truman. There isn't anybody who can touch Reagan." In a column of the same year, William Buckley wrote, with typical prescience, "Reagan is indisputably a part of America. And he may become a part of American history."

During the presidential election of 1968, Reagan entered the contest too late to challenge Richard Nixon effectively. South Carolina's Senator Strom Thurmond told him at the convention, "Son, you'll be President some day, but this isn't your year." In 1976, Reagan did well in the presidential primaries, supported by many Republican conservatives, but lost to President Ford at the convention. But by 1980, America's stagnant economy and slipping national position brought Reagan his opportunity. Underestimated by liberals as an actor and dismissed as a dangerous warmonger, he was elected president with a clear program of lower taxes, smaller government, and stronger defense. And Americans were captivated by his humor and confidence. After debating President Carter on national television for the first time, a reporter asked Reagan if he had been nervous. "No, not at all," he answered. "I've been on the same stage with John Wayne."

Ronald Reagan intended his presidency to be the extension and expression of the conservative movement. His favorite magazine was *National Review*. His nightstand reading was Whittaker Chambers's *Witness* and George Gilder's *Wealth and Poverty*. "A revolution of ideas," he later reflected, "became a revolution of governance on January 20, 1981." He planned not just a change of administrations, but a change of national assumptions.

Since the 1930s, our ruling political assumption had been that a growing government was necessary to tame the business cycle and move society closer and closer to equality. Both Democrats and Republicans ("We're all Keynesians now") seemed to accept these ideas as inevitable. Reagan attacked them root and branch, and transformed American politics in the process. He argued that we had crippled democracy by empowering bureaucracy—that the government's desire to help us had become an excuse to rule us. He condemned reckless spending, endless tax increases, an overgrown establishment, and a grasping judiciary. "There's a clear cause and effect here that is as neat and predictable as a law of physics: As government expands, liberty contracts."

Reagan's inauguration marked the final, exhausted end of the Great Society. "The liberals," he announced, "had had their turn at bat in the 1960s and they had struck out." In place of the Great Society, he set out on a new path, still being traveled by American politics. He moved toward a tax system that rewards accomplishment and effort rather than punishing these things. He started the shift from federal paternalism to true federalism. And he initiated welfare reform, not because of welfare's cost, but because of welfare's casualties—measured in illegitimacy, fatherlessness, crime, and despair. By the close of the Reagan decade, Stuart Eizenstat of the Carter Administration complained, "He has captured the high ground on virtually every major issue of consequence and controlled the debate as well as any President since Roosevelt." When Reagan left office, a strong plurality of Americans described themselves as conservatives. Our politics has never been the same.

In his farewell address to the nation in 1988, Reagan referred to "two great triumphs": an economic recovery "in which the people of America created—and filled—19 million new jobs" and the fact that America had "stood, again, for freedom." Both achievements have grown even larger from a decade's distance.

Beginning with high inflation, unindexed taxes, high interest rates, and declining income, Ronald Reagan created an American economic miracle. After a three-stage tax cut and a reduction in government growth, the American economy began to expand—by 31 percent from 1983 to 1989 in real terms. Americans of every class—rich, middle-class, and poor—saw their wealth increase. It was our nation's longest peacetime expansion in a long and prosperous history. By the end of the decade, we had added the economic equivalent of a whole new Germany to our Gross National Product. Inflation was cut by two-thirds, interest rates by half; unemployment dropped to the lowest level in fifteen years. Reagan's America was *not* characterized by a spirit of gain and greed, but by the greatest flood of private charity in our history—increasing by over 5 percent each year. Yes, our nation became more prosperous, but it also became more generous.

If Reaganomics was a failure, the *Wall Street Journal* has commented, it is the "most imitated failure in history." Its influence can be found from China to Mexico to India to Argentina—from the Pearl River Delta to the ruins of the Soviet Empire. Nations everywhere have found success by lowering tax rates, cutting government, and opening their borders to trade. Pyotr Filipov of the Leningrad City Council has said, "We must quickly move through Marxism-Leninism, through Socialism, to Reaganism."

But even this economic achievement was overshadowed by international events. Reagan notes, "We meant to change a nation, and instead we changed a world." The Reagan Administration determined that the Cold War, after forty years of fear, needed an end game. And the victory it won is perhaps the greatest conservative triumph.

After he took office, the intelligence briefings Reagan received left a clear impression. "The Soviet economy," he writes in his memoirs, "was being held together with baling wire; it was a basket case, partly because of massive spending on armaments ... I wondered how we as a nation could use these cracks in the Soviet system to accelerate the process of collapse." This was a major shift in strategic thinking, equal in breathtaking boldness to Reagan's domestic policy ideas. "He believed, simply," comments Richard Allen, "that democracy and freedom, resolutely asserted and eloquently articulated, could ultimately prevail."

This required a rejection of the whole post-war framework of containment. The objective was no longer to protect the *status quo* from aggression, but to roll back Soviet power, even radically change the nature of the Soviet system itself. Charles Krauthammer called it a new "democratic militance." America's goal shifted from coexistence to victory.

Foreign policy "experts," of course, were hostile. Strobe Talbott, then of *Time* and now of the Clinton Administration, called this "bear baiting." "Though some second-echelon hard-liners in the Reagan Administration," he wrote, "espouse the early 1950s goal of rolling back Soviet domination in Eastern Europe, the U.S. simply does not have the military or political power to do that." Recognizing this kind of foreign policy "realism" as defeatism, Reagan carefully set out to harass the Soviet empire at the limits of its influence—what came to be called the Reagan Doctrine.

In Afghanistan, the Reagan Administration set out to deflate Soviet imperial ambitions with a major strategic defeat. Again, the media were dismissive. *Newsweek* wrote in 1984, "The mujaheddin can never be strong enough to drive the Soviet out of Afghanistan." Richard Cohen of the *Washington Post* commented, "We are covertly supplying arms to guerrillas who don't stand the slightest chance of winning. Afghanistan is not the Soviet version of Vietnam."

All told, Reagan sent about two billion dollars in aid to the Afghan freedom fighters: Stinger anti-aircraft missiles, satellite data on Soviet targets, long-range sniper rifles, anti-tank missiles. Eventually, the mujaheddin carried their attacks into the Soviet provinces of Central Asia. Several weeks after Stinger missiles arrived, a meeting of the Politburo was called to discuss the escalating crisis. A few months later, the first deadline for Soviet withdrawal was announced. By late 1986, after heavy causalities had caused growing public unrest, the Soviet army retreated in defeat.

In Poland, the Reagan Doctrine took another shape. In June of 1982, after a personal meeting between President Reagan and Pope John Paul II at the Vatican, a plan was devised to funnel covert support to the Solidarity trade union, outlawed in a communist crackdown. The two men, according to one administration official, shared "a unity of spiritual view and a unity of vision on the Soviet empire: that right or correctness would ultimately prevail in the divine plan." It was a secret alliance that would help shatter the Yalta imperial system.

This time the tools of liberation were not weapons but tons of communication equipment: copy machines, computers, radio broadcasting stations, fax machines, telephones, video cameras, photocopiers. By 1985, there were over four hundred underground newsletters in Poland, some counting circulations over thirty thousand. Solidarity often interrupted government radio programming with messages like "Solidarity Lives!" or "Resist!" This movement of conscience, aided by the spread of information, eventually defeated a totalitarian dictator. "This was," writes Zbigniew Brzezinski, "the first time that communist police suppression didn't succeed."

This new American assertiveness was accompanied by renewed American power. President Reagan set out to reverse the military weakness that had drained American foreign policy of its confidence. Defense procurement rose by 25 percent each year in the early years of the Administration. By the mid-1980s, America outspent the Soviets on defense for the first time since the 1960s. In six years of the Reagan buildup, the U.S. bought ten thousand tanks, three thousand combat aircraft, and thirty-seven hundred strategic missiles. The Reagan legacy included the B-1 bomber, stealth technology, cruise missiles, Trident submarines, and heavy funding for research and development.

With the invasion of Grenada, the United States overcame its Vietnam-era loss of confidence. With the deployment of Pershing and cruise missiles in Western Europe, the Soviets were forced into real negotiations for the first time. And with the development of SDI, the Soviet leadership was presented with a Hobson's choice between its military preparedness and solving its economic problems—a choice that hastened its eventual fall.

Finally, Ronald Reagan understood that of all the battles of the Cold War none was more important than the spiritual battle—the need, as Alexander Solzhenitsyn put it, "to admit the existence of evil on earth." This conflict, in Reagan's view, was not just a political test of wills but a moral test of ideals. He concluded that if we "ignore the aggressive impulses of an evil empire" we will "remove ourselves from the struggle between right and wrong, good and evil."

The word "evil" is rarely used in polite diplomatic discourse. But never has it been more appropriate. The Soviet regime was more than a geopolitical rival. It was a prison nation, convicted of crimes against humanity by the mute testimony of the innocent dead. To this day, we are discovering mass graves near many Russian cities, in parks and mine shafts where victims were buried. One site next to Minsk yielded two hundred thousand bodies. If this is not evil, the term has no meaning.

By calling evil by its name, President Reagan showed respect for the survivors of tyranny and honored those who died fighting it. He took the side of dissidents and exiles and countless prisoners in icy Gulags. Reagan's moral clarity exposed the illegitimacy of Soviet communism to the world, and eventually to the Russian people themselves.

There is, predictably, an attempt to deny President Reagan's role in the end of Soviet communism—a revisionist campaign by academics and experts who seem disappointed the Cold War did not end in a tie. Strobe Talbott calls Reagan a "bystander" in the struggle. The *Chronicle of Higher Education* argues that America *lost* the Cold War, suffering from the "self-inflicted wounds" caused by a public willing "to compromise American principles and ideals ... in the name of fighting communism."

After Reagan left office, Peggy Noonan wrote him to ask him how he felt about this. "I'm not the sort to lose sleep over what a few revisionists say," he wrote back. "Let history decide; it usually does."

Rarely has the answer of history been so clear. It comes first from the vanquished. A senior KGB general put it bluntly: "American policy in the 1980s was the catalyst for the collapse of the Soviet Union." A Communist Party official wrote, "There was a widespread concern and actual fear of Reagan on the Central Committee." Former Soviet Foreign Minister Alexander Bessmertnykh said Reagan's policies, particularly SDI, "accelerated the decline of the Soviet Union."

The testimony also comes from the newly liberated. One Polish leader calls Reagan "the first world leader of the post-détente era who was willing to express ideas about the Soviets which were shared by most Poles." In 1990, when Reagan toured Poland, there was a particularly moving moment at a monument to shipyard workers in Gdansk. Seven thousand Poles chanted "Thank you, thank you!" and sang "Sto Lat," a hymn for Polish heroes. A prominent priest gave a saber to Reagan with the words, "I am giving you the saber for helping us to chop off the head of Communism." To these people, the Reagan legacy was clear because it included their very freedom.

At a 1991 Heritage Foundation dinner in Washington, former British Prime Minister Margaret Thatcher concluded of Reagan, "He won the Cold War without firing a shot." Michael Novak has written, "More than anyone else, Ronald Reagan made recent history happen as it did, and this marked his presidency with greatness. Ronald Reagan toppled communism."

The "Westminster Speech" is one of the most important documents of the Cold War, and a continuing tribute to the power and appeal of freedom. Reagan himself called it "one of the most important speeches I gave as president."

It is easy to forget how dark the international situation seemed when Reagan took office. An aggressive Soviet Union had placed missiles in Europe aimed at Western capitals, had invaded Afghanistan with great brutality, and was aggressively assisting communist groups in the Third World. In the West, there was a sense of danger and decay, a loss of will, a spiritual exhaustion. French writer Jean-François Revel wrote of "How Democracies Perish." "Democracy may, after all," he argued, "turn out to have been an historical accident, a brief parenthesis that is closing before our eyes."

Western intellectuals came back from pilgrimages to Moscow with glowing reports. Historian Arthur Schlesinger Jr. wrote in

1981, "Those in the U.S. who think the Soviet Union is on the verge of economic and social collapse are ... only kidding themselves." Economist John Kenneth Galbraith added, "The Russian system succeeds because, in contrast to Western industrial economies, it makes full use of its manpower." Moral equivalence was in full swing. British historian E. P. Thompson wrote in the *Nation* that the United States was "more dangerous and provocative" than the Soviet Union. A Soviet occupation, he argued, was preferable to a nuclear war because an occupation, at least, offered "the possibility, after some years, of resurgence and recuperation."

It is in this context that Ronald Reagan addressed the British Parliament on June 8, 1982. He delivered his "Westminster Speech" in Westminster Hall, within the Houses of Parliament complex. Westminster Hall has held many historic events over the centuries. Certainly, two of the most significant of the twentieth century were these remarks and Churchill's lying in state in 1965, where tens of thousands could pass by and pay their last respects. I was one of those—as a graduate student at the London School of Economics who stood in a "queue" for more than five hours to see Churchill one last time.

Reagan would later call this speech an attempt to "speak the truth about [the Soviets] for a change, rather than hiding behind the niceties of diplomacy." "In retrospect, I am amazed that our national leaders had not philosophically and intellectually taken on the principles of Marxist-Leninism. We were always too worried we would offend the Soviets if we struck at anything so basic. Well, so what? Marxist-Leninist thought is an empty cupboard. Everyone knew it by the 1980s, but no one was saying it. I decided to articulate a few of these things."

Reagan refused to accept the preemptive suicide of the West. He argued it was possible and essential to preserve *both* freedom and peace. In fact, it was freedom, not communism, that had a kind of historical inevitability, rooted in the hopes of a world weary of poverty and oppression. It is the "march of freedom and democracy" that will "leave Marxism-Leninism on the ash-heap of history as it has left other tyrannies which stifle the freedom and muzzle the self-expression of the people." Reagan grasped that American and Western strength was based not just on a balance of power, but on the superiority of "great civilized ideas: individual liberty, representative government, and the rule of law under God." Our nation, Reagan proclaimed to the world, is more than a place on a map; it is a bright signal in history's darkness. A central part of its purpose is to introduce the wonders of freedom to struggling men and women in every nation.

The *New York Times* called the speech one of the "dark spots" of Reagan's trip to Britain. "The stark, democracy-versus-Communism language of Mr. Reagan's speech," it concluded, "stunned many Britons." The *International Herald Tribune* sniffed, "It seems hard to be a sophisticated European and also an admirer of Ronald Reagan."

But history has come to a different conclusion about Reagan's campaign to renew America's purpose. "He has achieved the most difficult of all political tasks," according to former British Prime Minister Margaret Thatcher, "changing attitudes and perceptions about what is possible. From the strong fortress of his convictions, he set out to enlarge freedom the world over at a time when freedom was in retreat—and he succeeded."

I first saw Ronald Reagan close up when he testified on welfare reform before the Senate Finance Committee in 1973, displaying his unique ability to express conservative ideas in ways that Americans found compelling. In November 1978, my old friend Richard Allen, who was doing foreign policy work for candidate Reagan, asked whether I could set up a meeting between Reagan and journalists in London. Bill Deedes, the then editor of the *Daily Telegraph,* moaned and groaned to me in advance about coming to a breakfast meeting—"a barbaric American custom"—with this man who used to be governor of California. He left telling me it was one of the most interesting, fruitful, and positive hour-and-a-half meetings he had ever attended on either side of the Atlantic.

Perhaps the most memorable moment of my personal encounters with President Reagan occurred on October 3, 1983, at the "Heritage 10" anniversary dinner at the Shoreham Hotel in Washington, D.C. My wife, Linda, stood next to President Reagan on the dais. He was so moved by the Color Guard's presentation of the colors, and the Navy Band's playing of the Heritage March and the National Anthem, that when it was finished, he whispered to Linda, "That was so moving, it makes me want to clap. Too bad no one else is." Linda immediately responded, "Mr. President, I bet if you did, everyone else would join in." "Do you really think so?" President Reagan asked, in genuine amazement—at which point the two of them began clapping for what became a standing ovation from the fourteen hundred people in attendance.

In 1984, Ronald Reagan posthumously gave Whittaker Chambers the Medal of Freedom, our nation's highest civilian award. Chambers was a formative influence on Reagan. He credits Chambers's autobiography, *Witness,* with encouraging his move away from New Deal liberalism and toward Goldwater conservatism. Thirty years after reading the book, he could still quote Chambers's moving passage about finding the hand of God in the design of his daughter's ear. Chambers is the only conservative intellectual quoted in Reagan's first autobiography, *Where's the Rest of Me?* "Chambers's story," he later commented, "represents a generation's disenchantment with statism and its return to eternal truths and fundamental values."

Both men shared a profoundly spiritual view of the conflict between freedom and tyranny. In 1983 Reagan praised Chambers for understanding that "the crisis of the Western world exists to the degree in which the West is indifferent to God, the degree to which it collaborates in communism's attempt to make man stand alone without God."

Chambers referred to a struggle between "two rival faiths"—of the necessary choice between "irreconcilable opposites—God or Man, Soul or Mind, Freedom or Communism." Yet in the end, though Chambers believed he had joined the right side, he could not escape the feeling he had joined the losing side. The world, he felt, was growing "colder and older." "History is cluttered with the wreckage of nations that became indifferent to God, and died."

In this, Ronald Reagan has honored Chambers's convictions by proving them wrong. He is convinced that American ideals rise above the clutter of history. His optimism is not just a matter of temperament, but the evidence of a basic conviction: that in the contest of light and shadow, the light will not be overcome. Reagan believes that the future is charted by a God impatient with injustice—a God who views oppression as treason because every man and woman is the child of a King. This has been the source of his contagious confidence, justified by the decade he shaped.

Ronald W. Reagan

The March of Freedom: The Westminster Speech

My Lord Chancellor, Mr. Speaker:

The journey of which this visit forms a part is a long one. Already it has taken me to two great cities of the West, Rome and Paris, and to the economic summit at Versailles. And there, once again, our sister democracies have proved that even in a time of severe economic strain, free peoples can work together freely and voluntarily to address problems as serious as inflation, unemployment, trade, and economic development in a spirit of cooperation and solidarity.

Other milestones lie ahead. Later this week, in Germany, we and our NATO allies will discuss measures for our joint defense and America's latest initiatives for a more peaceful, secure world through arms reductions.

Each stop of this trip is important, but among them all, this moment occupies a special place in my heart and in the hearts of my countrymen—a moment of kinship and homecoming in these hallowed halls.

Speaking for all Americans, I want to say how very much at home we feel in your house. Every American would, because this is, as we have been so eloquently told, one of democracy's shrines.

The "Westminster Speech": An address to the British Parliament, June 8, 1982.

Here the rights of free people and the processes of representation have been debated and refined.

It has been said that an institution is the lengthening shadow of a man. This institution is the lengthening shadow of all the men and women who have sat here and all those who have voted to send representatives here.

This is my second visit to Great Britain as President of the United States. My first opportunity to stand on British soil occurred almost a year and a half ago when your Prime Minister graciously hosted a diplomatic dinner at the British Embassy in Washington. Mrs. Thatcher said then that she hoped I was not distressed to find staring down at me from the grand staircase a portrait of His Royal Majesty King George III. She suggested it was best to let bygones be bygones, and in view of our two countries' remarkable friendship in succeeding years, she added that most Englishmen today would agree with Thomas Jefferson that "a little rebellion now and then is a very good thing."

Well, from here I will go to Bonn and then Berlin, where there stands a grim symbol of power untamed. The Berlin Wall, that dreadful gray gash across the city, is in its third decade. It is the fitting signature of the regime that built it.

And a few hundred kilometers behind the Berlin Wall, there is another symbol. In the center of Warsaw, there is a sign that notes the distances to two capitals. In one direction it points toward Moscow. In the other it points toward Brussels, headquarters of Western Europe's tangible unity. The marker says that the distances from Warsaw to Moscow and Warsaw to Brussels are equal. The sign makes this point: Poland is not East or West. Poland is at the center of European civilization. It has contributed mightily to that civilization. It is doing so today by being magnificently unreconciled to oppression.

Poland's struggle to be Poland and to secure the basic rights we often take for granted demonstrates why we dare not take those rights for granted. Gladstone, defending the Reform Bill of 1866, declared, "You cannot fight against the future. Time is on our side." It was easier to believe in the march of democracy in Gladstone's day—in that high noon of Victorian optimism.

We're approaching the end of a bloody century plagued by a terrible political invention—totalitarianism. Optimism comes less easily today, not because democracy is less vigorous, but because democracy's enemies have refined their instruments of repression. Yet optimism is in order, because day-by-day democracy is proving itself to be a not-at-all-fragile flower. From Stettin on the Baltic to Varna on the Black Sea, the regimes planted by totalitarianism have had more than thirty years to establish their legitimacy. But none— not one regime—has yet been able to risk free elections. Regimes planted by bayonets do not take root.

The strength of the Solidarity movement in Poland demonstrates the truth told in an underground joke in the Soviet Union. It is that the Soviet Union would remain a one-party nation even if an opposition party were permitted, because everyone would join the opposition party

America's time as a player on the stage of world history has been brief. I think understanding this fact has always made you patient with your younger cousins—well, not always patient. I do recall that on one occasion, Sir Winston Churchill said in exasperation about one of our most distinguished diplomats: "He is the only case I know of a bull who carries his china shop with him."

But witty as Sir Winston was, he also had that special attribute of great statesmen—the gift of vision, the willingness to see the future based on the experience of the past. It is this sense of history, this understanding of the past that I want to talk with you about today, for it is in remembering what we share of the past that our two nations can make common cause for the future.

We have not inherited an easy world. If developments like the Industrial Revolution, which began here in England, and the gifts of science and technology have made life much easier for us, they have also made it more dangerous. There are threats now to our freedom, indeed to our very existence, that other generations could never even have imagined.

There is first the threat of global war. No President, no Congress, no Prime Minister, no Parliament can spend a day entirely free of this threat. And I don't have to tell you that in today's world the existence of nuclear weapons could mean, if not the extinction of mankind, then surely the end of civilization as we know it. That's why negotiations on intermediate-range nuclear forces now underway in Europe and the START talks—Strategic Arms Reduction Talks—which will begin later this month, are not just critical to American or Western policy; they are critical to mankind. Our commitment to early success in these negotiations is firm and unshakable, and our purpose is clear: reducing the risk of war by reducing the means of waging war on both sides.

At the same time there is a threat posed to human freedom by the enormous power of the modern state. History teaches the dangers of government that overreaches—political control taking precedence over free economic growth, secret police, mindless bureaucracy, all combining to stifle individual excellence and personal freedom.

Now, I'm aware that among us here and throughout Europe there is legitimate disagreement over the extent to which the public sector should play a role in a nation's economy and life. But on one point all of us are united—our abhorrence of dictatorship in all its forms, but most particularly totalitarianism and the terrible inhumanities it has caused in our time—the great purge, Auschwitz and Dachau, the Gulag, and Cambodia.

Historians looking back at our time will note the consistent restraint and peaceful intentions of the West. They will note that it was the democracies who refused to use the threat of their nuclear monopoly in the forties and early fifties for territorial or imperial gain. Had that nuclear monopoly been in the hands of the Communist world, the map of Europe—indeed, the world—would look very different today. And certainly they will note it was not the democracies that invaded Afghanistan or suppressed Polish Solidarity or used chemical and toxin warfare in Afghanistan and Southeast Asia.

If history teaches anything it teaches self-delusion in the face of unpleasant facts is folly. We see around us today the marks of our terrible dilemma—predictions of doomsday, antinuclear demonstrations, an arms race in which the West must, for its own protection, be an unwilling participant. At the same time we see totalitarian forces in the world who seek subversion and conflict around the globe to further their barbarous assault on the human spirit. What, then, is our course? Must civilization perish in a hail of fiery atoms? Must freedom wither in a quiet, deadening accommodation with totalitarian evil?

Sir Winston Churchill refused to accept the inevitability of war or even that it was imminent. He said, "I do not believe that Soviet Russia desires war. What they desire is the fruits of war and the indefinite expansion of their power and doctrines. But what we have to consider here today while time remains is the permanent prevention of war and the establishment of conditions of freedom and democracy as rapidly as possible in all countries."

Well, this is precisely our mission today: to preserve freedom as well as peace. It may not be easy to see; but I believe we live now at a turning point.

In an ironic sense Karl Marx was right. We are witnessing today a great revolutionary crisis, a crisis where the demands of the economic order are conflicting directly with those of the political order. But the crisis is happening not in the free, non-Marxist West, but in the home of Marxist-Leninism, the Soviet Union. It is the Soviet Union that runs against the tide of history by denying human freedom and human dignity to its citizens. It also is in deep economic difficulty. The rate of growth in the national product has been steadily declining since the fifties and is less than half of what it was then.

The dimensions of this failure are astounding: A country which employs one-fifth of its population in agriculture is unable to feed its own people. Were it not for the private sector, the tiny private sector tolerated in Soviet agriculture, the country might be on the brink of famine. These private plots occupy a bare 3 percent of the arable land but account for nearly one-quarter of Soviet farm output and nearly one-third of meat products and vegetables. Over centralized, with little or no incentives, year after year the Soviet system pours its best resources into the making of instruments of destruction. The constant shrinkage of economic growth combined with the growth of military production is putting a heavy strain on the Soviet people. What we see here is a political structure that no longer corresponds to its economic base, a society where productive forces are hampered by political ones.

The decay of the Soviet experiment should come as no surprise to us. Wherever the comparisons have been made between free and closed societies—West Germany and East Germany, Austria and Czechoslovakia, Malaysia and Vietnam—it is the democratic countries that are prosperous and responsive to the needs of their people. And one of the simple but overwhelming facts of our time is this: Of all the millions of refugees we've seen in the modern world, their flight is always away from, not toward the Communist world. Today on the NATO line, our military forces face east to prevent a possible invasion. On the other side of the line, the Soviet forces also face east to prevent their people from leaving.

The hard evidence of totalitarian rule has caused in mankind an uprising of the intellect and will. Whether it is the growth of the new schools of economics in America or England or the appearance of the so-called new philosophers in France, there is one unifying thread running through the intellectual work of these groups—rejection of the arbitrary power of the state, the refusal to subordinate the rights of the individual to the super-state, the realization that collectivism stifles all the best human impulses.

Since the exodus from Egypt, historians have written of those who sacrificed and struggled for freedom—the stand at Thermopylae, the revolt of Spartacus, the storming of the Bastille, the

Warsaw uprising in World War II. More recently we've seen evidence of this same human impulse in one of the developing nations in Central America. For months and months the world news media covered the fighting in El Salvador. Day after day we were treated to stories and film slanted toward the brave freedom-fighters battling oppressive government forces in behalf of the silent, suffering people of that tortured country.

And then one day those silent, suffering people were offered a chance to vote, to choose the kind of government they wanted. Suddenly the freedom-fighters in the hills were exposed for what they really are—Cuban-backed guerrillas who want power for themselves, and their backers, not democracy for the people. They threatened death to any who voted, and destroyed hundreds of buses and trucks to keep the people from getting to the polling places. But on election day, the people of El Salvador, an unprecedented 1.4 million of them, braved ambush and gunfire, and trudged for miles to vote for freedom.

They stood for hours in the hot sun waiting for their turn to vote. Members of our Congress who went there as observers told me of a woman who was wounded by rifle fire on the way to the polls, who refused to leave the line to have her wound treated until after she had voted. A grandmother, who had been told by the guerrillas she would be killed when she returned from the polls, told the guerrillas, "You can kill me, you can kill my family, kill my neighbors, but you can't kill us all." The real freedom-fighters of El Salvador turned out to be the people of that county—the young, the old, the in-between.

Strange, but in my own country there's been little if any news coverage of that war since the election. Now, perhaps they'll say it's—well, because there are newer struggles now.

On distant islands in the South Atlantic young men are fighting for Britain. And, yes, voices have been raised protesting their sacrifice for lumps of rock and earth so far away But those young men aren't fighting for mere real estate. They fight for a cause—for the belief that armed aggression must not be allowed to succeed, and the people must participate in the decisions of government—the decisions of government under the rule of law. If there had been firmer support for that principle some forty-five years ago, perhaps our generation wouldn't have suffered the bloodletting of World War II.

In the Middle East now the guns sound once more, this time in Lebanon, a country that for too long has had to endure the tragedy of civil war, terrorism, and foreign intervention and occupation. The fighting in Lebanon on the part of all parties must stop, and Israel should bring its forces home. But this is not enough. We must all work to stamp out the scourge of terrorism that in the Middle East makes war an ever-present threat.

But beyond the trouble spots lies a deeper, more positive pattern. Around the world today, the democratic revolution is gathering new strength. In India a critical test has been passed with the peaceful change of governing political parties. In Africa, Nigeria is moving in remarkable and unmistakable ways to build and strengthen its democratic institutions. In the Caribbean and Central America, sixteen of twenty-four countries have freely elected governments. And in the United Nations, eight of the ten developing nations which have joined that body in the past five years are democracies.

In the Communist world as well, man's instinctive desire for freedom and self-determination surfaces again and again. To be sure, there are grim reminders of how brutally the police state attempts to snuff out this quest for self-rule—1953 in East Germany, 1956 in Hungary, 1968 in Czechoslovakia, 1981 in Poland. But the struggle continues in Poland. And we know that there are even those who strive and suffer for freedom within the confines of the Soviet Union itself. How we conduct ourselves here in the Western democracies will determine whether this trend continues.

No, democracy is not a fragile flower. Still it needs cultivating. If the rest of this century is to witness the gradual growth of freedom and democratic ideals, we must take actions to assist the campaign for democracy.

Some argue that we should encourage democratic change in right-wing dictatorships, but not in Communist regimes. Well, to accept this preposterous notion—as some well-meaning people have—is to invite the argument that once countries achieve a nuclear capability, they should be allowed an undisturbed reign of terror over their own citizens. We reject this course.

As for the Soviet view, Chairman Brezhnev repeatedly has stressed that the competition of ideas and systems must continue and that this is entirely consistent with relaxation of tensions and peace.

Well, we ask only that these systems begin by living up to their own constitutions, abiding by their own laws, and complying with the international obligations they have undertaken. We ask only for a process, a direction a basic code of decency, not for an instant transformation.

We cannot ignore the fact that even without our encouragement there has been and will continue to be repeated explosions against repression and dictatorships. The Soviet Union itself is not immune to this reality. Any system is inherently unstable that has no peaceful means to legitimize its leaders. In such cases, the very repressiveness of the state ultimately drives people to resist it, if necessary, by force.

While we must be cautious about forcing the pace of change, we must not hesitate to declare our ultimate objectives and to take concrete actions to move toward them. We must be staunch in our conviction that freedom is not the sole prerogative of a lucky few, but the inalienable and universal right of all human beings. So states the United Nations Universal Declaration of Human Rights, which, among other things, guarantees free elections.

The objective I propose is quite simple to state: to foster the infrastructure of democracy, the system of a free press, unions, political parties, universities, which allows a people to choose their own way to develop their own culture, to reconcile their own differences through peaceful means.

This is not cultural imperialism, it is providing the means for genuine self-determination and protection for diversity. Democracy already flourishes in countries with very different cultures and historical experiences. It would be cultural condescension, or worse, to say that any people prefer dictatorship to democracy. Who would voluntarily choose not to have the right to vote, decide to purchase government propaganda handouts instead of independent newspapers, prefer government to worker-controlled unions, opt for land to be owned by the state instead of those who till it, want government repression of religious liberty, a single political party instead of a free choice, a rigid cultural orthodoxy instead of democratic tolerance and diversity?

Since 1917 the Soviet Union has given covert political training and assistance to Marxist-Leninists in many countries. Of course, it also has promoted the use of violence and subversion by these same forces. Over the past several decades, West European and other Social Democrats, Christian Democrats, and leaders have offered open assistance to fraternal, political, and social institutions to bring about peaceful and democratic progress. Appropriately, for a vigorous new democracy, the Federal Republic of Germany's political foundations have become a major force in this effort.

We in America now intend to take additional steps, as many of our allies have already done, toward realizing this same goal. The chairmen and other leaders of the national Republican and Democratic Party organizations are initiating a study with the bipartisan American Political Foundation to determine how the United States can best contribute as a nation to the global campaign for democracy now gathering force. They will have the cooperation of congressional leaders of both parties, along with representatives of business, labor, and other major institutions in our society. I look forward to receiving their recommendations and to working with these institutions and the Congress in the common task of strengthening democracy throughout the world.

It is time that we committed ourselves as a nation—in both the public and private sectors—to assisting democratic development.

We plan to consult with leaders of other nations as well. There is a proposal before the Council of Europe to invite parliamentarians from democratic countries to a meeting next year in Strasbourg. That prestigious gathering could consider ways to help democratic political movements.

This November in Washington there will take place an international meeting on free elections. And next spring there will be a conference of world authorities on constitutionalism and self-government hosted by the Chief Justice of the United States. Authorities from a number of developing and developed countries—judges, philosophers, and politicians with practical experience—have agreed to explore how to turn principle into practice and further the rule of law.

At the same time, we invite the Soviet Union to consider with us how the competition of ideas and values—which it is committed to support—can be conducted on a peaceful and reciprocal basis. For example, I am prepared to offer President Brezhnev an opportunity to speak to the American people on our television if he will allow me the same opportunity with the Soviet people. We also suggest that panels of our newsmen periodically appear on each other's television to discuss major events.

Now, I don't wish to sound overly optimistic, yet the Soviet Union is not immune from the reality of what is going on in the world. It has happened in the past—a small ruling elite either mistakenly attempts to ease domestic unrest through greater repression and foreign adventure, or it chooses a wiser course. It begins to allow its people a voice in their own destiny. Even if this latter process is not realized soon, I believe the renewed strength of the democratic movement, complemented by a global campaign for freedom, will strengthen the prospects for arms control and a world at peace.

I have discussed on other occasions, including my address on May 9th, the elements of Western policies toward the Soviet Union to safeguard our interests and protect the peace. What I am describing now is a plan and a hope for the long term—the march of freedom and democracy which will leave Marxism-Leninism on the ash-heap of history as it has left other tyrannies which stifle the freedom and muzzle the self-expression of the people. And that's why we must continue our efforts to strengthen NATO even as we move forward with our Zero-Option initiative in the negotiations on intermediate-range forces and our proposal for a one-third reduction in strategic ballistic missile warheads.

Our military strength is a prerequisite to peace, but let it be clear we maintain this strength in the hope it will never be used, for the ultimate determinant in the struggle that's now going on in the world will not be bombs and rockets, but a test of wills and ideas, a trial of spiritual resolve, the values we hold, the beliefs we cherish, the ideals to which we are dedicated.

The British people know that, given strong leadership, time and a little bit of hope, the forces of good ultimately rally and triumph over evil. Here among you is the cradle of self-government, the Mother of Parliaments. Here is the enduring greatness of the British contribution to mankind, the great civilized ideas: individual liberty, representative government, and the rule of law under God.

I've often wondered about the shyness of some of us in the West about standing for these ideals that have done so much to ease the plight of man and the hardships of our imperfect world. This reluctance to use those vast resources at our command reminds me of the elderly lady whose home was bombed in the Blitz. As the rescuers moved about, they found a bottle of brandy she'd stored behind the staircase, which was all that was left standing. And since she was barely conscious, one of the workers pulled the cork to give her a taste of it. She came around immediately and said, "Here now—there now, put it back. That's for emergencies."

Well, the emergency is upon us. Let us be shy no longer. Let us go to our strength. Let us offer hope. Let us tell the world that a new age is not only possible but probable.

During the dark days of the Second World War, when this island was incandescent with courage, Winston Churchill exclaimed about Britain's adversaries, "What kind of a people do they think we are?" Well, Britain's adversaries found out what extraordinary people the British are. But all the democracies paid a terrible price for allowing the dictators to underestimate us. We dare not make that mistake again. So, let us ask ourselves, "What kind of people do we think we are?" And let us answer, "Free people, worthy of freedom and determined not only to remain so but to help others gain their freedom as well."

Sir Winston led his people to great victory in war and then lost an election just as the fruits of victory were about to be enjoyed. But he left office honorably, and, as it turned out, temporarily, knowing that the liberty of his people was more important than the fate of any single leader. History recalls his greatness in ways no dictator will ever know. And he left us a message of hope for the future, as timely now as when he first uttered it, as opposition leader in the Commons nearly twenty-seven years ago, when he said, "When we look back on all the perils through which we have passed and at the mighty foes that we have laid low and all the dark and deadly designs that we have frustrated, why should we fear for our future? We have," he said, "come safely through the worst."

Well, the task I've set forth will long outlive our own generation. But together, we too have come through the worst. Let us now begin a major effort to secure the best—a crusade for freedom that will engage the faith and fortitude of the next generation. For the sake of peace and justice, let us move toward a world in which all people are at last free to determine their own destiny.

CHAPTER 15

Jeane J. Kirkpatrick

Commentary by Edwin J. Feulner Jr. (2002)

President Jimmy Carter's foreign policy—with one notable exception—was characterized by one calamity after another: the ousting of the pro-West Shah of Iran and his replacement by the fanatical Ayatollah Khomeini; the coming to power of the Marxist Sandinistas in Nicaragua; the surrender of the Panama Canal to a drug-running dictator; the deliberate derecognition of a long-time ally, the Republic of China on Taiwan; the Soviet invasion of Afghanistan; the establishment of Marxist regimes in Angola and Mozambique ... the litany seemed almost endless. The exception was Carter's historic Camp David summit meeting and the ensuing agreement between President Anwar Sadat of Egypt and Prime Minister Menachem Begin of Israel. But that single success did not begin to compensate for the many failures.

At the core of the dysfunctional Carter diplomacy was a utopian irrationality that alarmed our friends and encouraged our enemies. Asked to explain Communism's unrelenting aggression, particularly in the Third World, Andrew Young, Carter's ambassador to the United Nations, suggested in all apparent seriousness that the thirty thousand Cuban troops in Angola brought "a certain stability and order" to the country and the region.

In sharp contrast, President-elect Ronald Reagan was determined, as he put it, to send a powerful message to the Soviets "that we weren't going to stand by anymore while they armed and financed terrorists and subverted democratic governments." He chose as his United States Permanent Representative to the United Nations someone who he knew would neither excuse nor disregard Soviet aggrandizement: Jeane J. Kirkpatrick. Reagan had read Kirkpatrick's penetrating article, "Dictatorships and Double Standards," published in the November 1979 issue of *Commentary* magazine and had sent her a highly complimentary three-page letter.

In her article, Kirkpatrick asserted that the failure of the Carter Administration's foreign policy was now "clear to everyone except for its architects." Referring to Nicaragua and Iran, she criticized the Administration for undermining pro-American, "right-wing" autocracies while accepting the rule of Communist regimes. She stated that the Carter Administration's idea of national interest bordered on doublethink.

It may not always be easy, Kirkpatrick wrote, "to distinguish between democratic and totalitarian agents of change, but it is also not too difficult." In words that anticipated the Reagan Doctrine, the Georgetown University professor of political science (and liberal Democrat) said that "authentic democratic revolutionaries" aimed at governments based on the consent of the governed and believed that "ordinary men are capable of using freedom, of knowing their own interest, of choosing rulers." They did not assume, like the Sandinistas in Nicaragua, that it was necessary to postpone elections for several years while they "cured" the false consciousness of the people. Such lucid analysis appealed strongly to Ronald Reagan.

In February 1980, Jeane Kirkpatrick was invited by Richard V. Allen, Reagan's national security aide, to meet with the presidential candidate and a group of foreign policy experts. Kirkpatrick was impressed by the serious questions that Reagan asked and what she called his "intuitive grasp" of the issues. That evening, she sat next to Reagan at a private dinner hosted by conservative columnist George Will. Afterward she told her husband, political scientist Evron Kirkpatrick, that Reagan's view of foreign affairs was "generally correct and very realistic."

This was high praise from Jeane Kirkpatrick, who throughout her academic and political career always stressed the importance of rationalism and reason in foreign policy. She now faced a dilemma. She wanted to be part of what she saw as an important and even historic presidential campaign, but how could she, a lifelong Democrat, join the Republicans? She then remembered that Reagan had teased her at the Will dinner, saying, "I was a Democrat once, you know."

In May 1980, the Reagan campaign announced the establishment of a twelve-member policy council, supplemented by two groups of advisers, one on foreign affairs, the other on defense. Prominent among the names was Jeane J. Kirkpatrick. When a reporter asked her if she was supporting Reagan, Kirkpatrick mentioned the dismissive treatment by liberal Democrats and the friendly messages from conservative Republicans that she and other "Jackson Democrats" (referring to Democratic Senator Henry Jackson of Washington) had been receiving. "After a certain time," she explained, "it begins to seem irresistible." And, always realistic, she added, "especially if the person seems likely to be the next president of the United States."

Jeane Kirkpatrick was the first Democrat to attain a Cabinet-rank position in the Reagan Administration when the president-elect named her on December 22, 1980, to be the U.S. ambassador to the United Nations, the first woman to hold that position. The professor turned diplomat promised to resign if she could not in good conscience represent the policies of the administration, but Jeane Kirkpatrick quickly became one of Ronald Reagan's most loyal and effective spokesmen in the U.N. and around the world.

The road from relatively unknown academic to political superstar began in Duncan, Oklahoma. Jeane Duane Jordan was the daughter of an oil wildcatter who moved his family to a succession of small towns in Oklahoma and Illinois. Always interested in philosophy and history, Jeane Jordan received an A.A. degree from Stephens College in Columbia, Missouri, and then, in a turning point in her life, moved to New York City to attend Barnard College, a women's college affiliated with Columbia University. She earned a B.A. from Barnard and an M.A. in political science from Columbia. She had thought about studying journalism at college, "but I felt I didn't know anything to write about ... so I decided to study ... the big ideas."

She did postgraduate work as a French government fellow at the University of Paris's Institute of Political Science where she developed a lasting interest in French politics, history, and cuisine. She still spends a large part of each summer in Provence in southern France reading and thinking and cooking for her family and friends. A second big change in her life came when she married the well-known political scientist Evron (Kirk) Kirkpatrick in 1955. She was then a research associate at George Washington University in Washington, D.C., and working on a history of the Marshall Plan.

The Kirkpatricks soon had the first of their three sons (Douglas Jordan, John Evron, and Stuart Alan), and the young mother was faced with the choice of rearing her children or actively pursuing an academic career. "I decided to stay home," she recalls. In fact she spent most of the next eight years at home until her youngest son entered school, although she continued to read and study and write. "If I had a goal," she says, "it was not to become rusty" and lose touch with the academic world. She did not and never has.

In 1962, she became an assistant professor of political science at Trinity College in Washington, and five years later was appointed associate professor of political science at Georgetown University. A clear sign of Kirkpatrick's superior academic ability was that she received both appointments without having a Ph.D. Completing her dissertation (on Peronist politics in Argentina), she obtained her doctorate from Columbia University in 1968. Only five years later,

Jeane Kirkpatrick was appointed a full professor at Georgetown, and became Thomas and Dorothy Leavey Professor in the Foundations of American Freedom in 1978. A quarter of a century later, she retains the position of Thomas and Dorothy Leavey University Professor and, with all her responsibilities, including that of a Senior Fellow at the American Enterprise Institute and co-director of Empower America, still offers two seminars in government at Georgetown.

Always a prolific writer, Kirkpatrick authored numerous scholarly articles and books, including the ground-breaking work, *Political Women*, often cited by academics. But she did not ignore what was happening outside the groves of academe. Like other liberal but strongly anti-Communist Democrats, Kirkpatrick became alarmed at the rapid rise of the counterculture and the antiwar movement of the 1960s. She argued that their leaders were fundamentally opposed to American institutions and advocated unrealistic and utopian reforms. Unwilling to sit on the political sidelines, she ran in May 1972 in the Maryland primary on a slate of delegates committed to former Vice President Hubert H. Humphrey—but the slate lost. To counter the influence of McGovernites within the Democratic Party, Kirkpatrick and like-minded liberals formed the Coalition for a Democratic Majority. The CDM's goal, she explained, following the resounding defeat of presidential candidate George McGovern in the fall, was to reclaim the Democratic Party from the "antiwar, antigrowth, antibusiness, antilabor activists."

Increasingly, Jeane Kirkpatrick found herself in the company of what came to be called the neoconservatives. "Mugged by reality" (Irving Kristol's pungent phrase), these former liberals attacked the radicals as despoilers of the liberal tradition. In place of liberal radicalism, Kristol and others called for a return to the "republican virtue" of the founding fathers and invoked the idea of a good society. They endorsed the notion of a "moral and political order" and conceded that a "hidden hand" had its place in the marketplace.

Jeane Kirkpatrick, however, remained a Democrat because she retained a belief in the welfare state (or at least much of it) and the importance of organized labor.

The neoconservatives had an extraordinary impact on American politics in the 1970s and 1980s because they were, as Theodore White put it, "action intellectuals," with connections to America's leading universities and the more important mass media, direct access to officeholders and the political elite, good relations with major elements of the labor movement, and strong roots in influential foundations and think tanks with multimillion-dollar budgets. With her 1980 appointment as U.S. ambassador to the United Nations, Jeane Kirkpatrick became one of the most influential action intellectuals in the world of politics.

She eloquently defended Reagan policy during such crises as Israel's invasion of Lebanon, the U.S. overturn of a Marxist regime in Grenada, and the Soviet downing of Korean Airlines flight 007, which killed everyone aboard. She justified the administration's policy of granting arms assistance to El Salvador's military junta, which was under attack by Cuban-backed Marxist guerrillas. In a debate with a former Carter official, she asserted that the alternatives were "whether we do anything at all, or whether we leave the government unsupplied while the Cubans or the Soviet Union supply the guerrillas." She was especially vocal in support of aid to the anti-Communist Contras in Nicaragua and was deeply moved when they named one of their 400-man brigades the Jeane Kirkpatrick Task Force. Americans were equally enthusiastic about their forthright U.N. representative. Evron Kirkpatrick recalled that once when he and Jeane were out for a walk in Manhattan, "a truck driver sticks his head out the window and says, 'Give 'em hell, Jeane.' Things like that happen all the time."

Understanding that the U.N. did not operate in a political vacuum, she sent the voting records of every member nation to Congress. As the *New York Times* reported, the message was clear: any country that opposed the United States on an issue important to

Washington might find its foreign aid significantly reduced. Her tough stance got results that had not been seen in years. An Arab resolution to expel Israel was rejected. A Cuban attempt to cite the U.S. for "colonizing" Puerto Rico was blocked. A Nicaraguan campaign castigating U.S. policy in Central America died.

She took every possible opportunity to stress the importance of public diplomacy, cognizant that the United Nations is not only a forum for relations between states but a forum to reach out to publics behind the governments around the world. The transforming power of public diplomacy was driven home to Jeane Kirkpatrick when she visited Managua, Nicaragua, in October 1987, two years after she left her U.N. post. Cries of "Viva Kirkpatrick!" filled the air as she addressed a public rally of Contra supporters. Reading her speech in Spanish, Kirkpatrick was repeatedly interrupted by applause as people in the audience waved small American flags. She referred to the Sandinista government as a dictatorship and said the Contras were fighting for "the right to live normal lives free of oppression and reprisals." Three years later, in an internationally monitored national election, the outspoken anti-Communist Violeta Chamorro defeated the Sandinista presidential candidate Daniel Ortega.

Jeane Kirkpatrick was criticized by U.N. diplomats and U.S. liberals for her "non-diplomatic" behavior in the United Nations, but one man in particular endorsed strongly what she was doing. With President Reagan's approval, William P. Clark, the national security adviser until 1983, made Kirkpatrick an independent counsel to the President. She could see the President whenever she wanted and telephone him at any time. "She had absolutely direct access to him," says Judge Clark. "When she put her feet under the desk of the Oval Office, the President listened and he usually agreed with her."

She was also a member of the Administration's top-level foreign- policy–making committee, the National Security Planning Group. Every week or so, the group gathered in the Situation Room in the White House basement; they included the President, the vice president, the secretaries of State and Defense, the director of Central Intelligence, the national security adviser, the chairman of the Joint Chiefs of Staff, the White House chief of staff, the White House counsel, and U.N. Ambassador Jeane Kirkpatrick. "She had a substantial impact," remembers Lawrence S. Eagleburger, the former under secretary of state for Political Affairs, who frequently joined the meetings.

And she had considerable help at the U.N. from a strong diplomatic team that included Charles M. Lichenstein, a former Yale instructor and research director for the Goldwater for President Committee; Kenneth L. Adelman, a former assistant to Secretary of Defense Donald Rumsfeld; Cuban émigré Jose S. Sorzano; and Alan L. Keyes, a blunt-talking black graduate of Harvard. Lichenstein, who served as Kirkpatrick's chief deputy, became famous for his 1983 response to a Soviet delegate who rose on the U.N. floor to express his country's "indignation" about the "illegal and unprecedented" act of denying landing rights to the plane of Soviet foreign minister Andrei Gromyko. Gromyko was scheduled to arrive at the United Nations a few days after Soviet jet fighters shot down Korean Air Lines flight 007 over international waters.

Such an act, said the Soviet official pompously, "raises the question of whether the U.N. should be in the United States." Lichenstein immediately responded in true Kirkpatrickian fashion: "If, in the judicious determination of the members of the United Nations, they feel they are not welcome and treated with the hostly consideration that is their due, the United States strongly encourages member states to seriously consider removing themselves and this organization from the soil of the United States. We will put no impediment in your way," he added, "and we will be at the dockside bidding you a farewell as you set off into the sunset."

The following year Ambassador Lichenstein came to The Heritage Foundation as a distinguished fellow in international relations and remained with us until his death earlier this year. America owes Chuck Lichenstein a great debt of gratitude for the passion and skill with which he conducted his duties at the United Nations and subsequently. He was a boundless source of knowledge, history, and expertise on international institutions and the shape of conservative government.

I was to see firsthand the profound difference that Ambassador Kirkpatrick made at the U.N. In the summer of 1982, I was appointed by President Reagan as the Public Representative to the United Nations Second Special Session on Disarmament (SSOD-2, in U.N.-speak). To an idealistic young Reaganaut, the notion that I would be a part of the "Kirkpatrick Team" was exhilarating. That the late Sam Stratton (D–NY) and John Warner (R–VA) would represent the U.S. House of Representatives and the U.S. Senate, respectively, was encouraging. Heritage had worked with both men on disarmament issues, and their presence would ensure that the United States—the executive branch and the Congress—would speak with one voice.

On the first evening of the Session, Ambassador Kirkpatrick hosted a small dinner at her official residence in the Waldorf Towers in New York—it was the last time the whole team would be together during SSOD-2. Since the General Assembly was not in session, Jeane had committed herself to an extended trip to Africa. In her absence, Ken Adelman was given the responsibility of handling the U.S. position at the SSOD-2. As I trudged around with Ken in subsequent weeks, I learned the secret kitchen exits from every hotel ballroom in the city, a mandatory learning experience for everyone expected to attend the National Day celebrations of all 160-odd members of the U.N. Knowing the quickest route out of a hotel ballroom after shaking hands with the ambassador and the senior government officials from the host country allowed us to attend either another reception or to get back to serious negotiations with the Soviet delegation or others who had a real stake in disarmament issues.

As the weeks went by and the deadline to conclude SSOD-2 approached, it was easy to be caught up in the deliberate rhythm of the U.N., where haggling over a phrase or even a word took on a life of its own—even when it was a minor change in a communiqué which no one would ever read, let along comply with. SSOD-2 was scheduled to terminate on June 30. However, the actual meetings went into the July 4 holiday period, and both Congressman Stratton and Senator Warner left New York City to honor commitments back home.

On the day of the final session, it turned out that I, with my seven weeks of service, was the ranking member of the American delegation and would therefore deliver the U.S. address from the podium. I was asked by the career advisers of the U.S. delegation if I had a preference as to when we should be on the agenda. I suggested that it should be four or five speakers after the Soviet speaker. This caused some consternation because he was not scheduled until late in the afternoon and listening to various and sundry delegates speak on the desirability of disarmament was not the way anyone at the U.S. Mission wanted to spend their holiday weekend. For me, however, it was essential to follow the Soviets rather than precede them so that if they made any wild and reckless charges an official U.S. reply could be made.

As it turned out the Soviet speech was more confrontational than had been anticipated, and a huddle of Americans began reworking my text. In a sidebar conversation, one of them reminded me that under the U.N. rules, alphabetically rotating seats meant that the front row would contain Iran, Iraq, and Libya—hardly the most supportive audience for an American speaker. With some trepidation, I mounted the dais, stood at the podium to be greeted by hisses from the front row, and gave an eminently forgettable speech to anyone who happened to be listening. Thus, did SSOD-2 pass into history.

I recount this incident in such detail because the teamwork, which was evident among both political appointees and career foreign service officers in the American delegation, was remarkable. We met frequently, worked from a common agenda, and realized that we were all representing the views not simply of a department but of an Administration which stood for certain principles. We were all determined that those principles would be reflected as best as possible in policy decisions and certainly in the rhetoric of any debate. It was, of course, Jeane Kirkpatrick who was the soul of this enterprise and whose leadership and unflagging good spirits kept us all working from that shared agenda.

Since her tenure at the United Nations, her relationship with The Heritage Foundation has been close and collaborative. When she co-founded Empower America, several Heritage people were intimately involved in that enterprise. When Heritage has put together a program on any aspect of foreign policy, one of the regular participants has usually been Ambassador Kirkpatrick. And when we sponsored a series of nation-wide lectures by leading men and women of ideas to mark our 1998–1999 "Leadership for America" campaign, Jeane Kirkpatrick delivered the address on Strength.

Ambassador Kirkpatrick probably reached the apogee of her political career at the 1984 Republican national convention when she blistered the Democrats, who had already met in San Francisco, as the "blame America first" party. The San Francisco Democrats, she pointed out, blamed America for the invasion of Grenada and not "Cuba and the communists for threatening American students and murdering Grenadians." When the Marine barracks in Lebanon were bombed, the San Francisco Democrats blamed America and not the terrorists who killed Americans in their sleep. These same Democrats blamed the United States and not the Soviet Union for the impasse in arms negotiating. And they had the effrontery to judge U.S. involvement in Central America without regard for the real issue— Marxist dictators who "shoot their way into power."

The following year, after serving longer than any other U.S. ambassador in decades, Jeane Kirkpatrick resigned her U.N. position, returned to Georgetown University, and officially joined the Republican Party. Echoing Ronald Reagan, she explained that she had changed philosophy "a long time before I changed parties." She said that Republicans were more sensitive to threats of communism and their foreign policy "was more sensible and more successful." And in an interview published in the Heritage Foundation's *Policy Review*, Kirkpatrick admitted that she had also modified her views about the welfare state during her service on the U.N.'s Economic and Social Council. "I learned how much more successful market strategies are than any sort of statist strategies." She was also influenced by the experience of the Reagan Administration, which demonstrated that "even incremental enhancement of reliance on the market stimulates the economy and helps achieve goals like lower employment far more effectively than any kind of state action."

There was widespread speculation in 1988 that Jeane Kirkpatrick might be the vice presidential candidate on the Republican ticket, and in 1996, she was on everyone's short list for secretary of state if Bob Dole were elected President. But in her post-U.N. years, for the most part, Kirkpatrick did what she had been doing for several decades—guide her students through the prickly thickets of history and philosophy, write widely respected books like *The Withering Away of the Totalitarian State and Other Surprises*, receive awards like the Presidential Medal of Freedom and the Distinguished Public Service Medal of the Department of Defense, serve on national panels like the Defense Policy Review Board and the President's Foreign Intelligence Advisory Board, and speak before a wide variety of associations, government and nongovernment institutions, and university audiences, always offering clear cool thinking about public policy and public diplomacy.

The following original essay, "Defending U.S. Interests and Principles in the United Nations," was first drafted in 1985 by Ambassador Kirkpatrick shortly after she left the U.N. She has revised and updated it for The Heritage Foundation, and we are very pleased to be able to publish this important analysis of U.S. foreign policy for the first time.

Essentially, the essay is Jeane Kirkpatrick's answer to the question, "What did you learn in your years at the United Nations?"

What she learned needs to be remembered as the United States exercises leadership in the U.N. and elsewhere. The lessons include: international relations depend, above all, "on the values and the relative power of nations." Power in international affairs is cumulative: "the more you have, the more you get and vice versa." And U.S. effectiveness and power in places like the U.N. require "absolutely that we have confidence in our values, our experience, our country."

Looking at the U.N. when she served there and today, Kirkpatrick asserts that it is not "a utopian arena" but a place "where a very hard game of politics is played." It may shock some, she concedes, but "it is not the merits of the case that determine who is condemned for what and when; it is the power structure inside the United Nations." Ambassador Kirkpatrick notes that the Soviet Union was more skillful and ruthless than the United States in securing support within the U.N. of countries in their own bloc. The problem was that there were neither rewards for helping the United States nor "a price for opposing us even on issues of concern to us."

The U.S. delegation learned that it was important for a nation seeking influence to practice what Thomas Jefferson called "the peaceable coercions" of international politics. The U.S. team came to understand that the complex politics of the United Nations— and by extension all of world politics—required cultivating and maintaining relations with a hundred-odd countries both inside and outside the U.N. And while it was not necessary that the United States dominate on every issue or even most issues, it was vital, in Kirkpatrick's words, that "we secure a decent respect for our values and our important principles." As she has stated frequently throughout her life, foremost among those principles is that "freedom works."

Ambassador Kirkpatrick concludes her essay by stating that she wished that "power, conflict and self-interest" did not play so large a role in the U.N. But we must accept the United Nations and the world as they are if we are "to protect ourselves, our principles, our values, our friends and indeed our civilization." If we are to survive in "this world of terrorists and weapons of mass destruction," she says, we should take care to remember the central role of power—and that "self-defense is not an aggressive act in the United Nations or out of it."

Jeane J. Kirkpatrick

Defending U.S. Interests and Principles in the United Nations

Preface, October 22, 2002

To pass a resolution of the fifteen-member U.N. Security Council at least nine positive votes are required with no "no" votes from the five Permanent Members. Even one "no" vote is enough to veto a resolution.

Normally negotiations on a resolution continue until a consensus is reached. Sometimes a resolution is abandoned by its sponsors if the necessary nine votes cannot be assembled or a veto avoided. That could happen on the U.S. resolution on Iraq. Whatever the outcome of negotiations on this resolution, many Americans, perhaps including those at the White House, will have learned that securing passage of a resolution by the Security Council may be neither easy nor certain. The pages which follow explain the many factors that influence the fate of a resolution —even one submitted by two such important Permanent Members as the United States and the United Kingdom.

People often asked me, what did you learn in your years at the United Nations? I replied, a great deal. The United Nations is a microcosm. All the countries in the world meet there to discuss all

This essay was written shortly after I ended my tenure as United States Permanent Representative to the United Nations, where I served from January 1981 through June 1985.

the issues in the world. It is the world writ small. To be sure, the United Nations is not an accurate reflection of the world. It has developed structures and institutions of its own, and they have their own influence. But it is nonetheless a place where very important lessons may be learned about the 159[1] nations which meet and interact there.

Much that can be learned about the behavior of nations inside the United Nations is true as well outside the United Nations. There is no substitute for experience inside the institution.

A book written in 1954 by one of America's most distinguished diplomats, George Kennan, called *The Realities of American Foreign Policy*, illuminates the interaction of nations inside the United Nations, as well as outside. Its brief, clear descriptions of the realities of American foreign policy are as accurate today as they were 40 years ago. Certainly, its major points coincide with the realities of my experience of the United Nations. I can summarize those points as follows:

- International relations depend, above all, on the values and the relative power of nations;
- The power in international affairs is cumulative; the more you have, the more you get and vice versa;
- The relative position of the United States and the Soviet Union depends in very important measure on our success in dealing with non-Communist nations in the world;
- Our influence with other nations depends in important measure on their hopes and fears—hopes of gains, fears of losses;
- And, finally, our effectiveness, our power, in places like the United Nations requires absolutely that we have confidence in our values, our experience, our country.

The bad news is that, even though we are a rich nation with great military strength and all the resources needed to protect ourselves, our values and our civilization, in the course of 20 years we

---

1 As of 2002, U.N. membership has grown to 191 nations.

came to be virtually powerless inside the United Nations—largely because we ignored those basic facts about politics.

The good news is that, by returning to the basic principles of international politics, we have been able to reverse the negative trend and restore America's position and capacity to act inside the United Nations. Maintaining decent respect for the United States requires behaving with the same kind of realism and common sense inside the United Nations that we regularly have in our private and political lives.

We got into trouble in the United Nations because we did not face realities about the behavior of nations. Getting out of trouble has been our principal preoccupation at the U.S. Mission and mine, quite specifically, during my four-plus years at the United Nations. I propose to share some of the lessons I learned as I observed and participated in the major processes that take place at the United Nations. You may not like those lessons much. Some people say America would rather preserve a sentimental, optimistic view of the world that is untrue, than face a less optimistic vision of the world that is true. I don't believe that. Anyway, I shall speak about realities.

A first fact, long since understood by most Americans, is that the United Nations, as of 1981, is not in any sense what its founders had intended or expected it to be. It is not in any sense a utopian arena where nations seek dispassionately, objectively to solve problems. It is, instead, a place where a very hard game of politics is played, whose outcome depends less on the merits of issues than on the relative power of the players within the U.N. system. It may appear that the behavior and the votes of nations at the United Nations are determined by rational debate about the issues. But we all know appearances are often deceiving. Reasoned debate plays a role inside the United Nations. But its role is often less to persuade than to justify. It is important always to demonstrate that we have good reasons for our position—because, if we don't and we do not respond persuasively to attacks against us, our silence will be interpreted as giving consent to the arguments of our adversaries. It is also true that debate inside the United Nations sometimes has a ripple effect in the world outside—because the journalists of all the world gather there.

But the fact is that normally it is less debate that determines decisions in the U.N. than decisions that determine debate. The interesting facts about the United Nations lie just beneath the surface in what determines the content of the resolutions that are offered there, the character of the debates, the votes, the efforts at implementation. At first glance, it isn't easy to understand what's going on in the U.N. or why. Some very strange things happen there. Some subjects are brought before the United Nations again and again. Some very important issues are never brought before the United Nations. Some countries are condemned by the United Nations again and again, and some countries are never condemned at all. That might seem reasonable enough; after all, some countries do cause many problems and some help solve them. Some countries are international outlaws and some are constructive citizens of the world. But the first big shock in looking closely at the U.N. is to realize that praise and blame inside the U.N. is awarded on a basis that is nearly opposite of what would be the case if it were determined by the merits of the issues.

Let me give you a few examples. Libya, a dictatorship which invades and threatens its neighbors, organizes assassination plots and sponsors terrorist groups, is never the object of U.N. condemnation. But Israel, a democracy which deeply desires peace with her neighbors and which is the victim, not the perpetrator, of terrorism is regularly the object of complaints and condemnation in the United Nations. The Soviet Union, which gives very little economic assistance to Third World countries, is never the object of pressure to give more. But the United States, which gives a great deal of help to the poorest people of the world, is frequently criticized for not giving more. Socialist economies, which have failed in every country in the world where they have been tried, are recommended in resolution after resolution. But market economics—the free enterprise system —which is responsible for growth in every developed country in the world, is regularly denounced.

The explanation of why such resolutions were proposed or passed lies not in the objective facts. The reasons lie in the power relations among the countries in that body. The first hard fact to be faced is that the United Nations is not a place where issues are decided on the merits of the case. It is not the merits of the case that determine who is condemned for what and when; it is the power structure inside the United Nations.

Again, I offer some examples: Libya is protected from condemnation by its political strength inside the U.N. Israel is attacked because of its lack of political strength inside the U.N. Libya is a member of the Organization of African Unity (OAU), the Organization of the Islamic Conference, the Non-Aligned Movement (NAM). Those memberships protect and empower it. The United States used to be attacked because of our lack of political strength in the U.N. as well. Neither the intellectual strength, nor the facts, nor the eloquence of our arguments, nor the morality of our positions could win fair play for us, or for any other nations. Influence in the Untied Nations depends on other factors. It does not depend on reason or morality.

Influence in the United Nations depends, in part, on the bloc system of voting: a bloc is rather like a political party. Inside the U.N., it helps to be part of a large bloc and it hurts to be part of no bloc. We are part of no bloc. Influence in the U.N. depends in part on the ability to influence decisions that are made inside one's blocs and also to have alliances in other blocs. It depends in part on understanding how the system in the U.N. works. It depends in part in persuading other countries that they have something to gain or something to dread from their treatment of the United States inside the United Nations. Being right will not win votes. Being eloquent will not win votes. Being well liked will not win votes inside the United Nations.

When power relations dominate, as they do in the U.N., then the content and the fate of resolutions are determined by these power relations. For example, when power relations dominate, a resolution on economic development will be less concerned with giving good advice to countries seeking development than it will be concerned with expressing the short-range political interests of the strongest bloc. A resolution on economic growth in a U.N. dominated by the Soviet bloc will have as its principal purpose not promoting growth but attacking what they call capitalism, and the United States, as responsible for all the poverty in the world. A resolution on the Middle East will not have as its purpose winning peace in the Middle East. A resolution on the Middle East will have as its purpose establishing the position of the most powerful Arab states in the United Nations. A resolution on human rights in El Salvador will be less concerned with the objective facts of the situation than with blaming the government of El Salvador for whatever is wrong in that country.

The thorough-going politicization of the United Nations took place long ago. Although the United Nations was created in the ashes of World War II as an antidote to international relations based on power and conflict, no one should be surprised it has itself developed a power structure and power processes which sometimes operate quite ruthlessly, with little regard for truth, fairness or friendship.[2] A country can count on being fairly treated if it has power within the system and uses it. Useful, constructive action can be accomplished inside the United Nations when constructive countries have power within the system. The United States lost its influence inside the United Nations in the mid-sixties. And for 20 years, the United States was not treated fairly inside the United Nations. The democracies lost their dominant role to other blocs in the mid-sixties. And with that, the United Nations lost much of its capacity to work for constructive purposes, exactly the constructive purposes it was established to achieve.

---

2 A recent example was when the United States was blocked from membership on the Human Rights Commission last year.

The United Nations can only act against terrorism if the nations which oppose terrorism have more power in the U.N. system than those which sponsor the terrorists. The United Nations can only help promote economic development if the nations which desire economic growth and know something about how it is achieved are more powerful that those which preach and practice failed policies. The United States can only help the United Nations or itself if we are strong inside that system. But the fact is that the United States sunk slowly to a position so impotent and isolated inside the United Nations that we could not even protect ourselves against the attacks of arrogant dictators who are dependent on us for help. Obviously, from such a position we couldn't protect anyone else, or accomplish anything useful.

Inside the United Nations, power feeds on itself—and so does the lack of power. Those who have power find it easy to get more. Countries that lack power are avoided because they are powerless. The United States' standing on the United Nations had sunk so low that even our best friends kept their distance from us and from our positions. On many issues, they preferred to position themselves as neutral or non-aligned or "moderate," between the American position and that of some other group like the non-aligned.

George Kennan said it: "one of the great realities of political life is the cumulative nature of power and the factor of momentum in human affairs" (what one president once called the "big M"). The support of the powerful is vigorously courted inside the United Nations because the support of the powerful is important to the success of any activity.

Conversely, those who lack power cannot expect to have their opinions taken into account. Inside the United Nations, not to be taken into account means not being consulted about resolutions that are being drafted. It means not having one's support sought for resolutions that are being drafted. It means not being able to protect one's country from slanderous attacks by anyone. It means not even being able to count on the normal courtesies that are available to all nations—for example, in the Security Council, the 24-hour delay before the Security Council votes. Being helpless before humiliating attacks further weakens a country's standing. Being denied normal courtesies further weakens a country's standing. And a downward spiral of isolation and humiliation continues. The United States traveled far down that vicious spiral of isolation and humiliation while momentum of the opposite kind swept the Soviet Union and associated radical states to more and more victories inside the United Nations. It gave them more voice in more proceedings of the United Nations.

Improving the position of the United States, breaking that momentum of American powerlessness, was our major task at the United Nations during my four years because it was a prerequisite to achieving any other goal. Inside the United Nations power is measured by numbers of votes, and votes are awarded on the basis of one country, one vote. That means, for example, St. Kitts, with its population of 120,000 at the height of the tourist season, has one vote and the United States has one vote. Our problem in the United Nations could be reduced to the simplest level: it was to persuade more countries to stop voting against us and to start voting with us. Some of those countries included our best friends. Most of the countries in the U.N. are small, poor, Third World countries. Many of them are countries with whom the United States has friendly relations outside the United Nations. Yet, in spite of those friendly relations outside the United Nations, we kept failing to get a hearing, and failing to get their vote. We kept being isolated, less because of the opposition of the Soviet Union than because of the behavior of the non-Communist Third World countries. Slowly, we came to realize that the Soviets' strength inside the United Nations derived, above all, from the fact that they were better than we Americans were at winning support from the non-Communist countries of the Third World. We realized, too, that we were confronted with a problem that was simultaneously more complex and more soluble than is often imagined. I don't mean the problem was simple, and it is not simple today; the fact is, it was very difficult. But it is a different problem than often supposed.

Why was it that the United States, which helped more countries than the Soviet Union, respected their independence, and really is a peace-loving nation, was continually doing less well than the Soviets with the Third World countries inside the United Nations? Because the Soviets had understood better than we the multilateral politics of the United Nations. Because they were more skillful and flexible than we at playing U.N. politics. So, we also came to realize, were the British, the French, the Dutch, the Arabs, the Africans, and almost everyone else.

The Soviets were succeeding where the United States was failing because they were more skillful and more ruthless than the United States in securing support inside the U.N. of countries in their own bloc. Bulgaria, for example, or Cuba, or Hungary, always voted with the Soviet Union; but Britain, France, our other NATO allies, and our Latin American friends, only sometimes voted with us. The Soviets were also more successful than we, because they were better at securing the votes of countries outside their own power bloc. India, for example, also regularly supported the Soviet Union but is clearly an independent nation. Thailand, a country quite friendly to the United States, but thoroughly independent, only sometimes supported the United States' position inside the United Nations. Finally, the Soviets were succeeding where we were failing because they were more skillful at securing the support of genuinely neutral states, like the Arab Gulf states, Nepal, Argentina, or Brazil.

The United States acted as though everything mattered to us, but nothing mattered much. There were neither rewards for helping the United States nor a price for opposing us even on issues of concern to us.

George Kennan's famous 1954 warning was clearly relevant to our predicament, but nobody had heeded it. In 1954, he had written:

> I view with skepticism our chances for exerting any useful influence unless we learn how to create respect for our possible disfavor, at least as great as the respect for our possible favor.

Kennan knew the behavior of nations is not normally motivated
or controlled by disinterested gratitude or friendship, but rather by
the hope of gain and the fear of loss. Kennan knew that it was important for a nation seeking influence to remember what Thomas Jefferson had called "the peaceable coercions" of international politics.

What could we do? We came to understand that the complex
politics of the United Nations required cultivating and maintaining
relations with a hundred-odd countries in the U.N. concerning the
U.N., and outside the U.N. concerning the U.N. But these relations
must be reciprocal. They must be based on mutual respect and not
on our respecting others while others fail to respect us. That reci-
procity, we came to understand, must be continually renewed. It
does not require that the United States dominate on every issue in
the U.N or even most issues in the U.N. In fact, in order to be effective, we must always respect the interests of other nations, and
sometimes give priority to their concerns.

U.S. effectiveness in the United Nations does not require that we
always prevail all times. It does require that we secure a decent
respect for our values and our important principles. That can be as
often achieved when others take a leadership role than when we
seek to dominate. George Kennan understood that, too, and he had
a warning that was relevant. In dealing with Third World nations,
he warned, being effective, friendly and supportive did not mean
we needed to "breathe down their necks all the time or try to
smother them with our influence."

This brings me to the final point: that to be effective inside the
United Nations the United States must have confidence in our
national experience, our principles and, of course, we must be faithful to them. Sometimes America's representatives have behaved as
though they secretly agreed with our adversaries. Sometimes they've
behaved as if they didn't believe that we had advice and experience
as well as money to share with others.

Having confidence in ourselves, being true to ourselves and our
standards, does not mean judging ourselves by the Sermon on the

Mount and everybody else on the curve. It does not require unilateral disarmament or unilateral risk; being true to ourselves does not require, it does not even permit, being indifferent to our security. Strong, the United States can help to build and preserve a world of independent countries living at peace with one another. Weak, the United States cannot even protect itself much less its principles or the independence of other nations.

The United States has had great difficulty in understanding and accepting the truth about how the United Nations works. Partly because we had been certain that this great "town meeting of the world" would behave differently than any town meeting ever did. We believed that reason would replace power, that peace would take priority over selfish interests, that decisions would be decided objectively. I cannot conceive why we ever supposed that countries would behave differently inside the U.N. than they ever had in history. Or why we ever supposed that they would behave differently than most people do in their own lives. The answer to that terribly important question lies in a national susceptibility to a nearly utopian optimism about the world.

Our nation's tendency to this brand of utopianism about international affairs has been noted, described and regretted by such distinguished students, writers and practitioners of world affairs as Hans Morgenthau, Walter Lippmann, Dean Acheson, George Kennan, Henry Kissinger.

Kennan traced the source of the problem to the long period of peace and security the United States enjoyed in the 19th century. During that period, he said, we had no problems on our borders and, largely because of the strength of the British during the 19th century, we felt safe and secure and did not find it necessary to defend ourselves. That long period of peace and security, Kennan said, served to eliminate from our consciousness all feeling of vulnerability.

It is strange that a people as realistic and skilled in practical conduct, personal affairs and domestic politics should lose its clear-eyed, hard-headed, common-sense views when it deals with international affairs. The history of the 20th century, probably the most violent century in human history, certainly does not support a romantic view of the world and of international affairs any more than the history of the United Nations supports a romantic or a utopian view of the United Nations. We wish that it were different.

I wish that power, conflict and self-interest did not play so large a role in the United Nations. But, we are stuck with living in the world as it is, with operating in the United Nations as it is, if we are to protect ourselves and our principles, our values, our friends and our civilization. If we are even to survive in this world of terrorists and weapons of mass destruction, we should take care to remember that doing so requires the necessary power and weapons.

Self defense is not an aggressive act in the United Nations or out of it.